W9-BWW-960

Fodor's

WASHINGTON, D.C.

WELCOME TO WASHINGTON, D.C.

With its neoclassical government buildings and broad avenues, Washington, D.C., looks its part as America's capital. Majestic monuments and memorials pay tribute to notable leaders and great achievements, and merit a visit. But D.C. also lives firmly in the present, and not just politically; new restaurants and bars continually emerge, upping the hipness factor in neighborhoods from Capitol Hill to U Street. Fun museums and tree-shaded parks make it a terrific place for families. You may come for the official sites, but you'll remember D.C.'s local flavor, too.

TOP REASONS TO GO

★ **Cherry Blossoms:** For a few weeks in spring, D.C. is awash in glorious pink blooms.

★ **The White House:** 1600 Pennsylvania may be the best-known address in the U.S.

★ **Memorials:** The lives of soldiers, presidents, and political figures are commemorated.

★ **Museums:** For every taste—whether you like spies, airplanes, history, or art.

★ **Globe-trotting Cuisine:** Diverse cultures support restaurants with authentic flavors.

★ **The Mall:** Ground zero for museums, picnics, festivals, and performances.

Fodor's WASHINGTON, D.C.

Editorial: Douglas Stallings, *Editorial Director*; Salwa Jabado and Margaret Kelly, *Senior Editors*; Alexis Kelly, Jacinta O'Halloran, and Amanda Sadlowski, *Editors*; Teddy Minford, *Associate Editor*; Rachael Roth, *Content Manager*

Design: Tina Malaney, *Associate Art Director*

Photography: Jennifer Arnow, *Senior Photo Editor*

Maps: Rebecca Baer, *Senior Map Editor*; David Lindroth and Mark Stroud (Moon Street Cartography), *Cartographers*

Production: Jennifer DePrima, *Editorial Production Manager*; Carrie Parker, *Senior Production Editor*; Elyse Rozelle, *Production Editor*

Business & Operations: Chuck Hoover, *Chief Marketing Officer*; Joy Lai, *Vice President and General Manager*; Stephen Horowitz, *Head of Business Development and Partnerships*

Public Relations: Joe Ewaskiw, *Manager*

Writers: Zach Everson, Mike Lillis, Robert Michael Oliver, Doug Rule, Cathy Sharpe

Editors: Amanda Sadlowski, Jacinta O'Halloran

Production Editor: Carrie Parker

Production Design: Liliana Guia

23rd Edition

ISBN 978-1-101-88009-8

ISSN 0743-9741

PRINTED IN THE UNITED STATES OF AMERICA

10 9 8 7 6 5 4 3 2

CONTENTS

1 EXPERIENCE
   WASHINGTON, D.C. 9
   Washington, D.C. Today........... 10
   Washington, D.C. Planner.......... 12
   What's Where..................... 14
   Washington, D.C.
   Top Attractions 16
   Great Itineraries 18
   Best Tours in D.C................. 20
   Washington, D.C.
   Black History Walk................ 22
   Free in D.C. 24
   D.C. with Kids.................... 25
   D.C.'s Top Festivals............... 26

2 EXPLORING 27
   The National Mall................. 30
   The White House Area
   and Foggy Bottom................ 54
   Capitol Hill and
   Northeast D.C..................... 62
   Downtown........................ 79
   Georgetown 89
   Dupont Circle and
   Logan Circle 94
   Adams Morgan 100
   U Street Corridor 104
   Upper Northwest 108
   Arlington and
   Northern Virginia 113

3 WHERE TO EAT 125
   Planning......................... 127
   Restaurant Reviews.............. 128
   Where to Eat and Stay
   in Washington, D.C............... 151

4 WHERE TO STAY............. 157
   Planning......................... 159
   Hotel Reviews 160

Fodor's Features

National Air and Space Museum 38
On the Hill, under the Dome:
Experiencing the Capitol 67
Arlington, the Nation's Cemetery..... 117

5 NIGHTLIFE 177
   Planning.......................... 179
   White House Area
   and Foggy Bottom................ 179
   Capitol Hill and
   Northeast D.C..................... 180
   Downtown........................ 182
   Georgetown 184
   Dupont Circle and
   Logan Circle 185
   Adams Morgan 188
   U Street Corridor 189
   Arlington and
   Northern Virginia 195

6 PERFORMING ARTS 197
   Planning.......................... 199
   White House Area 199
   Foggy Bottom 201
   Capitol Hill and
   Northeast D.C..................... 203
   Downtown........................ 205

Georgetown 207

Dupont Circle and
Logan Circle 207

Adams Morgan 209

U Street Corridor 209

Upper Northwest 210

Arlington and
Northern Virginia 211

7 SPORTS AND
   THE OUTDOORS............. 213

Planning........................... 214

Parks and Nature................. 216

Sports 225

8 SHOPPING................... 233

Planning........................... 234

White House Area 235

Foggy Bottom 237

Capitol Hill........................ 238

Downtown......................... 240

Georgetown 242

Dupont Circle and Logan Circle... 247

Adams Morgan 250

U Street Corridor 251

Upper Northwest 253

9 SIDE TRIPS FROM
   WASHINGTON, D.C. 255

Welcome to Side Trips
from Washington, D.C............. 256

Planning........................... 258

Alexandria, Virginia 259

Mount Vernon, Woodlawn,
and Gunston Hall................. 267

Annapolis, Maryland.............. 273

TRAVEL SMART
WASHINGTON, D.C. 283

ABOUT OUR WRITERS....... 320

MAPS

Black History Walk................. 23

The National Mall.................. 32

The White House and
Foggy Bottom 56

Capitol Hill and Northeast D.C..... 64

Downtown.......................... 80

Georgetown 90

Dupont Circle and Logan Circle.... 96

Adams Morgan 102

U Street Corridor 106

Upper Northwest 110

Arlington and
Northern Virginia 114

Dining and Lodging Map 1... 152–153

Dining and Lodging Map 2... 154–155

Alexandria, Virginia 261

Mount Vernon, Woodlawn,
and Gunston Hall................. 271

Annapolis, Maryland.............. 275

ABOUT THIS GUIDE

Fodor's Recommendations

Everything in this guide is worth doing—we don't cover what isn't—but exceptional sights, hotels, and restaurants are recognized with additional accolades. **Fodor's** Choice★ indicates our top recommendations. Care to nominate a new place? Visit Fodors.com/contact-us.

Trip Costs

We list prices wherever possible to help you budget well. Hotel and restaurant price categories from **$** to **$$$$** are noted alongside each recommendation. For hotels, we include the lowest cost of a standard double room in high season. For restaurants, we cite the average price of a main course at dinner or, if dinner isn't served, at lunch. For attractions, we always list adult admission fees; discounts are usually available for children, students, and senior citizens.

Hotels

Our local writers vet every hotel to recommend the best overnights in each price category, from budget to expensive. Unless otherwise specified, you can expect private bath, phone, and TV in your room. *For expanded hotel reviews, visit Fodors.com.*

Top Picks	Hotels &
★ **Fodor's** Choice	Restaurants
	⌂ Hotel
Listings	↵ Number of
✉ Address	rooms
✉ Branch address	❘O❘ Meal plans
☎ Telephone	✕ Restaurant
🖷 Fax	⌖ Reservations
⊕ Website	⌂ Dress code
✉ E-mail	▭ No credit cards
🎟 Admission fee	Ⓢ Price
◷ Open/closed	
times	**Other**
Ⓜ Subway	⇨ See also
⊹ Directions or	☞ Take note
Map coordinates	⅄ Golf facilities

Restaurants

Unless we state otherwise, restaurants are open for lunch and dinner daily. We mention dress code only when there's a specific requirement and reservations only when they're essential or not accepted. *For expanded restaurant reviews, visit Fodors.com.*

Credit Cards

The hotels and restaurants in this guide typically accept credit cards. If not, we'll say so.

EUGENE FODOR

Hungarian-born Eugene Fodor (1905–91) began his travel career as an interpreter on a French cruise ship. The experience inspired him to write *On the Continent* (1936), the first guidebook to receive annual updates and discuss a country's way of life as well as its sights. Fodor later joined the U.S. Army and worked for the OSS in World War II. After the war, he kept up his intelligence work while expanding his guidebook series. During the Cold War, many guides were written by fellow agents who understood the value of insider information. Today's guides continue Fodor's legacy by providing travelers with timely coverage, insider tips, and cultural context.

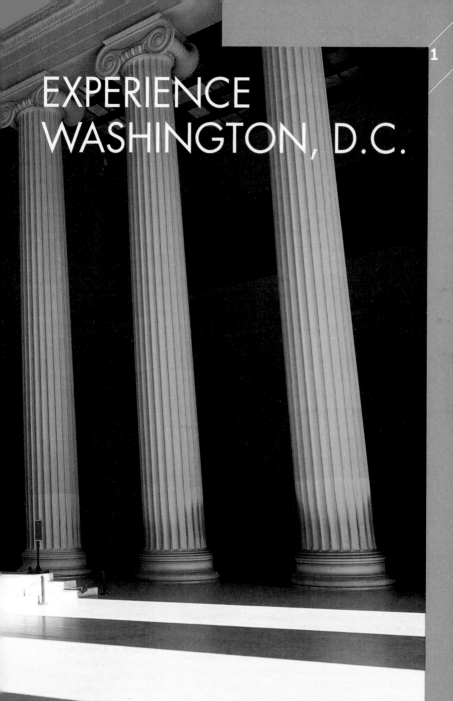

EXPERIENCE WASHINGTON, D.C.

WASHINGTON, D.C. TODAY

Classically majestic and stunningly beautiful, the Capitol, the White House, and the Supreme Court stand at the heart of Washington, D.C., symbols of the stability and strength of the nation. But the city that revolves around this axis is in a constant state of change, lived on a more human scale.

Politics

Donald Trump moved into the White House in 2017, but don't expect to find many fans among his Washington neighbors. The city is overwhelmingly Democratic (Trump won just 4% of the vote here) and many residents are still coming to uneasy grips with his arrival. On the day of Trump's inauguration, violent protesters set fire to trash cans near the White House. A day later, it was estimated that half a million people marched through the city to protest his views in the historic Women's March. Those dynamics may change, but for now the tensions still simmer, as visitors will likely find as they bellyup to the bars around town. At one popular H Street haunt, the coasters read: "He may be the most powerful man on earth, but he'll never drink a beer in The Pug."

Sports

First and foremost, this is a football town, as the hoards of loyal Redskins fans demonstrate each fall Sunday at bars around town. Still, the team has struggled under billionaire owner Danny Snyder, who has shelled out big bucks to attract top players but has yet to return the team to the Super Bowl under his watch. Frustrated fans have noticed, and tickets are much easier to come by than they once were (though they still aren't cheap). Filling the void, the Nationals baseball team has wowed D.C. in recent years, with all-star talents like Max Scherzer, the 2016 Cy Young winner, and slugger Bryce Harper leading the team to a string of playoff appearances. Not to be outdone, the Capitals hockey team, led by perennial all-star Alex Ovechkin, has emerged as a yearly contender for the Stanley Cup. And even the Wizards basketball team has shed its once-lowly reputation, joining the playoff ranks on the wings of scoring sensation John Wall.

WHAT'S NEW

Streetcars: More than 60 years after Washington retired streetcars from Downtown, residents celebrated their return in 2016 with the opening of a new rail line running east from Union Station to the Anacostia River. The 2.4-mile H/Benning line is designed to bring more traffic to one of D.C.'s fastest-growing commercial districts: the bustling H Street Corridor. And that's not all. Ultimately, the system is expected to extend to 37 miles of track fanning into all parts of the city—a network that will put Washington in league with Portland, Oregon, and Seattle, Washington, when it comes to streetcar options.

Smithsonian National Museum of African American History and Culture: This $540 million project opened on the National Mall in 2016 with much fanfare, and a

Marijuana

D.C. has been on the cutting edge of the growing national movement to legalize marijuana, but with some complications. In 2014, D.C. voters overwhelmingly approved a measure permitting those over 21 to possess up to 2 ounces of marijuana, grow a small number of cannabis plants in their homes, and transfer up to an ounce of the drug to another adult—if no money accompanies the exchange. The law means you can smoke pot in private places, but you cannot buy it legally, which doesn't allow any pot tourism seen in states like Colorado in recent years. Still, that nuance has not dissuaded faithful users, and visitors should not be surprised if, on occasion, they encounter a waft of pot smoke in the air.

Demographics

Washington's postrecession economic boom has only accelerated the demographic face-lift that was already transforming the city. This shift is highlighted by several recent population milestones: an increase in residents, and a median age that has fallen below 34—almost four years younger than the country as a whole.

Hardly unrelated, the trends reveal that, after years of fleeing D.C. due to high crime rates and underperforming schools, more and more suburban families are opting to live in the city where they work. These younger professionals—mostly white, mostly drawn by the government and related industries—have helped bolster Washington's economy, but not without a price. Indeed, the gentrification—heightened by enormous stadium projects like Nationals Park—has reached deep into the traditionally black areas of Northeast and Southeast, stirring resentment, driving up costs, and pricing many longtime residents out of their childhood homes. Indeed, D.C. has one of the widest income gaps between rich and poor in the country, leaving local officials to seek ways to strengthen commercial interests without sacrificing community and culture.

Food

It ain't quite New York City, but Washington has made great culinary strides in recent years. No longer known only for stuffy steak houses catering to lobbyists, D.C. now offers options to satisfy the most eclectic tastes. And top-tier chefs from around the country have taken notice, with many descending on D.C. to catch the wave.

speech by then-President Obama, the nation's first black president. The almost 37,000 items on display examine all aspects of the African American experience, including slavery, the Harlem Renaissance, and the Civil Rights March on Washington.

The Wharf: Stretching east along the Washington Channel from the Maine Avenue fish market, this 47-acre, $2 billion project—slated to open its first phase in 2017—will include residential, office, and retail development wrapped

around a waterfront promenade with restaurants, parks, boat slips, and a museum of maritime history.

WASHINGTON, D.C. PLANNER

When to Go

D.C. has two delightful seasons: spring and autumn. In spring the city's ornamental fruit trees are blossoming, and its many gardens are in bloom. Summers can be uncomfortably hot and humid. By autumn most of the summer crowds have left and you can enjoy the sights in peace.

Winter weather is mild by East Coast standards, but a handful of modest snowstorms each year bring this southern city to a standstill.

Getting Here

D.C. is served by three airports: **Ronald Reagan Washington National Airport (DCA)** in Virginia, 4 miles south of Downtown Washington; **Dulles International Airport (IAD)**, 26 miles to the west; and **Baltimore/ Washington International–Thurgood Marshall Airport (BWI)** in Maryland, about 30 miles to the northeast.

Amtrak trains arrive and depart from Union Station, in Northeast D.C.

Getting Around

Car Travel: Driving in D.C. can be a headache. Traffic is usually congested, and the road layout is designed for frustration, with one-way streets popping up at just the wrong moment. Once you've reached your destination, the real challenge begins: D.C. must be among the most difficult cities in America in which to find parking. All of this means that you'd be wise to use public transit whenever possible.

Metro and Bus Travel: The Washington Metropolitan Area Transit Authority operates a network of subway lines (known locally as the Metro) and bus routes throughout D.C. Most popular tourist attractions are near Metro stops, though certain areas are accessible only by bus, most notably Georgetown and Adams Morgan in Northwest and the Atlas District in Northeast.

All Metro train rides require SmarTrip cards, rechargeable passes, which can be purchased online, at any Metro station, and at some tourist retailers around the city. They cost $10, but $8 of that goes to future trips. Metro fares vary by the distance traveled and the time of day—information about trips is posted on each vending machine in the Metro. Fares range from $2.15 to $5.90 during "peak" hours—which include the morning and evening commutes and the after-midnight hours of weekends—and from $1.75 to $3.60 at all other times. One-day passes for unlimited Metro travel are also available for $14.50, while weekly passes cost $59.25 and monthly cards run $237.

Bus fares are $1.75 (exact change only) for regular routes, regardless if you use cash or a SmarTrip card. A special bus, the 5A, runs from D.C. to Dulles airport for $7. SmarTrip cards will grant users free transfers between buses within a two-hour window, and $0.50 discounts on transfers between buses and the Metro.

D.C. Streetcar Launched in 2016, the streetcar is a limited, but unique, way to get around one of the city's newer hot spots. The tracks currently run for 2.4 miles along the H Street corridor from Union Station to the Anacostia River. The ride is free, for an introductory period, but that's expected to change sometime in 2017. Check the streetcar website for updates.

Information Washington Metropolitan Area Transit Authority. ☎ *202/637–7000* ⊕ *www. wmata.com.*

Taxi Travel: Taxis in D.C. charge a $3.25 minimum base rate, which covers the first eighth of a mile, plus $0.27 for every additional eighth of a mile ($2.16 per mile). Riders stuck in traffic will pay more, as wait fees cost $35 per hour, or $0.58 per minute. A $2 charge applies to cabs hailed by phone, and surcharges also apply for airport travelers.

Taxi Information District of Columbia Taxicab Commission. ☎ *855/484–4966* ⊕ *www. dfhv.dc.gov.*

Getting Your Bearings

Four Quadrants: The address system in D.C. takes some getting used to. The city is divided into the four quadrants of a compass (NW, NE, SE, SW), with the U.S. Capitol at the center. Because the Capitol doesn't sit in the exact center of the city (the Washington Monument does), Northwest is the largest quadrant. Northwest also has most of the important landmarks, although Northeast and Southwest have their fair share.

Numbered Streets and Lettered Streets: Within each quadrant, numbered streets run north to south, and lettered streets run east to west (the letter *J* was omitted to avoid confusion with the letter *I*).

The streets form a fairly logical grid—for example, 900 G Street NW is the intersection of 9th and G Streets in the northwest quadrant of the city. Likewise, if you count the letters of the alphabet, skipping J, you can get a good sense of the location of an address on a numbered street. For instance, 1600 16th Street NW is close to Q Street, Q being the 16th letter of the alphabet if you skip J.

In short, this means it's vital to know which quadrant you're headed to, because 14th Street NW is a long way from 14th Street NE—about 28 blocks, in fact.

Avenues on the Diagonal: As if all this weren't confusing enough, Major Pierre L'Enfant, the Frenchman who originally designed the city, threw in diagonal avenues recalling those of Paris.

Most of D.C.'s avenues are named after U.S. states. You can find addresses on avenues the same way you find those on numbered streets, so 1200 Connecticut Avenue NW is close to M Street, because M is the 12th letter of the alphabet when you skip J. Furthering the chaos, L'Enfant devised a number of traffic circles as well—aesthetically pleasing additions that can nonetheless frustrate even the best out-of-town drivers.

Motorcades

Among D.C.'s natural hazards, motorcades rank near the top. These inconvenient affairs—occurring each time President Trump dines out, Vice President Mike Pence is whisked home from the White House, or visiting dignitaries travel in the city—lead to street closings that span dozens of blocks. For pedestrians, proximity to the fanfare might prove exciting. For drivers, motorcades are a hassle and another reason to stick with the Metro during your stay.

Safety Tips

D.C. is a relatively safe city, but crimes do occur, even in typically "safe" neighborhoods. The best way to protect yourself is to stick to well-lighted and populated areas and avoid walking alone after dark.

Many of the city's business and government districts become deserted at night, but the public transportation system is exceptionally safe, with only a few incidents of crime reported each year.

Visitor Information

Washington, D.C. Convention and Tourism Corporation. ✉ *901 7th St. NW, 4th fl., Downtown* ☎ *202/789–7000, 800/422–8644* ⊕ *www.washington.org.*

WHAT'S WHERE

1 **The National Mall.** This expanse of green is at the heart of D.C., stretching from the Capitol to the Washington Monument, and is lined by some of America's finest museums. D.C.'s most famous monuments are concentrated west of the Mall and along the Tidal Basin.

2 **The White House Area and Foggy Bottom.** There's great art at the Renwick Gallery, as well as performances at the Kennedy Center and a whiff of scandal at the Watergate.

3 **Capitol Hill and Northeast D.C.** The Capitol itself, along with the Supreme Court and Library of Congress, dominates this area. Follow Hill staffers to find restaurants, bars, and a thriving outdoor market. Also explore the ever-growing H Street Corridor.

4 **Downtown.** The Federal Triangle and Penn Quarter attract visitors to museums and galleries by day. By night, crowds head to the Verizon Center and Chinatown's bars, restaurants, and movie theaters.

5 **Georgetown.** The capital's wealthiest neighborhood is great for strolling and shopping, with the scene centering on Wisconsin Avenue and M Street. The C&O Canal starts here, providing recreation in, on, and alongside the water.

6 **Dupont Circle and Logan Circle.** This hub of fashionable restaurants, shops, and embassies is also home to the most visible segment of the gay community. Moving east, beautiful Logan Circle is largely residential, though a few hip new bars and eateries are just a short block away.

7 **Adams Morgan.** One of D.C.'s most ethnically diverse neighborhoods has offbeat restaurants and shops and a happening nightlife. Grand 19th-century apartment buildings and row houses have lured young professionals here.

8 **U Street Corridor.** Revitalization has brought trendy boutiques and hip eateries to the area around 14th and U, which was a hotbed of African American culture in the early 20th century.

9 **Upper Northwest.** This mostly residential swath of D.C. holds two must-see attractions: the National Cathedral and the National Zoo.

10 **Arlington and Northern Virginia.** Technically the suburbs, this easy-to-reach region is also home to the Pentagon and Arlington National Cemetery.

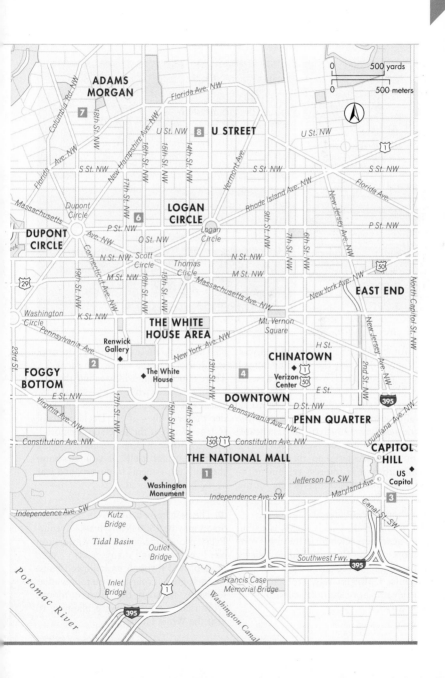

ADAMS MORGAN

Florida Ave. NW

U St. NW **8** **U STREET**

U St. NW

7

Columbia Rd. NW

18th St. NW

16th St. NW

15th St. NW

14th St. NW

New Hampshire Ave. NW

S St. NW

S St. NW

S St. NW

Florida Ave.

Vermont Ave.

Rhode Island Ave. NW

New Jersey Ave. NW

LOGAN CIRCLE

P St. NW

Dupont Circle

17th St. NW

P St. NW

6

Logan Circle

9th St. NW

7th St. NW

6th St. NW

DUPONT CIRCLE

O St. NW

N St. NW

Scott Circle

N St. NW

Thomas Circle

M St. NW

EAST END

Massachusetts

Ave. NW

Connecticut Ave. NW

19th St. NW

M St. NW

16th St. NW

15th St. NW

Massachusetts Ave. NW

New York Ave. NW

North Capitol St. NW

29

Washington Circle

K St. NW

Mt. Vernon Square

New Jersey Ave. NW

2nd St. NW

THE WHITE HOUSE AREA

Pennsylvania Ave.

Renwick Gallery

New York Ave. NW

H St.

CHINATOWN

FOGGY BOTTOM

23rd St.

2

The White House

13th St. NW

4

Verizon Center

E St.

395

E St. NW

Virginia Ave. NW

17th St. NW

15th St. NW

14th St. NW

DOWNTOWN

Pennsylvania Ave. NW

D St. NW

Louisiana Ave. NW

Constitution Ave. NW

Constitution Ave. NW

PENN QUARTER

CAPITOL HILL

THE NATIONAL MALL

1

Jefferson Dr. SW

US Capitol

3

Washington Monument

Independence Ave. SW

Maryland Ave.

Canal St. SW

Independence Ave. SW

Kutz Bridge

Outlet Bridge

Southwest Fwy.

395

Tidal Basin

Inlet Bridge

Francis Case Memorial Bridge

Washington Canal

Potomac River

395

0   500 yards
0   500 meters

WASHINGTON, D.C. TOP ATTRACTIONS

Capitol

(A) Home of the Senate and the House of Representatives, the marble Capitol is an architectural marvel filled with frescoes and statues. Tours begin at the underground Capitol Visitor Center. The Capitol grounds are equally stunning— Frederick Law Olmsted, the landscape architect famous for New York City's Central Park, designed them. A tour of the interior is impressive, but nothing beats attending a live debate on the House or Senate floor.

Washington Monument

(B) This 555-foot, 5-inch obelisk is visible from nearly everywhere in the city. From the top, it also offers unparalleled views of the city, reaching out to Maryland and Virginia. Unfortunately, problems with the elevator have shut off access until at least 2019.

Lincoln, Jefferson, and FDR memorials

(C) The key to these memorials is to stop, stand, and read the writing on the walls. There's nothing quite like reading the Gettysburg Address while the massive marble statue of Lincoln broods behind you. Ponder the first lines of the Declaration of Independence at the Jefferson Memorial, and remember the line "We have nothing to fear but fear itself" as you encounter the stark monuments to poverty and war at the FDR Memorial.

White House

(D) The best-known address in the United States may be 1600 Pennsylvania Avenue. Every president but George Washington has lived here, and many heads of state have passed through its hallowed halls. The self-guided tour lets you follow their footsteps through the historic rooms. Note that it takes advance planning to visit the White House.

National Cathedral

(E) Like its medieval European counterparts, this 20th-century cathedral has a nave, transepts, and vaults that were built stone by stone. Unlike those historic buildings, the National Cathedral has a gargoyle in the shape of Darth Vader.

Dumbarton Oaks

(F) If you enjoy formal gardens, visit the 10-acre grounds of Dumbarton Oaks in upper Georgetown, one of the loveliest spots for a stroll.

Arlington National Cemetery

(G) The hills across the Potomac from the Tidal Basin are the final resting place for some 340,000 members of the armed services. A visit here can be both sobering and moving.

Smithsonian museums

(H) Mostly flanking the National Mall, these illustrious galleries hold everything from Kermit the Frog to the *Spirit of St. Louis* and the Hope Diamond to Rodin's *Burghers of Calais*.

Martin Luther King Jr. Memorial

Among the newest additions to the Mall, this 30-foot sculpture of solid granite pays tribute to King, the giant of the civil rights movement killed by an assassin's bullet in 1968.

Vietnam Veterans, Korean War Veterans, and World War II memorials

Touch a name of a Vietnam vet, see your reflection alongside the statues of Korean War soldiers, search for the stories of those who lost their lives in World War II. These memorials are interactive and unforgettable.

National Zoo

The pandas may be the zoo's most famous attraction, but they're not the only highlight. Monkeys, elephants, lions, and other exotic residents never fail to delight.

GREAT ITINERARIES

ONE DAY IN D.C.

If you have a day or less in D.C., your sight-seeing strategy is simple: take the Metro to the Smithsonian stop and explore the area around the Mall. You'll be at the heart of the city—a beautiful setting where you'll find America's greatest collection of museums, with the city's monuments and the halls of government a stone's throw away.

Facing the Capitol, to your left are the **Museum of Natural History,** the **National Gallery of Art,** and the **National Archives.** To your right are the **Museum of African Art,** the **Hirshhorn Museum and Sculpture Garden,** the **National Air and Space Museum,** and more. Head in the other direction, toward the **Washington Monument,** and you're also on your way to the **National World War II Memorial,** the **Lincoln Memorial,** the **Vietnam Veterans Memorial,** and more monuments to America's presidents and its past. A lover of American history and culture could spend a thoroughly happy month, much less a day, wandering the Mall and its surroundings.

If you're here first thing in the morning: You can hit monuments and memorials early. They're open 24 hours a day and staffed beginning at 8 am. The sculpture garden at the Hirshhorn opens at 7:30, and the Smithsonian Institution Building ("the Castle") opens at 8:30. In the Castle you can grab a cup of coffee, watch an 18-minute film about D.C., and see examples of objects from many of the Smithsonian's 19 museums and galleries.

If you have only a few hours in the evening: Experience the beauty of the monuments at dusk and after dark. Many people think they're even more striking when the sun goes down. National Park Service rangers staff most monuments until midnight.

FIVE DAYS IN D.C.

Day 1

With more time, you have a chance both to see the sights and to get to know the city. A guided bus tour is a good way to get oriented; a hop-on, hop-off tour will give you genuine insights without a lot of tourist hokum.

Because you can get on and off wherever you like, it's a good idea to use a bus tour to explore **Georgetown** and the **Washington National Cathedral,** neither of which is easily accessible by Metro.

Day 2

Devote your next day to the Mall, where you can check out the museums and monuments that were probably your prime motivation for visiting D.C. in the first place. There's no way you can do it all in one day, so just play favorites and save the rest for next time. Try visiting the monuments in the evening: they remain open long after the museums are closed and are dramatically lit after dark.

Keep in mind that the **National Museum of Natural History** is the most visited museum in the country, while the **National Air and Space Museum,** the **National African-American Museum of History and Culture,** the **National Gallery of Art,** and the **Museum of American History** aren't far behind; plan for crowds almost any time you visit. If you visit the **United States Holocaust Memorial Museum,** plan on spending two to three hours. If you're with kids on the Mall, take a break by riding the carousel.

Cafés and cafeterias within the museums are your best option for lunch. Two excellent picks are the Cascade Café at the **National Gallery of Art** and the Mitsitam Café at the **National Museum of the American Indian,** where they serve creative dishes inspired by native cultures. Just north of the Mall, the **Newseum**, while not free to enter, features a food court with a menu designed by celebrity-chef Wolfgang Puck. If you have more time (and more money to spend), drop by The Source, a ritzy Puck-owned restaurant behind the museum.

If the weather permits—and you're not already weary—consider the healthy walk from the **Washington Monument** to the **Lincoln Memorial** and around the **Tidal Basin**, where you can see the **Jefferson Memorial**, the **Franklin Delano Roosevelt Memorial**, and the **Martin Luther King Jr. National Memorial**. Nearby, nestled north of the Mall's reflecting pool, is the **Vietnam Veterans Memorial**, "The Wall," a sobering black granite monolith commemorating the 58,272 Americans who never returned from the Vietnam War—a design that's "not so much a tombstone or a monument as a grave," in the somber words of writer Michael Ventura.

Day 3

Make this your day on **Capitol Hill**, where you'll have the option of visiting the **Capitol**, the **U.S. Botanic Gardens**, the **Library of Congress**, the **Supreme Court**, and the **Folger Shakespeare Library.**

Call your senators or congressional representative (or your country's embassy, if you are a visitor from outside the U.S.) for passes to see Congress in session. You can also venture into one of the congressional office buildings adjacent to the Capitol, where congressional hearings are almost always open to the public. (Visit ⊕ *www.house.gov* and ⊕ *www.senate.gov* for schedules.) Likewise, check the Supreme Court's website (⊕ *www.supremecourtus.gov*) for dates of oral arguments. If you arrive early enough, you might gain admission for either a short (three-minute) visit or the full morning session.

Day 4

Head to the **National Zoo** and say good morning to the pandas. If the weather is bad, you can still enjoy the numerous indoor animal houses. Then hop on the Metro to **Dupont Circle** for lunch. Walk west on tree-lined P Street NW to **Georgetown**, where you can shop, admire the architecture, and people-watch.

If you got a good dose of Georgetown on your first day, consider instead visiting the **International Spy Museum**, a Chinatown attraction that tends to be less crowded after 2 pm. From there you can easily walk to the **Smithsonian American Art Museum** and **National Portrait Gallery**, which stay open until 7.

Day 5

Spend the morning at **Arlington National Cemetery.** While you're there, don't miss the changing of the guard at the Tomb of the Unknowns, every hour or half hour, depending on the time of year. A short detour north of the cemetery brings you to the **Marine Corps War Memorial**, a giant bronze rendering of American soldiers planting the flag on Iwo Jima during World War II—one of the most famous images in U.S. military history.

After your contemplative morning, head back across the Potomac to spend the afternoon in **Adams Morgan** and **Dupont Circle.** Lunch at one of Adams Morgan's Ethiopian, El Salvadoran, or Mexican restaurants, and browse the Dupont Circle art scene—there are offbeat galleries tucked into the side streets, as well as the renowned **Phillips Collection.**

BEST TOURS IN D.C.

If ever there was a "do it yourself" city, it's D.C. The Metro system is safe and easy to navigate, and most major sights and museums are concentrated in a single area. Armed with a Metro map, a guide to the Mall, and a comfortable pair of shoes, you can do it all by yourself.

Nevertheless, the underground train is notably lacking in city views and driving tempts the fate of the parking gods, so sometimes a guided tour makes the most sense, especially if you're seeking the inside scoop from a local expert. Consider one of the following options if you're looking for chaperoned convenience.

For even more tours, please see the Tours section in the Travel Smart chapter.

Bus Tours

City Sights. This bus tour offers double-decker fun for those seeking to take advantage of warmer weather and get an elevated view of Washington. The group runs multiple loops around the city, some of which extend well beyond the Mall to include Georgetown, the National Cathedral, Arlington National Cemetery, and the Pentagon. All trips offer hop-on, hop-off convenience, and several multiday options are available for those on longer stays. City Sights also offers night tours, boat trips, and guided bike tours. ☎ 202/650–5444 ⊕ *www.citysightsdc.com* ✆ *From $39.*

DC Ducks. Ready for a unique take on Washington? DC Ducks takes the traditional jaunt through the city and adds a thrilling twist: the 90-minute guided tour ends with a splashdown in the Potomac River, where the amphibious Duckmobile gives visitors a rousing water leg to their trip. Tours, which run from mid-March to November, begin at Union Station, leaving every hour between 10 am and 4 pm. ☎ 866/754–5039 ⊕ *www. dcducks.com* ✆ *From $42.*

Old Town Trolley Tours. D.C.'s longest-running tour company offers one of the best narrated glimpses of the city's many historic wonders, with the option of hop-on, hop-off service at 14 different stops. Two loops are available: one wraps around the Mall and Capitol; the other extends from the Lincoln Memorial to Arlington National Cemetery in Virginia. (Transfers between the loops are part of the deal.) Visitors can begin their tour at any of the stops, and buses swing by every 30 minutes. ☎ 844/356–2603 ⊕ *www.trolleytours.com/washington-dc* ✆ *From $35.*

Bike Tours

Bike and Roll. Based at both Union Station and L'Enfant Plaza, just off the National Mall, Bike and Roll offers a series of guided tours through D.C.'s top sites, including the Capitol, Supreme Court, and WWII Memorial. Bike rentals and Segway tours are also offered, and self-guided options stretch as far as Mount Vernon and even Pittsburgh. ✉ *955 L'Enfant Plaza SW, Washington* ☎ *202/842–2453* ⊕ *www.bikeandrolldc. com* ✆ *From $40.*

Capital City Bike Tours. Yet another option for touring the monuments on your own time, Capital Bike Tours offers guided day tours, sunset trips, Segway rentals, and packages that include entrance into the Newseum and Spy Museum. A typical tour is three hours of easy peddling. ✉ *502 23rd St. NW, Foggy Bottom* ☎ *202/626–0017* ⊕ *dc.capitalcitybik-etours.com* ✆ *From $39.*

Boat Tours

Dandy Cruises. Departing from Alexandria, the glass-enclosed *Nina's Dandy* cruises up the Potomac to Georgetown year-round, passing many of D.C.'s monuments along the way. Lunch, champagne brunch, and dinner cruises are offered, and there are special holiday cruises, too. ⊠ *Prince St., between Duke and King Sts., Alexandria* ☎ *703/683–6076* ⊕ *www.dandydinnerboat.com* ✆ *From $50.*

Thompson Boat Center. Another way to see the monuments from the Potomac River is through Thompson Boat Center in Georgetown, which offers boat rentals for self-guided tours. Pack a lunch and paddle over to Roosevelt Island for a picnic. A double kayak rents for $22 per hour, while a canoe goes for $14 per hour. Sculls are also available for certified rowers. ⊠ *2900 Virginia Ave. NW, Georgetown* ☎ *202/333–9543* ⊕ *www. thompsonboatcenter.com* ✆ *From $16.*

Specialty Tours

Gross National Product's Scandal Tours. For almost three decades this comedy troupe has delighted tourists with juicy bits from Washington's rumor mill. The circuit features stops at the Tidal Basin, where a powerful congressman and his stripper girlfriend ran afoul of the law, and the Watergate Hotel, where the country's most infamous burglary led to the fall of a president. ☎ *202/783–7212* ⊕ *www.gnpcomedy.com/ScandalTours. html* ✆ *From $30.*

Smithsonian Associates. For a walk through the battles and strategies that shaped Civil War history, take a multiday tour with Smithsonian Associates. Stops include such historic sites as Manassas National Battlefield Park in Virginia, Antietam National Battle Field in Maryland, and Harpers Ferry, West Virginia, site of John Brown's last stand. ☎ *202/633–3030* ⊕ *www.smithsonianassociates.org* ✆ *From $30.*

Walking Tours

Cultural Tourism DC. This nonprofit group has 15 self-guided Neighborhood Heritage Trails, plus a citywide African American Heritage Trail, all of which are highlighted with historic markers. All the tours can be downloaded from their website. One week each fall, the group leads free guided walking tours that highlight the history and architecture of certain neighborhoods, from the southwest waterfront to points much farther north. You can also check out other cultural events, many free, happening around the city on their website. ☎ *202/661–7581* ⊕ *www.culturaltourismdc.org* ✆ *Free.*

DC by Foot. Dozens of tours, including the Tidal Basin and National Mall, Arlington National Cemetery, Capitol Hill, Georgetown, and U Street, are led by guides who work for tips, guaranteeing a highly entertaining experience. Tours last two to four hours, and are available year-round, but days and times vary by season and advance reservations are required. ☎ *202/370–1830* ⊕ *www.freetoursbyfoot.com* ✆ *Guides work for tips.*

Washington Walks. The wide range of tours offered by Washington Walks includes the self-explanatory "Memorials by Moonlight" and "The Most Haunted Houses." "Get Local Saturdays" goes in depth into Washington neighborhoods, and there are tours of Georgetown and Dupont Circle. ☎ *202/484–1565* ⊕ *www. washingtonwalks.com* ✆ *From $20.*

WASHINGTON, D.C.
BLACK HISTORY WALK

A walk along U Street and the eastern rim of Adams Morgan gives a taste of D.C. that most tourists never get. This tour through "Black Broadway" bounces from lively commercial streets brimming with hip bars, cafés, and boutiques to quiet, tree-lined, residential blocks, and highlights African American culture and history.

"Black Broadway" — U Street Corridor

The Howard Theatre at T Street and Florida Avenue is a good place to start. Opened in 1910, this landmark of black culture found its way onto the National Register of Historic Places for hosting some of the greatest musical acts of the last century—a list that includes such notables as Ella Fitzgerald and native son Duke Ellington in the 1930s and, more recently, Lena Horne, James Brown, and Marvin Gaye. All but destroyed in 1968, following the assassination of Martin Luther King Jr., the theater was renovated beautifully in 2012 and now features live acts almost nightly. A short hike west, at 10th and U Streets, sits the **African American Civil War Memorial,** where the names of more than 200,000 black soldiers who fought for their freedom are inscribed. Across 11th Street is **Washington Industrial Bank,** which thrived by offering African Americans a service that others in the city wouldn't: the option to borrow money. One block south and another west you'll find the **12th Street YMCA,** the oldest black Y in the country (1853). Head back to U Street to explore the **African American Civil War Museum,** featuring wonderful photographs from the era and an extensive on-site database for searching individual soldiers. Next, grab a half-smoke at **Ben's Chili Bowl.** A D.C. landmark, Ben's refused to close its doors during the fierce riots that followed King's assassination. While most of U Street was being destroyed, Ben's fed the police officers and black activists trying to keep order. Next door is the **Lincoln Theater,** another exceptional jazz venue and, from 1922 until desegregation, one of the largest and most elegant "colored-only" theaters. Given the area's history, it's probably little wonder that 15th and U marked the epicenter of the spontaneous celebration that erupted in the streets following the 2008 election of Barack Obama, the country's first African American president.

North of U Street

Venture northwest to marvel at **St. Augustine's Catholic Church**—a gorgeous, two-tower cathedral now home to a black congregation that seceded from its segregated church (St. Matthews) in 1858. Feel free to walk inside to glimpse the striking stained-glass portrait of a black St. Augustine and St. Monica. A few steps north is sprawling **Meridian Hill (or Malcolm X) Park,** where a number of civil rights marches have originated over the years. Cutting through the park to 16th Street, you'll spot **Meridian Hill Hall,** Howard University's first coed dorm. Alumni of the elite African American school include Thurgood Marshall and Toni Morrison. Continuing north, past some beautiful working embassies, you'll find **All Souls Unitarian Church.** Its pastor in the 1940s, Reverend A. Powell Davies, led the push to desegregate D.C. schools.

1

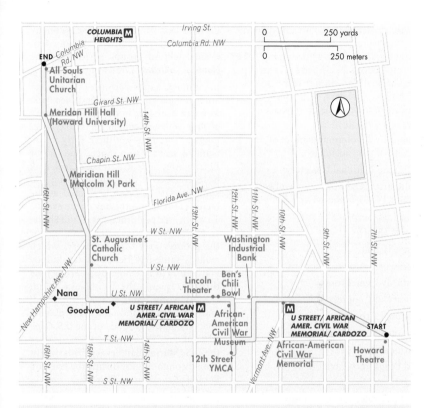

Highlights:	U Street was the center of black culture before Harlem was Harlem. See where Duke Ellington played, indulge in a half-smoke at Ben's Chili Bowl, and learn a bit about African American history along the way.
Where to Start:	Howard Theatre, just east of Metro's U St./Cardozo stop on the Green or Yellow lines
Length:	About 1½ miles; 1–2 hours, with window-shopping
Where to Stop:	All Souls Unitarian Church. The S1, S2, or S4 bus lines on 16th Street will whisk you back Downtown.
Best Time to Go:	While the sun is up, though the nightlife on U Street is an attraction in itself.
Worst Time to Go:	Avoid walking through Meridian Hill Park after dark.
Shopping Detour:	Check out Nana (*1528 U St. NW between 15th and 16th Sts., upstairs*) for new and vintage women's clothing, and browse Goodwood (*1428 U St. NW between 14th and 15th Sts.*) for antique wood furniture and estate jewelry.

FREE IN D.C.

For the thrifty, D.C. is a dream come true. All Smithsonian museums and national memorials are free, as are many other top attractions like Ford's Theatre and the National Zoo. Summertime is heaven for budget travelers, with free outdoor concerts and festivals every week.

Free Attractions

American Revolution Institute of the Society of the Cincinnati

Arlington National Cemetery

Dumbarton Oaks (free November 1 to March 14; $10 otherwise)

Folger Shakespeare Library

Ford's Theatre

Gravelly Point

Kenilworth Aquatic Gardens

Kennedy Center tours

Library of Congress

National Arboretum

National Postal Museum

National Zoo

Old Post Office Pavilion

Old Stone House

Phillips Collection (donations recommended)

Rock Creek Park

Sculpture Garden at the National Gallery of Art

Supreme Court of the United States

U.S. Botanic Garden

U.S. Capitol/Capitol Visitors Center

Washington National Cathedral

White House

Free Performances

The **Kennedy Center** hosts free performances 365 days a year at 6 pm on the Millennium Stage. Every September the Prelude Festival kicks off the Kennedy Center's fall schedule with many free events. Choral groups perform at the **National Cathedral**, often at no charge.

In summer, bands perform on Monday and Thursday nights atop **Fort Reno Park.** You can hear jazz in the **National Gallery of Art's sculpture garden** on Friday evenings in summer—get there early if you want to secure lawn space. The Carter Barron Amphitheatre in **Rock Creek Park** hosts free events throughout spring and summer with tickets distributed at the facility's box office the day of the events. To catch free performances of the **Shakespeare Theatre Company,** sign up online for the group's Free-for-All lottery, which awards same-day tickets at the Sidney Harman Hall in Chinatown. From June through August the U.S. Navy Band, U.S. Air Force Band, U.S. Marine Band, and U.S. Army Band take turns playing concerts on the grounds of the **U.S. Capitol** weekdays at 8 pm. You can also see the U.S. Marine Band every Friday night May through August during the Evening Parade at the Marine Barracks.

Almost every day of the year, the **Politics and Prose** bookstore on Connecticut Avenue invites authors to the store for readings, talks, and Q&A sessions. **Busboys and Poets,** another bookstore with two Downtown locations, offers readings, films, and political discussions almost every night as well.

Free Festivals

D.C. is a city of festivals, many of which are free to the public. For a complete list of events, visit the Washington, D.C. Convention and Tourism Corporation at ⊕ *www.washington.org.*

D.C. WITH KIDS

D.C. is filled with kid-friendly attractions. These sights are sure winners:

Bureau of Engraving and Printing

Any youngster who gets an allowance will enjoy watching bills roll off the presses. Despite the lack of free samples, the self-guided, 35-minute bureau tour is one of the city's most popular attractions.

DC Ducks

What do you get when you cross a tour bus with a boat? A duck—DC Ducks, that is. Tour the city by both land and water without leaving your seats aboard these unusual amphibious vehicles: standard 2½-ton GM trucks in watertight shells with propellers.

Discovery Theater

Within the Smithsonian's Ripley Center on the Mall, this lively theater began as a low-key puppet show before expanding to feature more than 300 programs a year exploring art, science, and global heritage—everything from robots to the Wright brothers to African drums.

International Spy Museum

This museum takes the art of espionage to new levels for junior James Bonds and Nancy Drews. Even the most cynical pre-teens and teenagers are usually enthralled with all the cool gadgetry. This museum is best for older tweens and teens—if you bring along a younger sibling, you could be in for a workout: there aren't many places to sit down, and strollers aren't allowed in the museum. Also, there is an entrance fee.

Mount Vernon

Farm animals, a hands-on discovery center, an interactive museum, and movies about the nation's first action hero make George Washington's idyllic home a place where families can explore all day.

National Air and Space Museum

There's a good reason why this place is one of the most popular museums in the world: kids love it. The 23 galleries here tell the story of aviation and space from the earliest human attempts at flight. All three gift shops sell freeze-dried astronaut food—not as tasty as what we eat on Earth, but it doesn't melt or drip. If you've never crunched into ice cream, it's worth the experience.

National Museum of American History

Oh, say, you can see ... the flag that inspired "The Star-Spangled Banner," Oscar the Grouch, the ruby slippers from *The Wizard of Oz,* an impressive collection of trains, and more Americana than anyone can digest in a day.

National Museum of Natural History

Say hello to Henry. One of the largest elephants ever found in the wild, this stuffed beast has greeted generations of kids in the rotunda of this huge museum dedicated to natural wonders. Take your kid to the O. Orkin Insect Zoo, home to live ants, bees, centipedes, tarantulas, roaches (some as large as mice), and other critters you wouldn't want in your house. Did we mention the dinosaurs?

National Zoo

Known more for its political animals than its real animals, D.C. nevertheless has one of the world's foremost zoos. If your child is crazy about animals, this is an absolute must—it's huge.

Paddleboat the Tidal Basin

How better to see the Jefferson Memorial and the world-famous cherry trees—gifts from Japan—than from the waters of the tidal basin? The paddleboats get the kids and you off your feet and into the sun!

D.C.'S TOP FESTIVALS

For a look at yearly events, visit ⊕ *www. washington.org*, the website of the tourism bureau.

Winter

National Christmas Tree Lighting/Pageant of Peace (☏ *202/208–1631* ⊕ *www.thenationaltree.org, Dec.*). Each year in early December, the president lights the tree at dusk on the Ellipse, with concerts, a Yule log, and Nativity scene held later in the month.

Restaurant Week (⊕ *www.ramw.org/restaurantweek, Jan. and Aug.*). More than 200 top restaurants offer lunch and dinner menus for around $20 and $35, respectively—often a steal.

Washington Auto Show (⊕ *www.washingtonautoshow.com, late Jan.*). Held at the Convention Center, this yearly event showcases the latest offerings from the world of automobiles.

Spring

National Cherry Blossom Festival (☏ *877/442–5666* ⊕ *www.nationalcherryblossomfestival.org, late Mar.–early Apr.*). D.C.'s most eye-catching annual festival opens with a Japanese lantern-lighting ceremony at the Tidal Basin.

Georgetown French Market (☏ *202/298–9222, late Apr.*). Shop, eat, wander, and enjoy strolling mimes and live musicians in one of D.C.'s most beautiful neighborhoods.

National Cathedral Flower Mart (☏ *202/365–3222, early May*). This 79-year-old free event on the Cathedral grounds features food, music, kids' activities and, of course, flowers.

Summer

Capital Pride Festival (☏ *202/719–5304* ⊕ *www.capitalpride.org, early June*). This weeklong festival with parade celebrates gay, lesbian, bisexual, and transgendered citizens.

Washington Shakespeare Theatre Free for All (☏ *202/547–1122* ⊕ *www.shakespearetheatre.org, June*). For two weeks, the theater company mounts free nightly performances at the Sidney Harman Hall, near Chinatown. Tickets are required.

Smithsonian's Folklife Festival (☏ *202/633–6440* ⊕ *www.folklife.si.edu, late June–early July*). This two-week festival includes traditional dance and music, storytelling, and ethnic food.

Independence Day Celebration (☏ *202/619–7222, July*). A parade fills Constitution Avenue, fireworks fly over the Washington Monument, and the NSO plays on the west lawn.

National Symphony Orchestra Labor Day Concert (☏ *202/416–8114* ⊕ *www.kennedycenter.org, Labor Day weekend*). This free concert is held on the grounds of the U.S. Capitol.

Fall

National Book Festival (☏ *202/707–1940, late Sept.*). This two-day event attracts some of the world's top authors and poets to the National Mall, where visitors can get books signed.

Washington International Horse Show (☏ *202/525–3679* ⊕ *www.wihs.org, late Oct.*). Held at Verizon Center, this annual show features jumping, dressage, barrel racing, and more.

Veterans Day (☏ *703/607–8000 for Cemetery Visitor Center,* ☏ *202/619–7222 for National Park Service, Nov. 11*). Services held at Arlington National Cemetery, Vietnam Veterans Memorial, and U.S. Navy Memorial, with a wreath-laying at 11 am at the Tomb of the Unknowns.

EXPLORING

Updated by
Catherine
Sharpe

With its neoclassical government buildings and broad avenues, Washington, D.C., looks its part as America's capital. Majestic monuments and memorials pay tribute to notable leaders and great achievements, and merit a visit. But D.C. also lives firmly in the present, and not just politically; new restaurants and bars continually emerge, upping the hipness factor in neighborhoods from Capitol Hill to U Street. Fun museums and tree-shaded parks make it a terrific place for families. You may come for the official sites, but you'll remember D.C.'s local flavor, too.

The internationally renowned collections of the Smithsonian—140 million objects, specimens, and artworks displayed in the world's largest museum complex—make Washington one of the great museum cities. The holdings of the 19 Smithsonian museums range from a 65-million-year-old *Tyrannosaurus rex* skeleton to masterpieces by Leonardo da Vinci and Pablo Picasso, the Hope Diamond, the original "Star-Spangled Banner," and the original 1903 *Wright Flyer*—and all are on view for free. Add in the legendary art treasures of the National Gallery, Portrait Gallery, the Phillips Collection, and Dumbarton Oaks, and Washington, D.C., becomes a true feast for the eyes.

Washington is a monumental city. In the middle of traffic circles, on tiny slivers of park, and at street corners and intersections, you'll find statues, plaques, and simple blocks of marble honoring the generals, artists, and statesmen who helped shape the nation. Of these tributes, the greatest and grandest are clustered west of the Mall on ground reclaimed from the marshy flats of the Potomac—which also happens to be the location of Washington's most striking display of cherry trees.

Given the heightened security concerns of present-day Washington, it might come as a surprise to learn that most government institutions continue to welcome the general public. The Founding Fathers' mandate of a free and open government lives on—just with metal detectors and bag searches. Though security checks are no one's idea of fun, most people find them a small price to pay for the opportunity to get a firsthand look at the government in action. Being in the famous halls of the Capitol or the Supreme Court is a heady experience. It's one part celebrity sighting and one part the world's best civics lesson.

Although the Capitol, White House, and Supreme Court get the lion's share of the attention, other government institutions hold their own, sometimes quirky, appeal. Art enthusiasts can gaze in wonder at the works on display at the Red Cross headquarters and the Interior Department, while military buffs can retrace the footsteps of four- and five-star generals in the seemingly endless hallways of the Pentagon.

HOW D.C. CAME TO BE

The city that invented American politicking, back-scratching, and delicate diplomatic maneuvering is itself the result of a compromise. Tired of its nomadic existence after having set up shop in eight locations, Congress voted in 1785 to establish a permanent federal city. Northern lawmakers wanted the capital on the Delaware River; Southerners wanted it on the Potomac. A deal was struck when Virginia's Thomas Jefferson agreed to support the proposal that the federal government assume the war debts of the colonies if New York's Alexander Hamilton and other Northern legislators would agree to locate the capital on the banks of the Potomac.

George Washington himself selected the site of the capital, a diamond-shape, 100-square-mile plot not far from his estate at Mount Vernon, near the confluence of the Potomac and Anacostia Rivers. To give the young city a head start, Washington included the already thriving tobacco ports of Alexandria, Virginia, and Georgetown, Maryland, in the District of Columbia. In 1791 Pierre-Charles L'Enfant, a French engineer who had fought in the Revolution, created the classic plan for the city.

It took the Civil War to energize the city first, attracting thousands of new residents and spurring a building boom that extended the capital in all directions. Streets were paved in the 1870s, and the first streetcars ran in the 1880s. The early 20th century witnessed the development of the city's monumental core: memorials to famous Americans such as Lincoln and Jefferson, along with the massive Federal Triangle, which includes the National Archives, the Internal Revenue Service, and the Department of Justice.

THE NATIONAL MALL

Sightseeing
★★★★★
Dining
★★
Lodging
★★★
Shopping
★★
Nightlife
★

It could be said that the National Mall—the heart of almost every visitor's trip to Washington—has influenced life in the U.S. more than any other expanse of lawn. The National Mall is a picnicking park, a jogging path, and an outdoor stage for festivals and fireworks. People come here from around the globe to tour the illustrious Smithsonian museums, celebrate special events, or rally to make the world a better place.

TOP ATTRACTIONS

Franklin Delano Roosevelt Memorial. This 7.5-acre memorial to the 32nd president, on the west side of the Tidal Basin, includes waterfalls and reflecting pools, four outdoor gallery rooms—one for each of Roosevelt's presidential terms (1933 to 1945)—and 10 bronze sculptures. The granite megaliths connecting the galleries are engraved with some of Roosevelt's famous statements, including, "The only thing we have to fear is fear itself."

Congress established the Franklin Delano Roosevelt Memorial Commission in 1955, and invited prospective designers to look to "the character and work of Roosevelt to give us the theme of a memorial." Several decades passed before Lawrence Halprin's design for a "walking environmental experience" was selected. It incorporates work by artists Leonard Baskin, Neil Estern, Robert Graham, Thomas Hardy, and George Segal, and master stone carver John Benson.

The statue of a wheelchair-bound Roosevelt near the entrance of the memorial was added in 2001. Originally, the memorial showed little evidence of Roosevelt's polio, which he contracted at age 39. He used a wheelchair for the last 24 years of his life, but kept his disability largely hidden from public view. The statue was added after years of debate about whether to portray Roosevelt realistically or to honor his desire not to display his disability.

You're encouraged to touch the handprints and Braille along the columns in the second room, which represent the working hands of the American people. A bronze statue of First Lady Eleanor Roosevelt stands in front of the United Nations symbol in the fourth room. She was a vocal spokesperson for human rights and one of the most influential women of her time. This was the first memorial designed to be wheelchair accessible. Several pillars with Braille lettering and tactile images help the visually impaired. At night the lighting over the waterfalls creates interesting shadows, and there's less noise from airplanes overhead. ⊠ *400 W. Basin Dr. SW, The Mall* ☎ *202/426–6841* ⊕ *www.nps.gov/fdrm* ⊡ *Free* Ⓜ *Smithsonian.*

Freer and Sackler galleries. The Smithsonian Institution has two museums of Asian art: the Freer Gallery of Art, which opened to the public in 1923, and the Arthur M. Sackler Gallery, which welcomed its first visitors in 1987. Both are physically connected by an underground passageway, and ideologically linked through the study, exhibition, and sheer love of Asian art. In addition, the Freer Gallery contains an important collection of 19th-century American art, punctuated by James McNeill Whistler's Peacock Room.

Explore a dramatic collection of 12th- to 19th-century Buddhist art from South Asia, including a majestic stone image of Shiva Dakshinamurti (Lord of the South) and a fierce gilded bronze of Palden Lhamo, the deity that protects Lhasa, the capital city of Tibet. You can further your understanding of Buddhism with an exhibition of art and immersive spaces that will run through October 2020. You'll step into a Tibetan shrine, visit a Sri Lankan stupa, and travel with an 8th-century Korean monk.

Be sure to marvel at the Peacock Room, a jewel box of a space designed by James McNeill Whistler, with gold murals on peacock-blue walls, and a peacock-feather-pattern gold-leaf ceiling. At noon on the third Thursday of every month, the floor-to-ceiling shutters are opened, bathing the room in glittering natural light.

Free highlight tours are held regularly. The museums also regularly host films, concerts, talks, and other events. Visit the website to see what's on. Enhance your visit with free mobile apps featuring the Peacock Room and select collection areas. ⊠ *Freer: 12th St. and Jefferson Dr. SW; Sackler: 1050 Independence Ave. SW, The Mall* ☎ *202/633–4880* ⊕ *www.asia.si.edu* ⊡ *Free* Ⓜ *Smithsonian.*

Fodor's Choice ★ **Hirshhorn Museum and Sculpture Garden.** Conceived as the nation's museum of modern and contemporary art, the Hirshhorn is home to nearly 12,000 works by masters who include Alexander Calder, Andy Warhol, and Louise Bourgeois, as well as contemporary superstars Anish Kapor and Yinka Shonibare. The art is displayed in a circular 1974 poured-concrete building, designed by Gordon Bunshaft, that was dubbed the "Doughnut on the Mall" when it was built. Most of the collection was bequeathed by the museum's founder, Joseph H. Hirshhorn, a Latvian immigrant who made his fortune in uranium mines.

Getting Oriented

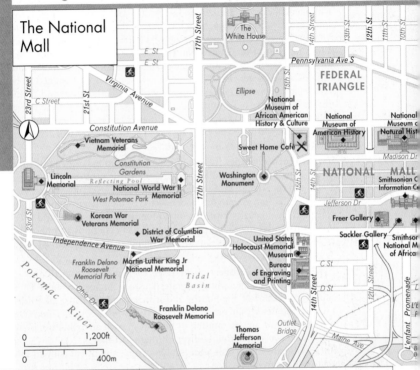

The National Mall

PLANNING YOUR TIME	GREAT EXPERIENCES IN THE NATIONAL MALL
With 12 museums spread out along 11 city blocks, you can't expect to see everything in one day. Few people have the stamina for more than half a day of museum- or gallery-hopping at a time; children definitely don't. To avoid mental and physical exhaustion, try to devote at least two days to the Mall.	**Monuments at night:** For a unique (and less crowded) historical experience, tour the many monuments at night. **National Air and Space Museum:** Touch a moon rock, see the original Spirit of St. Louis and Apollo Lunar Module, learn about the night sky, and catch an exciting IMAX movie. **National Museum of African American History and Culture:** D.C.'s newest museum is also its most moving. Learn about when captive slaves were first brought to the New World, the resilient African Americans who lived during the era of segregation, and the artists, filmmakers, writers, actors, musicians, and cultural leaders who have contributed so much to the history of the country. **Smithsonian museums.** The museums in the Smithsonian collection span the gauntlet of history, art, and culture. Spend the day bouncing between them (they're all free), and learning more about the United States.

2

GETTING HERE

You can access the National Mall from several Metro stations. On the Blue and Orange lines, the Federal Triangle stop is convenient to the Natural History and American History museums, and the Smithsonian stop is close to the Holocaust Memorial Museum and Hirshhorn Museum. On the Yellow and Green lines, Archives/Navy Memorial takes you to the National Gallery of Art. The L'Enfant Plaza stop, accessible from the Blue, Orange, Yellow, and Green lines, is the best exit for the Hirshhorn and Air and Space Museum. Walking from the Holocaust Memorial Museum to the National Gallery of Art is quite a trek. Many visitors take advantage of the D.C. Circulator National Mall Route buses that cost just $1 and run daily.

QUICK BITES

Garden Café. After marveling at the masterpieces in the National Gallery West Building, grab a quick bite on the ground floor with its lovely courtyard and fountain. ⊠ *6th and Constitution, The Mall* ☎ *202/712-7453* Ⓜ *Archives/Navy Memorial/Penn Quarter.*

Mitsitam Cafe. The café within the National Museum of the American Indian offers food stations with traditional and contemporary native dishes from throughout the Western Hemisphere. Don't miss the fry bread and corn totopos. ⊠ *4th St. SW and Independence Ave. SW, The Mall* ☎ *202/868-7774* ⊕ *www.nmai.si.edu* Ⓜ *Federal Station.*

Sweet Home Cafe. Located in the National Museum of African American History & Culture, the menu here offers rotating dishes based on the seasons and showcases the rich history of African American cuisine from four distinct geographic regions. ⊠ *1400 Constitution Ave. NW, The Mall* ☎ *202/633-1000* ⊕ *www.nmaahc.si.edu* Ⓜ *Smithsonian or Federal Triangle.*

The sculpture collection has masterpieces by Henry Moore, Alberto Giacometti, and Constantin Brancusi. Outside, sculptures dot a grass-and-granite garden. Among them is a 32-foot-tall yellow cartoon sculpture by pop-art iconographer Roy Lichtenstein that has become a beloved local landmark.

Inside, the third level is the place to see dramatic postwar art from the museum's permanent collection, displayed thematically, with works by artists such as Joseph Cornell, Isa Genzken, Alighiero e Boetti, and Sol LeWitt. Be sure to check out Cornell's *Untitled (Aviary with Yellow Birds)* and Yoko Ono's *Sky TV for Washington*. Large-scale text works by conceptual artist Lawrence Weiner round out the space.

The second level houses exhibits that rotate about three times a year, curated by museum staff and devoted to particular artists or themes. The lower level houses recent and experimental works from the permanent collection, as well as the Black Box, a space for moving-image installations. The sculpture garden makes an inspiring spot for a picnic. The museum also regularly screens premieres of independent, experimental, and documentary films. ⊠ *Independence Ave. and 7th St. SW, The Mall* ☎ *202/633–2829* ⊕ *www.hirshhorn.si.edu* ⊠ *Free* Ⓜ *Smithsonian or L'Enfant Plaza (Maryland Ave. exit).*

Korean War Veterans Memorial. At the west end of Mall, this memorial to the 1.5 million United States men and women who served in the Korean War (1950–53) highlights the cost of freedom. Nearly 37,000 Americans were killed on the Korean peninsula, 8,000 were missing in action, and more than 103,000 were wounded. The privately funded memorial was dedicated on July 27, 1995, the 42nd anniversary of the Korean War Armistice.

In the *Field of Service*, 19 oversize stainless-steel soldiers toil through rugged terrain toward an American flag; look beneath the helmets to see their weary faces. The reflection in the black granite wall to their right doubles their number to 38, symbolic of the 38th parallel, the latitude established as the border between North and South Korea in 1953, as well as the 38 months of the war.

Unlike many memorials, this one contains few words. The 164-foot-long granite wall etched with the faces of 2,400 unnamed servicemen and servicewomen says, "Freedom is not free." The plaque at the flagpole base reads, "Our nation honors her sons and daughters who answered the call to defend a country they never knew and a people they never met." The only other words are the names of 22 countries that volunteered forces or medical support, including Great Britain, France, Greece, and Turkey.

The adjacent circular Pool of Remembrance honors all who were killed, captured, wounded, or missing in action; it's a quiet spot for contemplation. ⊠ *Daniel French Dr. SW and Independence Ave. SW, The Mall* ☎ *202/426–6841* ⊕ *www.nps.gov/kwvm* ⊠ *Free* Ⓜ *Foggy Bottom.*

Fodor'sChoice
★

Lincoln Memorial. Many consider this to be the most inspiring monument in Washington, but that hasn't always been the case; early detractors thought it inappropriate that a president known for his humility should be honored with what some felt amounts to a

CLOSE UP

Introduction to the Smithsonian Museums

Be amazed by the history of air and space travel as you look up and see the 1903 Wright brothers' *Flyer*, and then hold your breath while watching astronauts repair the International Space Station in a mesmerizing IMAX movie at the National Air and Space Museum. Imagine yourself as Thomas Jefferson composing documents at his "writing box," or as Judy Garland playing Dorothy in *The Wizard of Oz*, when she clicked her ruby slippers three times—both are on display at the National Museum of American History.

Thought-provoking modern art is on view at the constantly changing Hirshhorn Museum, where you'll see Kenneth Snelson's *Needle Tower* in the outdoor sculpture garden and Yoko Ono's *Sky TV for Washington* inside the museum, or you can simply contemplate color or spend a few meditative moments in the Phillips Collection's intimate Rothko Room or Laib Wax Room. At the National Building Museum you can design and build your own monument, city, or structure.

VISITING THE SMITHSONIAN
Most of the 19 Smithsonian museums are open between 10 and 5:30 more than 360 days a year, and all are free, though there may be charges for some special exhibits. During the spring and summer, many of the museums offer extended hours and close at 7:30. To get oriented, start with a visit to the Smithsonian building—aka the "Castle," for its towers-and-turrets architecture—which has information on all the museums.

SPECIAL EVENTS
Smithsonian museums regularly host an incredible spectrum of special events, from evenings of jazz and dance nights to food and wine tastings, films, lectures, and events for families and kids. A full schedule is available at ⊕ *www.si.edu/events*. Popular events include live jazz on Friday evenings in summer from 5 to 8:30 at the National Gallery of Art sculpture garden and Take Five performances every third Thursday from 5 to 7 at the Smithsonian American Art Museum. The National Museum of the American Indian often holds weekend festivals that showcase the history and culture of native peoples from the around the world, complete with workshops, film screenings, hands-on activities for all ages, craft shows, and cooking demonstrations.

grandiose Greek temple. The memorial was intended to be a symbol of national unity, but over time it has come to represent social justice and civil rights.

Daniel Chester French's statue of the seated president gazes out over the Reflecting Pool. The 19-foot-high sculpture is made of 28 pieces of Georgia marble. The surrounding white Colorado-marble memorial was designed by Henry Bacon and completed in 1922. The 36 Doric columns represent the 36 states in the Union at the time of Lincoln's death; their names appear on the frieze above the columns. Over the frieze are the names of the 48 states in existence when the memorial was dedicated. Alaska and Hawaii are represented with an inscription on the terrace leading up to the memorial. At night the memorial is illuminated, creating a striking play of light and shadow across Lincoln's face.

The view from inside the Lincoln Memorial captures its reflecting pool and the iconic Washington Monument.

Two of Lincoln's great speeches—the second inaugural address and the Gettysburg Address—are carved on the north and south walls. Above each is a Jules Guerin mural: the south wall has an angel of truth freeing a slave; the unity of North and South is opposite.

The memorial's powerful symbolism makes it a popular gathering place; in its shadow Americans marched for integrated schools in 1958, rallied for an end to the Vietnam War in 1967, and laid wreaths in a ceremony honoring the Iranian hostages in 1979. It may be best known, though, as the site of Martin Luther King Jr.'s "I Have a Dream" speech.

Lincoln's face and hands look especially lifelike because they're based on castings done while he was president. Those who know sign language might recognize that the left hand is shaped like an A and the right like an L. It's unlikely this was intentional, but the sculptor, Daniel Chester French, did have a deaf son. ✉ *23rd St. SW and Independence Ave. SW, The Mall* ✛ *West end of Mall* ☎ *202/426–6841* ⊕ *www.nps. gov/linc* ✉ *Free* Ⓜ *Foggy Bottom.*

Martin Luther King Jr. National Memorial. A "King" now stands tall among the presidents on the National Mall. At the dedication on October 16, 2011, President Barack Obama said, "This is a day that would not be denied." The memorial opened 15 years after Congress approved it in 1996 and 82 years after the famed civil rights leader was born in 1929.

Located strategically between the Lincoln and Jefferson memorials and adjacent to the FDR Memorial, the crescent-shape King Memorial sits on a 4-acre site on the curved bank of the Tidal Basin. There are two main ways to enter the memorial. From West Basin Drive, walk through a center walkway cut out of a huge boulder, the Mountain of Despair.

From the Tidal Basin entrance, a 28-foot-tall granite boulder shows King looking out toward Jefferson. The symbolism of the mountain and stone are explained by King's words: "With this faith, we will be able to hew out of the mountain of despair a stone of hope." The centerpiece stone was carved by Chinese sculptor Lei Yixin; his design was chosen from more than 900 entries in an international competition. Fittingly, Yixin first read about King's "I Have a Dream" speech at age 10 while visiting the Lincoln Memorial.

The themes of democracy, justice, hope, and love are reflected through quotes on the south and north walls and on the Stone of Hope. The quotes reflect speeches, sermons, and writings penned by King from 1955 through 1968. Waterfalls in the memorial reflect King's use of the biblical quote: "Let justice roll down like waters and righteousness like a mighty stream. ⊠ *1964 Independence Ave. SW, The Mall* ☎ *202/426–6841* ⊕ *www.nps.gov/mlkm* ⊠ *Free* Ⓜ *Smithsonian.*

Fodor's Choice
★

National Air and Space Museum. *For more information, see the highlighted feature in this section.* ⊠ *Independence Ave. at 6th St. SW* ☎ *202/633–1000* ⊕ *www.airandspace.si.edu* ⊠ *Free; IMAX or planetarium $9; IMAX feature film $15; flight simulators $7–$8.*

National Gallery of Art, East Building. The East Building opened in 1978 in response to the changing needs of the National Gallery, especially to house a growing collection of modern and contemporary art. The building itself is a modern masterpiece. The trapezoidal shape of the site prompted architect I.M. Pei's dramatic approach: two interlocking spaces shaped like triangles provide room for galleries, auditoriums, and administrative offices. Despite its severe angularity, Pei's building is inviting. The ax-blade-like southwest corner has been darkened and polished smooth by thousands of hands irresistibly drawn to it. Inside, the sunlit atrium is dominated by a colorful 76-foot-long Alexander Calder mobile. Visitors can view a dynamic 500-piece collection of photography, paintings, sculpture, works on paper, and media arts in thought-provoking chronological, thematic, and stylistic arrangements.

Highlights include galleries devoted to Mark Rothko's giant, glowing canvases, Barnett Newman's 14 stark black, gray, and white canvas paintings from *The Stations of the Cross, 1958–1966,* and several colorful and whimsical Alexander Calder mobiles and sculptures. You can't miss Katharina Fritsch's *Hahn/Cock, 2013,* a tall blue rooster that appears to be standing guard over the street and federal buildings below from the museum's roof terrace that also offers views of the Capitol. The Upper Level gallery showcases modern art from 1910–80 including masterpieces by Constantin Brancusi, Marcel Duchamp, Sam Gilliam, Henri Matisse, Joan Miró, Piet Mondrian, Jackson Pollock, and Andy Warhol, among others. Ground-level galleries are devoted to American art from 1900–50, including pieces by George Bellows, Edward Hopper, Georgia O'Keeffe, Charles Sheeler, and Alfred Stieglitz. With the theme "Markers, Signs and Flow," the concourse level presents showpieces like Glenn Ligon's neon sculpture/sign *Double America, 2012*; Jasper Johns' *Target, 1958* and Jessica Stockholder's expressive sculptural installation, *No Title, 1994.*

Continued on page 44

NATIONAL AIR AND SPACE MUSEUM

(above) Neil Armstrong and Buzz Aldrin's spacesuits.
(left) You can see into the cockpit of the Airbus A320.

The country's second most-visited museum, attracting 9 million people annually to its vast and diverse collection of historic aircraft and spacecraft, is the perfect place to amaze the kids with giant rocket ships, relive the glory days of fighter jets, and even learn to fly. Its 22 galleries tell the story of humanity's quest for flight—from the Wright brothers' experiments with gliders to space exploration.

PLANNING YOUR TIME

If you only have short time take the free ninety-minute docent-led tour of the museum's highlights, which leaves daily at 10:30 and 1 from the Welcome Center.

To get the most from the museum, plan your must-sees in advance and allow plenty of time—at least two hours—to take everything in. The museum has three basic types of exhibits: aircraft and spacecraft; galleries of history and science; and experiences, such as IMAX films and hands-on workshops. An ideal visit would include a mix of these.

Before your visit, buy timed tickets online up to two weeks in advance for the popular IMAX films and planetarium shows to bypass the long lines and sold-out screenings.

When you arrive at the museum, consult the guides at the welcome desk; they can help you fine-tune your plan. If you didn't buy tickets for IMAX online, buy them now.

If you're traveling with kids, arrive early to avoid lines and pick up a kids' guide with games and activities at the welcome desk. Ask for the daily schedule of science demonstrations and (Thursday–Saturday only) Story Times for kids ages 2 to 8. If it's a clear day, visit the Public Observatory for daytime telescopic viewing and a chat with an astronomer. Strollers are allowed through security; there is a family bathroom on the first floor near the food court and a baby changing station near the Early Flight gallery.

If you just can't get enough, the Steven F. Udvar-Hazy Center, a companion museum near Dulles International Airport, features two massive hangars filled with hundreds more aircraft, spacecraft, aviation artifacts and a hangar where you can see restoration work in progress.

MUSEUM HIGHLIGHTS

AIRCRAFT AND SPACECRAFT

On entering the museum, visitors will find the **Boeing Milestones of Flight Hall,** which traces the evolution of air and space travel.

Albatros D.va

Make like Buzz Lightyear and head to infinity and beyond with a walk through the **Skylab Orbital Workshop,** the largest component of America's first space station in the **Space Race** gallery. Also on display are an arsenal of rockets and missiles, from the giant **V-2 rocket** to the devastatingly accurate **Tomahawk Cruise missile.** The **Apollo Lunar Module** is also a must-see in **Exploring the Moon.**

HISTORY AND SCIENCE

Even those who don't like history flock to the fascinating **Wright Brothers** gallery to see the first machine to achieve piloted flight, the **1903 Wright Flyer** and the Barron Hilton **Pioneers of Flight** gallery with Amelia Earhart's Lockheed Vega.

For history buffs, the **Great War in the Air, World War II,** and **Sea-Air Operations** galleries are essential, with legendary fighter planes such as the **Supermarine Spitfire.**

In the history of space exploration, **Apollo to the Moon** is packed with artifacts from moon missions.

Is there life on Mars? Find out in the science-oriented **Explore the Universe, Looking at Earth,** and **Moving Beyond Earth** galleries.

IMAX AND PLANETARIUM SHOWS

Lift off with an **IMAX** film. You'll feel like you've left the ground with the swooping aerial scenes in **To Fly!** or **Hidden Universe 3D.** Or take a trip into deep space with Hubble 3D. In the **Albert Einstein Planetarium,** you can watch the classic tour of the nighttime sky as well as shows like **Dark Universe.**

HANDS-ON

Test your top gun skills at one of the popular **Flight Simulators** where you'll get full-on fighter plane experience—barrel rolls and all.

TOURING TIPS

Avoid the Crowds: Between April and September (and on holiday weekends) the museum is slammed with visitors; it is least crowded September to March. It's always a good idea to come before noon to beat the rush.

Where to Eat: A huge food court offers McDonald's, Boston Market, and Donato's Pizzeria, and is the most simple and practical eating option around.

Souvenirs: The three-story museum store is the largest in all the Smithsonian museums, and one of the best. Along with souvenirs, books, and collectors' items, it also displays a model of the *USS Enterprise,* used in the filming of the first *Star Trek* television series. If you have kids, don't start your tour here or you may never leave!

Flight Simulators: Tickets can be purchased at the IMAX box office or in the **Flight Simulators** gallery.

Soviet SS-20 nuclear missile.

Apollo capsule   Breitling Orbiter   Apollo 11 module   Lockheed Vega

FIRST FLOOR

National Air and Space Museum

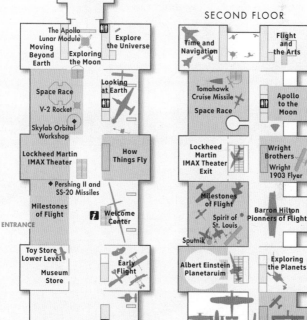

The Wright Place
Food Court

The Apollo
Lunar Module
Moving
Beyond
Earth

Explore
the Universe

Exploring
the Moon

Looking
at Earth

Space Race
V-2 Rocket

Skylab Orbital
Workshop

Lockheed Martin
IMAX Theater

How
Things Fly

◆ Pershing II and
SS-20 Missiles

Milestones
of Flight

ENTRANCE

Welcome
Center

Toy Store
Lower Level

Museum
Store

Early
Flight

America
By Air

Jet
Aviation

Flight
Simulators

West
Gallery

Golden
Age of
Flight

SECOND FLOOR

Time and
Navigation

Flight
and
the Arts

Tomahawk
Cruise Missile

Space Race

Apollo
to the
Moon

Lockheed
Martin
IMAX Theater
Exit

Wright
Brothers
Wright
1903 Flyer

Milestones
of Flight

Spirit of
St. Louis

Barron Hilton
Pioneers of Flight

Sputnik

Albert Einstein
Planetaruim

Exploring
the Planets

Great War
in the Air

Supermarine
Spitfire

Sea-Air
Operations

Military
Unmanned
Aerial
Vehicles
(UAV)

World War II
Aviaton

KEY

⊥ *Hanging Artifacts*

🍴 *Food court*

🚻 *Restroom*

ℹ️ *Tourist information*

0 ——————— 90 feet

0 ——————— 30 m

Staggerwing

The East Building Shop is located on the concourse level and Terrace Café looks out over the atrium from the upper level. You can access an audio tour on your mobile device, and docent-led tours are available most days at 1:30 pm. ⊠ *Constitution Ave., between 3rd and 4th Sts. NW, The Mall* ☎ *202/737–4215* ⊕ *www.nga.gov* ⊠ *Free* Ⓜ *Archives/ Navy Memorial.*

National Gallery of Art, West Building. The two buildings of the National Gallery hold one of the world's foremost art collections, with paintings, sculptures, and graphics that date from the 13th to the 21st centuries. Opened in 1941, the museum was a gift to the nation from treasury secretary Andrew W. Mellon. The rotunda, with marble columns surrounding a fountain, sets the stage for the masterpieces on display in more than 100 galleries.

Ginevra de' Benci, the only painting by Leonardo da Vinci on display in the Americas, is the centerpiece of the collection's comprehensive survey of Italian Renaissance paintings and sculpture. Rembrandt van Rijn and Johannes Vermeer, masters of painting light, anchor the magnificent collection of Dutch and Flemish works. The 19th-century French Galleries house gorgeous French impressionist masterworks by such superstars as Vincent van Gogh, Paul Cézanne, Claude Monet, Auguste Renoir, and Edgar Degas.

Walk beneath flowering trees in the sculpture garden, on the Mall between 7th and 9th Streets. Granite walkways take you through a shaded landscape featuring works from the Gallery's growing collection, as well as loans for special exhibitions.

There are many free docent-led tours every day, and a recorded tour of highlights of the collection is available free on the main floor adjacent to the rotunda. For a quick tour, pick up the laminated "What to See in One Hour," which pinpoints 12 must-see masterworks. The Information Room maintains a database of more than 1,700 works of art from the collection. Touch-screen monitors provide access to color images, text, animation, and sounds to help you better understand the works. ⊠ *4th St. and Constitution Ave. NW, The Mall* ☎ *202/737–4215* ⊕ *www.nga.gov* ⊠ *Free* Ⓜ *Archives/ Navy Memorial.*

Fodor's Choice
★

National Museum of African American History & Culture. Washington's newest, most powerful museum is perhaps best summed up with a quote by founding director Lonnie Bunch: "the African American experience is the lens through which we understand what it is to be an American." This serves as that lens, thanks to the 12 exhibitions that display nearly 3,000 historical artifacts, documents, photographs, memorabilia, and media.

The building's structure resembles nothing else on the Mall. The shape of its bronze-color corona was inspired by a Nigerian artist's carving, which is prominently displayed in one of the galleries. The corona's filigree design was patterned after railings made by enslaved 19th-century craftsmen. The museum's three tiers are hung at the same angle as the Washington Monument's capstone (it makes for a dramatic photo). Powerful quotes from African Americans are strategically placed

TO WORK AND FIGH...
WN LIKE ...TER AND
...MIGHTY STREAM

ING JR 1955

...CHERISH MY OWN FREEDOM DEARLY,
BUT I CARE EVEN MORE FOR YOUR FREEDOM

NELSON MANDELA 199...

DID YOU KNOW

Within the National Museum
of African American History
& Culture, you'll find a collection of the country's most
moving and powerful exhibits.
If necessary, visitors can take
time to emotionally recharge
within the contemplative
space known as the reflection
room, where a glass structure
called the oculus allows light
in from above and a waterfall
effect offers a quiet space for
reflection.

throughout the space. The museum is divided into two parts: 60% of the museum is underground and the remaining 40% is aboveground. Exhibits underground share a somber and wrenching historical time line from slavery through civil rights. Aboveground, galleries celebrate the cultural contributions of African Americans.

To best experience this museum, start at the underground Concourse History Galleries. Here you'll see wreckage from a slave ship that broke apart off Cape Town, South Africa, in 1794 that drowned 212 people; a 19th-century slave cabin from Edisto Island, South Carolina, that was occupied until 1980; the original casket of 14-year-old Emmett Till, who was murdered in Mississippi in 1955 for allegedly flirting with a white woman; a railcar with its very different first-class and "colored" sections; and a biplane used to train the Tuskegee Airmen who fought in WWII. Also on the main Concourse level is the 350-seat Oprah Winfrey Theater that hosts musical performances, lectures and discussions, film presentations, and other programming. The Center for African American Media Arts is on the second floor, where visitors can research their families in a genealogy center.

The third- and fourth-floor galleries have a more spirited vibe. Highlights include sports memorabilia like Jesse Owens's cleats, Michael Jordan's 1996 jersey, Joe Louis's gloves, Muhammad Ali's robe, Gabby Douglas's leotard, and nine Olympic medals won by Carl Lewis. Other collection gems include a lobby card from the 1967 movie *Guess Who's Coming to Dinner*; Louis Armstrong's trumpet; Michael Jackson's sequined jacket; and Marian Anderson's jacket and skirt that she wore when she performed a 1939 concert from the Lincoln Memorial, among many others.

You must have a timed pass to enter the museum. Same-day, timed passes are available online daily beginning at 6:30 am. A limited number of walk-up passes are given out weekdays beginning at 1 pm, but they go fast. Download the NMAAHC mobile app to further enhance your visiting experience. ✉ *1400 Constitution Ave. NW, The Mall* ☎ *202/633–1000* ⊕ *www.nmaahc.si.edu* 🖾 *Free* Ⓜ *Smithsonian or Federal Triangle.*

FAMILY   **National Museum of American History.** The 3 million artifacts and archival
Fodor's Choice   collections in the country's largest American history museum explore
★   America's cultural, political, and scientific past, with holdings as diverse and iconic as Abraham Lincoln's top hat, Thomas Edison's lightbulbs, Julia Child's kitchen, and Judy Garland's ruby slippers.

The centerpiece of the **Star-Spangled Banner** gallery is the banner that in 1814 was hoisted to show that Fort McHenry had survived 25 hours of British rocket attacks, inspiring Francis Scott Key to write the lyrics that became the national anthem. **American Stories** showcases historic and cultural touchstones of American history through more than 100 objects from the museum's vast holdings that rotate frequently: a walking stick used by Benjamin Franklin, a sunstone capital from a Mormon temple, Archie Bunker's chair, Muhammad Ali's boxing gloves, a fragment of Plymouth Rock, and a Jim Henson puppet.

Highlights Tours are offered daily at 10:15 and 1 from the welcome desks. This is also the only museum in the world with an active program of using its historical musical instruments for live performances; the Smithsonian Chamber Music Society holds regular concerts here. ✉ *Constitution Ave. and 14th St. NW, The Mall* ☎ *202/633–1000* ⊕ *www.americanhistory.si.edu* ✆ *Free* Ⓜ *Smithsonian or Federal Triangle.*

National Museum of the American Indian. Visually and conceptually, the National Museum of the American Indian stands apart from the other cultural institutions on the Mall. The exterior, clad in pinkish-gold limestone from Minnesota, evokes natural rock formations. Inside, four floors of galleries cover 10,000 years of history of the thousands of native tribes of the Western Hemisphere. However, only 5% of the museum's holdings are on display at any one time. Touring with one of the Native American guides helps bring the history and legends to life. Live music, dance, theater, and storytelling are central to experiencing this museum. Tribal groups stage performances in the two theaters and sunlit ceremonial atrium.

The Great Inka Road: Engineering an Empire explores the 20,000-mile road that crosses rivers, deserts, and mountains, and linked Cusco, the center of the Inkas, to the farthest reaches of its empire. The *Our Universe* exhibit tells the unique creation legends of eight different tribes, with carvings, costumes, and videos of tribal storytellers. *Nation to Nation: Treaties Between the United States and American Indian Nations* shares the history and legacy of U.S.–American Indian diplomacy from the colonial period to the present. This exhibit showcases the influence of Native diplomats and leaders of Indian nations.

Visit between 10 and 2 on a sunny day to see the central atrium awash in rainbows created by the light refracted through prisms in the ceiling aligned with Earth's cardinal points. Free tours are offered weekdays at 1:30, and the museum's 6,000-square-foot family-friendly imagiNATIONS Activity Center includes hands-on activities throughout the year. ✉ *4th St. and Independence Ave. SW, The Mall* ☎ *202/633–1000* ⊕ *www.americanindian.si.edu* ✆ *Free* Ⓜ *L'Enfant Plaza.*

FAMILY **National Museum of Natural History.** This is one of the world's great natural history museums, with 18 exhibition halls, one of the largest IMAX screens in the world, giant dinosaur fossils, glittering gems, creepy-crawly insects, and other natural delights. There are more than 126 million specimens in all, attracting more than 7 million visitors annually. Marvel at the enormous 12-ton, 14-foot-tall African bush elephant that greets visitors in the rotunda of the museum and learn about elephant behavior and conservation efforts.

Discover **Q?RIUS**, a state-of-the-art, hands-on space featuring 6,000 objects, on-site experts, and an array of digital tools that focus on the natural world. Walk among hundreds of live butterflies in the **Butterfly Pavilion** (for a separate fee). Check out giant millipedes and furry tarantulas in the **O. Orkin Insect Zoo** (don't miss the daily live tarantula feedings). See perfectly preserved male and female giant squids, a jaw-dropping replica of a whale, and the ecosystem of a living coral reef in the **Sant Ocean Hall,** the museum's largest exhibit. The **Ocean Explorer Theater** stimulates a dive into the sea. Watch as paleobiologists study the newest addition to the museum's collection of 46 million fossils, including the Wankel T. rex found in Montana in 1988. One of the most complete T. rex skeletons ever discovered, it will form the centerpiece of the new 25,000-square-foot dinosaur hall that's currently scheduled for completion in 2019.

The IMAX theater shows three-dimensional natural history films throughout the day. Buy advance tickets at the box office when you arrive, then tour the museum. ⊠ *Constitution Ave. and 10th St. NW, The Mall* ☎ *202/633–1000* ⊕ *www.mnh.si.edu* ⊠ *Free; IMAX $9; Butterfly Pavilion $6 (free Tues.)* Ⓜ *Smithsonian or Federal Triangle.*

National World War II Memorial. This symmetrically designed monument, in a parklike setting between the Washington Monument and Lincoln Memorial, honors the 16 million Americans who served in the armed forces, the more than 400,000 who died, and all who supported the war effort at home.

An imposing circle of 56 granite pillars, each bearing a bronze wreath, represents the U.S. and its territories of 1941–45. Four bronze eagles, a bronze garland, and two 43-foot-tall arches inscribed with "Atlantic" and "Pacific" surround the large circular plaza. The roar of the water comes from the Rainbow Pool, here since the 1920s and renovated to form the centerpiece of the memorial. There are also two fountains and two waterfalls.

The Field of Stars, a wall of 4,000 gold stars, commemorates the more than 400,000 Americans who lost their lives in the war. Bas-relief panels tell the story of how World War II affected Americans by depicting women in the military, V-J Day, medics, the bond drive, and more activities of the time. The 24 panels are divided evenly between the Atlantic front and the Pacific front. ⊠ *17th St. SW and Home Front Dr. SW, between Independence Ave. SW and Constitution Ave. NW, The Mall* ☎ *202/426–6841* ⊕ *www.nps.gov/nwwm* ⊠ *Free* Ⓜ *Smithsonian.*

FAMILY **Smithsonian National Museum of African Art.** This unique underground building houses stunning galleries, a library, photographic archives, and educational facilities. The rotating exhibits illuminate African visual arts, including sculpture, textiles, photography, archaeology, and modern art. *Currents: Water in African Art* showcases the power of art through pieces like intricately carved wooden masks and figures paying tribute to water spirits and deities. *African Mosaic: Celebrating a Decade of Collecting* presents a dynamic exhibition of paintings, sculpture, carvings, jewelry, clothing, and face masks, presented thematically so that visitors are encouraged to reflect on the connections between the artworks and what they communicate to the viewer. The museum's educational programs for both children and adults include films with contemporary perspectives on African life, storytelling programs, and festivals including Community Day. The hands-on workshops, such as traditional basket weaving, bring Africa's oral and cultural traditions to life. Workshops and demonstrations by African and African American artists offer a chance to meet and talk to practicing artists. ⊠ *950 Independence Ave. SW, The Mall* ☎ *202/633–4600* ⊕ *africa.si.edu* ⊠ *Free* Ⓜ *Smithsonian.*

Fodor'sChoice
★

Thomas Jefferson Memorial. In the 1930s Congress decided that Thomas Jefferson deserved a monument positioned as prominently as those honoring Washington and Lincoln. Workers scooped and moved tons of the river bottom to create dry land for the spot directly south of the White House where the monument was built. Jefferson had always admired the Pantheon in Rome, so the memorial's architect, John Russell Pope, drew on it for inspiration. His finished work was dedicated on April 13, 1943, the bicentennial of Jefferson's birth.

Early critics weren't kind to the memorial—rumor has it that it was nicknamed "Jefferson's muffin" for its domed shape. The design was called outdated and too similar to that of the Lincoln Memorial. Indeed, both statues of Jefferson and Lincoln are 19 feet, just 6 inches shorter than the statue of Freedom atop the Capitol.

The bronze statue of Jefferson, standing on a 6-foot granite pedestal, looms larger than life. You can get a taste of Jefferson's keen intellect from his writings about freedom and government inscribed on the marble walls surrounding his statue. Check out the view of the White House from the memorial's steps—it's one of the best in the city.

Learn more about Jefferson by visiting the exhibit called *Light and Liberty* on the memorial's lower level. It chronicles highlights of Jefferson's life and has a time line of world history during his lifetime. ✉ *Tidal Basin, south bank, off Ohio Dr. SW, The Mall* ☎ *202/426–6841* ⊕ *www.nps.gov/thje* ✆ *Free* Ⓜ *Smithsonian.*

Fodor'sChoice
★

United States Holocaust Memorial Museum. This museum asks visitors to consider how the Holocaust was made possible by the choices of individuals, institutions, and governments, and what lessons they hold for us today. The permanent exhibition, *The Holocaust*, tells the stories of the millions of Jews, Gypsies, Jehovah's Witnesses, homosexuals, political prisoners, the mentally ill, and others killed by the Nazis between 1933 and 1945. The exhibitions are detailed and sometimes graphic; the experiences memorable and powerful.

Upon arrival, you are issued an "identity card" containing biographical information on a real person from the Holocaust. As you move through the museum, you read sequential updates on your card. Hitler's rise to power and the spread of European anti-Semitism are thoroughly documented in the museum's early exhibits, with films of Nazi rallies, posters, newspaper articles, and recordings of Hitler's speeches immersing you in the world that led to the Holocaust. Exhibits include footage of scientific experiments done on Jews, artifacts such as a freight car like those used to transport Jews to concentration camps, and oral testimonies from Auschwitz survivors.

Also on view is *Some Were Neighbors: Collaboration & Complicity in the Holocaust,* which examines how the Holocaust was made possible by decisions made by ordinary individuals. *I Want Justice* details the past and current judicial efforts to hold perpetrators accountable from the Nuremberg to Cambodia trials. *Genocide: The Threat Continues* looks at the people and places who are currently at risk. As part of this exhibit, visitors can speak in real time with people who have escaped genocidal and war crimes in northern Iraq and Syria.

The United States Holocaust Memorial Museum is the country's official memorial remembering those lost in the Holocaust.

After this powerful experience, the *Hall of Remembrance*, filled with candles, provides a much-needed space for quiet reflection.

Timed-entry passes (distributed on a first-come, first-served basis at the 14th Street entrance starting at 9:45 am or available in advance through the museum's website with a $1 per ticket service fee) are necessary for the permanent exhibition from March through August. Allow extra time to enter the building in spring and summer, when long lines can form. From September through February, no passes are required. ✉ *100 Raoul Wallenberg Pl. SW or 14th St. SW, The Mall* ☎ *202/488–0400, 800/400–9373 for tickets* ⊕ *www.ushmm. org* ✉ *Free; $1 per ticket service fee for advance online reservations* Ⓜ *Smithsonian.*

Fodor's Choice
★

Vietnam Veterans Memorial. "The Wall," as it's commonly called, is one of the most visited sites in Washington. The names of more than 58,000 Americans who died in the Vietnam War are etched in its black granite panels, creating a powerful memorial. It was conceived by Jan Scruggs, a corporal who served in Vietnam, and designed by Maya Lin, then a 21-year-old architecture student at Yale.

Thousands of offerings are left at the wall each year; many people leave flowers, others leave the clothing of soldiers or letters of thanks. In 2003, President George W. Bush signed a law authorizing the Vietnam Veterans Memorial Fund to build an education center at The Wall, which will pay tribute to service members who lost their lives not only in the Vietnam War, but in the Iraq and Afghanistan wars. The project is currently expected to break ground in 2018, for completion in 2020.

In 1984 Frederick Hart's statue of three soldiers and a flagpole was erected to the south of the wall, with the goal of winning over veterans who considered the memorial a "black gash of shame." In 2004, a plaque was added to honor veterans who died after the war as a direct result of injuries in Vietnam, but who fall outside Department of Defense guidelines for remembrance at the wall.

The Vietnam Women's Memorial was dedicated in 1993. Glenna Goodacre's bronze sculpture depicts two women caring for a wounded soldier while a third kneels nearby; eight trees around the plaza commemorate the eight women in the military who died in Vietnam.

Names on the wall are ordered by date of death. To find a name, consult the alphabetical lists found at either end of the wall. You can get assistance locating a name at the white kiosk with the brown roof near the entrance. At the wall, rangers and volunteers wearing yellow caps can look up the names and supply you with paper and pencils for making rubbings. Every name on the memorial is preceded (on the west wall) or followed (on the east wall) by a symbol designating status. A diamond indicates "killed, body recovered." A plus sign (found by a small percentage of names) indicates "killed, body not recovered." ⊠ *Constitution Gardens, 23rd St. NW and Constitution Ave. NW, The Mall* ☎ *202/426–6841* ⊕ *www.nps.gov/vive* ▦ *Free* Ⓜ *Foggy Bottom.*

Washington Monument. The 555-foot, 5-inch Washington Monument punctuates the capital like a huge exclamation point. The monument was part of Pierre L'Enfant's plan for Washington, but his intended location proved to be marshy, so it was moved 100 yards southeast. Construction began in 1848 and continued until 1884. Upon completion, the monument was the world's tallest structure and weighed more than 81,000 tons.

Six years into construction, members of the anti-Catholic Know-Nothing Party stole and smashed a block of marble donated by Pope Pius IX. This action, combined with funding shortages and the onset of the Civil War, brought construction to a halt. After the war, building finally resumed, and though the new marble came from the same Maryland quarry as the old, it was taken from a different stratum with a slightly different shade. Inserted into the walls of the monument are 193 memorial stones from around the world.

While visitors are usually allowed to visit the top, the Monument is currently closed for a two-year elevator modernization project. It is scheduled to reopen in the spring of 2019. As always, you can have a glorious view of this beloved landmark from the steps of the Lincoln Memorial. ⊠ *15th St. NW, between Constitution Ave. NW and Independence Ave. SW, The Mall* ☎ *202/426–6841* ⊕ *www.nps.gov/ wamo* Ⓜ *Smithsonian.*

ASK A RANGER

You may think of park rangers as denizens of the woods, but they're a conspicuous presence at Washington's memorials—look for the olive-green-and-gray uniforms. Rangers lead talks about each memorial run by the Park Service (every hour on the hour, from 10 to 9) unless they are short staffed, which does happen. They are an invaluable source of information; don't hesitate to ask questions of them. Kids can get Junior Park Ranger activity booklets from the ranger booths at the Lincoln, Roosevelt, Vietnam, World War II, and King memorials. The National Park Service also has two wonderful programs: "Walk with a Ranger" is a 1½- to 2-hour daily walk to the monuments and memorials, often with a theme. They start at the Lincoln Memorial at 10 am and 2 pm and from the base of the Washington Monument at 7 pm. and "Run with a Ranger," on the second and fourth Saturdays of every month March through November, is a 3- to 4-mile ranger-led themed run that includes short lectures at key monuments and statues.

WORTH NOTING

FAMILY **Bureau of Engraving and Printing.** Paper money has been printed here since 1914, when the bureau relocated from the redbrick-towered Auditors Building at the corner of 14th Street and Independence Avenue. In addition to paper currency, military certificates and presidential invitations are printed here, too. You can only enter the bureau on tours, which last about 40 minutes. From March 6 through September 1, free same-day timed-entry tour passes are issued starting at 8 am (plan on being in line no later than 7 am) at the Raoul Wallenberg Place SW ticket booth. For the rest of the year, tickets are not required and visitors can simply wait in line. You also can arrange a tour through your U.S. senator or representative. ✉ *14th and C Sts. SW, The Mall* ☎ *202/874–2330, 866/874–2330 tour information* ⊕ *moneyfactory. gov* 🖾 *Free* Ⓜ *Smithsonian.*

District of Columbia War Memorial. Despite its location and age, visitors often overlook this memorial on the National Mall that President Herbert Hoover dedicated in 1931. Unlike the neighboring memorials on the Mall, this relatively small structure isn't a national memorial. The 47-foot-high, circular, domed, columned temple is dedicated to the 499 men and women (military and civilian) from Washington, D.C., who died in the Great War. Unofficially referred to as the World War I memorial, the marble structure was in disrepair and hidden by trees for decades. Through the American Recovery and Reinvestment Act of 2009, the memorial was restored to its original grandeur and is now maintained by the National Park Service. ✉ *Independence Ave. SW, The Mall* ✛ *North side, between World War II Memorial and Lincoln Memorial* ☎ *202/426–6841* ⊕ *www.nps.gov/nacc* Ⓜ *Foggy Bottom.*

Smithsonian Castle Information Center. The original home of the Smithsonian Institution is an excellent first stop on the Mall to help you get your bearings and plan your exploration of the museums. Built of red sandstone, this Medieval Revival style building, better known

Every Memorial Day, thousands flock to the Vietnam Veterans Memorial to pay their respects to those lost in the conflict.

as the Castle, was designed by James Renwick Jr., the architect of St. Patrick's Cathedral in New York City. Although British scientist and founder James Smithson never visited America, his will stipulated that, should his nephew, Henry James Hungerford, die without an heir, Smithson's entire fortune would go to the United States, "to found at Washington, under the name of the Smithsonian Institution, an establishment for the increase and diffusion of knowledge." The museums on the Mall are the Smithsonian's most visible example of this ideal, but the organization also sponsors traveling exhibitions and maintains research posts in the Chesapeake Bay area and the tropics of Panama.

A 10-minute video gives an overview of the Smithsonian museums and the National Zoo, and the exhibition *The Smithsonian Institution: America's Treasure Chest* features objects representing all the museums, which reveal the breadth and depth of the Smithsonian's collections. James Smithson's crypt is in a small chapel-like room here. The Castle also has *Views from the Tall Tower,* an exhibit that lets you see how the Washington skyline has changed since 1863, a good café, brochures in several languages, and a museum store. Kids appreciate the historic carousel at the north entrance; at the south entrance you'll find the beautifully manicured Haupt Garden and copper-domed kiosk called the S. Dillon Ripley Center, which houses the Discovery Theater (delightful and affordable live, family-oriented shows on selected weekday mornings—usually geared for kids 2–12—are held here). ⊠ *1000 Jefferson Dr. SW, The Mall* ☎ *202/633–1000* ⊕ *www.si.edu* ▣ *Free* Ⓜ *Smithsonian.*

THE WHITE HOUSE AREA AND FOGGY BOTTOM

Sightseeing
★★★★★
Dining
★★★
Lodging
★★
Shopping
★
Nightlife
★★

Foggy Bottom includes some of D.C.'s most iconic attractions, the top being the White House, the home of every U.S. president but George Washington. Visitors may have a tough time deciding what to see first: the numerous war memorials on the National Mall, the Tidal Basin, or some of Washington's better, if smaller, museums. Adding to the variety, you will find the Kennedy Center along the Potomac River and George Washington University's campus. Surprisingly, the area has a strong residential character as well, and is home to some of D.C.'s oldest houses.

TOP ATTRACTIONS

Department of State. U.S. foreign policy is administered by battalions of brainy analysts in the huge Department of State building (often referred to as the State Department). All is presided over by the secretary of state, who is fourth in line for the presidency (after the vice president, speaker of the House, and president pro tempore of the Senate). On the top floor are the opulent Diplomatic Reception Rooms, decorated like the great halls of Europe and the rooms of wealthy colonial American plantations. Furnishings include a Philadelphia highboy (antique chest of drawers), a Paul Revere bowl, and the desk on which the Treaty of Paris, which ended the Revolutionary War, was signed in 1783. ■ TIP➔ **To visit the reception rooms, register online for a tour three months in advance.** ⊠ *2201 C St. NW, Foggy Bottom* ☎ *202/647–3241* ⊕ *receptiontours. state.gov* ⊡ *Free* ⊗ *No tours weekends* Ⓜ *Foggy Bottom.*

Fodor's Choice ★

Renwick Gallery. This luscious French Second Empire–style building is across the street from the White House and the Eisenhower Executive Office Building, and even with such lofty neighbors, it is still the most appealing architecture on the block. This was the first purpose-built museum in Washington, D.C., and it was known at the time as "the American Louvre." The words "dedicated to art" are engraved above the entrance. Designed by James Renwick in 1859 to hold the art collection of Washington merchant and banker William Wilson Corcoran, the National Historic Landmark building today is a branch of the Smithsonian American Art Museum.

The Renwick's exhibits of craft and decorative arts are showcased in a captivating, interactive environment designed to illustrate not only the history of craft in America, but also its future. Here you'll discover exciting contemporary artists who are using materials in innovative ways, redefining what craft is, and taking contemporary craft in bold new directions. Highlights include gorgeous glass-blown pieces by artists including Dale Chihuly, Cliff Lee, and Lino Tagliapietra; Judith Schechter's *The Birth of Eve,* made with five layers of cut, sandblasted, and enameled glass; a stunning hammered-brass necklace by Alexander Calder; and quilts by Kathryn Clark and Marie Watt.

Unlike at other museums, photography is encouraged here. Be sure to tag your favorites on social media with #therenwickgallery and your post may show up on the museum's website. The museum also hosts quarterly Handi-Hours, themed craft nights with arts-and-crafts activities, live music, food, and craft beer; these popular events sell out fast so buy tickets in advance. ⊠ *Pennsylvania Ave. at 17th St. NW, White House area* ☎ *202/633–2850* ⊕ *www.renwick.americanart.si.edu* ☒ *Free* Ⓜ *Farragut W.*

The White House. America's most famous house was designed in 1792 by Irish architect James Hoban. It was known officially as the Executive Mansion until 1902, when President Theodore Roosevelt renamed it The White House, long its informal name. The house has undergone many structural changes: Andrew Jackson installed running water; James Garfield put in the first elevator; Harry Truman had the entire structure gutted and restored, adding a second-story porch to the south portico; and Richard Nixon installed a one-lane bowling alley in 1969.

To see the White House you need to contact your U.S. representative or senator (or embassy if you aren't a U.S. citizen). Requests can be made up to three months in advance (especially for spring, summer, or December tour requests) and no less than 21 days in advance. You'll be asked for the names, birth dates, and Social Security numbers of everyone in your group. On the morning of your tour, call the White House Visitors Office information line for any updates; tours are subject to last-minute cancellations. Arrive 15 minutes early. Your group will be asked to line up in alphabetical order. Everyone 18 years and older must present government-issued photo ID, and no purses, backpacks, or bags are allowed on the tour (and no storage lockers are provided so leave them in your hotel room). Photography is prohibited and there are no public restrooms. The security process will probably last as long as the tour itself, 20–25 minutes.

Getting Oriented

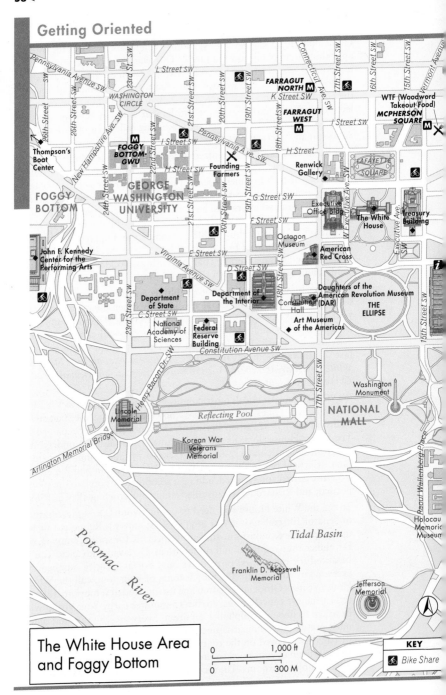

L Street SW

FARRAGUT NORTH M

K Street SW

FARRAGUT WEST M

WTF (Woodword Takeout Food)
MCPHERSON SQUARE M

WASHINGTON CIRCLE

Pennsylvania Avenue SW

Connecticut Ave. SW

Pennsylvania Ave. SW

I Street SW

H Street

FOGGY BOTTOM-GWU M

Thompson's Boat Center

Founding Farmers

Renwick Gallery

LAFAYETTE SQUARE

GEORGE WASHINGTON UNIVERSITY

FOGGY BOTTOM

H Street SW

G Street SW

F Street SW

Executive Office Bldg.

The White House

Treasury Building

John F. Kennedy Center for the Performing Arts

New Hampshire Ave. SW

Virginia Avenue SW

E Street SW

D Street SW

Octagon Museum

American Red Cross

W. Executive Ave. SW

Executive Ave.

Department of State

Department of the Interior

Daughters of the American Revolution Museum (DAR)

THE ELLIPSE

Constitution Hall

National Academy of Sciences

C Street SW

Federal Reserve Building

Art Museum of the Americas

Constitution Avenue SW

Washington Monument

Arlington Memorial Bridge

Henry Bacon Dr. SW

Lincoln Memorial

Reflecting Pool

17th Street SW

NATIONAL MALL

Korean War Veterans Memorial

Potomac River

Tidal Basin

Holocau Memoric Museum

Raoul Wallenberg Place

Franklin D. Roosevelt Memorial

Jefferson Memorial

The White House Area and Foggy Bottom

0   1,000 ft

0   300 M

KEY
Bike Share

GREAT EXPERIENCES IN THE WHITE HOUSE AND FOGGY BOTTOM AREA

Department of State Diplomatic Reception Rooms: One of D.C.'s best-kept secrets, this suite of rooms is filled with museum-quality art and historical treasures inspired by the country's founding years. You must reserve well in advance.

John F. Kennedy Center for the Performing Arts: See a free performance by anyone from the Joffrey Ballet to the National Symphony Orchestra here on the Millennium Stage, daily at 6 pm.

Thompson's Boat Center: Take in Washington's marble monuments, lush Roosevelt Island, and the Virginia coastline with a canoe ride down the Potomac.

Touring the White House: The White House website has up-to-date information on White House tours.

GETTING HERE

The White House can be reached by the Red Line's Farragut North stop or the Blue and Orange lines' McPherson Square and Farragut West stops. Foggy Bottom has its own Metro stop, also on the Blue and Orange lines. A free shuttle runs from the station to the Kennedy Center. Many of the other attractions are a considerable distance from the nearest subway stop. If you don't relish long walks or if time is limited, check the map to see if you need to make alternate travel arrangements to visit specific sights.

PLANNING YOUR TIME

Touring the area around the White House could easily take a day or even two. If you enjoy history, you may be most interested in the buildings in the Lafayette Square Historic District, **DAR Museum**, and **State Department.** Save the **Kennedy Center** for the evening.

QUICK BITES

Founding Farmers. Enjoy American comfort and farm food at this always-busy restaurant that serves breakfast, lunch, and dinner, plus weekend and holiday-Monday brunches. Owned by farmers, the eco-friendly restaurant uses ingredients and products from sustainable farms across the country. ⊠ *1924 Pennsylvania Ave. NW, Foggy Bottom* ☎ *202/822–8783* ⊕ *www. wearefoundingfarmers.com* Ⓜ *Farragut W or Foggy Bottom.*

WTF (Woodward Takeout Food). You can eat in or grab takeout for an outdoor picnic at this casual spot. Choose from breakfast sandwiches, pastries, egg specialties, oatmeal, and granola. For lunch, there are soups and salads, individual pizzas, and sandwiches. The bar, with its windows along H Street, is also a great spot for people-watching. ⊠ *1426 H St. NW, White House area* ☎ *202/347–5355* ⊕ *www. woodwardtable.com.*

The self-guided tour includes rooms on the ground floor, but the State Floor has the highlights. The East Room is the largest room in the White House, the site of ceremonies and press conferences; this is also where Theodore Roosevelt's children roller-skated and one of Abraham Lincoln's sons harnessed a pet goat to a chair and went for a ride. The portrait of George Washington that Dolley Madison saved from torch-carrying British soldiers in 1814 hangs in the room, and the White House Christmas tree stands here every winter. The only president to get married in the White House, Grover Cleveland, was wed in the Blue Room. Esther, the second daughter of President Cleveland and First Lady Frances, holds the distinction of being the only child born in the White House. The Red Room, decorated in early-19th-century American Empire style, has been a favorite of first ladies. Mary Todd Lincoln had her coffee and read the morning paper here. In 1961, First Lady Jacqueline Kennedy undertook an extensive restoration of the White House to preserve and showcase the historical and architectural significance of the home and its contents. The East Garden, which now bears her name, honors her contributions. Michelle Obama installed a vegetable and herb garden to promote healthy eating, as well as an apiary and pollinator garden for bees and other insects.

Your tour of the White House will be enhanced by visiting the White House Visitor Center at 1450 Pennsylvania Avenue NW, featuring displays, photos, and a 30-minute video about the White House. ✉ *1600 Pennsylvania Ave. NW, White House area* ☎ *202/208–1631, 202/456–7041 24-hr info line* ⊕ *www.whitehouse.gov* ✉ *Free* ☉ *No tours Mon.* Ⓜ *Federal Triangle, Metro Center, or McPherson Sq.*

WORTH NOTING

American Red Cross. The national headquarters for the American Red Cross, a National Historic Landmark since 1965, is composed of four buildings. Guided tours show off the oldest, a neoclassical structure of blinding-white marble built in 1917 to commemorate women who cared for the wounded on both sides during the Civil War. Three stained-glass windows designed by Louis Comfort Tiffany illustrate the values of the Red Cross: faith, hope, love, and charity. Other holdings included on the 60-minute tour include an original Norman Rockwell painting, sculptures, and two signature quilts. Weather permitting, the tour includes a visit to the courtyard. Reservations are required for the free tour; schedule via email or phone. ✉ *430 17th St. NW, White House area* ☎ *202/303–4233* ⊕ *www.redcross.org* ✉ *Free* ☉ *No tours Thurs.–Tues.* Ⓜ *Farragut W.*

Art Museum of the Americas. Changing exhibits highlight modern and contemporary Latin American and Caribbean artists in this small gallery, part of the Organization of American States (OAS). The collection has 2,000 objects reflecting the diversity of expression found in the region. A public garden connects the Art Museum and the OAS building. ✉ *201 18th St. NW, White House area* ☎ *202/370–0147* ⊕ *www.amamuseum. org* ✉ *Free* ☉ *Closed Mon.* Ⓜ *Farragut W.*

A statue of Andrew Jackson during the battle of New Orleans presides over Lafayette Square.

FAMILY **Daughters of the American Revolution Museum (DAR).** The beaux arts–style Memorial Continental Hall was the site of the DAR's annual congress until the larger Constitution Hall was built, and now serves as its headquarters. An entrance on D Street leads to the museum, where the 30,000-item collection includes fine examples of colonial and Federal furniture, textiles, quilts, silver, china, porcelain, stoneware, earthenware, and glass. Thirty-one period rooms are decorated in styles representative of various U.S. states, ranging from an 1850 California adobe parlor to a New Hampshire attic filled with 18th- and 19th-century toys. Two galleries—one featuring changing exhibitions—hold decorative arts. Docent tours of the period rooms are available weekdays 10–2:30 and Saturday 9–4:30. The museum also hosts regular Family Saturdays with fun hands-on activities; check the website for dates. ⊠ *1776 D St. NW, White House area* ☎ *202/628–1776* ⊕ *www.dar.org* ⬛ *Free* ⊘ *Closed Sun.* Ⓜ *Farragut W.*

Department of the Interior. The outside of the building is plain, but inside a wealth of art, contained in two separate collections, reflects the department's work. The **Secretary's Collection**, featuring heroic oil paintings of dam construction, gold panning, and cattle drives, is found throughout the building's hallways, offices, and meeting rooms. The **Department of the Interior Museum** outlines the work of the Bureau of Land Management, the U.S. Geological Survey, the Bureau of Indian Affairs, the National Park Service, and other department branches. On Tuesday and Thursday at 2 pm, you can view more than 75 of the museum's dramatic murals created in the 1940s by photographer Ansel Adams and other artists such as

CLOSE UP

Inside Congress: How Laws Are Made

Amid the grand halls of the Capitol building, members of Congress and their aides are busy crafting the laws of our land. It's not a pretty process; as congressional commentators have quipped, laws are like sausages—it's best not to know how they're made. But for iron stomachs, here's a brief tour through Washington's sausage factory.

THE IDEA STAGE

Most laws begin as proposals that any of Congress's 535 members may offer in the form of bills. Many are trivial, such as renaming post-office branches. Others are vital, like funding the federal government. Once introduced, all proposals move to a relevant congressional committee.

CONGRESSIONAL COMMITTEES AND COMMITTEE HEARINGS

Although thousands of proposals are introduced each year, almost all die in committee. Congress never has enough time to entertain each bill, so committee leaders prioritize. Some bills are dismissed for ideological reasons.

Others simply lack urgency. Efforts to rein in fuel costs, for instance, are popular when gas prices are high. Lobbying and special-interest money are other major factors influencing the content and even success or failure of individual bills.

For bills that advance, merits and drawbacks are debated in committee hearings. These hearings—staged in the congressional office buildings adjacent to the Capitol—are usually open to the public; check ⊕ *www.house.gov* and ⊕ *www.senate.gov* under the "committee" headings for schedules. Committee members then vote on whether to move bills to the chamber floor.

PASSING THE HOUSE, SENATE, AND WHITE HOUSE

A bill approved by committee still faces three formidable tests before becoming a law: it must pass the full House, the full Senate, and usually the White House.

Each legislative chamber has different rules for approving bills. In the House, proposals that clear a committee and have the blessing of House leaders need only a simple majority. In the Senate, legislation can be delayed by filibustering—a time-honored process of talking nonstop on the Senate floor—until at least 60 senators vote to end the delay. If the House and Senate pass different versions of the same proposal, then those differences are reconciled in a joint conference committee before returning to the respective floors for another round of voting.

A bill passed by both the House and Senate then proceeds to the White House. The president can either sign it—in which case it becomes law—or veto it, in which case it returns to Congress. Lawmakers can override a veto, but two-thirds of each chamber must support the override to transform a vetoed bill into law. When President George W. Bush twice vetoed a popular children's health care proposal, House supporters couldn't rally the two-thirds majority to override it. The bill enjoyed President Obama's support and became law after he took office.

Maynard Dixon and John Steuart Curry. Reservations are required for the Murals Tour; call at least two weeks in advance. The **Indian Craft Shop** across the hall from the museum sells Native American pottery, dolls, carvings, jewelry, baskets, and books. ⊠ *1849 C St. NW, White House area* 🕾 *202/208-4743* ⊕ *www.doi.gov/interior-museum* 🎫 *Free* Ⓜ *Farragut W.*

Federal Reserve Building. This imposing marble edifice, its bronze entryway topped by a massive eagle, was designed by Folger Library architect Paul Cret. Its appearance seems to say, "Your money's safe with us." Even so, there's no money here, as the Fed's mission is to set interest rates and keep the economy on track. The stately facade belies a friendlier interior, with a varied collection of art and three special art exhibitions every year. Tours of the building are available for groups of 10 or more, all aged 18 years or more; they must be booked at least two weeks in advance. ⊠ *20th St. and Constitution Ave. NW, Foggy Bottom* 🕾 *202/452-3324 to arrange a tour* ⊕ *www.federalreserve.gov/finearts* 🎫 *Free* ☉ *Closed weekends* Ⓜ *Foggy Bottom.*

Treasury Building. Once used to store currency, this is the largest Greek Revival edifice in Washington. Robert Mills, the architect responsible for the Washington Monument and the Smithsonian American Art Museum, designed the colonnade on 15th Street. After the death of President Lincoln, the Andrew Johnson Suite was used as the executive office while Mrs. Lincoln moved out of the White House. Tours must be arranged through your congressperson; participants must be U.S. citizens or legal residents. ⊠ *15th St. and Pennsylvania Ave. NW, White House area* 🕾 *202/622-2000* ⊕ *www.treasury.gov/about/ history/Pages/tours.aspx* 🎫 *Free* Ⓜ *McPherson Sq. or Metro Center.*

CAPITOL HILL AND NORTHEAST D.C.

Sightseeing
★★★★
Dining
★★★
Lodging
★★★
Shopping
★★★
Nightlife
★★★★

The people who live and work on "the Hill" do so in the shadow of the edifice that lends the neighborhood its name: the gleaming white Capitol. This is where political deals and decisions are made. Beyond these grand buildings lies a vibrant and diverse group of neighborhoods with charming residential blocks lined with Victorian row houses and a fine assortment of restaurants and bars where senators, members of Congress, and lobbyists come to unwind or to continue their deal making. D.C.'s favorite market and newest sporting attraction are also here. A little farther afield, the rapidly developing H Street Corridor to the north and east offers hip and edgy shopping, dining, and nightlife.

CAPITOL HILL

TOP ATTRACTIONS

Fodor'sChoice
★

The Capitol Building. *See the highlighted feature in this chapter for more information.* ⊠ *East end of The Mall* ☎ *202/226–8000* ⊕ *www.visit-thecapitol.gov* ✉ *Free* ☉ *Closed Sun.*

Fodor'sChoice
★

Library of Congress. Founded in 1800, the largest library in the world has more than 164 million items on approximately 838 miles of bookshelves. Only 38 million of its holdings are books—the library also has 3.6 million recordings, 14 million photographs, 5.5 million maps, 8.1 million pieces of sheet music, and 70 million manuscripts. Also here is the Congressional Research Service, which, as the name implies, works on special projects for senators and representatives.

Built in 1897, the copper-domed **Thomas Jefferson Building** is the oldest of the three buildings that make up the library. The dome, topped with the gilt "Flame of Knowledge," is ornate and decorative, with busts of Dante, Goethe, and Nathaniel Hawthorne perched above its entryway. The *Court of Neptune*, Roland Hinton Perry's fountain at the front steps, rivals some of Rome's best fountains.

The Jefferson Building opens into the Great Hall, richly adorned with mosaics, paintings, and curving marble stairways. The octagonal Main Reading Room, its central desk surrounded by mahogany readers' tables under a 160-foot-high domed ceiling, inspires researchers and readers alike. Computer terminals have replaced card catalogs, but books are still retrieved and dispersed the same way: readers (16 years or older) hand request slips to librarians and wait for their materials to be delivered. Researchers aren't allowed in the stacks, and only members of Congress and other special borrowers can check books out. Items from the library's collection—which includes one of only three perfect Gutenberg Bibles in the world—are on display in the Jefferson Building's second-floor Southwest Gallery and Pavilion. ■TIP➔ To even begin to come to grips with the scope and grandeur of the library, one of the free hourly tours is highly recommended. ✉ *Jefferson Bldg., 1st St. and Independence Ave. SE, Capitol Hill* ☎ *202/707–9779* ⊕ *www.loc.gov* ⊠ *Free* ⊗ *Closed Sun.* Ⓜ *Capitol S.*

Fodor's Choice
★

The Supreme Court. It wasn't until 1935 that the Supreme Court got its own building: a white-marble temple with twin rows of Corinthian columns designed by Cass Gilbert. Before then, the justices had been moved around to various rooms in the Capitol; for a while they even met in a tavern. William Howard Taft, the only man to serve as both president and chief justice, was instrumental in getting the court a home of its own, though he died before the building was completed. Today you can sit in the gallery and see the court in action. Even when court isn't in session, there are still things to see.

The court convenes on the first Monday in October and hears cases until April (though court is in session through June). There are usually two arguments a day at 10 and 11 in the morning, Monday through Wednesday, in two-week intervals.

On mornings when court is in session, two lines form for people wanting to attend. The "three-to-five-minute" line shuttles you through, giving you a quick impression of the court at work. The full-session line gets you in for the whole show. If you want to see a full session, it's best to be in line by at least 8:30. For the most-contentious cases, viewers have been known to queue up days before. In May and June the court takes to the bench Monday morning at 10 to release orders and opinions. Sessions usually last 15 to 30 minutes and are open to the public.

The *Washington Post* carries a daily listing of what cases the court will hear. The court displays its calendar of cases a month in advance on its website; click on "Oral Arguments." You can't bring your overcoat or electronics such as cameras and cell phones into the courtroom, but you can store them in a coin-operated locker. When court isn't in session,

Getting Oriented

Capitol Hill and Northeast D.C.

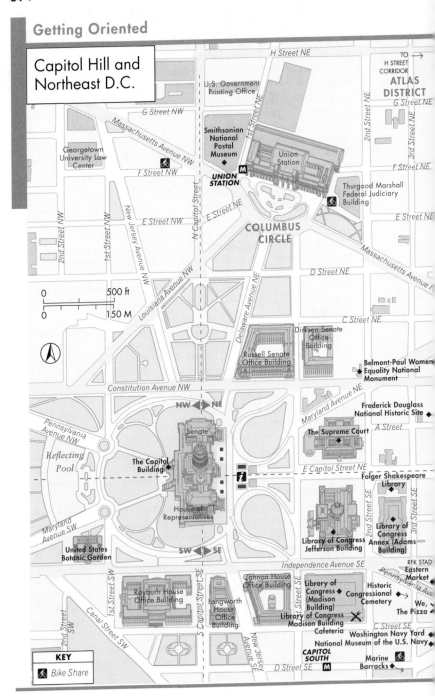

H Street NE

U.S. Government Printing Office

G Street NW

Massachusetts Avenue NW

Georgetown University Law Center

Smithsonian National Postal Museum

F Street NW

Union Station

TO →
H STREET CORRIDOR
ATLAS DISTRICT

G Street NE

F Street NE

UNION STATION

Thurgood Marshall Federal Judiciary Building

E Street NW

E Street NE

E Street NE

COLUMBUS CIRCLE

Massachusetts Avenue NE

D Street NE

0 ———— 500 ft
0 ———— 150 M

Louisiana Avenue NW

Delaware Avenue NE

C Street NE

Dirksen Senate Office Building

Russell Senate Office Building

Belmont-Paul Women's Equality National Monument

Constitution Avenue NW

Pennsylvania Avenue NW

Reflecting Pool

NW | NE

Senate

The Capitol Building

Maryland Avenue NE

The Supreme Court

Maryland Avenue SW

United States Botanic Garden

House of Representatives

SW | SE

Frederick Douglass National Historic Site

A Street

E Capitol Street NE

Folger Shakespeare Library

Library of Congress Annex (Adams Building)

Library of Congress Jefferson Building

Independence Avenue SE

Cannon House Office Building

Library of Congress (Madison Building)

RFK STAD

Eastern Market

Historic Congressional Cemetery

Pennsylvania Ave

We, The Pizza

Rayburn House Office Building

Canal Street SW

Longworth House Office Building

Library of Congress Madison Building Cafeteria

C Street SE

Washington Navy Yard

National Museum of the U.S. Navy

CAPITOL SOUTH

D Street SE

Marine Barracks

KEY
🚲 Bike Share

GREAT EXPERIENCES ON CAPITOL HILL
AND NORTHEAST D.C.

Barracks Row: Founded in 1801, it's one of the oldest neighborhoods in D.C. and was central to the defense of the city during the War of 1812 and Civil War. The commercial corridor boasts bars, shops, restaurants, and access to two landmarks, the Navy Yard and Washington Nationals Stadium.

The Capitol: See where democracy is put into action. Start your tour at the Visitors Center, then walk among marble American heroes and gape at the soaring Rotunda.

Eastern Market: One of D.C.'s most beloved weekend destinations is the place to pick up fresh produce, baked goods, and locally made crafts.

The Library of Congress: Contemplate George Washington's drafts of the Constitution and other historic documents, the lavishly sculpted Great Hall, and the splendor of the gilded Main Reading Room.

The Supreme Court: Round out your firsthand look at the three branches of government by watching the justices hear precedent-setting arguments.

United States Botanic Garden: Wrinkle your nose at the corpse flower, explore the jungle, gawk at the orchids, or stroll the paths of the National Garden.

GETTING HERE

From the Red Line's Union Station, you can walk to most destinations on Capitol Hill. From the Blue and Orange lines, the Capitol South stop is close to the Capitol and Library of Congress, and the Eastern Market stop leads to the market and the Marine Corps Barracks. Bus Nos. 31, 32, 36, and Circulator buses run from Friendship Heights through Georgetown and Downtown to Independence Avenue, the Capitol, and Eastern Market.

PLANNING YOUR TIME

Touring Capitol Hill should take you about three hours, allowing for about an hour each at the **Capitol**, the **Botanic Garden**, and the **Library of Congress**.

If you want to see **Congress** in session, contact your legislator (or, if you are visiting from abroad, your country's embassy) in advance, and bear in mind that the House and the Senate are usually not in session in August.

Supreme Court cases are usually heard October through April, Monday through Wednesday, two weeks out of each month.

QUICK BITES

Library of Congress's Madison Building Cafeteria. Steps from the Capitol, this eatery gets raves for its varied breakfast and lunch, and panoramic views of Washington. ✉ *Madison Bldg., Library of Congress, Independence Ave. SE, between 1st and 2nd Sts., Capitol Hill* ☎ *202/707–8300* ⊕ *www.loc.gov* ⊘ *Closed weekends* Ⓜ *Capitol S.*

We, the Pizza. *Top Chef's* Spike Mendelsohn flips specialty pies with creative ingredients. Eat in or take out. ✉ *305 Pennsylvania Ave. SE, Capitol Hill* ☎ *202/544–4008* ⊕ *www.wethepizza.com* ⊘ *Closed Sun.* Ⓜ *Capitol S.*

you can hear lectures about the court, typically given every hour on the half hour from 9:30 to 3:30. On the ground floor you can also find revolving exhibits, a video about the court, a gift shop, an information desk, and a larger-than-life statue of John Marshall, the longest-serving chief justice in Supreme Court history. ⊠ *1 1st St. NE, Capitol Hill* ☎ *202/479–3030* ⊕ *www.supremecourt.gov* ⊠ *Free* ☉ *Closed weekends* Ⓜ *Union Station or Capitol S.*

WORTH NOTING

Belmont-Paul Women's Equality National Monument. Standing strong on Capitol Hill for more than 200 years, this house witnessed the construction of the U.S. Capitol and Supreme Court, and its early occupants participated in the formation of Congress. In 1929, the National Woman's Party (NWP), founded by Alice Paul, an outspoken suffragist and feminist, purchased the house, and it soon evolved into a center for feminist education and social change. For more than 60 years, the trailblazing NWP utilized its strategic location, steps from the U.S. Capitol and its Congressional offices, to lobby for women's political, social, and economic equality. Today, an expansive collection of artifacts from the suffrage and equal rights campaigns brings the story of the women's rights movement to life. The innovative tactics and strategies these women devised became the blueprint for women's progress throughout the 20th century. In 2016, President Obama designated the home as a national monument. ⊠ *144 Constitution Ave. NE, Capitol Hill* ✛ *Entrance on 2nd St., next to Hart Senate Office Bldg.* ☎ *202/546–1210* ⊕ *www. sewallbelmont.org* ⊠ *Free* ☉ *Closed Mon. and Tues.* Ⓜ *Union Station.*

Folger Shakespeare Library. This Elizabethan monument, a white marble art deco building decorated with sculpted scenes from the Bard's plays, was designed by architect Paul Philippe Cret and dedicated in 1932. Inside, the design is Tudor England with oak paneling, high plaster ceilings, and ornamental floor tiles. Henry Clay Folger, the Library's founder, personally selected the inscriptions by and about Shakespeare that are found throughout the property. The Great Hall is simply stunning, and holds rotating exhibits from the library's collection. Terracotta floor tiles feature titles of Shakespeare's plays and the masks of comedy and tragedy while the First Folio of Shakespeare is always on view and may be thumbed through here digitally.

Visitors are greeted at the entrance to the Elizabethan Theatre with a marble statue of Puck from *A Midsummer Night's Dream*. With its overhead canopy, wooden balconies, and oak columns, the Theatre is a reproduction of a 16th-century inn-yard playhouse. This is the site for performances of Shakespearean plays, chamber music, readings, lectures, and family programs; check the website for a calendar of events. Understandably, the collection of works by and about Shakespeare and his times is second to none and both the Paster and New Reading Rooms are devoted to scholarly research. On Saturdays at noon you can tour both rooms; advance reservations are required. A manicured Elizabethan garden on the grounds is open to the public, and the gift shop contains many collectibles featuring the Bard and English theater. ⊠ *201 E. Capitol St. SE, Capitol Hill* ☎ *202/544–4600* ⊕ *www.folger. edu* ⊠ *Free* Ⓜ *Capitol S.*

Continued on page 75

ON THE HILL, UNDER THE DOME: EXPERIENCING THE CAPITOL

In Washington, the Capitol literally stands above it all: by law, no other building in the city can reach the height of the dome's peak.

Beneath its magnificent dome, the day-to-day business of American democracy takes place: senators and representatives debate, coax, and cajole, and ultimately determine the law of the land.

For many visitors, the Capitol is the most exhilarating experience Washington has to offer. It wins them over with a three-pronged appeal:

- It's the city's most impressive work of architecture.

- It has on display documents, art, and artifacts from 400 years of American history.

- Its legislative chambers are open to the public. You can actually see your lawmakers at work, shaping the history of tomorrow.

(Clockwise from top left) Moving into the new Capitol circa 1800; 19th-century print by R. Brandard; Thornton sketch circa 1797; the Capitol before the dome.

1792–1807
A Man with a Plan

William Thornton, a physician and amateur architect from the West Indies, wins the competition to design the Capitol. His plan, with its central rotunda and dome, draws inspiration from Rome's Pantheon. On September 18, 1793, George Washington lays the Capitol's cornerstone. In November 1800, Congress moves from Philadelphia to take up residence in the first completed section, the boxlike area between the central rotunda and today's north wing. In 1807, the House wing is completed, just to the south of the rotunda; a covered wooden walkway joins the two wings.

1814–1826
Washington Burns

In 1814, British troops march on Washington and set fire to the Capitol, the White House, and other government buildings. The wooden walkway is destroyed and the two wings gutted, but the walls remain standing after a violent rainstorm douses the flames. Fearful that Congress might leave Washington, residents fund a temporary "Brick Capitol" on the spot where the Supreme Court is today. By 1826, reconstruction is completed under the guidance of architects Benjamin Henry Latrobe and Charles Bulfinch; a low dome is made of wood sheathed in copper.

1850s–1880s
Domed if You Do

North and south wings are added through the 1850s and '60s to accommodate the growing government of a growing country. To maintain scale with the enlarged building, work begins in 1885 on a taller, cast-iron dome. President Lincoln would be criticized for continuing the expensive project during the Civil War, but he calls the construction "a sign we intend the Union shall go on."

(Clockwise from top left) The east front circa 1861; today the Capitol is a tourist mecca with its own visitor center; *Freedom* statue.

1960s – Today

Expanding the Capitol

The east front is extended 33½ feet, creating 100 additional offices. In 1983 preservationists fight to keep the west front, the last remaining section of the Capitol's original facade, from being extended; in a compromise the facade's crumbling sandstone blocks are replaced with stronger limestone. In 2000 the ground is broken on the subterranean Capitol Visitor Center, to be located beneath the grounds to the building's east side. The extensive facility, three-fourths the size of the Capitol itself, was finally completed on December 2, 2008 to the tune of $621 million.

Freedom atop the Capitol Dome

The twin-shelled Capitol dome, a marvel of 19th-century engineering, rises 285 feet above the ground and weighs 4,500 tons. It can expand and contract as much as 4 inches in a day, depending on the outside temperature.

The allegorical figure on top of the dome is *Freedom*. Sculpted in 1857 by Thomas Crawford, *Freedom* was cast with help from Philip Reid, a slave. Crawford had first planned for the 19½-foot-tall bronze statue to wear the cloth liberty cap of a freed Roman slave, but Southern lawmakers, led by Jefferson Davis, objected. An "American" headdress composed of a star-encircled helmet surmounted with an eagle's head and feathers was substituted. A light just below the statue burns whenever Congress is in session.

Before the visitor center opened, the best way to see the details on the *Freedom* statue atop the Capitol dome was with a good set of binoculars. Now, you can see the original plaster model of this classical female figure up close. Her right hand rests on a sheathed sword, while her left carries a victory wreath and a shield of the United States with 13 stripes. She also wears a brooch with "U.S." on her chest.

THE CAPITOL VISITOR CENTER

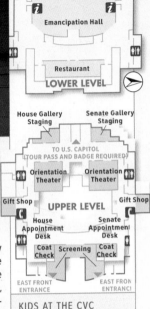

The enormous and sunlit Capitol Visitor Center (CVC) is the start for all Capitol tours, and brings a new depth to the Capitol experience with orientation theaters, an interactive museum, and live video feeds from the House and Senate. It also provides weary travelers with welcome creature comforts, including a 530-seat restaurant.

DESIGN
At 580,000 square feet, the visitor center is approximately three-quarters the size of the 775,000-square-foot Capitol. The center's belowground location preserves the historic landscape and views designed by Frederick Law Olmsted in 1874. Inside, skylights provide natural light and views of the majestic Capitol dome. The center opened in December 2008, three years late and $356 million over budget.

EMANCIPATION HALL
The center's largest space is a gorgeous sunlit atrium called Emancipation Hall in honor of the slaves who helped to build the Capitol in the 1800s. The plaster model of the *Freedom* statue, which tops the Capitol's dome, anchors the hall. Part of the Capitol's National Statuary Hall collection is also on display here.

MUSEUM
Other attractions include exhibits about the Capitol, historical artifacts, and documents. A marble wall displays historic speeches and decisions by Congress, like President John F. Kennedy's famous 1961 "Man on the Moon" speech and a letter Thomas Jefferson wrote to Congress in 1803 urging the funding of the Lewis and Clark Expedition.

KIDS AT THE CVC

The Capitol Visitor Center is a great place for families with children who may be too young or too wiggly for a tour of the Capitol. In the Exhibition Hall, the 11-foot tall touchable model of the Capitol, touch screen computers, and architectural replicas welcome hands-on exploration.

Challenge younger kids to find statues of a person carrying a spear, a helmet, a book, and a baby.

Tweens can look for statues of the person who invented television, a king, a physician, and a representative who said, "I cannot vote for war."

PLANNING YOUR CAPITOL DAY

LOGISTICS

To tour the Capitol, you can book free, advance passes at ⊕ *www.visitthecapitol.gov* or through your representative's or senator's offices. In addition, a limited number of same-day passes are available at the Public Walk-Up line on the lower level of the visitor center. Tours run every 15 minutes; the first tour begins at 8:50 and the last at 3:20, Monday through Saturday. The center is closed on Sunday.

Plan on two to four hours to tour the Capitol and see the visitor center. You should arrive at least 30 minutes before your scheduled tour to allow time to pass through security. Tours last about one hour.

If you can't get a pass to tour the Capitol, the Capitol Visitor Center is still worth a visit. You can also take one of the free guided tours that do not require reservations.

To get passes to the chambers of the House and Senate, contact your representative's or senator's office. Many will also arrange for a staff member to give you a tour of the Capitol or set you up with a time for a Capitol Guide Service tour. When they're in session, some members even have time set aside to meet with constituents. You can link to the e-mail of your representative at ⊕ *www.house.gov* and of your senators at ⊕ *www.senate.gov*.

SECURITY

Expect at least a 30-minute wait going through security when you enter the Capitol Visitor Center. Bags can be no larger than 14 inches wide, 13 inches high, and 4 inches deep. View the list of prohibited items on ⊕ *www.visitthecapitol.gov*. (There are no facilities for storing prohibited belongings.) For more information, call ☎ *202/226–8000, 202/224–4049 TTY.*

BEAN SOUP AND MORE

A favorite with legislators, the Senate bean soup has been served every day for more than 100 years in the exclusive Senate Dining Room. It's available to the general public in the restaurant of the CVC on a rotating basis. You can also try making your own with the recipe on the Senate's Web site (⊕ www.senate.gov).

GETTING HERE— WITHOUT GETTING VOTED IN

The Union Station, Capitol South and Federal Center, SW Metro stops are all within walking distance of the Capitol. Follow the people wearing business suits— chances are they're headed your way. Street parking is extremely limited, but Union Station to the north of the Capitol has a public garage and there is some metered street parking along the Mall to the west of the Capitol.

TOURING THE CAPITOL

National Statuary Hall

Your 30- to 40-minute tour conducted by the Capitol Guide Service includes stops at the Rotunda, followed by the National Statuary Hall, the Hall of Columns, the old Supreme Court Chamber, the crypt (where there are exhibits on the history of the Capitol), and the gift shop. Note that you *don't* see the Senate or House chambers on the tour. (Turn the page to learn about visiting the chambers.) The highlights of the tour are the first two stops. . . .

THE ROTUNDA
You start off here, under the Capitol's dome. Look up and you'll see *Apotheosis of Washington,* a fresco painted in 1865 by Constantino Brumidi. The figures in the inner circle represent the 13 original states; those in the outer ring symbolize arts, sciences, and industry. Further down, around the Rotunda's rim, a frieze depicts 400 years of American history. The work was started by Brumidi in 1877 and continued by another Italian, Filippo Costaggini. American Allyn Cox added the final touches in 1953.

NATIONAL STATUARY HALL
South of the Rotunda is Statuary Hall, which was once the chamber of the House of Representatives. When the House moved out, Congress invited each state to send statues of two great deceased residents for placement in the hall. Because the weight of the statues threatened to make the floor cave in, and to keep the room from being cluttered, more than half of the sculptures have ended up in other spots in the Capitol. Ask your guide for help finding your state's statues.

ARTIST OF THE CAPITOL
Constantino Brumidi (1805-80) devoted his last 25 years to frescoing the Capitol; his work dominates the Rotunda and the Western Corridor. While painting the section depicting William Penn's treaty with the Indians for the Rotunda's frieze (pictured above), a 74-year-old Brumidi slipped from the 58-foot scaffold, hanging on until help arrived. He would continue work for another four months, before succumbing to kidney failure.

TRY THIS
Because of Statuary Hall's perfectly elliptical ceiling, a whisper uttered along the wall can be heard at the point directly opposite on the other side of the room. Try it when you're there—if it's not noisy, the trick should work.

ONE BIG HAWAIIAN
With a solid granite base weighing six tons, Hawaii's Kamehameha I in Statuary Hall is among the heaviest objects in the collection. On Kamehameha Day (June 11, a state holiday in Hawai'i), the statue is draped with leis.

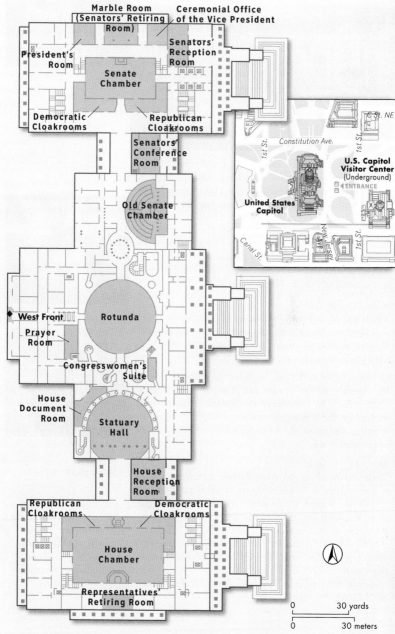

United States Capitol

Marble Room
(Senators' Retiring
Room)

Ceremonial Office
of the Vice President

President's
Room

Senate
Chamber

Senators'
Reception
Room

Democratic
Cloakrooms

Republican
Cloakrooms

Senators'
Conference
Room

Old Senate
Chamber

West Front

Rotunda

Prayer
Room

Congresswomen's
Suite

House
Document
Room

Statuary
Hall

House
Reception
Room

Republican
Cloakrooms

Democratic
Cloakrooms

House
Chamber

Representatives'
Retiring Room

Constitution Ave.

1st St.

C St. NE

1st St.

U.S. Capitol
Visitor Center
(Underground)

ENTRANCE

United States
Capitol

Canal St.

New Jersey Ave.

1st St.

0   30 yards

0   30 meters

GOING TO THE FLOOR

ONE IF BY LAND...?

When flags fly over their respective wings of the Capitol, you'll know the House and Senate are in session. The House is on the south side, the Senate on the north.

A tour of the Capitol is impressive, but the best part of a visit for many people is witnessing the legislators in action. Free gallery passes into the House and Senate chambers have to be obtained from your representative's or senator's office. They aren't hard to come by, but getting them takes some planning ahead. Once you have a pass, it's good for any time the chambers are open to public, for as long as the current Congress is sitting. Senate chambers are closed when the Senate is not in session, but the House is open.

Judiciary Committee

HOUSE CHAMBER

The larger of two chambers may look familiar: it's here that the president delivers the annual State of the Union. When you visit, you sit in the same balcony from which the First Family and guests watch the address.

Look carefully at the panels above the platform where the Speaker of the House sits. They're blue (rather than green like the rest of the panels in the room), and when the House conducts a vote, they light up with the names of the representatives and their votes in green and red.

House session

SENATE CHAMBER

With 100 members elected to six-year terms, the Senate is the smaller and ostensibly more dignified of Congress's two houses. Desks of the senators are arranged in an arc, with Republicans and Democrats divided by the center aisle. The vice president of the United States is officially the "president of the Senate," charged with presiding over the Senate's procedures. Usually, though, the senior member of the majority party oversees day-to-day operations, and is addressed as "Mr. President" or "Madam President."

SWEET SPOT IN THE SENATE

In the sixth desk from the right in the back row of the Senate chamber, a drawer has been filled with candy since 1968. Whoever occupies the desk maintains the stash.

The Supreme Court officially began meeting in this Corinthian-column-lined building in 1935.

Historic Congressional Cemetery. Established in 1807 "for all denomination of people," this cemetery is the final resting place for such notables as U.S. Capitol architect William Thornton, Marine Corps march composer John Philip Sousa, Civil War photographer Mathew Brady, FBI director J. Edgar Hoover, and many members of Congress. Air Force veteran and gay rights activist Leonard Matlovich is also buried here under a tombstone that reads "When I was in the military, they gave me a medal for killing two men and a discharge for loving one." The cemetery is about a 20-minute walk from the Capitol. You can take your own self-guided tour year-round during daylight hours; pick up a map at the gatehouse or download one from the cemetery website. On Saturday from April through October, you can join one of the free docent-led tours at 11. Additionally, on the third Saturday of the month at 1 pm, there are Civil War–themed tours. ⊠ *1801 E St. SE, Capitol Hill* ☎ *202/543–0539* ⊕ *www.congressionalcemetery. org* Ⓜ *Stadium Armory or Potomac Ave.*

FAMILY **Smithsonian National Postal Museum.** The National Museum of Natural History has the Hope Diamond, but the National Postal Museum has the envelope wrapping used to mail the gem to the Smithsonian—part of a collection that consists of more than 6 million stamps. Exhibits, underscoring the important part the mail has played in America's development, include horse-drawn mail coaches, railroad mail cars, airmail planes, and a collection of philatelic rarities. Learn about stamp collecting and tour *Systems at Work,* an exhibit that demonstrates how mail has gone from the mailbox to its destination for the past 200 years, featuring a high-def film highlighting amazing technologies. The **William Gross Stamp**

Gallery, the largest of its kind in the world, has an additional 20,000 objects never before on public display, showing how closely stamps have intertwined with American history. The museum is housed in the old Washington City Post Office, designed by Daniel Burnham and completed in 1914. ✉ *2 Massachusetts Ave. NE, Capitol Hill* ☎ *202/633–5555* ⊕ *www.postalmuseum.si.edu* ▨ *Free* Ⓜ *Union Station.*

NORTHEAST D.C.

Frederick Douglass National Historic Site. **Cedar Hill,** the Anacostia home of abolitionist Frederick Douglass, was the first Black National Historic Site that Congress designated. Douglass, a former slave who escaped to freedom and delivered rousing abolitionist speeches at home and abroad, resided here from 1877 until his death in 1895. The house has a wonderful view of Washington across the Anacostia River and contains many of Douglass's personal belongings. The home has been meticulously restored to its original grandeur; you can view Douglass's hundreds of books displayed on his custom-built bookshelves, and Limoges china on the family dining table. A short film on Douglass's life is shown at a nearby visitor center. Entry to the home requires participation in a 30-minute ranger-led tour, for which you must arrive 30 minutes in advance; reserve by phone or online. ✉ *1411 W St. SE, Anacostia* ☎ *202/426–5961, 202/444–6777 museum tours* ⊕ *www.nps. gov/frdo, www.recreation.gov for online ticket reservations* ▨ *House: $1.50; garden and visitor center: free* Ⓜ *Anacostia.*

Marine Barracks. In early 1801, President Thomas Jefferson and the second commandant of the Marine Corps, Lt. Col. William Ward Burrows, made a horseback tour through Washington, D.C., looking for a proper site for the Marine Barracks and a home for the commandant. They selected "Square 927" and construction began later that year; the house was completed in 1806 and the Barracks in 1808. It was one of the few buildings not burned by the British when they destroyed much of the Capitol in 1814. Over the years, the home underwent several renovations and additions. The Georgian-Federalist style home now boasts 15,000 square feet of space and more than 30 rooms. Still used for its original purpose, the **Home of the Commandants** on 8th and I Street has been home to all but the first two commandants, and is said to be the oldest continuously occupied public building in Washington, D.C. "Square 927," now the block surrounded by 8th, I, 9th, and G Streets SE, was designated a National Historic Landmark in 1976. Although you can't tour the home, you can see the outside of this impressive home for the commandant of the Marine Corps and the historic Marine Barracks. ✉ *801 G St. SE, Southeast* ☎ *202/433–6040* ⊕ *www.barracks. marines.mil* Ⓜ *Eastern Market or Potomac Ave.*

National Museum of the US Navy. The history of the U.S. Navy, from the Revolution to the present, is chronicled here, with exhibits ranging from the fully rigged foremast of the USS *Constitution* (better known as *Old Ironsides*) to a U.S. Navy Corsair fighter plane dangling from the ceiling. All around are models of fighting ships, a real Vietnam-era Swift boat, working periscopes, displays on battles, and portraits of the sailors who

Visiting Government Buildings

You can visit many of Washington's government offices, but you have to do some advance planning in many cases. Here's a rundown of how far in advance you need to make arrangements.

NO ADVANCE PLANNING REQUIRED

Two of the most impressive places in Washington don't require advance reservations. The **Library of Congress** and the **Washington National Cathedral** are architectural and artistic treasures.

The cathedral was dubbed at its creation a "House of Prayer for All People," and does indeed draw people from all over the world seeking comfort and reflection. Statues of George Washington and Abraham Lincoln make it clear that this is a place where church and state are welcome to coexist. With its murals, paintings, sculptures and statues, and, of course, millions of books and manuscripts, the Library of Congress

is truly impressive. Even if you're not a bookworm, the free docent-led tour is one of the best things going in the city.

CAPITOL VISITOR CENTER

One of the most visited attractions, the **Capitol Visitor Center** is the starting point for tours of the Capitol and where you'll discover a plethora of historical treasures, including a table used by Abraham Lincoln during his 1865 inaugural address. Crowds in spring and summer can number in the thousands, so plan for at least three hours here. The five-football-fields-size underground complex is a destination in itself, with the model of the statue of *Freedom*, a 530-seat dining room that serves the famous Senate bean soup, and exhibits on the Capitol. Tours of the Capitol run Monday through Saturday from 8:40 to 3:30. Allow extra time to go through security.

To visit the Capitol, you'll need to either reserve tickets online at ⊕ *www.visitthecapitol.gov* or contact your representative or senator.

---

fought them. In front of the museum is a collection of guns, cannons, and missiles, and the decommissioned U.S. Navy destroyer USS *Barry* floats a short distance away on Riverwalk by the Anacostia River. The **Navy Art Collection,** including many works by Navy artists, is also housed in the museum. A new addition to the Navy Museum is the **Cold War Gallery** in Building 70 with exhibits that explore the Navy's response to the threat of Soviet military power and communist ideology. ⚠ **All visitors to the museum must have a valid photo ID and report to the Visitor Control Center (VCC) at the Washington Navy Yard's primary access gate at 11th and O Streets. The VCC is only open weekdays until 3:30. If you're planning to visit the museum on the weekend, you must be prevetted. A Base Access Pass Registration must be submitted at least seven days before your visit. Call 202/433–4882 for access-related questions.** ✉ *Bldg. 76, Navy Yard, 805 Kidder Breese St. SE, Southeast* ⊹ *Enter through visitor gate at 11th and O Sts. SE (weekdays) or 6th and M Sts. SE (weekends) and show a valid photo ID; you'll receive a pass and map of surroundings* ☏ *202/433–3815 museum, 202/433–4882 USS Barry* ⊕ *www.history.navy.mil* ▨ *Free* Ⓜ *Eastern Market.*

FAMILY **Washington Navy Yard.** A 115-acre historic district with its own street system, the Washington Navy Yard is the Navy's oldest outpost on shore. Established in 1799 as a shipbuilding facility, the district was burned by the Americans during the War of 1812 to keep the British from capturing the base and the four Navy ships docked there. Rebuilt and converted to weapons production by the mid-19th century, the Navy Yard became integral to the defense of Washington during the Civil War, and the Lincoln assassination conspirators were held there. Charles Lindbergh landed at the Navy Yard after his famous transatlantic flight.

The Navy Yard gradually fell into disuse, until the 1960s when it was revived as a thriving administrative and cultural center. It currently houses the **National Museum of the US Navy.** The west side of the Yard is flanked by a waterfront promenade, the **Anacostia Riverwalk**, which is popular for cyclists, runners, skaters, and walkers.

On weekdays, enter the Navy Yard on 11th and O Street; on weekends, you enter on 6th and M Street. Visitors 18 and older must show valid government-issued identification (a driver's license or passport). Access and ID requirements are subject to change; check the website for the latest information. The Metro stations are several blocks from the entrance to Navy Yard, so prepare to walk some distance. ⊠ *O and 11th Sts. SE, Southeast* ⊕ *www.history.navy.mil* ✉ *Free* Ⓜ *Eastern Market or Navy Yard.*

DOWNTOWN

Sightseeing
★★★★
Dining
★★★★
Lodging
★★★★
Shopping
★★★
Nightlife
★★★★

Downtown D.C. is where government, commerce, and entertainment meet. The streets are wide, the buildings are tall (as they get in Washington), and D.C. feels like a big city (almost). This extensive area encompasses some distinct districts, packed with historic and cultural attractions, with still more in the pipeline. Downtown is compact; you can see the main sights in an hour and a half, not counting time spent inside museums. Travel light, however, for you'll have your bag screened before entering almost everywhere.

TOP ATTRACTIONS

FAMILY
Fodor'sChoice
★

Ford's Theatre. The events that took place here on the night of April 14, 1865, shocked the nation: during a performance of *Our American Cousin,* John Wilkes Booth entered the Presidential Box at Ford's Theatre and shot Abraham Lincoln in the back of the head; he died later that night. This block-long, Lincoln-centered cultural campus encompasses four sites. In the **Museum,** you'll explore Lincoln's presidency and Civil War milestones and learn about Booth and those who joined his conspiracy to topple the government. Artifacts include Lincoln's clothing and weapons used by Booth. The **Theatre,** which stages performances throughout the year, is restored to look as it did when Lincoln attended, including the Presidential Box draped with flags as it was on the night he was shot. During the spring and summer you can also watch a 30-minute one-act performance titled "One Destiny" that tells the story of the night from the eyes of those who were in the theater. In the restored **Petersen House,** you can see the room where Lincoln died and the parlor where his wife, Mary Todd Lincoln, waited in anguish through the night.

Getting Oriented

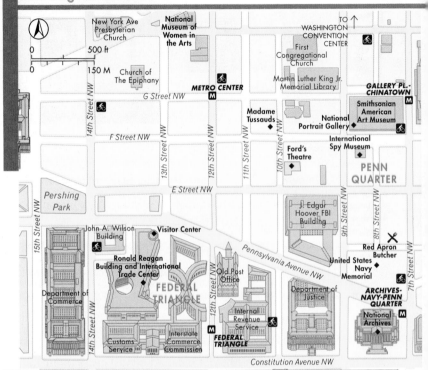

GETTING HERE

Take the Metro to Federal Triangle or Archives–Navy Memorial to visit the government buildings along Pennsylvania Avenue. The Gallery Place–Chinatown stop gives direct access to the Verizon Center, Chinatown, and the American Art and Spy museums. Judiciary Square has its own stop, and Metro Center is the best choice for the National Theatre and Penn Quarter. Bus routes crisscross the area as well. Limited street parking is available on nights and weekends away from the main Chinatown and Verizon Center area.

GREAT EXPERIENCES DOWNTOWN

International Spy Museum: Indulge your inner James Bond with a look at 007's Aston Martin from *Goldfinger*—along with more serious toys used by the CIA, FBI, and KGB.

The National Archives: Stand in awe as you read the Declaration of Independence, Constitution, Bill of Rights, and a 1297 Magna Carta. Then lose yourself in the treasures of the Public Vault.

National Portrait Gallery and Smithsonian American Art Museum: These masterful museums have something for everyone.

Newseum: See parts of the Berlin Wall, and play the role of a journalist. The roof-deck terrace provides postcard-perfect views of the Capitol and is a pleasure in good weather.

Theater District: Performances ranging from Shakespeare to contemporary dramas and musicals are mounted in Penn Quarter, Washington's answer to Broadway.

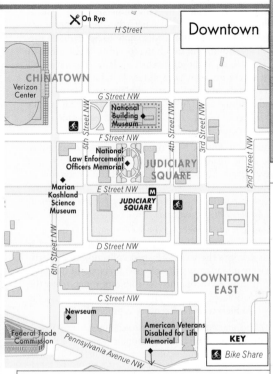

Downtown

FORD'S THEATRE

U.S. Department Of The Interior
National Park Service

BOX
FO
THE

PLANNING YOUR TIME

Downtown is densely packed with major attractions—far too many to see in one day. You'll need at least an hour inside each attraction, so pick the two that appeal most and stroll past the rest. Art lovers might focus on the **National Portrait Gallery** and **Smithsonian American Art Museum**; history buffs might limit themselves to touring the **National Archives** and the **National Building Museum**; families with kids may prefer the **International Spy Museum**; and media junkies will want to visit the **Newseum** and the **Marian Koshland Science Museum**, which looks at the real story behind science topics that are widely reported.

SAFETY

Downtown's blocks of government and office buildings still become a bit of a ghost town when the working day is done, but a revitalized Penn Quarter remains energized late into the evenings, especially when there are events at the Verizon Center or at one or more of Downtown's major theaters.

QUICK BITES

On Rye. At this deli in Chinatown, veggies take center stage with offerings like a portobello and broccoli Reuben or a roasted beet salad. Meat lovers shouldn't despair, as you can get a very fine traditional Reuben here, too. ⊠ 740 6th St. NW, Chinatown ☎ 202/794–8400 ⊕ www.onrye.com Ⓜ Gallery Pl./Chinatown.

Red Apron Butcher. As its name implies, you can get a very meaty sandwich here, but there are excellent choices for vegetarians as well. The breakfast and lunch tigelles (crisp and chewy Italian flatbreads with assorted toppings) are especially good. ⊠ 709 D St. NW, Penn Quarter ☎ 202/524–5244 ⊕ www.redapronbutchery.com ▭ No credit cards Ⓜ Archives.

The centerpiece of the **Aftermaths Exhibits at the Center for Education and Leadership** is a jaw-dropping, three-story tower of 6,800 books written about Lincoln. Here, visitors take an immersive step back in time, entering a 19th-century street scene where they find a reproduction of Lincoln's funeral train car and see its route to Springfield, Illinois. Visitors also learn about the manhunt for John Wilkes Booth and his co-conspirators' trial, and they interact with an "escape map" to the tobacco barn where Booth was captured. Exhibits also explore the fate of Lincoln's family after his death, explain the milestones of Reconstruction, and describe Lincoln's legacy and his enduring impact on U.S. and world leaders. A visit ends with a multiscreen video wall that shows how Lincoln's ideas resonate today.

Visits to Ford's Theatre require a free, timed-entry ticket. Same-day tickets are available at the theater box office beginning at 8:30 am on a first-come, first-served basis. You can also reserve tickets in advance at *www.fords.org* with a $3 fee per ticket. ⊠ *511 10th St. NW, Downtown* ☎ *202/426–6924* ⊕ *www.fords.org* ✉ *Free, except for performances* Ⓜ *Metro Center or Gallery Pl./Chinatown.*

FAMILY
Fodor'sChoice
★

International Spy Museum. It's believed that there are more spies in Washington than in any other city in the world, making it a fitting home for this museum, which displays the world's largest collection of spy artifacts. Museum advisers include top cryptologists, masters of disguise, and former CIA, FBI, and KGB operatives. Exhibits range from the coded letters of Revolutionary War überspy Benedict Arnold and the KGB's lipstick pistol, to high-tech 21st-century espionage toys.

The Secret History of History takes you behind the headlines, from Moses's use of spies in Canaan and Abraham Lincoln's employment of the Pinkerton National Detective Agency as a full-scale secret service in the Civil War, to the birth of Lenin's state-run espionage ring—later known as the KGB. Check out the spy gadgets, weapons, vehicles, and disguises and then see if you have what it takes to be a spy in *School for Spies. Exquisitely Evil: 50 Years of Bond Villains* brings you face-to-face with Bond villains. More than 100 movie artifacts are exhibited, from the steel teeth worn by Richard Kiel as "Jaws" in 1979's *Moonraker* to Raoul Silva's laptop in *Skyfall.* And—of course—Bond's famous Aston Martin is on display. *Operation Spy,* a one-hour "immersive experience," works like a live-action game, dropping you in the middle of a foreign intelligence mission. Each step—which includes decrypting secret audio files, a car chase, and interrogating a suspect agent—is taken from actual intelligence operations.

Advance tickets (purchased at the museum or on its website) are highly recommended. All tickets are date- and time-specific. Tickets are most likely available on Tuesday, Wednesday, and Thursday or daily after 2 pm. ⊠ *800 F St. NW, Downtown* ☎ *202/393–7798* ⊕ *www.spymuseum. org* ✉ *Permanent exhibition $21.95; Operation Spy and Spy in the City $14.95 (discounted combo tickets are available)* Ⓜ *Gallery Pl./Chinatown.*

FAMILY
Fodor'sChoice
★

National Archives. Monument, museum, and the nation's memory, the National Archives, headquartered in a grand marble edifice on Constitution Avenue, preserves more than 12 billion paper records dating back to 1774 and billions of recent electronic records. The National

Kids love the International Spy Museum, where they can adopt a cover identity and try out being a spy in an interactive mission.

Archives and Records Administration is charged with preserving and archiving the most historically important U.S. government records at its records centers nationwide and in presidential libraries.

Charters of Freedom—the Declaration of Independence, the Constitution, and the Bill of Rights—are the star attractions. They are housed in the Archives' cathedral-like rotunda, each on a marble platform, encased in bulletproof glass.

On display at the entrance to the David M. Rubenstein Gallery is a 1297 Magna Carta, the document of English common law whose language inspired the Constitution. One of four remaining originals, the Magna Carta sets the stage for the *Records of Rights* exhibit in this interactive gallery that traces the civil rights struggles of African Americans, women, and immigrants. Highlights include the discharge papers of a slave who fought in the Revolutionary War to gain his freedom; the mark-up copy of the 1964 Civil Rights Act; and letters to the president from children who questioned segregation.

The Public Vaults go deep into the stacks. You can find records that give a glimpse into Federal investigations, from the Lincoln assassination to Watergate. Watch films of flying saucers, used as evidence in congressional UFO hearings, listen to the Nuremberg trials or Congress debating Prohibition. Reservations to visit the Archives are highly recommended. Reservations for guided tours, or for timed visit entries, should be made at least six weeks in advance. ⊠ *Constitution Ave., between 7th and 9th Sts., Downtown* ☎ *866/272–6272, 877/444–6777 tours and reservations* ⊕ *www.archives.gov* ⊠ *Free; $1.50 convenience fee for online reservations* Ⓜ *Archives/Navy Memorial.*

FAMILY **National Building Museum.** Architecture, design, landscaping, and urban planning are the themes of this museum, the nation's premier cultural organization devoted to the built environment. The open interior of the mammoth redbrick edifice is one of the city's great spaces, and has been the site of many presidential inaugural balls. The eight central Corinthian columns are among the largest in the world, rising to a height of 75 feet. Although they resemble Siena marble, each is made of 70,000 bricks that have been covered with plaster and painted.

The long-term exhibition *House and Home* features a kaleidoscopic array of photographs, objects, models, and films that takes visitors on a tour of houses both surprising and familiar, through past and present, exploring American domestic life and residential architecture. Among the most popular permanent exhibits is the *Building Zone,* where kids ages two to six can get a hands-on introduction to building by constructing a tower, exploring a kid-size playhouse, or playing with bulldozers and construction trucks. ⊠ *401 F St. NW, between 4th and 5th Sts., Downtown* ☎ *202/272–2448* ⊕ *www.nbm.org* ✉ *$10; Tool Kits $3 with admission or $5 without admission; docent-led tour of building and entrance to Great Hall, shop, and café free* Ⓜ *Judiciary Sq. or Gallery Pl./Chinatown.*

FAMILY
Fodor's Choice
★
National Portrait Gallery. The intersection of art, biography, and history is illustrated here through images of men and women who have shaped U.S. history. There are prints, paintings, photos, and sculptures of subjects from George Washington to Madonna.

This museum shares the National Historic Landmark building Old Patent Office with the Smithsonian American Art Museum. Built between 1836 and 1863, and praised by Walt Whitman as the "noblest of Washington buildings," it is deemed one of the country's best examples of Greek Revival architecture.

"America's Presidents" shares the stories of the country's leaders and the times in which they governed. In this gallery, you'll see the only complete collection of presidential portraits outside the White House. Highlights include Gilbert Stuart's 1796 "Landsdowne" portrait of George Washington, Alexander Gardner's "cracked-plate" image of Abraham Lincoln from Lincoln's last formal portrait session before his assassination in 1865, a sculpture of Andrew Jackson on a horse, and political cartoonist Pat Oliphant's sculpture of George H.W. Bush playing horseshoes.

From portraits of World War II generals Eisenhower and Patton to Andy Warhol's *Time* magazine cover of Michael Jackson, the third-floor gallery, Twentieth-Century Americans, offers a vibrant tour of the people who shaped the country and culture of today. And, don't miss the *Bravo* and *Champions* exhibits on the mezzanine, especially if you enjoy the performing arts or are a sports buff. The displays of entertainers and American sports figures are dynamic and engaging.

There are free docent-led tours weekdays at noon and 2:30, and most weekends at 11:45, 1:30, 3:15 and 4:30. Check the website to confirm times. At the Lunder Conservation Center on the third and fourth floors, you can watch conservators restoring works. ⊠ *8th and F Sts. NW, Downtown* ☎ *202/633–8300* ⊕ *www.npg.si.edu* ✉ *Free* Ⓜ *Gallery Pl./Chinatown.*

On the exterior of the Newseum, the first amendment is inscribed in its entirety.

Newseum. The setting, in a dramatic glass-and-silver structure on Pennsylvania Avenue, smack between the White House and the Capitol, is a fitting location for a museum devoted to the First Amendment and the role of a free press in democracy. Visitors enter the 90-foot-high media-saturated atrium, overlooked by a giant breaking-news screen and a news helicopter suspended overhead. From there, 15 galleries display 500 years of news history, including exhibits on the First Amendment; global news; the rise of multimedia; and how radio, TV, and the Internet transformed worldwide news dissemination.

The largest piece of the Berlin Wall outside Germany, including a guard tower, is permanently installed in an exhibit explaining how a free press was a key contributor to the fall of the wall. One of only 19 copies of *The Pennsylvania Evening Post* from July 6, 1776, that published the Declaration of Independence is also here in an exhibit that explores how news of freedom led delegates in the 13 colonies to unite for independence.

Fifteen state-of-the art theaters, including an eye-popping "4-D" theater and another with a 90-foot-long screen, show features, news, sports, and documentaries throughout the day. In the Interactive Newsroom you can play the role of journalist, try your hand at investigative reporting to solve a mysterious animal breakout at the zoo, or step behind a camera and try to capture the most compelling photograph of a river rescue. Evocative press photos are on display at the Pulitzer Prize Photographs gallery.

There's a lot to take in here, but luckily tickets for the Newseum are valid for two consecutive days. On one of those days, be sure to visit the top-floor terrace, which offers one of the best views of the Capitol in the city. ✉ *555 Pennsylvania Ave. NW, Downtown* ☏ *888/639–7386* ⊕ *www.newseum.org* 💲 *$24.95* Ⓜ *Archives/Navy Memorial or Judiciary Sq.*

Smithsonian American Art Museum. From Childe Hassam's *The South Ledges, Appledore* to Nelson Shanks's *The Four Justices,* the Smithsonian American Art Museum features one of the world's largest collections of American art that spans more than four centuries. Over the past few decades, the museum has broadened its collection to include modern and contemporary art, too. Among the artists represented are Benny Andrews, José Campechi, Robert Indiana, Roy Lichtenstein, Isamu Noguchi, Robert Rauschenberg, Mickalene Thomas, and Charlie Willeto. The museum shares a National Historic Landmark building with the National Portrait Gallery.

On the first floor, you'll discover an enormous tinfoil altarpiece by James Hampton and more than 60 sculptures and paintings by Emery Blagdon that represent his thought-provoking and constantly changing *Healing Machine*. You can also experience American artwork from the 1930s, many created as part of New Deal programs. Highlights here include Marvin Beerbohm's Automotive Industry, Lily Furedi's Subway, and Edward Hopper's Ryder's House. Also on the first floor is the *Direct Carving* exhibit which showcases artists who work directly on a piece of stone or wood.

Art from the colonial period to the dawn of modernism is displayed throughout the galleries on the second floor. Discover masterpieces by Mary Cassatt, Frederick Carl Frieseke, Thomas Moran, Harriett Whitney Frishmuth, George Catlin, Albert Bierstadt, Winslow Homer, and John Singer Sargent, to name just a few.

The museum's third floor features modern and contemporary paintings and sculpture and the Watch This! gallery, where you can see a selection of works from the museum's media art and film collection. Highlights include Nam June Paik's billboard-size piece with 215 monitors showing video images from the Seoul Olympics, Korean folk rituals, and modern dance.

At any given time, much of the museum's holdings are in storage, but you can view more than 3,000 artworks in its Luce Foundation Center, a visible storage space on the third and fourth floors, where visitors can also watch the museum's conservators at work. Free docent-led tours of the museum are available every day at 12:30 and 2. ✉ *8th and G Sts. NW, Downtown* ☏ *202/633–7970* ⊕ *www.americanart. si.edu* 💲 *Free* Ⓜ *Gallery Pl./Chinatown.*

WORTH NOTING

American Veterans Disabled for Life Memorial. Located on a 2.4 acre tract adjacent to the Mall and within full view of the U.S. Capitol, this memorial illustrates the disabled veteran's journey, from injury and healing to rediscovery of purpose. The plaza, with a star-shape fountain and low triangular reflecting pool, features bronze sculptures, glass panels, and granite walls engraved with quotations from 18 veterans describing their experiences. With its single ceremonial flame, the fountain is the focal point of this memorial. It's a powerful icon, expressing the healing, cleansing properties of water and the enlightenment, power, and eternal nature of fire. A grove of trees adjacent to the pool signifies the persistence of hope. The needs of the disabled are front and center in the memorial's design. The low fountain can easily be surveyed by someone in a wheelchair; there are numerous benches in front of text panels and unobtrusive metal bars are placed strategically to help visitors who need assistance to sit or stand. Designed by Michael Vergason Landscape Architects, of Alexandria, Virginia, the memorial is a fitting reminder of the cost of human conflict. ⊠ *150 Washington Ave. SW, Downtown* ⊕ *www.avdlm.org* ⊡ *Free* Ⓜ *Federal Center.*

Madame Tussauds. A branch of the famous London-based waxworks franchise focuses on U.S. presidential history. You can see and pose for pictures (some for a small fee) with uncanny likenesses of the Founding Fathers or any of the presidents, including Barack Obama and his wife, or sit inside the Oval Office, painstakingly re-created in wax. The Civil Rights room features Martin Luther King Jr. and Rosa Parks. There are cultural icons, sports figures, and a behind-the-scenes exhibit where experts demonstrate wax sculpting. The Glamour Room is populated with waxen re-creations of George Clooney, Beyoncé, Zac Efron, and Taylor Swift, among others. ⊠ *1025 F St. NW, Downtown* ☎ *202/942–7300, 866/823–9565 to confirm hrs* ⊕ *www.madametussaudsdc.com* ⊡ *$22* Ⓜ *Metro Center or Gallery Pl./Chinatown.*

FAMILY **Marian Koshland Science Museum.** Part of the National Academy of Sciences, this small but engaging museum invites older kids and adults to interact with current scientific issues in a thought-provoking setting. Visitors have the opportunity to use science to solve problems and engage in conversation. There's a driving simulator, a 3-D look inside the brain, plus exhibits on the science of healthy eating through the life span. In the Idea Lab, you'll explore the concept of resilience in your life and community. Map risk and resilience, play a disaster-simulation game, and create an emergency plan. ■ TIP→ **Though the interactive exhibits are fun and educational, they are aimed at ages 12 and up.** ⊠ *525 E St. NW, Downtown* ☎ *202/334–1201* ⊕ *www.koshland-dc.org* ⊡ *$5* ⊙ *Closed Tues.* Ⓜ *Gallery Pl./Chinatown or Judiciary Sq.*

National Law Enforcement Officers Memorial. These 3-foot-high walls bear the names of 20,267 American police officers killed in the line of duty since 1791. On the third line of panel 13W are the names of six officers killed by William Bonney, better known as Billy the Kid. J. D. Tippit, the Dallas policeman killed by Lee Harvey Oswald, is honored on the ninth line of panel 63E. Other names include the 72 officers who died due to the events of 9/11. Directories there allow you to look up officers by name, date of death, state, and department. Call to arrange for a free tour. A National Law Enforcement Museum is in the works; until then, a small visitor center (*400 7th St.*) has a computer for looking up names, a display on the history of law enforcement, and a small gift shop. ⊠ *400 block of E St. NW, Penn Quarter* ☎ *202/737–3400* ⊕ *www.lawmemorial.org* ⊠ *Free* Ⓜ *Judiciary Sq.*

National Museum of Women in the Arts. This museum, in a beautifully restored 1907 Renaissance Revival building designed by Waddy B. Wood, brings to light remarkable female artists of the past, while promoting the best female artists working today. Founded in 1987, this is the only major museum in the world solely dedicated to recognizing women's creative contributions. In addition to hosting special exhibitions, the museum holds a collection of 5,000 artworks including paintings, drawings, sculpture, prints, videos, and photographs by Frida Kahlo, Camille Claudel, Mary Cassatt, Alma Thomas, Judy Chicago, Magdalena Abakanowicz, Nan Goldin, Louise Dahl-Wolfe, Helen Frankenthaler, and Élisabeth Vigée-Lebrun, among others. The installations highlight connections between historical and contemporary artworks. Gallery and artist talks, hands-on art workshops, and concerts are held regularly; check the museum's website for the calendar of events. ⊠ *1250 New York Ave. NW, Downtown* ☎ *202/783–5000* ⊕ *www. nmwa.org* ⊠ *$10* Ⓜ *Metro Center.*

Ronald Reagan Building and International Trade Center. At more than 3 million square feet, this is the largest federal building in Washington, and the only structure used by both government and private entities. A blend of classical and modern architecture, it is also officially the World Trade Center, Washington, D.C. The Reagan Building hosts special events throughout the year, in addition to its permanent art collection including a section of the Berlin Wall and the Woodrow Wilson Presidential Memorial Exhibit and Learning Center. In summer, check out Live!, a free concert series, performed daily from noon to 1:30. A farmers' market takes over the plaza on Friday during the spring and summer. ⊠ *1300 Pennsylvania Ave. NW, Downtown* ☎ *202/312–1300* ⊕ *www. itcdc.com* ⊠ *Free* Ⓜ *Federal Triangle.*

United States Navy Memorial. Although Pierre L'Enfant included a Navy Memorial in his plans for Washington, D.C., it wasn't until 1987 that one was built. The main attraction here is a 100-foot-diameter granite map of the world, known as the Granite Sea. It's surrounded by fountains, benches, and six ship masts. The *Lone Sailor*, a 7-foot-tall statue, stands on the map in the Pacific Ocean between the United States and Japan. The Naval Heritage Center, next to the memorial in the Market Square East Building, displays videos and exhibits of uniforms, medals, and other aspects of Navy life. If you've served in the Navy, you can enter your record of service into the Navy Log here. Bronze relief panels on the Pennsylvania Avenue side of the memorial depict 26 scenes commemorating events in the nation's naval history and honoring naval communities. ⊠ *701 Pennsylvania Ave. NW, Downtown* ☎ *202/737– 2300* ⊕ *www.navymemorial.org* ⊠ *Free* Ⓜ *Archives/Navy Memorial.*

2

GEORGETOWN

Sightseeing
★★★
Dining
★★★★★
Lodging
★★★★
Shopping
★★★★★
Nightlife
★★★★★

At first glance, Washington's oldest and wealthiest neighborhood may look genteel and staid, but don't be fooled: this is a lively part of town. Georgetown is D.C.'s top high-end shopping destination, with everything from eclectic antiques and housewares to shoes and upscale jeans. At night, particularly on weekends, revelers along M Street and Wisconsin Avenue eat, drink, and make merry. Perfect for strolling, this neighborhood's historic, tree-lined streets and waterfront parks have wonderful views of the Potomac. Although the coveted brick homes north of M Street are the province of Washington's high society, the rest of the neighborhood offers ample entertainment for everyone.

Fodor's Choice
★

Dumbarton Oaks. Career diplomat Robert Woods Bliss and his wife, Mildred, bought the property in 1920 and tamed the sprawling grounds into acres of splendid gardens designed mainly by Beatrix Farrand. In 1940, the Blisses gave the estate to Harvard University as a study center, library, museum, and garden. The museum holds a world-renowned collection of Byzantine and pre-Columbian art. Both collections are small but selective, reflecting the enormous skill and creativity developed at roughly the same time in two very different parts of the world. The Byzantine collection includes beautiful examples of both religious and secular items executed in mosaic, metal, enamel, stone, textile, and ivory. Pre-Columbian works—artifacts and textiles from Mexico and Central and South America by peoples such as the Aztec, Maya, Inca, and Olmec—are arranged in an enclosed glass pavilion designed by Philip Johnson.

Getting Oriented

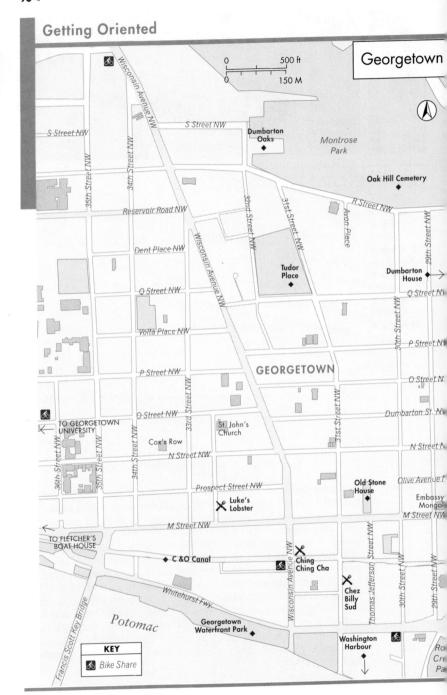

Georgetown

0 ——— 500 ft
0 ——— 150 M

Wisconsin Avenue NW

S Street NW

S Street NW

Dumbarton Oaks

Montrose Park

Oak Hill Cemetery

R Street NW

34th Street NW

35th Street NW

Reservoir Road NW

32nd Street NW

31st Street NW

Avon Place

29th Street NW

Dent Place NW

Wisconsin Avenue NW

Dumbarton House

Tudor Place

Q Street NW

Q Street NW

Volta Place NW

30th Street NW

P Street NW

P Street NW

GEORGETOWN

O Street N

33rd Street NW

O Street NW

31st Street NW

Dumbarton St. N

TO GEORGETOWN UNIVERSITY

St. John's Church

N Street N

36th Street NW

35th Street NW

34th Street NW

Cox's Row

N Street NW

Olive Avenue

Prospect Street NW

Old Stone House

Embassy Mongol

TO FLETCHER'S BOAT HOUSE

Luke's Lobster

M Street NW

M Street NW

C &O Canal

Wisconsin Avenue NW

Ching Ching Cha

Thomas Jefferson Street NW

30th Street NW

29th Street NW

Whitehurst Fwy

Chez Billy Sud

Francis Scott Key Bridge

Potomac

Georgetown Waterfront Park

Washington Harbour

Ro Cre Pa

KEY

Bike Share

GREAT EXPERIENCES IN GEORGETOWN

C&O Canal: Walk or bike along the path here, which offers bucolic scenery from the heart of Georgetown across Maryland.

Dumbarton Oaks: Stroll through the 10 acres of formal gardens—Washington's loveliest oasis.

M Street: Indulge in some serious designer retail therapy (or just window-shopping). Reward your willpower or great find with a great meal afterward—all on the same street.

Tudor Place: Step into Georgetown's past with a visit to the grand home of the Custis-Peter family. On view are antiques from George and Martha Washington's home at Mount Vernon and a 1919 Pierce Arrow roadster.

Washington Harbour and Waterfront Park: Come on a warm evening to enjoy sunset drinks while overlooking the Watergate, Kennedy Center, and Potomac River. Board a sightseeing cruise at the dock.

GETTING HERE

There's no Metro stop in Georgetown, so you have to take a bus or taxi or walk to this part of Washington. It's about a 20-minute walk from Dupont Circle and the Foggy Bottom Metro stations. Perhaps the best transportation deal in Georgetown is the Circulator. For a buck you can ride from Union Station along Massachusetts Avenue and K Street to the heart of Georgetown. Or try the Georgetown Circulator route, which connects M Street to the Dupont Circle and Rosslyn Metro stops. The Circulator runs daily at varying hours (⊕ www.dccirculator.com).

Other options include the G2 Georgetown University bus, which goes west from Dupont Circle along P Street, and Friendship Heights bus Nos. 31, 32, and 36 , which go south down Wisconsin Avenue and west down Pennsylvania Avenue toward Georgetown. From the Foggy Bottom Metro stop catch Bus 38B to M Street.

PLANNING YOUR TIME

You can easily spend a pleasant day in Georgetown, partly because some sights (**Tudor Place, Dumbarton Oaks, Oak Hill Cemetery,** and **Dumbarton House**) are somewhat removed from the others and partly because the street scene, with its shops and people-watching, invites you to linger.

Georgetown is almost always crowded at night. Driving and parking are difficult, so the wise take a bus or taxi.

QUICK BITES

Chez Billy Sud. A cozy gem in Georgetown is this French restaurant, which serves lunch, dinner, and weekend brunch. If it's a nice day, request a table on the lovely patio. ⊠ *1039 31st St. NW, Georgetown* ☎ *202/965–2606* ⊕ *www.chezbillysud.com* ⊙ *Closed Mon. No lunch weekends.*

Ching Ching Cha. Step into Ching Ching Cha, a teahouse where tranquillity reigns supreme. In addition to tea, lunch and dinner may be ordered from a simple menu with light, healthy meals. ⊠ *1063 Wisconsin Ave. NW, Georgetown* ☎ *202/333–8288* ⊕ *www.chingchingcha.com* ⊙ *Closed Mon.*

A History of Georgetown

The area that would come to be known as George (after George II), then George Towne, and finally Georgetown, was part of Maryland when it was settled in the early 1700s by Scottish immigrants, many of whom were attracted by the region's tolerant religious climate.

Georgetown's position—at the farthest point up the Potomac that's accessible by ship—made it an ideal transit and inspection point for farmers who grew tobacco in Maryland's interior. In 1789 the state granted the town a charter, but two years later Georgetown—along with Alexandria, its counterpart in Virginia—was included by George Washington in the Territory of Columbia, site of the new capital.

While Washington struggled, Georgetown thrived. Wealthy traders built their mansions on the hills overlooking the river; merchants and the working class lived in modest homes closer to the water's edge.

In 1810 a third of Georgetown's population was African American—both free people and slaves. The Mt. Zion United Methodist Church on 29th Street is the oldest organized black congregation in the city, and when the church stood at 27th and P Streets it was a stop on the Underground Railroad (the original building burned down in the mid-1800s).

Georgetown's rich history and success instilled in all its residents a feeling of pride that persists today. When Georgetowners thought the capital was dragging them down, they asked to be given back to Maryland, the way Alexandria was given back to Virginia in 1845.

Tobacco's star eventually fell, and Georgetown became a milling center, using waterpower from the Potomac. When the Chesapeake & Ohio (C&O) Canal was completed in 1850, the city intensified its milling operations and became the eastern end of a waterway that stretched 184 miles to the west.

The C&O took up some of the slack when Georgetown's harbor began to fill with silt and the port lost business to Alexandria and Baltimore, but the canal never became the success that George Washington had envisioned.

In the years that followed, Georgetown was a malodorous industrial district, a far cry from the fashionable spot it is today. Clustered near the water were a foundry, a fish market, paper and cotton mills, and a power station for the city's streetcar system.

Georgetown still had its Georgian, Federal, and Victorian homes, though, and when the New Deal and World War II brought a flood of newcomers to Washington, Georgetown's tree-shaded streets and handsome brick houses were rediscovered. Pushed out in the process were many of Georgetown's renters, including many of its black residents.

In modern times some of Washington's most famous residents have called Georgetown home, including former *Washington Post* executive editor Ben Bradlee, political pundit George Stephanopoulos, Secretaries of State John Kerry and Madeleine Albright, Senator John Warner and his wife at the time, Elizabeth Taylor, and *New York Times* op-ed doyenne Maureen Dowd, who lives in a town house where President Kennedy lived as a senator.

Normally on public view are the lavishly decorated music room, special changing exhibits, and selections from Mrs. Bliss's collection. On weekends, visitors can see the Rare Book Reading Room, and docents are on hand to share the history of the room and its furnishings and artwork. The gorgeous gardens are currently closed for maintenance work, but plans are to reopen them in March 2018, just in time for the peonies bloom. ⊠ *1703 32nd St. NW, Georgetown* ☎ *202/339–6401, 202/339–6409 tours* ⊕ *www.doaks.org* ✉ *Free; gardens $8* ☉ *Closed Mon.* Ⓜ *Dupont Circle.*

Old Stone House. Washington's oldest surviving building, this fieldstone house in the heart of Georgetown was built in 1765 by a cabinetmaker named Christopher Layman. It was used as both a residence and place of business by a succession of occupants until 1953 when it was purchased by the National Park Service. Over the next seven years, the park service conducted an extensive restoration that has preserved the building's Revolutionary-war era architecture and design. Five of the house's rooms are furnished with the simple, sturdy artifacts—plain tables, spinning wheels, and so forth—of 18th-century middle-class life. You can take a self-guided tour of the house and its lovely English-style gardens. ⊠ *3051 M St. NW, Georgetown* ☎ *202/895–6070* ⊕ *www.nps. gov/olst* ✉ *Free* Ⓜ *Foggy Bottom.*

Tudor Place. Stop at Q Street between 31st and 32nd Streets; look through the trees to the north, to the top of a sloping lawn, and you can see the neoclassical Tudor Place, designed by Capitol architect Dr. William Thornton for one of Martha Washington's granddaughters. Completed in 1816, the house remained in the family for six generations and during these 178 years, many politicians, dignitaries, and military leaders spent time here. On the house tour you can see the largest collection of George and Martha Washington items on public display outside Mount Vernon, Francis Scott Key's law desk, and spurs belonging to soldiers who were executed as spies in the Civil War. You can only visit the house by guided tour (given hourly; last tour at 3), but before and afterward, until 4 pm, you can wander freely, with a map, through the formal garden full of roses and boxwoods, many planted in the early 19th century. ⊠ *1644 31st St. NW, Georgetown* ☎ *202/965–0400* ⊕ *www.tudorplace.org* ✉ *$10; garden only $3 ($1 in Feb.)* ☉ *Closed Mon. and Jan.* Ⓜ *Dupont Circle.*

DUPONT CIRCLE AND LOGAN CIRCLE

Sightseeing
★★★★
Dining
★★★★★
Lodging
★★★★
Shopping
★★★★
Nightlife
★★★★

Dupont Circle, named for Civil War hero Admiral Samuel F. Dupont, is the grand hub of D.C., literally. This traffic circle is essentially the intersection of the main thoroughfares of Connecticut, New Hampshire, and Massachusetts Avenues. More important though, the area around the circle is a vibrant center for urban and cultural life in the District.

Along with wealthy tenants and basement-dwelling young adults, museums, art galleries, and embassies call this upscale neighborhood home. Offbeat shops, specialty bookstores, coffeehouses, and varied restaurants help the area stay funky and diverse.

The Logan Circle neighborhood runs to the east along P Street and stretches north along the 14th Street Corridor, where sidewalk cafés, a handful of sights, and two theaters—Source DC and Studio—draw a lively nightlife crowd.

Add to the mix stores and clubs catering to the neighborhood's gay community and this area becomes a big draw for nearly everyone. Perhaps that's why the fountain at the center of the Dupont traffic island is such a great spot for people-watching.

TOP ATTRACTIONS

FAMILY **National Geographic Museum.** Founded in 1888, the National Geographic Society is best known for its magazine, and entering this welcoming 13,000-square-foot exhibition space feels like stepping into its pages. The small museum has child-friendly interactives and is home to a rotating display of objects from the society's permanent collections—cultural, historical, and scientific—as well as traveling exhibitions. It also has weekend showings in its 3-D movie theater. Nat Geo Nights—presentations by explorers with interactive activities, music, and food and drink specials—are held the third Thursday of every month. The M Street Lobby photography exhibit, as well as the outdoor photo display around the perimeter of the museum, are free. ⊠ *17th and M Sts. NW, Dupont Circle* ☎ *202/857–7588, 202/857–7689 group tours* ⊕ *www.nationalgeographic.org/dc* ⊠ *$15; 3-D movies $7* Ⓜ *Farragut N.*

Fodor's Choice
★
Phillips Collection. The first museum of modern art in the country, the masterpiece-filled Phillips Collection is unique in origin and content. It opened in 1921 in the Georgian Revival mansion of collector Duncan Phillips, who wanted to showcase his art in a museum that would stand as a memorial to his father and brother. Having no interest in a painting's market value or its faddishness, Phillips searched for pieces that impressed him as outstanding products of a particular artist's unique vision. At the heart of the collection are impressionist and modern masterpieces by Pierre-Auguste Renoir, Vincent van Gogh, Paul Cézanne, Edgar Degas, Pablo Picasso, Paul Klee, Pierre Bonnard, and Henri Matisse. By combining works of different nationalities and periods in displays that change frequently, the Phillips makes for a museum-going experience that is as intimate as it is inspiring. The domestic scale and personal atmosphere encourage visual conversations among the works.

The collection's most famous piece is Renoir's magnificent work of impressionism, *Luncheon of the Boating Party*. Other celebrity works include Degas's *Dancers at the Barre* and van Gogh's *Entrance to the Public Gardens at Arles*. The chapel-like Rothko Room emerged when modern master Mark Rothko said he preferred to exhibit in intimately scaled rooms; Phillips designed the gallery specifically for him. You can see four of Rothko's dramatic color abstracts here.

On Thursdays, the Phillips is open until 8:30 pm and, on the first Thursday of the month, Phillips after 5 ($12) combines live music, gallery talks, food, and a cash bar. Reservations are strongly advised. Music at the Phillips, a tradition since 1941, is a concert series held on Sunday at 4 from October through May in the oak-paneled music room. Tickets are $40 and include museum admission that day. Reservations are recommended. ⊠ *1600 21st St. NW, Dupont Circle* ☎ *202/387–2151* ⊕ *www.phillipscollection.org* ⊠ *Free weekdays; $10 weekends for permanent collection; $12 for special ticketed exhibitions (includes permanent collection)* ⊗ *Closed Mon.* Ⓜ *Dupont Circle.*

WORTH NOTING

The American Revolution Institute of the Society of the Cincinnati. The palatial Gilded Age Anderson House is the headquarters of the Society of the Cincinnati, the nation's oldest historical organization promoting knowledge and appreciation of America's independence. The Society was founded by Revolutionary War veterans in 1783—George Washington was its first president general—and this has been its home since 1938. Guided tours of the first and second floors reveal the history of the Society, the significance of the American Revolution, and the lives and collections of the home's first owners, Larz and Isabel Anderson. Built in 1905, the home was the Andersons' winter residence and retains much

Getting Oriented

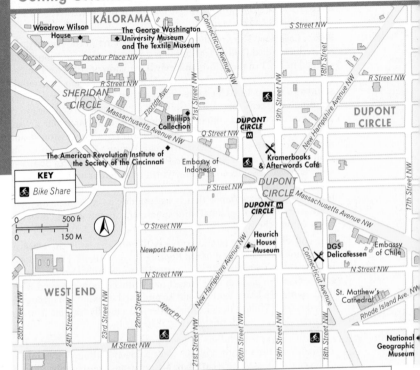

🚲 Bike Share

0 — 500 ft
0 — 150 M

QUICK BITES

DGS Delicatessen. DGS pickles, cures, and smokes all its food in-house. Their smoked salmon, pastrami, and corned beef are top sellers. ✉ 1317 Connecticut Ave. NW, Dupont Circle ☎ 202/293–4400 ⊕ www.dgsdelicatessen.com Ⓜ Dupont Circle.

Kramerbooks & Afterwords Café. Grab a table at this vibrant bookstore-café that offers an eclectic American menu, including cocktails. ✉ 1517 Connecticut Ave. NW, Dupont Circle ☎ 202/387–1400 ⊕ www.kramers.com Ⓜ Dupont Circle.

GREAT EXPERIENCES AROUND DUPONT CIRCLE AND LOGAN CIRCLE

Dupont Circle: Grab a cup of coffee and a *CityPaper* and soak up the always-buzzing scene around the fountain.

Logan Circle: Take in a contemporary play at the Studio Theatre, then stay out late in the restaurants and bars on 14th and P Streets.

National Geographic Society: See *National Geographic* magazine come to life in rotating exhibits at the society's Explorers Hall.

Phillips Collection: Admire masterpieces such as Renoir's *Luncheon of the Boating Party* and Degas's *Dancers at the Barre* at the country's first museum of modern art.

Woodrow Wilson House: Glimpse the life of the 28th American president, who lived here during his retirement, surrounded by all the modern luxuries of the early 1900s.

2

Dupont Circle and Logan Circle

A GOOD WALK: KALORAMA

To see the embassies and luxurious homes that make up the Kalorama neighborhood, begin your walk at the corner of S and 23rd Streets.

Head north up 23rd, keeping an eye out for the emergency call boxes now turned into public art.

At the corner of Kalorama Road, head west, but don't miss the Tudor-style mansion at 2221 Kalorama Road, now home to the French ambassador.

Turn right on Kalorama Circle, where you can look down at Rock Creek Park and into Adams Morgan. Kalorama means "beautiful view" in Greek, and this is the sight that inspired the name.

From here you can retrace your steps, or take Kalorama Circle back to Kalorama Road, turn right, and make a left on Wyoming to bring you back to 23rd.

GETTING HERE

Dupont Circle has its own stop on the Metro's Red Line. Exit on Q Street for the Phillips Collection, Anderson House, and Kalorama attractions. Take the Connecticut Avenue exit for the National Geographic Society, Christian Heurich House museum, or shopping between Dupont Circle and Farragut North. Follow P Street to the east for Logan Circle. On-street parking in residential areas is becoming increasingly difficult to find, especially on weekend evenings.

PLANNING YOUR TIME

Visiting the Dupont Circle area takes at least half a day, although you can find things to keep you busy all day and into the evening. You'll likely spend the most time at the **Phillips Collection, Anderson House,** and **Woodrow Wilson House.** The hours will also fly if you linger over lunch or indulge in serious browsing in area shops.

The many fountains in Dupont Circle make it a nice place for a walk.

of its original contents—an eclectic mix of furniture, tapestries, paintings, sculpture, and Asian art. Larz, a U.S. diplomat from 1891 to 1913, and his wife, Isabel, an author and benefactress, assembled their collection as they traveled the world during diplomatic postings. Today, the house also features an exhibition gallery and research library. ✉ *2118 Massachusetts Ave. NW, Dupont Circle* ☎ *202/785–2040* ⊕ *www.societyofthecincinnati.org* ✉ *Free* ⊗ *Closed Mon.* Ⓜ *Dupont Circle.*

The George Washington University Museum and The Textile Museum. Designed to foster the study and appreciation of art, history, and culture, this 46,000-square-foot LEED Gold-certified museum facility is located on the campus of George Washington University. Galleries dedicated for The Textile Museum showcase weavings, carpets, and tapestries that date from 3000 BC to the present. Rotating exhibits are taken from a permanent collection of 19,000 rugs, textiles, and related objects, including Coptic and pre-Columbian textiles, Kashmir embroidery, and Turkmen tribal rugs. Also within this impressive building are the Arthur D. Jenkins Library for the Textile Arts, a museum shop, and galleries displaying art from the university's collection. The building is linked to the renovated Woodhull House, which holds the Albert H. Small Washingtoniana Collection: 1,000 maps, photographs, books, newspapers, manuscripts, and other artifacts that document D.C.'s history from the 18th to the mid-20th century. The museum also offers a dynamic range of lectures, tours, and activities that explore the textile arts. ✉ *701 21st St. NW, Foggy Bottom* ☎ *202/994–5200* ⊕ *www.museum.gwu.edu* ✉ *$8 suggested donation* ⊗ *Closed Tues.* Ⓜ *Foggy Bottom/GWU.*

2

Heurich House Museum. This opulent Romanesque Revival mansion, also known as the Brewmaster's Castle, was the home of Christian Heurich, a German immigrant who made his fortune in the beer business. Heurich's brewery was in Foggy Bottom, where the Kennedy Center stands today. During the late 19th century, he was the second-largest landowner and the largest private employer in the city. The building, a National Register of Historic Places landmark, is considered one of the most intact Victorian houses in the country, and all the furnishings were owned and used by the Heurichs. The interior is an eclectic gathering of plaster detailing, carved wooden doors, and painted ceilings. The downstairs Breakfast Room, which also served as Heurich's *bierstube* (or beer hall), is decorated like a Rathskeller and adorned with German sayings such as "A good drink makes old people young." Heurich must have taken proverbs seriously. He drank beer daily, had three wives, and lived to be 102. A History & Hops event is held the third Thursday of every month with beer tastings and house tours. ⊠ *1307 New Hampshire Ave. NW, Dupont Circle* ☎ *202/429–1894* ⊕ *www.heurichhouse.org* ▨ *$5* ⊙ *Closed Sun.–Wed.* Ⓜ *Dupont Circle.*

Woodrow Wilson House. President Wilson and his second wife, Edith Bolling Wilson, retired in 1921 to this Georgian Revival house designed by Washington architect Waddy B. Wood. It was on this quiet street that Wilson lived out the last few years of his life.

Toward the end of his second term, President Wilson suffered a stroke. Edith made sure he was comfortable in their home; she had a bed constructed that had the same dimensions as the large Lincoln bed Wilson had slept in while in the White House. She also had the house's trunk lift (a sort of dumbwaiter for luggage) converted to an Otis elevator so the partially paralyzed president could move from floor to floor.

Wilson died in 1924—Edith survived him by 37 years—and bequeathed the house and its contents to the National Trust for Historic Preservation. Tours of the home provide a wonderful glimpse into the lives of this couple and the dignitaries who visited them here. You'll be able to view such items as Wilson's clothing, his collection of canes, a Gobelins wall-size tapestry that was a gift from the people of France, a mosaic from Pope Benedict XV, the pen used by Wilson to sign the declaration of war that launched the U.S. into World War I, and the shell casing from the first shot fired by U.S. forces in the war. The house also contains memorabilia related to the history of the short-lived but influential League of Nations, including the colorful flag Wilson hoped would be adopted by that organization. ⊠ *2340 S St. NW, Dupont Circle* ☎ *202/387–4062* ⊕ *www.woodrowwilsonhouse.org* ▨ *$10* ⊙ *Closed Mon. and Tues. year-round and Wed. and Thurs. in Jan. and Feb.* Ⓜ *Dupont Circle.*

ADAMS MORGAN

Sightseeing
★

Dining
★★★★

Lodging
★

Shopping
★★★

Nightlife
★★★★★

To the urban and hip, Adams Morgan is like a beacon in an otherwise stuffy landscape. D.C. may have a reputation for being staid and traditional, but drab suits, classical tastes, and bland food make no appearance here. Adams Morgan takes its name from two elementary schools that came together in 1958 after desegregation. It remains an ethnically diverse neighborhood with a blend of cuisines, offbeat shops, and funky bars and clubs.

Adams Morgan and its neighboring Columbia Heights comprise the city's Latin Quarter. The area wakes up as the sun goes down, and young Washingtonians in their weekend best congregate along the sidewalks, crowding the doors of this week's hot bar or nightclub. Typical tourist attractions are sparse, but the scene on a Saturday night has its own appeal. If you're here on the second Saturday in September, sample the vibrant neighborhood culture at the Adams Morgan Day Festival.

As you walk around Adams Morgan, note the many colorful and striking murals. Champorama Mural is one of the best; it is located in a tiny park just off 18th Street on the corner of Kalorama Road and Champlain Street. Among others, Toulouse-Lautrec is on 18th near Belmont Street. Find more on Columbia Road, including the oldest remaining mural in the neighborhood at 17th Street.

Getting Oriented

Adams Morgan

TO WOODLEY PARK-ZOO METRO →

Calvert Street NW

Columbia Road

TO COLUMBIA HEIGHTS ↗

TO ALL SOULS ↑
UNITARIAN CHURCH &
MEXICAN CULTURAL INSTITUTE

Euclid Street NW

Meridian H
(Malcolm
Pa

Rock Creek Park

Biltmore Street NW

Madam's Organ ◆

Tryst Coffeehouse-Bar-Lounge ◆

Ontario Road

17th Street NW

Kalorama Road

16th Street

Julia's Empanadas

18th Street NW

Champlain Street NW

Crescent Pl.

Habana Village ◆

Mintwood Pl.

The Black Squirrel ◆

Belmont St.

Belmont Rd

Kalorama Park

19th Street NW

Belmont Rd NW

Amsterdam Falafel ✕

Columbia Road

Bourbon ◆

Ashmead Pl.

Belmont Rd

20th Street NW

Kalorama Road NW

Kalorama Road

Wyoming Avenue NW

Wyoming Avenue NW

California Street NW

V Street NW

California Street NW

U Street NW

U Street NW

16th Street NW

ADAMS MORGAN

Florida Avenue NW

Willard Street NW

17th Street NW

T Street NW

T Street NW

19th Street NW

18th Street NW

Bancroft Place

Swann St. NW

Embassy of Thailand

21st Street NW

20th Street NW

S Street NW

S Street NW

Decatur Place

New Hampshire Avenue NW

R Street NW

Connecticut Avenue NW

R Street NW

R Street NW

Corcoran St. NW

Florida Ave.

DUPONT CIRCLE

Q Street NW

Q Street NW

16th Street NW

Massachusetts Avenue NW

Embassy of Botswana

KEY
🚲 Bike Share

0 ___ 500 ft

St. Thomas Parish

0 ___ 150 M

DUPONT CIRCLE

Embassy of Iraq

GREAT EXPERIENCES IN ADAMS MORGAN

Eat ethnic food: Adams Morgan rivals U Street with its plentiful and delicious Ethiopian restaurants. If you'd rather dine using utensils, you can choose among Japanese, Brazilian, Salvadorian, Mexican, Indian, and other cuisines.

Hang out like a local: The residents of Adams Morgan make an art of relaxing. Follow their lead and settle into one of Tryst's overstuffed armchairs with a laptop or a copy of the *New Republic* and a coffee, or kill hours browsing the "rare and medium-rare" selections at Idle Time Books.

Move to the beat: Every evening from 3 to 9 pm and on Sunday afternoon, drummers from all walks of life form the Drum Circle in Meridian Hill Park, bashing out the beats while some dance and others simply sit back and watch.

Stay out all night: If you want to party on until the break of dawn, this is the place to do it. Don't miss the live blues music at Madam's Organ, the salsa dancing at Habana Village, and the cool kids making the scene at the Black Squirrel or Bourbon.

GETTING HERE

Adams Morgan has two Metro stops that are a pleasant 10-minute walk away. From the Woodley Park/Zoo Metro station take a short walk south on Connecticut, then turn left on Calvert Street, and cross over Rock Creek Park on the Duke Ellington Bridge. If you get off at the Dupont Circle Metro stop walk east, turning left on 18th Street.

The heart of Adams Morgan is at the intersection of Columbia Road and 18th Street. Don't even dream about finding parking here on weekend evenings.

If you take the Metro, remember that stations close at midnight, or 3 am on Friday and Saturday nights. If you're not ready to turn in by then, you'll need to hail a cab.

PLANNING YOUR TIME

Window-shopping around Adams Morgan and surrounding environs can occupy the better part of an afternoon, and if you take advantage of the restaurants and nightlife here, there's no telling when your head will hit the pillow.

The few tourist attractions in this area are not time-intensive, but they can be a long walk from restaurants.

QUICK BITES

Amsterdam Falafel. Here you can garnish your authentic falafel balls with a choice of 21 toppings. ✉ 2425 18th St. NW, Adams Morgan ☎ 202/234–1969 ⊕ www.falafelshop.com Ⓜ Woodley Park-Adams Morgan.

Julia's Empanadas. Empanadas here are served in paper bags to go, so you can eat standing up. ✉ 2452 18th St. NW, Adams Morgan ☎ 202/328–6232 ⊕ www.juliasempanadas.com Ⓜ Columbia Heights.

Tryst Coffeehouse-Bar-Lounge. Stop in for breakfast, lunch, brunch, or dessert, or sip something stronger after hours—as late as 1 am on weekends. There's live jazz Monday to Thursday evenings. ✉ 2459 18th St. NW, Adams Morgan ☎ 202/232–5500 ⊕ www.trystdc.com Ⓜ Columbia Heights.

U STREET CORRIDOR

Sightseeing
★★
Dining
★★★★
Lodging
★
Shopping
★★★★
Nightlife
★★★★★

Home-style Ethiopian food, offbeat boutiques, and live music are fueling the revival of the U Street area. Just a few years back, this neighborhood was surviving on memories of its heyday as a center of black culture and jazz music in the first half of the 20th century.

The neighborhood was especially vibrant from the 1920s to the 1950s, when it was home to jazz genius Duke Ellington, social activist Mary McLeod Bethune, and poets Langston Hughes and Georgia Douglas Johnson. The area's nightclubs hosted Louis Armstrong, Cab Calloway, and Sarah Vaughn. In the 1950s Supreme Court Justice Thurgood Marshall, then still a lawyer, organized the landmark *Brown v. Board of Education* case at the 12th Street YMCA. Now this diverse neighborhood has experienced a lively resurgence of culture, nightlife, and renovation of many historic buildings—and the crowds are back.

You'll need a couple of hours to explore U Street fully, especially if you want to stop at the African American Civil War Museum. For maps, shopping, and dining information, stop in the Greater U Street Neighborhood and Visitor Center next to Ben's Chili Bowl, and don't stray too far off the main drag, especially at night.

Getting Oriented

U Street Corridor

KEY
Bike Share

W Street NW

V Street NW

Busboys and Poets

Ben's Chili Bowl

U Street Music Hall

9:30 Club

Lincoln Theatre

U Street NW

U Street/Cardozo

African-American Civil War Museum

U Street/Cardozo

African-American Civil War Memorial

15th Street NW

14th Street NW

16th Street NW

New Hampshire Avenue NW

Vermont Avenue NW

12th Street

11th Street NW

T Street NW

Swann Street NW

CARDOZO

Westminster St. NW

S Street NW

Black Cat

13th Street NW

10th Street NW

TO HOWARD → UNIVERSITY

R Street NW

Corcoran Street NW

Q Street NW

Church Street NW

Vermont Avenue NW

11th Street NW

Rhode Island Avenue NW

LOGAN CIRCLE

P Street NW

P Street NW

LOGAN CIRCLE/SHAW

O Street NW

Rhode Island Avenue NW

14th Street NW

13th Street NW

O Street NW

16th Street NW

SCOTT CIRCLE

N Street NW

Embassy of Tunisia

Massachusetts Avenue NW

Vermont Avenue NW

THOMAS CIRCLE

12th Street NW

11th Street NW

10th Street NW

16th Street NW

15th Street NW

M Street NW

Massachusetts Ave.

0   500 ft

0   150 M

GREET EXPERIENCES ON U STREET CORRIDOR

African American Civil War Memorial and Museum: Learn about the lives of slaves and freedmen, and discover whether your ancestors fought in black regiments during the Civil War.

Ben's Chili Bowl: This D.C. institution has perfected its recipe over the last 50 years and satisfies meat eaters and vegetarians alike.

Boutiques: Whether you're after funky footwear or flashy housewares, hit the shops on U and 14th Streets for trendy finds.

Ethiopian food: Nothing brings you closer to your meal than eating with your hands. Use the spongy injera bread to scoop up delectable dishes from East Africa.

Live music: Music greats like Duke Ellington made this neighborhood famous back in the 1920s. Dance the night away at the U Street Music Hall or rock out to today's music at the 9:30 Club or Black Cat.

GETTING HERE

The Green Line Metro stops at 13th and U, in the middle of the main business district. To get to the African American Civil War Memorial, get out at the 10th Street exit. Limited parking can be found on the residential streets north and south of U Street, but as the area gets more popular, spots are getting harder to find on weekend nights.

The area is within walking distance from Dupont Circle and Adams Morgan, but at night you are better off on the bus or in a cab, especially if you are alone. Buses 90 and 92 travel from Woodley Park through Adams Morgan to 14th and U, while Buses 52, 53, and 54 travel north from several downtown Metro stops up 14th Street (check ⊕ *www.wmata. com* for information).

PLANNING YOUR TIME

You'll need half a day at most to see U Street's attractions and visit its boutiques. You can also fill an evening with dinner on U Street, a show at the **9:30 Club, U Street Music Hall,** or **Lincoln Theatre,** and drinks afterward. If you're not driving, allow plenty of time for public transportation.

QUICK BITES

Ben's Chili Bowl. This U Street institution still serves its original chili half-smoke, plus burgers, sandwiches, and breakfast platters. ⊠ *1213 U St. NW, U Street* ☎ *202/667–0909* ⊕ *www. benschilibowl.com* Ⓜ *U St.*

Busboys and Poets. For a more intellectual snack, step into this bookstore–cum–restaurant–cum performance space that serves up omelets, sandwiches, pizzas, and poems. Named in honor of Langston Hughes, this gathering place holds readings and musical performances. ⊠ *2021 14th St. NW, U Street* ☎ *202/387–7638* ⊕ *www.busboysandpoets.com* Ⓜ *U St.*

SAFETY

The blocks between 10th and 16th Streets are well lit and busy, but the area gets grittier to the north and east. Use your street sense, especially at night, when it's a good idea to take a cab.

UPPER NORTHWEST

Sightseeing
★★★★
Dining
★★
Lodging
★★
Shopping
★★★★
Nightlife
★

The upper northwest corner of D.C. is predominantly residential and in many places practically suburban. However, there are several good reasons to visit the leafy streets, including the National Zoo and National Cathedral. If the weather is fine, spend an afternoon strolling through Hillwood Gardens or tromping through Rock Creek Park's many acres. You'll have to travel some distance to see multiple attractions in one day, but many sights are accessible on foot from local Metro stops.

TOP ATTRACTIONS

Hillwood Estate, Museum and Gardens. Long before the age of Paris Hilton, cereal heiress Marjorie Merriweather Post was the most celebrated socialite of the 20th century, famous for her fabulous wealth and beauty, as well as her passion for collecting art and creating some of the world's most lavish homes. Of these, the 25-acre Hillwood Estate, which Merriweather Post bought in 1955, is the only one now open to the public. The 36-room Georgian mansion, where she regularly hosted presidents, diplomats, and royalty, is sumptuously appointed, with a formal Louis XVI drawing room, private movie theater and ballroom, and magnificent libraries filled with portraits of the glamorous hostess and her family and acquaintances, as well as works from her rich art collection. She was especially fascinated with Russian art, and her collection of Russian icons, tapestries, gold and silver work, and Fabergé eggs is considered to be the largest and most significant outside Russia. She devoted equal attention to her gardens; you can wander through 13 acres of them. You should allow two to three hours to take in the estate, gardens, and museum shop. ✉ *4155 Linnean Ave. NW, Upper Northwest* ☎ *202/686–5807, 202/686–8500* ⊕ *www.hillwoodmuseum.org* ✉ *$18, ($15 weekdays if purchased online)* ⊘ *Closed Mon.* Ⓜ *Van Ness/UDC.*

FAMILY
Fodor's Choice
★

Smithsonian National Zoological Park. Carved out of wooded hills in Rock Creek Park, The National Zoo houses 1,800 animals, representing 300 species, in innovative compounds showing animals in their native settings. Step inside the Great Flight Cage to observe the flight of many species of birds; this walk-in aviary is open from May to October. Between 11 am and 2 pm on mild days you can catch the orangutans traveling on the "O Line," a series of cables and towers near the Great Ape House that allows the primates to swing hand over hand about 35 feet over your head.

On the giant panda front, Tian Tian and Mei Xiang have been the zoo's most famous residents since 2000. In 2005 the pandas had their first cub, Tai Shan, who was moved to China in 2010. Then Bao Bao, born in the late summer of 2013, moved to China in the winter of 2017. The panda's third cub, Bei Bei, born in late summer of 2015, is currently delighting visitors with his bamboo eating and lounging.

Part of the Smithsonian Institution, the National Zoo was designed by landscape architect Frederick Law Olmsted, who also designed the U.S. Capitol grounds and New York's Central Park. ■ TIP→ **Visit early in the morning or late afternoon for your best chance of seeing active animals. Many sleep at midday.** Or opt for the rare but enchanting experience of seeing the zoo at night during the annual ZooLights event, starting just after Thanksgiving and lasting until January 1. ✉ *3001 Connecticut Ave. NW, Upper Northwest* ☎ *202/673–4800, 202/673–4717* ⊕ *nationalzoo.si.edu* ▭ *Free* Ⓜ *Cleveland Park or Woodley Park/Zoo.*

Fodor's Choice
★

Washington National Cathedral. Construction of the sixth-largest cathedral in the world began in 1907, and what is officially known as the Cathedral Church of St. Peter and St. Paul was finished and consecrated in 1990. Like its 14th-century Gothic counterparts, the stunning National Cathedral has a nave, flying buttresses, transepts, and vaults that were built stone by stone. The cathedral is Episcopalian, but it's the site of frequent ecumenical and interfaith services. State funerals for presidents Eisenhower, Reagan, and Ford were held here, and the tomb of Woodrow Wilson, the only president buried in Washington, is on the nave's south side. ■ TIP→ **The expansive view of the city from the Pilgrim Observation Gallery is exceptional.** You can even enjoy a traditional English afternoon tea in the gallery most Tuesdays and Wednesdays following a one-hour cathedral tour.

The compact, English-style **Bishop's Garden** provides a counterpoint to the cathedral towers with boxwoods, ivy, tea roses, yew trees, and an assortment of arches, bas-reliefs, and stonework from European ruins.

The cathedral's Flower Mart is held annually on the first Friday and Saturday in May and is one of Washington's premiere festivals. Each year, one Washington embassy is honored and festivalgoers are treated to the culture, traditions, food, and art of the selected country, though lobster rolls are traditionally on offer on the Friday evening of the festival. This is one of only two times during the year that you can climb the 333 steps to the cathedral's tower.

Getting Oriented

Upper Northwest

TO PLANETARIUM

FRIENDSHIP HEIGHTS
Garrison St. NW
42nd St. NW
Bell Rd. NW
Wisconsin Ave. NW
River Rd. NW
43rd Pl. NW
4th St. NW
45th St. NW
44th St. NW
Fessenden St. NW
39th St. NW
38th St. NW
Fort Reno Park
Everett St. NW
Ellicott St. NW
Reno Reservoir
Davenport St. NW
Davenport St. NW
Linnean Ave. NW
Chesapeake St. NW
Connecticut Ave. NW
30th St.
Brandywine St. NW

Murdock Mill Rd. NW
Nebraska Ave. NW
TENLEYTOWN
Appleton St. NW
Albemarle St. NW
Albemarle St. NW
TENLEYTOWN-AU
Alton Pl. NW
Yuma St. NW
Windom Pl. NW
Tenley Circle
Reno Rd. NW
36th St.
Audubon Ter. NW
Soapstone Valley Park
Alton Pl. NW
Yuma St. NW
Warren St. NW
43rd St. NW
University of the District of Columbia
35th St. NW
Howard University Law School
Van Ness St. NW
38th St. NW
37th St. NW
Van Ness St. NW
Hillwood Estat Museum a Garde
VANESS-UDC
Upton St. NW
Tilden St. NW
Wisconsin Ave. NW

Tindall St.
Nebraska Ave. NW
Melvin Hazen Park
Rodman St. NW
Ward Circle
CLEVELAND PARK
Porter St.
American University
Porter St. NW
CLEVELAND PARK
Ordway St. NW
Glover-Archbold Park
Idaho Ave. NW
38th St. NW
President Lincoln's Cottage
Newark St. NW
Newark St. NW
Macomb St. NW
Macomb St. NW
34th St.
Smithsonian Nationa Zoological Par
Lowell St. NW
Lowell St. NW
WOODLEY PARK
Klingle St. NW
Woodley Rd.
TO WOODLEY PARK-ZOO METRO AND WARDMAN TOWER
Cathedral Ave. NW
Massachusetts Ave. NW
Washington National Cathedral
Connecticut
33rd St.
32nd St.
Cathedral Ave. NW
Hawthorne St. NW
39th St. NW
38th St. NW
Garfield St. NW
34th St.
35th Pl. NW
29th St. NW
28th St. NW
27th St. NW
4th St. NW
Fulton St. NW
36th Pl. NW
36th St. NW
Cleveland Ave. NW
Woodland Dr.
Foxhall Rd.
Glover-Archbold Park
Davis Pl.
MN St.
45th St. NW
Calvert St. NW
40th Pl. NW
40th St. NW
39th St. NW
39th Pl. NW
Circle
Observatory
U.S. Naval Observatory
Kahil Gibran Memorial Garden
Massachusetts Ave. NW
Rock Cree
Kreeger Museum
FOXHALL
37th St. NW
Wisconsin Ave. NW

0 ——— 400 yards
0 ——— 400 meters

Dumbarton Oaks Park

KEY
🚲 Bike Share

GREAT EXPERIENCES IN UPPER NORTHWEST

House museums: The Hillwood Estate, Museum and Gardens showcase cereal heiress Marjorie Merriweather Post's collection of Imperial Russian art and Fabergé eggs, and 25 gorgeous acres of formal French and Japanese gardens. Chagalls, Picassos, and Monets inside contrast with the architecture at the modernist Kreeger Museum.

National Zoo: Visit the giant pandas, elephants, lions, and other members of the animal kingdom while you enjoy a stroll outdoors.

Shopping in Friendship Heights: The city's most glamorous shopping lines Wisconsin Avenue at the Maryland border. Want to actually buy something? Plenty of stores cater to shoppers on a budget, too.

U.S. Naval Observatory: View the heavens through one of the world's most powerful telescopes (on Monday evening with a reservation).

Washington National Cathedral: Look for the Darth Vader gargoyle on the soaring towers of this landmark, then relax among the rosebushes in the Bishop's Garden. Concerts are held here, too.

GETTING HERE

Connecticut Avenue attractions, such as the zoo, are accessible from the Red Line Metro stops between Woodley Park/Zoo and Van Ness. The Friendship Heights bus travels north from Georgetown along Wisconsin Avenue and takes you to the National Cathedral.

Parking can be tricky along Massachusetts Avenue. It is more practical for good walkers to hoof it up the street or take Bus N2, N3, N4, or N6 between Dupont Circle and Friendship Heights. For more-outlying sights, driving or cabbing it may be the best way to visit.

PLANNING YOUR TIME

The amount of time you spend at the zoo is up to you; animal enthusiasts could easily spend a full day here. You may want to plan your trip around daily programs, such as the elephant-training session or the small-mammal feeding. For the optimal experience, see the animals when they are most active—in the early morning and late afternoon.

For other itineraries, be sure to leave room in your schedule for travel between sights and, if you have a car, for parking. To maximize your time, call ahead to inquire whether on-site parking is available and when the next tour will begin.

QUICK BITES

If you've got the time, skip lunch at the zoo's eateries and head north or south on Connecticut to find a wealth of dining options. The streets immediately surrounding the Woodley Park and Cleveland Park Metro stations are chockablock with restaurants, bakeries, and ice-cream stores.

In 2011, the cathedral sustained earthquake damage (the same quake caused extensive damage to the Washington Monument). Using limestone from the quarry that supplied material for the building of the cathedral, stone carvers continue to restore damaged carvings and repairs are still being made to the exteriors. Restoration work is expected to continue for several years, but the cathedral remains open during the process. ⊠ *Wisconsin and Massachusetts Aves. NW, Upper Northwest* ☎ *202/537–6200, 202/537–6207 tour information* ⊕ *www.nationalcathedral.org* ✉ *$12; tours $22–$30* Ⓜ *Cleveland Park or Tenleytown-AU, then take any 30 series bus.*

WORTH NOTING

Kreeger Museum. The cool white domes and elegant lines of this post-modern landmark stand in stark contrast to the traditional feel of the rest of the Foxhall Road neighborhood. Designed in 1963 by iconic architect Philip Johnson, the building was once the home of GEICO insurance executive David Lloyd Kreeger and his wife, Carmen. Music is a central theme of the art and the space: the Kreegers wanted a showpiece residence that would also function as a gallery and recital hall. The art collection includes works by Renoir, Degas, Cézanne, and Munch, African artifacts, and outstanding examples of Asian art. Especially stunning are the outdoor sculptures, including works by Henry Moore and Leonardo Nierman, among others, and six large-scale John L. Dreyfuss pieces that surround the museum's reflecting pool. The domed rooms also have wonderful acoustics, and serve as an excellent performance venue for the classical concerts that are regularly performed here. The museum is not reachable by Metro; you need to take a car or taxi to get here. ⊠ *2401 Foxhall Rd. NW, Upper North-west* ☎ *202/338–3552* ⊕ *www.kreegermuseum.org* ✉ *$10, Sculpture Garden free* ⊙ *Closed Sun. and Mon.*

President Lincoln's Cottage. In June 1862 President Lincoln moved from the White House to this Gothic Revival cottage on the grounds of the Soldiers' Home to escape the oppressive heat of Washington and to grieve for the loss of his son Willie. Lincoln and his wife, Mary, lived in the cottage until November of that year, and because they found it to be a welcome respite from wartime tensions, they returned again during the summers of 1863 and 1864. Lincoln ultimately spent a quarter of his presidency at this quiet retreat; he was here just one day before he was assassinated. Considered the most significant historic site of President Lincoln's presidency outside the White House, it was here that the president developed the Emancipation Proclamation.

Visitors may picnic on the cottage grounds, which have been landscaped to look as they did when Lincoln lived here. ■ TIP➔ **As you go up the hill toward the Cottage, there's a panoramic view of the city, including the Capitol dome. The 251-acre Soldier's Home sits atop the third-tallest point in D.C.** ⊠ *Armed Forces Retirement Home, 140 Rock Creek Church Rd. and Upshur St. NW, Columbia Heights* ☎ *202/829–0436* ⊕ *www.lincolncottage.org* ✉ *$15* Ⓜ *Georgia Ave./Petworth.*

2

ARLINGTON AND NORTHERN VIRGINIA

Discover American treasures, historical attractions, diverse dining, first-class shopping, and eclectic arts and entertainment in the northern Virginia city of Arlington. Just across the Potomac River from D.C. (complete with easy Metro access), this area offers a great blend of history and urban excitement.

Spend a day or two visiting Arlington National Cemetery, the Marine Corps War Memorial, the Air Force Memorial, and the National 9/11 Pentagon Memorial. If you're traveling with kids or just want to ooh and aah over very cool planes and rockets, don't miss the Udvar-Hazy Center in Chantilly near Dulles International Airport. This companion facility to the National Air and Space Museum on the National Mall displays thousands of aviation and space artifacts in huge hangars; you can even watch restoration projects in progress.

TOP ATTRACTIONS

Fodor'sChoice **Arlington National Cemetery.** *For more information, see the highlighted*
★ *feature in this chapter.* ✉ *West end of Memorial Bridge* ☎ *877/907–8585* ⊕ *www.arlingtoncemetery.mil* 🎫 *Free; parking $1.75 per hr for 1st 3 hrs, $2.50/hr thereafter; Arlington National Cemetery Tours $13.50.*

Pentagon. The headquarters of the United States Department of Defense is the largest low-rise office building in the world. Approximately 24,000 military and civilian workers arrive daily. Astonishingly, the mammoth structure, completed in 1943, took less than two years to construct.

Following the September 11, 2001, crash of hijacked American Airlines Flight 77 into the northwest side of the building, the damaged area was removed in just over a month and repaired in a year. In this same area is the America's Heroes Memorial and Chapel, which pays tribute to the civilians and military members killed in the attack. South of the building is the 2-acre outdoor Pentagon Memorial, with its 184 benches

Getting Oriented

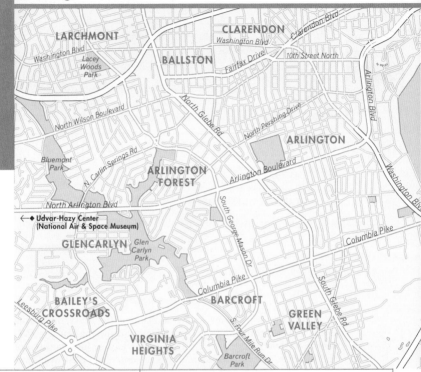

GETTING HERE	TOP EXPERIENCES
You can reach Arlington Cemetery and the U.S. Air Force and Marine Corps Memorials by Metro (Arlington Cemetery on the Blue Line, Pentagon City on the Blue or Yellow lines, Rosslyn on the Orange, Blue, or Silver lines) or Metrobus, although there will be some walking involved. You can also get to these sites with a car or via Big Bus Tours or Old Town Trolley Tours. Your best bet is to use Metro to visit the Pentagon and 9/11 Memorial (Pentagon stop via Blue or Yellow line). You'll need a car to visit the Udvar-Hazy Center.	**Arlington National Cemetery:** The most visited cemetery in the country is the final resting place for more than 400,000 Americans, from unknown soldiers to John F. Kennedy and his wife, Jacqueline Kennedy Onassis. **Udvar-Hazy Center (National Air and Space Museum):** See the Boeing B-29 *Enola Gay*, Bücker Bü-133C Jungmeister, Lockheed SR-71 Blackbird, space shuttle *Discovery*, and hundreds of other aviation and space artifacts in the immense hangars that make up this museum near Dulles International Airport. **United States Air Force Memorial:** Just south of Arlington Cemetery, this memorial honors members of the Air Force who've given their lives in service to the country. **United States Marine Corps War Memorial:** Commonly called the *Iwo Jima Memorial*, it's located just north of Arlington cemetery and is a powerful tribute to all of the marines who have lost their lives in battle since 1775.

Arlington and
Northern Virginia

QUICK BITES

Epic Smokehouse. For barbe-cue lovers, the smoked brisket, ribs, and pulled pork here are standouts. There also are sandwiches, salads, steaks, and seafood available. ⊠ *1330 S. Fern St., Arlington* ☏ *571/319–4001* ⊕ *www.epicsmokehouse. com* Ⓜ *Pentagon City.*

Extreme Pizza. Pizzas with wonderfully creative toppings are served here, alongside tasty salads, sandwiches, calzones, and wings. ⊠ *1419 S. Fern St., Arlington* ☏ *703/271–1020* ⊕ *extremepizza.hungerrush. com* Ⓜ *Pentagon City.*

Shake Shack. This NYC phenomenon has grown into a nationwide chain of burger shops including this location in the Fashion Centre at Pentagon City. Get the burger with special sauce, and one of the frozen custard shakes to wash it down. ⊠ *1100 S. Hayes St., Arlington* ☏ *703/454–0552* ⊕ *www.shake-shack.com* Ⓜ *Pentagon City.*

PLANNING YOUR TIME

You can easily combine a visit to Arlington Cemetery with visits to the DEA Museum, the Pentagon and 9/11 Memorial, and U.S. Air Force and Marine Corps memorials; it will be a full day and require advance planning for the Pentagon tour. A visit to the Udvar-Hazy Center (National Air and Space Museum) will require a good part of a day due to its location; a car is needed and you'll probably encounter some traffic. If you're flying out of nearby Dulles Airport, you can combine a morning visit to the center with a late afternoon or evening departure.

commemorating the lives lost on 9/11. Tours of the Pentagon are free; reserve online through the Pentagon Tour Office at least two weeks, but no more than three months, in advance. ⊠ *I–395 at Columbia Pike and Rte. 27, Arlington* ☎ *703/697–1776* ⊕ *pentagontours.osd.mil* ✉ *Free* ⊗ *No tours weekends* Ⓜ *Pentagon.*

Pentagon Memorial. Washington's own "9/11 memorial" honors the 184 people who perished when the hijacked American Airlines Flight 77 crashed into the northwest side of the Pentagon. Stainless-steel-and-granite benches engraved with the victims' names are arranged in order by date of birth and where they were when they died. The names of the victims who were inside the Pentagon are arranged so that visitors reading their names face the Pentagon, and names of the victims on the plane are arranged so that visitors reading their names face skyward. At each bench is a lighted pool of flowing water. Designed by Julie Beckman and Keith Kaseman, the memorial opened to the public on September 11, 2008, the seventh anniversary of the attacks. Volunteer docents periodically stand near the entrance and answer questions. There is no public parking, with the exception of five stalls for handicap-permitted vehicles. ⊠ *1 Rotary Rd., Pentagon, Arlington* ☎ *301/740–3388* ⊕ *www.pentagonmemorial.org* ✉ *Free* Ⓜ *Pentagon.*

FAMILY **Udvar-Hazy Center (National Air and Space Museum).** For giant jets and spaceships, visit the National Air and Space Museum's Steven F. Udvar-Hazy Center, near Washington Dulles International Airport in northern Virginia. Unlike the museum on the Mall, which is divided into smaller galleries with dense history and science exhibits, the Udvar-Hazy Center displays large aircraft and spacecraft, hung as though in flight throughout two vast, multilevel hangars. This focus makes the center more appealing for families with kids who may not be old enough to take in detailed historical narratives, but will certainly ooh and aah over the marvelous planes. It is also much less crowded than the Mall museum, with room to move.

One giant three-level hangar is devoted to historic aircraft, such as the Lockheed SR-71 Blackbird, the fastest jet in the world; the sleek, supersonic Concorde; and the *Enola Gay,* which in 1945 dropped the first atomic bomb to be used in war on Hiroshima, Japan. A second hangar is largely taken up by space shuttle *Discovery,* the first of the flown orbiters to be on display anywhere, as well as satellites, Mars rovers, missiles, and even a human-size android. It also features a fascinating display of astronaut paraphernalia, including space food (chicken and peas for American astronauts, borscht for Russians) and special space underwear required for spacewalks.

In a separate wing, visitors can take an elevator to the observation tower (for free)—you can watch airplanes take off and land at nearby Dulles Airport. There is also an eight-story IMAX theater in this wing.

If you want to combine a morning visit with an afternoon departure from Dulles, Fairfax Connector Bus 983 runs daily between the museum and airport for $1.75 (SmarTrip card or cash); the trip takes 15 minutes. ⊠ *14390 Air and Space Museum Pkwy., Chantilly* ☎ *703/572–4118, 866/868–7774 IMAX information* ⊕ *www.airandspace.si.edu* ✉ *Free; IMAX film $9; IMAX feature film $15; flight simulators $8–$10.*

Continued on page 124

ARLINGTON, THE NATION'S CEMETERY

The most famous, most visited cemetery in the country is the final resting place for close to 400,000 Americans, from unknown soldiers to John F. Kennedy. With its tombs, monuments, and "sea of stones," Arlington is a place of ritual and remembrance, where even the most cynical observer of Washington politics may find a lump in his throat or a tear in his eye.

EXPERIENCING THE SEA OF STONES

In 1864, a 200-acre plot directly across the Potomac from Washington, part of the former plantation home of Robert E. Lee, was designated America's national cemetery. Today, the cemetery covers 624 acres.

Today, Arlington's major monuments and memorials are impressive, but the most striking experience is simply looking out over the thousands upon thousands of headstones aligned across the cemetery's hills.

Most of those buried here served in the military—from reinterred Revolutionary War soldiers to troops killed in Iraq and Afghanistan. As you walk through the cemetery, you're likely to hear a trumpet playing taps or the report of a gun salute. An average of 27 funerals a day are held here, Monday through Friday. There currently are nearly 400,000 graves in Arlington; it's projected that the cemetery will be filled by 2060.

FINDING A GRAVE

At the Welcome Center, staff members and computers can help you find the location of a specific grave. You need to provide the deceased's full name and, if possible, the branch of service and year of death.

WHO GETS BURIED WHERE

With few exceptions, interment at Arlington is limited to active-duty members of the armed forces, veterans, and their spouses and minor children. In Arlington's early years as a cemetery, burial location was determined by rank (as well as, initially, by race), with separate sections for enlisted soldiers and officers. Beginning in 1947, this distinction was abandoned. Grave sites are assigned on the day before burial; when possible, requests are honored to be buried near the graves of family members.

ABOUT THE HEADSTONES

Following the Civil War, Arlington's first graves were marked by simple whitewashed boards. When these decayed, they were replaced by cast-iron markers covered with zinc to prevent rusting. Only one iron marker remains, for the grave of Captain Daniel Keys (Section 13, Lot 13615, Grid G-29/30).

In 1873, Congress voted in the use of marble headstones, which continues to

be the practice today. The government provides the standard-issue stones free of charge. Next of kin may supply their own headstones, though these can only be used if space is available in one of the sections where individualized stones already exist.

THE SAME, BUT DIFFERENT

Regulation headstones can be engraved with one of 54 symbols indicating religious affiliation. In section 60, the headstones of soldiers killed in Afghanistan and Iraq reflect the multicultural makeup of 21st-century America. Along with a variety of crosses and the Star of David, you see the nine-pointed star of the Baha'i; a tepee and three feathers representing the Native American faiths; the Muslim crescent and star; and other signs of faith. (Or lack of it. Atheism is represented by a stylized atom.)

Opposite: Sea of Stones; Upper left: Burial ceremony; Bottom left: A soldier placing flags for Memorial Day. Right: Coast Guard headstone.

PLANNING YOUR VISIT TO ARLINGTON

ARLINGTON BASICS

Getting Here: You can reach Arlington on the Metro, by foot over Arlington Memorial Bridge (southwest of the Lincoln Memorial), or by car—there's a large parking lot by the Visitors Center on Memorial Drive. Also, the Big Bus Tours (☎ 877/332–8689 ⊕ www.bigbustours.com) and Old Town Trolley (☎ 202/832–9800 ⊕ www.oldtowntrolley.com) both have Arlington National Cemetery stops in their loops.

✉ Cemetery free, parking $1.75 per hr for the first three hours, $2.50 per hr thereafter.

☎ 877/907–8585 for general information and to locate a grave.

⊕ www.arlingtoncemetery.mil

✗ No food or drink is allowed at the cemetery. There are water fountains in the Welcome Center, and from fall through spring a water fountain operates near the amphitheater at the Tomb of the Unknowns. You can also purchase bottled water at the Women's Memorial.

TOURING OPTIONS

Your first stop at the cemetery should be the Welcome Center, where you can pick up a free brochure with a detailed map. Once there you have a choice: tour by bus or walk.

Arlington by Bus. Arlington National Cemetery Tours leave every 15 to 25 minutes from just outside the Welcome Center April through September, daily 8:30–6, and October through March, daily 8:30–4. The 45 to 60-minute tour includes stops at the Kennedy grave sites, The Tomb of the Unknown Soldier, and Arlington House. Your bus driver will provide basic facts about the cemetery.

Arlington on Foot. Walking the cemetery requires some stamina, but it allows you to take in the thousands of graves at your own pace. On the facing page is a walking tour that includes the major points of interest. Audio tours are available in the Welcome Center.

Above: 3rd Infantry Honor Guard

2

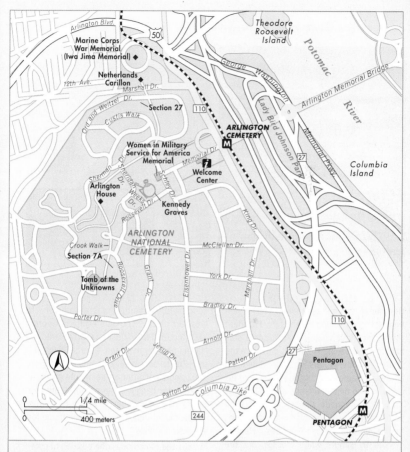

A WALKING TOUR

■ Head west from the Welcome Center on Roosevelt Drive and turn right on Weeks Drive to reach the **Kennedy graves**; just to the west is **Arlington House**. (¼ mile)

■ Take Crook Walk south, following the signs, to the **Tomb of the Unknowns**; a few steps from the tomb is **Section 7A**, where many distinguished veterans are buried. (³⁄₁₀ mile)

■ To visit the graves of soldiers killed in Afghanistan and Iraq, take Roosevelt Drive past Section 7 and turn right on McClellan Drive, turn right when you get to Eisenhower Drive, then go left onto York Drive. The graves will be on your right. (⁶⁄₁₀ mile)

■ Walk north along Eisenhower Drive, which becomes Schley Drive; turn right onto Custis Walk, which brings you to **Section 27**, where 3,800 former slaves are buried. (¾ mile)

■ Leave the cemetery through the Ord and Weitzel Gate, cross Marshall Drive carefully, and walk to the 50-bell **Netherlands Carillon**, where there's a good vista of Washington. To the north is the **United States Marine Corps War Memorial**, better known as the **Iwo Jima Memorial**. (¼ mile)

ARLINGTON'S MAIN ATTRACTIONS

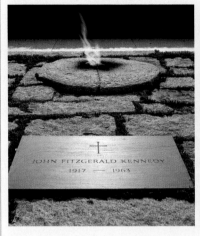

The Kennedy Graves

Once while taking in the view of Washington from Arlington National Cemetery, President John F. Kennedy commented, "I could stay here forever." Seeing Kennedy's grave is a top priority for most visitors. He's buried beneath an eternal flame, next to graves of two of his children who died in infancy, and of his wife, Jacqueline Kennedy Onassis. Across from them is a low wall engraved with quotations from Kennedy's inaugural address. Nearby, marked by simple white crosses, are the graves of Robert F. Kennedy and Ted Kennedy.

The gas-fueled flame at the head of John F. Kennedy's grave was lit by Jacqueline Kennedy during his funeral. A continuously flashing electric spark reignites the gas if the flame is extinguished by rain, wind, or any other cause.

Many visitors ask where Kennedy's son John F. Kennedy Jr. is buried. His ashes were scattered in the Atlantic Ocean, near the location where his plane went down in 1999.

Arlington House

Long before Arlington was a cemetery, it was part of the 1,100-acre estate of George Washington Parke Custis, a grandchild of Martha and (by marriage) George Washington. Custis built Arlington House between 1802 and 1818. After his death, the property went to his daughter, Mary Anna Randolph Custis, who wed Robert E. Lee in 1831. The couple made Arlington House their home for the next 30 years.

In 1861 Lee turned down the position of commander of the Union forces and left Arlington House, never to return. Union troops turned the house into an Army headquarters, and 200 acres were set aside as a national cemetery. By the end of the Civil War headstones dotted the estate's hills.

The house looks much as it did in the 19th century and a quick tour takes you past objects once owned by the Custises, the Lees, and the Washingtons. The views from Arlington House remain spectacular.

Robert E. Lee

The Tomb of the Unknown Soldier

The first burial at the Tomb of the Unknowns, one of the cemetery's most imposing monuments, took place on November 11, 1921. In what was part of a world-wide trend to honor the dead after the unparalleled devastation of World War I, an unidentified soldier was interred under the large white-marble sarcophagus. Unknown servicemen killed in World War II and Korea joined him in 1958.

The Memorial Amphitheater west of the tomb is used for ceremonies on Veterans Day, Memorial Day, and Easter. Decorations awarded to the unknowns are displayed in an indoor trophy room.

One of the most striking activities at Arlington is the precision and pageantry of the changing of the guard at the Tomb of the Unknowns. From April through September, soldiers from the Army's U.S. Third Infantry (known as the Old Guard) change guard every half hour during the day. For the rest of the year, and at night all year long, the guard changes every hour.

The Iwo Jima Memorial

Ask the tour bus driver at Arlington where the Iwo Jima is, and you might get back the quip "very far away." The memorial commonly called the Iwo Jima is officially named the United States Marine Corps War Memorial, and it's actually located just north of the cemetery. Its bronze sculpture is based on one of the most famous photos in American military history, Joe Rosenthal's February 23, 1945, shot of five marines and a navy corpsman raising a flag atop Mt. Suribachi on the Japanese island of Iwo Jima. By executive order, a real flag flies 24 hours a day from the 78-foot-high memorial.

On Tuesday evening at 7 PM from early June to mid-August there's a Marine Corps sunset parade on the grounds of the Iwo Jima Memorial. On parade nights a free shuttle bus runs from the Arlington Cemetery visitors' parking lot.

The Old Guard are not making a fashion statement in their sunglasses—they're protecting their eyes from the sun's glare off the white marble of the tomb.

WORTH NOTING

United States Air Force Memorial. On a beautiful hillside in Arlington, the Air Force Memorial honors the service and sacrifice of America's airmen. Three stainless-steel, asymmetrical spires slice through the skyline up to 270 feet, representing flight, the precision of the "bomb burst" maneuver performed by the Air Force Thunderbirds, and the three core values of the Air Force: Integrity first, Service before self, and Excellence in all we do. The spires are adjacent to the southern portion of Arlington National Cemetery and visible from the Tidal Basin and I–395 near Washington. At the base of the spires is an 8-foot statue of the honor guard, a glass wall engraved with the missing man formation, and granite walls inscribed with Air Force values and accomplishments. On Friday evenings throughout the summer, the United States Air Force Band performs concerts on the memorial lawn. ⊠ *1 Air Force Memorial Dr., off Columbia Pike, Arlington* ☎ *703/979–0674* ⊕ *www.airforcememorial.org* ✉ *Free* Ⓜ *Pentagon City or Pentagon.*

WHERE TO EAT

Updated by
Zach Everson

Washington has long benefited from a constant infusion of different cultures, making it a stellar culinary host for visitors and transplants from around the world. But recent years have made the fifth or sixth banana of American haute cuisine into a foodie town in its own right. You can find almost any cuisine here, from Salvadoran to Ethiopian, despite the lack of true ethnic neighborhoods in the city. You can now also sample cooking from some of the country's hottest new chefs, find already established celebrity chefs who have just made their D.C. debuts, and sip craft cocktails on par with some of the world's best.

Although most neighborhoods lack a unified culinary flavor, make no mistake: D.C. is a city of distinctive areas, each with its own style. Chinatown, for example, is known for chic small plates of various origins. You'll find Japanese noodle shops next to Mexican taquerias and Indian bistros. These spots wax and wane on the popularity scale with each passing season; it's worth taking a stroll down the street to see what's new. Downtown, you'll find many of the city's blue-chip law firms and deluxe, expense-account restaurants, as well as stylish lounges, brewpubs, and upscale eateries that have sprung up to serve the crowds that attend games at the Verizon Center.

Wherever you venture forth in the city, there are a few trends worth noting: artisanal cocktails, charcuterie-and-cheese plates, and back-to-basics new American cuisine are in vogue. You'll find tapas-style portions pervasive, whether you're at a Greek, Asian, or American restaurant. High-end restaurants in town also have begun to add bar menus with smaller plates that are much less expensive than their entrées, but created with the same finesse.

Though Italian, French, and fusion spots continue to open at a ferocious pace, Washingtonians are always hungry to try something new, whether it's Chinese smoked lobster, fiery Indian curry, or crunchy and addictive Vietnamese spring rolls.

PLANNING

RESERVATIONS

Plan ahead if you're determined to snag a sought-after reservation. Some renowned restaurants are booked weeks in advance and others do not accept advance requests. But you can get lucky at the last minute if you're flexible—and friendly. Most restaurants keep a few tables open for walk-ins and VIPs, and many spots offer their full menus at the bar, where it's easier to nab a seat. Show up for dinner early (5:30 pm) or late (after 10 pm) and politely inquire about any last-minute vacancies or cancellations. If you're calling a few days ahead of time, ask if you can be put on a waiting list. Occasionally, an eatery may ask you to call the day before your scheduled meal to reconfirm: don't forget, or you could lose out.

HOURS

Washington has less of an around-the-clock mentality than other big cities, with many big-name restaurants shutting down between lunch and dinner and closing their kitchens by 11 pm. Weekend evenings spent Downtown can also be a hassle for those seeking quick bites, because many popular chain eateries cater to office workers and shut down on Friday at 6 pm. For a midnight supper, the best bets are Dupont Circle and the U Street Corridor, while families looking for late lunches should head north from the Mall to find kitchens that stay open between mealtimes.

WHAT TO WEAR

As unfair as it seems, the way you look can influence how you're treated—and where you're seated. Generally speaking, jeans and a button-down shirt will suffice at most table-service restaurants in the $–$$ range. Some pricier restaurants require jackets, and some insist on ties. In reviews, we mention dress only where men are required to wear a jacket or a jacket and tie. But even when there's no formal dress code, we recommend wearing jackets and ties in $$$ and $$$$ restaurants. If you have doubts, call the restaurant and ask.

PRICES

If you're watching your budget, be sure to ask the price of daily specials recited by the waiter or captain. The charge for specials at some restaurants is noticeably out of line with the other prices on the menu. Beware of the $10 bottle of water; ask for tap water instead. And always review your bill.

If you eat early or late you may be able to take advantage of prix-fixe deals not offered at peak hours. Most upscale restaurants offer great lunch deals with special menus at cut-rate prices designed to give customers a true taste of the place.

Credit cards are widely accepted, but many restaurants (particularly smaller ones Downtown) accept only cash. If you plan to use a credit card, it's a good idea to double-check its acceptability when making reservations or before sitting down to eat.

WHAT IT COSTS			
$	$$	$$$	$$$$
AT DINNER under $17	$17–$26	$27–$35	over $35

Prices in the reviews are the average cost of a main course at dinner or, if dinner is not served, at lunch.

TIPPING AND TAXES

In most restaurants, tip the waiter 16%–20%. (To figure the amount quickly, just double the sales tax noted on the check—it's 10% of your bill.) Tip at least $1 per drink at the bar and $1 for each coat checked. Never tip the maître d' unless you're out to impress your guests or expect to pay another visit soon.

If you're dining with a group, make sure not to overtip; review your check to see if a gratuity has been added, as many restaurants automatically tack on an 18% tip for groups of six or more.

DINING WITH KIDS

Though it's unusual to see children in the dining rooms of D.C.'s most elite restaurants, eating with youngsters in the nation's capital does not have to mean culinary exile. Many of the restaurants reviewed here are excellent choices for families and are marked with a "Family" symbol.

SMOKING

Smoking is banned in all restaurants and bars, with the exception of a few spaces that have enclosed and ventilated rooms—usually for cigar aficionados.

RESTAURANT REVIEWS

Restaurant reviews have been shortened. For full information, visit Fodors.com. Listed alphabetically within neighborhood. Use the coordinate at the end of the review (✛ 2:B2) to locate a property on the Where to Eat and Stay map.

THE WHITE HOUSE AREA AND FOGGY BOTTOM

The history-steeped Foggy Bottom area boasts architectural landmarks like the Watergate Hotel. Around George Washington University there's cheaper, college-friendly fare like burrito joints and coffee shops. Nearby, the Kennedy Center draws a more mature crowd with tastes that have evolved past burgers and nachos.

$$$$

MODERN

AMERICAN

Fodor'sChoice

★

✕ **Blue Duck Tavern.** With a kitchen firmly committed to artisanal and local ingredients, this high-end tavern, located in the Park Hyatt Hotel, wows with East Coast–inspired dishes like moulard duck breast and oven-roasted bone marrow. Thanks to its much-deserved Michelin star, a visit here means being on the lookout for the city's biggest political names to claim their favorite tables (yes, that includes the Obamas). **Known for:** hand-cut steak fries doused in duck fat; modern American dishes that change with the seasons; stylish, rustic dining room; intimate chef's table with tasting menu. [$] *Average main: $38* ✉ *Park Hyatt Hotel, 1201 24th St. NW, Foggy Bottom* ☎ *202/419–6755* 🌐 *www.blueducktavern.com* [M] *Foggy Bottom/GWU* ✥ *1:D5.*

$$$$ BELGIAN 🍴 **Marcel's.** The French-inspired Belgian cuisine at Marcel's are well-designed multicourse meals served in an elegant setting. The menus change daily, and often include multiple seafood choices (like perfectly seared diver scallops and Blue Bay mussels), succulent duck breast, and a selection of foie gras. **Known for:** very upscale multicourse menus that change daily; flavorful Blue Bay mussels; affordable pretheater menu. [$] *Average main: $125* ✉ *2401 Pennsylvania Ave. NW, Foggy Bottom* ☎ *202/296–1166* 🌐 *www.marcelsdc.com* ⏲ *No lunch* [M] *Foggy Bottom/GWU* ✥ *1:D6.*

3

CAPITOL HILL

"The Hill," as locals know it, was once an enclave of congressional boardinghouses in the shadow of the Capitol building but is now D.C.'s largest historic district, with an eclectic mix of restaurants. Around the Capitol South Metro station, government offices end and neighborhood dining begins. Here, along tree-lined streets, some of the city's most acclaimed restaurant have joined the local bars and eateries that have long catered to lunch and happy-hour crowds during the week.

Neighborhood establishments and all-American pubs line historic Barracks Row, with Eastern Market anchoring the homey House side of the Hill; the Senate end is given a more hustle-and-bustle vibe with the chain dining and upscale boîtes of Union Station. A few blocks northeast is Union Market, where dozens of local food and beverage purveyors sell everything from arepas to Zinfandels.

$$$ SOUTHERN 🍴 **Art and Soul.** Best known as Oprah's longtime personal chef, Art Smith is now serving the Washington crowd at this funky Southern-fried spot that gives down-home cravings an upscale twist. The chic kitchen draws some of the city's biggest movers and shakers (including Michelle Obama), but still maintains a homey and welcoming atmosphere. **Known for:** the best biscuits in the city; Southern hospitality and the cuisine to go along with it; dog-friendly outdoor patio (complete with menu for Fido). [$] *Average main: $31* ✉ *Liaison Capitol Hill, 415 New Jersey Ave. NW, Capitol Hill* ☎ *202/393–7777* 🌐 *www.artandsouldc.com* [M] *Union Station* ✥ *2:F3.*

$$ BELGIAN 🍴 **Belga Café.** Belgium culture aficionados can go traditional with mussels and the crispiest of french fries or dabble in what the chef calls Eurofusion at this sleek café done up with dark wood and exposed brick. Classic dishes such as Flemish beef stew made with Corsendonk Brune beer sauce help capture that Belgian charm. **Known for:** 10 styles of mussels you can choose from; huge 12-page beer menu; waffle-centric brunch menu. [$] *Average main: $25* ✉ *514 8th St. SE, Capitol Hill* ☎ *202/544–0100* 🌐 *www.belgacafe.com* [M] *Eastern Market* ✥ *2:H6.*

$$$ FRENCH 🍴 **Bistro Bis.** The zinc bar, cherrywood interior, and white tablecloths create great expectations at Bistro Bis, where the seasonal menu serves a modern take on a French bistro. Thanks to its prime location,

acclaimed menu, deep wine list, and classic cocktails, it's a popular spot for Washington power brokers and insiders. **Known for:** excellent steak frites and steak tartare; sophisticated ambience that attracts a powerful clientele. [$] *Average main: $29* ✉ *Hotel George, 15 E St. NW, Capitol Hill* ☎ *202/661–2700* 🌐 *www.bistrobis.com* [M] *Union Station* ⊕ *2:F3.*

$$ GREEK Fodor's Choice ★ 🍴 **Cava Mezze.** This modern mecca for mezes (small plates for sharing) delivers delicious, chic Mediterranean cuisine without the whiz-bang conceits of its pricier cousins. There are few surprises on the menu, save for the feta hush puppies, but the wood-and-brick interior and gallant service make the traditional dishes feel new again. **Known for:** no-frills Mediterranean meze plates; crazy feta hush puppies and spicy lamb sliders; lots of vegan and gluten-free options; all-you-can-eat brunch with 25¢ mimosas. [$] *Average main: $24* ✉ *527 8th St. SE, Capitol Hill* ☎ *202/543–9090* 🌐 *www.cavamezze.com* ⏲ *No lunch Mon.* [M] *Eastern Market* ⊕ *2:H6.*

$ CONTEMPORARY 🍴 **EatBar.** A quintessential gastropub, EatBar has all the necessities for an easygoing dining experience: good beers, good tunes, and good eats. While the menu offers full-on entrées like smoked chicken and waffles and a double pimento cheeseburger, it mostly features shareable small plates like wild boar pâté and fried brussels sprouts with bacon. **Known for:** meat-heavy small plates created by a butcher-cum-chef; eclectic jukebox options; superb selection of beer, wine, and cocktails; ham fries, aka ham and potatoes whipped in ham fat. [$] *Average main: $15* ✉ *415 8th St. SE, Capitol Hill* ☎ *202/847–4827* 🌐 *www.eat-bar.com* [M] *Eastern Market* ⊕ *2:H6.*

$$ ETHIOPIAN 🍴 **Ethiopic.** The spongy rolls of sourdough *injera* bread (ubiquitous on Ethiopian plates) used in place of utensils can make traditional Ethiopian feel decidedly undelicate, but the bright surroundings and friendly service here make for a downright romantic experience. Venture off the well-beaten path of spicy lamb and lentils to try the spicy chickpea dumplings or fragrant simmered split peas, laden with garlic and served in a clay pot. **Known for:** minimalist yet friendly atmosphere; Ethiopian standards like beef tibs and injera; great Ethiopian coffee and beer options. [$] *Average main: $23* ✉ *401 H St. NE, Capitol Hill* ☎ *202/675–2066* 🌐 *www.ethiopicrestaurant.com* ⏲ *Closed Mon. No lunch Tues.–Thurs.* [M] *Union Station* ⊕ *2:H2.*

$ AMERICAN FAMILY Fodor's Choice ★ 🍴 **Good Stuff Eatery.** Fans of Bravo's *Top Chef* will first visit this brightly colored burgers-and-shakes joint hoping to spy charismatic celebrity chef Spike Mendelsohn, but they will return for the comfort-food favorites. The lines can be long, as it's a favorite lunch spot of congressional aides, but Spike's inventive beef dishes are worth the wait. **Known for:** fun burgers like the "Prez Obama"; thick malted milk shakes; cafeteria-style ordering; variety of dipping sauces for hand-cut skinny fries. [$] *Average main: $8* ✉ *303 Pennsylvania Ave. SE, Capitol Hill* ☎ *202/543–8222* 🌐 *www.goodstuffeatery.com* ⏲ *Closed Sun.* [M] *Eastern Market* ⊕ *2:H5.*

$$ BELGIAN 🍴 **Granville Moore's Brickyard.** This Belgian beer hall with a gourmet soul is worth a visit for both its intense beer list and mussels and frites. Snag a seat at the bar or at one of the first-come, first-served tables,

and linger over unfiltered artisanal brews that range from Chimay to obscure options from the reserve and limited-stock beer selection. **Known for:** steamed mussels served with crunchy fries and homemade dipping sauces; wide-ranging Belgian beer list; unique salads and burgers. [$] *Average main: $18* ✉ *1238 H St. NE, Capitol Hill* ☎ *202/399–2546* 🌐 *www.granvillemoores.com* ⏲ *No lunch Mon.–Thurs.* [M] *Union Station* ✥ *2:H2.*

3

$ AMERICAN
🍴 **Jimmy T's Place.** This D.C. institution is tucked in the first floor of an old row house only five blocks from the Capitol where talkative regulars and the boisterous owner pack the place daily. Enjoy favorites like eggs Benedict made with a toasted English muffin, a huge piece of ham, and lots of hollandaise sauce. **Known for:** classic greasy spoon atmosphere; breakfast combos like grits and pumpkin pancakes; absolutely no substitutions; cash-only. [$] *Average main: $7* ✉ *501 E. Capitol St. SE, Capitol Hill* ☎ *202/546–3646* 💳 *No credit cards* ⏲ *Closed Mon. No dinner* [M] *Capitol S* ✥ *2:H5.*

$ AMERICAN FAMILY
🍴 **The Market Lunch.** Digging into a hefty pile of pancakes from this casual counter in Eastern Market makes for the perfect end to a stroll around the Capitol. Favorites include eggs, grits, and pancakes in the morning and crab cakes, fried shrimp, and fish for lunch. **Known for:** blueberry buckwheat pancakes; long lines and lots of kids; cash-only policy. [$] *Average main: $14* ✉ *Eastern Market, 225 7th St. SE, Capitol Hill* ☎ *202/547–8444* 🌐 *www.marketlunchdc.com* 💳 *No credit cards* ⏲ *Closed Mon. No dinner* [M] *Eastern Market* ✥ *2:H6.*

$$$$ CONTEMPORARY Fodor's Choice ★
🍴 **Pineapple and Pearls.** For his follow-up to the smash hit Rose's Luxury, chef Aaron Silverman opened this dining room next door that offers a 13-course (give or take) tasting menu for $250 per person (and yes, that means beverages and tips, too). While that price point often comes with a heaping serving of pretension, that's not the case here, where dishes have included roasted potato ice cream that tastes an awful lot like french fries dipped into a milk shake. **Known for:** expensive (but all-inclusive) tasting menu; fun and low-key dishes with zero pretension; intense reservation process. [$] *Average main: $250* ✉ *715 8th St. SE, Capitol Hill* ☎ *202/595–7375* 🌐 *www.pineappleandpearls.com* ⏲ *Closed Sun., Mon., and most Sat.* [M] *Eastern Market* ✥ *2:H6.*

$$$ MODERN AMERICAN Fodor's Choice ★
🍴 **Rose's Luxury.** A darling of both diners and the media, Rose's Luxury lives up to the hype as one of the city's most welcoming and groundbreaking dining destinations. The dishes are as delightful as they are shocking, and cause visitors to wait in line for hours to visit the supremely stylish re-creation of a hipster's dream dinner party. **Known for:** innovative small plates; the sausage, lychee, and habanero salad; long waits for a table (with reservations only for big groups). [$] *Average main: $32* ✉ *717 8th St. SE, Washington* ☎ *202/580–8889* 🌐 *www.rosesluxury.com* ⏲ *No lunch* ✥ *2:H6.*

$ PIZZA
🍴 **Seventh Hill.** The breezy charm of this casual bistro quickly vaulted its pizza to the top of the list of D.C.'s best places for pies. Each is named for a nearby neighborhood—the zesty mating of basil and anchovies on the "Southwest Waterfront" pie is matched only by the creamy goat cheese of the "Eastern Market." Pizzas match well with

the small cast of bottled beers available. **Known for:** locally named wood-fired pizzas; bright and welcoming atmosphere; Nutella calzone for dessert. $ *Average main: $16* ⊠ *327 7th St. SE, Capitol Hill* ☎ *202/544–1911* ⊕ *www.montmartredc.com/seventhhill* ☾ *Closed Mon.* Ⓜ *Eastern Market* ✛ *2:H6.*

$$ ✕ **Sonoma.** This chic multilevel wine bar has pours aplenty (in both tast-
WINE BAR ing portions and full glasses) along with well-thought-out charcuterie boards piled with prosciutto and fluffy, grill-charred focaccia. There's more-filling fare, too, like potato gnocchi with mushrooms. **Known for:** hip and vast wine menu; happy hour catering to a congressional crowd; house-made charcuterie and thin-crust pizzas. $ *Average main: $22* ⊠ *223 Pennsylvania Ave. SE, Capitol Hill* ☎ *202/544–8088* ⊕ *www. sonomadc.com* ☾ *No lunch Sat.* Ⓜ *Capitol S* ✛ *2:H5.*

$$ ✕ **Ted's Bulletin.** This cheeky homage to mid-20th-century diners is styled
DINER after a newspaper office, with menus printed in broadsheet format and
FAMILY specials mounted on the wall in mismatched plastic lettering. But one bite of the grilled cheese with tomato soup or the "'Burgh" burger, served on Texas toast with coleslaw, french fries, and a runny egg, will convince you that the kitchen's skills are no joke. **Known for:** fun newsroom-meets-diner ambience; boozy milk shakes with clever names; homemade Pop-Tarts. $ *Average main: $17* ⊠ *505 8th St. SE, Capitol Hill* ☎ *202/544–8337* ⊕ *www.tedsbulletincapitolhill.com* Ⓜ *Eastern Market* ✛ *2:H6.*

DOWNTOWN

Until recently, tourists who trekked north from the Mall hungry for something more than Smithsonian cafeteria food were stranded Downtown with little but high-end options. Now young Washingtonians are taking advantage of residential development and moving off Capitol Hill to Downtown, pulling trendy and affordable dining choices up north. You can also give credit to chef José Andrés; in the early 2000s, his Spanish tapas restaurant Jaleo was one of the rare establishments in the Penn Quarter to garner critical acclaim. His success led to other restaurateurs following suit—along with a highly regarded culinary empire of his own. Nearby Chinatown, home of the Verizon Center, is also a bustling hub of restaurants offering excellent Asian food and much more.

$$ ✕ **The Arsenal at Bluejacket.** Most restaurants pair beers with food, but
CONTEMPORARY here you'll find the opposite: refined but hearty new American fare designed to complement the rotating 20 craft brews. If you're not sure whether an herbal saison or the spicy fruit of a Scotch ale would go best with a bone-in beef short rib in a Kansas City rub, don't be afraid to ask the gracious cast of servers. **Known for:** in-house brewery that produces excellent speciality beer; industrial vibe; fantastic Sunday brunch. $ *Average main: $22* ⊠ *300 Tingey St. SE, D.C. Waterfront* ☎ *202/524–2862* ⊕ *www.bluejacketdc.com* ☾ *No lunch Sat.* ✛ *2:F6.*

$ ✕ **Beau Thai.** This dream of a local haunt was founded by an experi-
THAI enced Thai chef and two American entrepreneurs inspired by her flair for spice. The drunken noodle is light yet flavorful, the green curry is

complex, and the sesame-crusted tofu appetizer achieves that nirvana of bean curd: carnivores can't get enough of it. **Known for:** Thai take on empanadas; plenty of gluten-free options; chic dining room. $ *Average main: $14* ✉ *1550 7th St. NW, Unit A, Downtown* ☎ *202/536–5636* ⊕ *www.beauthaidc.com* Ⓜ *Columbia Heights* ✛ *1:H3.*

$$ ✕ **Bibiana Osteria and Enoteca.** You might call this the Italian version
ITALIAN of the überpopular Indian spot Rasika, and you'd be correctly noting the modernist fingerprints of local impresario Ashok Bajaj. The 120-seat dining room, decorated in Bajaj's favored spare tones and metallic accents, specializes in hearty Italian cuisine dished out by uncommonly attentive and knowledgeable servers. **Known for:** being a Milan-inspired osteria; unexpected Italian dishes; affordable lunch specials. $ *Average main: $26* ✉ *1100 New York Ave. NW, entrance at 12th and H Sts., Downtown* ☎ *202/216–9550* ⊕ *www.bibianadc.com* ☽ *No lunch Sat. Closed Sun.* Ⓜ *Metro Center* ✛ *2:C2.*

$$ ✕ **Bombay Club.** One block from the White House, the beautiful Bombay
INDIAN Club tries to re-create the refined aura of British private clubs in colonial India. On the menu are unusual seafood specialties and a large number of vegetarian dishes, but the real standouts are the aromatic curries. **Known for:** great Indian curries; British colonial club vibe; upscale Sunday buffet brunch. $ *Average main: $24* ✉ *815 Connecticut Ave. NW, Downtown* ☎ *202/659–3727* ⊕ *www.bombayclubdc.com* ☽ *No lunch Sat.* Ⓜ *Farragut W* ✛ *1:G6.*

$$$ ✕ **Brasserie Beck.** Give in to sensory overload at this homage to the
BELGIAN railway dining rooms that catered to the prewar European elite. The food is just as rich as you'd expect: entrée-size salads with Belgian frites, *fruits de mer* platters with enough shellfish for a small army, and a dizzying lineup of artisanal beers. **Known for:** luxurious vintage-inspired interiors; excellent brunch that includes Belgian waffles and unlimited mimosas; great outdoor patio. $ *Average main: $32* ✉ *1101 K St. NW, Downtown* ☎ *202/408–1717* ⊕ *www.brasseriebeck.com* Ⓜ *McPherson Sq.* ✛ *2:C2.*

$$$ ✕ **DBGB Kitchen and Bar.** After leaving D.C. in 1982, famed chef Dan-
FRENCH iel Boulud finally returned 32 years and 18 restaurants later to open this interpretation of a classic French brasserie in downtown D.C. The small plates of house-made sausage, coq au vin, and baked Alaska for dessert demonstrate the impressive culinary chops he picked up while away. **Known for:** world-famous chef's prodigal return home; variety of house-made sausages; fun cocktail menu. $ *Average main: $28* ✉ *931 H St. NW, Downtown* ☎ *202/695–7660* ⊕ *www.dbgb.com/dc* Ⓜ *Gallery Pl./Chinatown* ✛ *2:C2.*

$ ✕ **District Taco.** The line out the door at lunchtime is a dead giveaway that
MEXICAN D.C.er's have taken to this fast casual Yucatan-style Mexican restaurant
FAMILY that got its start as a food truck in 2009. While you can customize the toppings of your tacos or burritos, ordering them the Mexican way (with cilantro and onion) is a sure bet. **Known for:** food truck origins; all-day breakfast tacos; extensive salsa bar. $ *Average main: $8* ✉ *1309 F St. NW, Downtown* ☎ *202/347–7359* ⊕ *www.districttaco.com* Ⓜ *Metro Center* ✛ *2:B3.*

$$$$ MODERN ITALIAN

🍴 **Fiola.** Chef Fabio Trabocchi's flights of fancy, such as oysters with granita and caviar or Nova Scotia lobster ravioli delight many area foodies. Happy hour and lunch menus offer more affordable small plates to go with inventive cocktails (head to the bar or patio for these à la carte options). **Known for:** upscale and innovative Italian dishes; date night crowd; encyclopedic beverage list. [$] *Average main: $47* ✉ *601 Pennsylvania Ave. NW, Penn Quarter* ✥ *Enter at 678 Indiana Ave.* ☎ *202/628–2888* 🌐 *www.fioladc.com* [M] *Archives/Navy Memorial* ✥ *2:D4.*

$$ ECLECTIC

🍴 **The Hamilton.** Formerly a Borders bookstore, the Hamilton (no relation to the hit musical) is now an enormous multiroom restaurant over a subterranean live music hall that can accommodate almost a thousand people. The menu is just as ambitious as the venue, offering burgers, sushi, pasta, steaks, salads, seafood, and one solitary vegetarian entrée. **Known for:** all-encompassing menu; huge space with live music; happy hour deals. [$] *Average main: $26* ✉ *600 14th St. NW, Downtown* ☎ *202/787–1000* 🌐 *www.thehamiltondc.com* [M] *Metro Center* ✥ *2:B3.*

$$ JAPANESE

🍴 **Kaz Sushi Bistro.** Traditional Japanese cooking is combined with often inspired improvisations ("freestyle Japanese cuisine," in the words of chef-owner Kaz Okochi) at this serene location. For a first-rate experience, sit at the sushi bar and ask for whatever is best—you're in good hands. **Known for:** one of D.C.'s original sushi spots; unique Japanese dishes and small plates. [$] *Average main: $26* ✉ *1915 I St. NW, Downtown* ☎ *202/530–5500* 🌐 *www.kazsushibistro.com* 🕒 *Closed Sun. No lunch Sat.* [M] *Farragut W* ✥ *1:F6.*

$$ ASIAN Fodor's Choice ★

🍴 **Momofuku CCDC.** New York City legend David Chang made his D.C. debut with this outpost of his original Asian-street-food-inspired restaurant. As at the other Momofukus, the soft buns are a must—you won't regret ordering a few different types (be sure to include the pork though). **Known for:** D.C's take on a NYC culinary legend; Asian street food like pork buns; delicious ramen noodles. [$] *Average main: $17* ✉ *1090 I St. NW, Downtown* ☎ *202/602–1832* 🌐 *ccdc.momofuku.com* [M] *Metro Center* ✥ *2:C2.*

$$$ AMERICAN

🍴 **Old Ebbitt Grill.** People flock here to drink at the several bars, which seem to go on for miles, and to enjoy well-prepared buffalo wings, hamburgers, and hearty sandwiches (the Reuben is a must). A 160-year-old institution (it claims Teddy Roosevelt may have "bagged animal heads" at the main bar), Old Ebbitt also has one of Washington's best raw bars. **Known for:** one of D.C.'s oldest bars; standard bar menu, including great oysters. [$] *Average main: $27* ✉ *675 15th St. NW, Downtown* ☎ *202/347–4800* 🌐 *www.ebbitt.com* [M] *Metro Center* ✥ *2:B3.*

$$$ ITALIAN

🍴 **Osteria Morini.** The stylish design and superlative pastas of this take on cuisine from northern Italy's Emilia-Romagna region might seem like an unexpected match for the sports fans flocking to Nationals Park. But you can't ask for a better way to cap off a day at the ballpark than the wood-grilled meats here. **Known for:** prosciutto, mortadella, and wood-grilled meats; fantastic brunch burger; proximity to the baseball stadium. [$] *Average main: $32* ✉ *301 Water St. SE, Washington* ☎ *202/484–0660* 🌐 *osteriamorini.com* [M] *Navy Yard* ✥ *2:F6.*

D.C. FOOD TRUCKS

The nation's capital loves celebrity chefs and pricey bistros, but its latest romance is both affordable and accessible: food trucks. The mobile-food rush reached its peak several years ago when local brick-and-mortar restaurateurs attempted to fight the trucks' appeal by passing an ordinance to keep them from staying too long in one place. That battle continues, but visitors keen to try the best D.C. trucks can always take advantage of Twitter. Even those without a Twitter account are free to visit the trucks' pages to track their locations—and in many cases, check out menus to see whether chicken vindaloo or red-velvet cupcakes are on the docket at these favorite spots.

Arepa Zone (⊕ *www.twitter. com/arepazone*) is a celebration of Venezuelan cuisine; arepas, *cachapas* (cheese sticks), and *cachapas* (tacolike sweet corn pancakes) all feature heavily.

PhoWheels (⊕ *www.twitter. com/PhoWheels*) makes pho so delicious you'll want a cup even on a hot D.C. day (go for the eye-round steak). Soup can be a bit difficult to eat when sitting on a curb or park bench, but luckily PhoWheels also offers impressive bánh mì sandwiches and Vietnamese-style tacos.

Red Hook Lobster Pound (⊕ *twitter.com/lobstertruckdc*) is the Washington outpost of the popular Brooklyn, New York, spot that purveys rolls filled with überfresh shellfish from Maine (tossed with light mayo) and Connecticut (kissed by creamy butter) variations—or try the equally good shrimp roll for $7 less. Add a decadent chocolate homemade whoopie pie for dessert.

$$$
CONTEMPORARY
✕ **The Oval Room.** The city is full of established restaurants that cater to lobbyists and the government officials they're wining and dining, but the Oval Room is a rare example of one that also has great food. The menu is largely split between Southern-influenced dishes, like shrimp and grits, and Mediterranean-inspired ones, such as smoked yellowfin potato agnolotti. **Known for:** clientele of D.C. insiders; classy and intimate dining room; modern American cuisine like yellowfin tuna crudo. Ⓢ *Average main: $28* ✉ *800 Connecticut Ave. NW, Downtown* ☎ *202/463–8700* ⊕ *www.ovalroom.com* ⊗ *Closed Sun. No lunch weekends* Ⓜ *Farragut W* ✛ *2:A2.*

$
FRENCH
FAMILY
✕ **Paul.** This chic, quick café is the Parisian equivalent of Starbucks, but that doesn't mean Americans won't be blown away by the fluff of its cheese *gougeres* puffs, the heft of its salty-sweet croque monsieur sandwiches, and the delicate crunch of its almond-flour *macaron* cookies. Although there can be lengthy lines, when you compare the prices and quality here to other Downtown lunch options, nothing else comes close. **Known for:** Parisian-style fast casual chain; huge pastry selection; big crowds during lunch. Ⓢ *Average main: $10* ✉ *801 Pennsylvania Ave. NW, Downtown* ☎ *202/524–4500* ⊕ *www.paul-usa.com* ⊗ *No dinner* Ⓜ *Archives* ✛ *2:D4.*

$ ASIAN FAMILY 🍴 **Teaism.** This informal teahouse stocks more than 50 imported teas (black, white, and green), and also serves healthy and delicious Japanese, Indian, and Thai food. You can mix small dishes—like udon noodle salad and grilled avocado—to create meals or snacks. **Known for:** impressive selection of teas; lunch dishes spanning several Asian cuisines; chocolate salty oat cookies. [$] *Average main: $12* ✉ *400 8th St. NW, Downtown* ☎ *202/638–6010* 🌐 *www.teaism.com* [M] *Archives/Navy Memorial* ✥ *2:D3.*

$$$$ ASIAN FUSION 🍴 **Wolfgang Puck's The Source.** Iconic chef Wolfgang Puck's first foray into Washington offers two different dining experiences, both with a focus on Asian flavors and with some of the city's most dedicated servers. The downstairs area is home to an intimate lounge where guests can try small plates while upstairs the focus is all on haute cuisine. **Known for:** one of the world's most well-known chefs; upscale Asian-fusion cuisine; location in the Newseum; dim sum brunch. [$] *Average main: $37* ✉ *The Newseum, 575 Pennsylvania Ave. NW, Downtown* ☎ *202/637–6100* 🌐 *www.wolfgangpuck.com/restaurants/fine-dining/3941* 🕒 *Closed Sun.* [M] *Archives/Navy Memorial* ✥ *2:D4.*

CHINATOWN

$$ PERUVIAN 🍴 **China Chilcano.** The José Andrés formula is pleasantly familiar to D.C. diners who have visited his ever-growing empire of endlessly kicky small plate restaurants since Jaleo first opened in 1993. This hybrid of Peruvian and Chinese-Japanese styles, inspired by a 19th-century wave of migration to South America, is one of the newer additions to the stylish family. **Known for:** part of chef José Andrés's empire; Peruvian-inspired shareable small plates; pisco fruit cocktails. [$] *Average main: $20* ✉ *418 7th St. NW, Washington* ☎ *202/783–0941* 🌐 *chinachilcano.com* 🕒 *No lunch* [M] *Gallery Pl./Chinatown* ✥ *2:D3.*

$ RAMEN 🍴 **Daikaya.** This no-reservations, Sapporo-style ramen shop is one of the city's best bets for the tasty Japanese noodle soup. It offers five excellent types of ramen, with the vegan version a welcome option. **Known for:** small spot serving ramen; loud, local-friendly vibe; fancier Izakaya upstairs. [$] *Average main: $14* ✉ *705 6th St. NW, Chinatown* ☎ *202/589–1600* 🌐 *www.daikaya.com* [M] *Gallery Pl./Chinatown* ✥ *2:D3.*

$$$ FUSION 🍴 **Dirty Habit.** Inside trendy Hotel Monaco, Dirty Habit woos diners with a towering skylit space that until 1901 was the general post office. Honing in on globally inspired shared plates, the chef conjures up such satisfying dishes as poached hen dumplings and smoked Chilean sea bass. **Known for:** alfresco dining (and drinking) in the courtyard; popular happy hour; small plates in a historic space. [$] *Average main: $30* ✉ *Hotel Monaco, 555 8th St. NW, Chinatown* ☎ *202/783–6060* 🌐 *www.dirtyhabitdc.com* [M] *Gallery Pl./Chinatown* ✥ *2:D3.*

$ CHINESE 🍴 **Full Kee.** Many locals swear by this standout from the slew of mediocre Chinese joints in the area. The style-free interior can be off-putting to some—reminiscent of the fluorescent-lit dives of Manhattan's Chinatown—but the cuisine is better than most similar options within the city limits. **Known for:** rare good spot for Chinese food in Chinatown; Catonese-style roasted meats; no-frills decor. [$] *Average main: $14*

✉ *509 H St. NW, Chinatown* ☎ *202/371–2233* ⊕ *www.fullkeedc.com* Ⓜ *Gallery Pl./Chinatown* ✛ *2:D2.*

$$
MODERN ITALIAN

✕ **Graffiato.** Manhattan-trained Mike Isabella brought a rock-star cool to his stints on *Top Chef* and *Top Chef All-Stars,* and his venture down I–95 gave the same instant pizzazz to Washington's culinary scene. Everyone does wood-fired pizzas, but Graffiato (the Italian word for "scratched," an excellent description of its artful-grunge ambience) does a Jersey Shore pie inspired by Isabella's home state that piles pink cherry-pepper aioli onto fried calamari. **Known for:** *Top Chef* celeb status; unique wood-fired pizzas; happy hour specials. Ⓢ *Average main: $25* ✉ *707 6th St. NW, Chinatown* ☎ *202/289–3600* ⊕ *graffiatodc.com* Ⓜ *Gallery Pl./Chinatown* ✛ *2:D3.*

$$
BARBECUE
FAMILY

✕ **Hill Country.** Few who stop by this bustling hive of smoky brisket and gooey ribs can deny that it does Texas meat right. This is evident down to the pay-by-the-pound ethos that lets you sample one slice of lean beef and one scoop of gooey white shoepeg corn pudding alongside a succulent turkey breast, so tender it drips juice down your chin. **Known for:** Texas-style brisket—with the rub; cafeteria-style, pay-by-the pound ordering; country western karaoke night every Wednesday. Ⓢ *Average main: $18* ✉ *410 7th St. NW, Chinatown* ☎ *202/556–2050* ⊕ *www.hillcountrywdc.com* Ⓜ *Archives/ Navy Memorial* ✛ *2:D3.*

$$
SPANISH

✕ **Jaleo.** Make a meal of the long list of tapas at chef José Andrés's lively Spanish bistro, although the five types of handcrafted paella are the stars of the ample entrée menu. Tapas highlights include the *gambas al ajillo* (sautéed garlic shrimp), tender piquillo peppers stuffed with goat cheese, and the grilled homemade chorizo, which also comes draped in creamy mashed potatoes. **Known for:** José Andrés original tapas eatery; sangria by the pitcher; different paella options. Ⓢ *Average main: $25* ✉ *480 7th St. NW, Chinatown* ☎ *202/628–7949* ⊕ *www.jaleo.com* Ⓜ *Gallery Pl./ Chinatown* ✛ *2:D3.*

$$$$
MODERN
AMERICAN

✕ **Kinship.** The unique menu divides Kinship's offerings into four categories; first there's craft, honoring a particular cooking technique, and then history, which offers a different take on a classic dish. The ingredients menu explores a certain product while the indulgence section is where you'll find dishes like caviar with potato chips or lobster French toast. **Known for:** themed menu with diverse selections; Chesapeake Bay soft-shell crabs (when in season); warm yet chic ambience. Ⓢ *Average main: $50* ✉ *1015 7th St. NW, Chinatown* ☎ *202/737–7700* ⊕ *www. kinshipdc.com* Ⓜ *Mt. Vernon Sq.* ✛ *2:D1.*

$$$$
CONTEMPORARY
Fodor's Choice
★

✕ **minibar by José Andrés.** For food fanatics who can afford it, a visit to chef José Andrés's cutting-edge culinary counter is as essential as a visit to the White House when visiting Washington. Here Andrés showcases his molecular-gastronomy techniques with the 20 or so courses on the tasting menu that vary regularly (no à la carte ordering allowed). **Known for:** pricey tasting menu of avant-garde cuisine; hard-to-get reservations required; chocolate-covered foie gras; experimental cocktails. Ⓢ *Average main: $275* ✉ *855 E. St. NW, Chinatown* ☎ *202/393–0812* ⊕ *www.minibarbyjoseandres.com/minibar* ✛ *2:D3.*

$$ MEXICAN 🍴 **Oyamel.** The specialty at chef José Andrés's Mexican stunner is *antojitos,* literally translated as "little dishes from the streets." But the high ceilings, gracious service, and gorgeous Frida Kahlo–inspired interior are anything but street, and even the smallest of dishes is larger than life when doused with chocolate mole poblano sauce or piquant lime-cilantro dressing. **Known for:** street-inspired Mexican small plates; grasshopper tacos; affordable lunch deals. [$] *Average main: $23* ✉ *401 7th St. NW, Chinatown* ☎ *202/628–1005* 🌐 *www.oyamel.com* [M] *Archives/Navy Memorial* ✥ *2:D3.*

$$$ MODERN AMERICAN 🍴 **The Partisan.** Charcuterie is more than just salami at this wood-paneled homage to all parts of the pig. Sample servings of meat under headings like rich + earthy, herbal + floral, and boozy, and complement the taste with one of the vibrant small plates like grilled octopus and brussels sprout slaw. **Known for:** pig-focused charcuterie menu; late-night hot spot; great dessert menu including hazelnut mudpies. [$] *Average main: $30* ✉ *709 D St. NW, Washington* ☎ *202/524–5322* 🌐 *thepartisandc.com* [M] *Gallery Pl.* ✥ *2:D3.*

$$$ CONTEMPORARY 🍴 **Proof.** The name should make this spot's beverage-centric disposition clear: Proof has more than 1,000 different wine varieties in bottles and 40 by the glass, dispensed via a stainless-steel Enomatic machine. Its modern American cuisine shows influences from across the globe in dishes like wagyu beef carpaccio, Hudson Valley foie gras, and Peking duck. **Known for:** expansive wine menu; cheese and charcuterie boards. [$] *Average main: $32* ✉ *775 G St. NW, Chinatown* ☎ *202/737–7663* 🌐 *www.proofdc.com* ⏲ *No lunch weekends* [M] *Gallery Pl./Chinatown* ✥ *2:D2.*

$$ INDIAN Fodor's Choice ★ 🍴 **Rasika.** Adventurous wine lists, stellar service, inventive presentations that don't scrimp on the spice—this Indian kitchen would have been a local legend even without the romantic yet supersleek decor that drives date-night crowds to snap up reservations weeks in advance. The menu highlights unique tandooris and grills, from lamb to chicken, and überpopular vegetarian dishes such as the fried spinach leaves with sweet yogurt sauce called *palak chaat.* **Known for:** upscale Indian with unique dishes; plenty of options for vegetarians; tables that book up weeks in advance. [$] *Average main: $25* ✉ *633 D St. NW, Chinatown* ☎ *202/637–1222* 🌐 *www.rasikarestaurant.com* ⏲ *Closed Sun. No lunch Sat.* [M] *Archives/Navy Memorial* ✥ *2:D3.*

$ AMERICAN FAMILY Fodor's Choice ★ 🍴 **Shake Shack.** Yes, it's a chain made most famous in Manhattan, but if you're craving a burger, there's no better place to address that problem than its D.C. Chinatown outpost. Juicy burgers with a special sauce, classic fries (get them with cheese), and tasty shakes make it worth the short wait—especially if you're looking for a tasty lunch between Downtown attractions at a reasonable price. **Known for:** classic Shack Burger (and that sauce!); vanilla milk shakes; long lines that go fast. [$] *Average main: $9* ✉ *800 F St. NW, Chinatown* ☎ *202/800–9930* 🌐 *www.shakeshack.com/location/f-street-dc* [M] *Gallery Pl./Chinatown* ✥ *2:C3.*

$$ MIDDLE EASTERN Fodor's Choice ★ 🍴 **Zaytinya.** This sophisticated urban dining room with soaring ceilings is a local favorite for meeting friends or dining with a group. Here chef José Andrés devotes practically the entire menu to Turkish, Greek, and Lebanese small plates, known as meze. **Known for:** variety of meze; roasted lamb shoulder to share; vegetarian friendly

options; hard-to-get reservations. Ⓢ *Average main: $26* ⊠ *701 9th St. NW, Chinatown* ☎ *202/638–0800* ⊕ *www.zaytinya.com* Ⓜ *Gallery Pl./Chinatown* ✛ *2:D3.*

GEORGETOWN

Georgetown's picturesque Victorian streetscapes make it D.C.'s most famous neighborhood, with five-star restaurants in historic row houses and casual cafés sandwiched between large national chain stores.

At its beginnings in the mid-1700s, Georgetown was a Maryland tobacco port. Today the neighborhood is one of D.C.'s premier shopping districts, as well as a tourist and architectural attraction. And while recent additions to the neighborhood seem more apt to be chains, there are some standout local restaurants that cater to the budgets of college students, middle-income travelers, and D.C.'s well-heeled elite.

$$
CAJUN
✕ **Bayou.** New Orleans and Washington, D.C., might seem to have little in common, but both cities share a common love of after-hours carousing and belt-stretching cuisine. The urban marriage is consummated beautifully at this two-level po'boy palace, where live bands often turn the top floor into a mini–Bourbon Street. **Known for:** New Orleans–style po'boys; live music; NOLA-inspired cocktails. Ⓢ *Average main: $22* ⊠ *2519 Pennsylvania Ave. NW, Georgetown* ☎ *202/223–6941* ⊕ *www.bayouonpenn.com* ☉ *Closed Mon. No lunch Tues. and Wed.* ✛ *1:D5.*

$$$$
STEAKHOUSE
✕ **Bourbon Steak.** In a city full of steak houses catering to business travelers on expense accounts, it'd be easy to write off this restaurant in the Four Seasons. But with expertly prepared all-natural meats, sides like tater tot and foie-gras poutine, and service that's attentive but not pretentious, if it's not the best steak house in town, it's at least a contender. **Known for:** one of the top steak houses in town; lively bar scene full of locals; more affordable lounge menu. Ⓢ *Average main: $75* ⊠ *Four Seasons, 2800 Pennsylvania Ave. NW, Georgetown* ☎ *202/944–2026* ⊕ *www.bourbonsteakdc.com* ☉ *No lunch weekends* Ⓜ *Foggy Bottom/GWU* ✛ *1:C5.*

$$
ETHIOPIAN
✕ **Das.** If Das marks your first foray into upscale Ethiopian dining, the delightful chicken and beef combination sampler and harvest vegetable specialty provide a taste of the genre at its best. And don't worry about running out of the pancakelike injera bread used in place of utensils—your server will keep bringing it. **Known for:** rare Ethiopian fine dining; excellent sampler option; patio dining in nice weather. Ⓢ *Average main: $18* ⊠ *1201 28th St. NW, Georgetown* ☎ *202/333–4710* ⊕ *www.dasethiopian.com* Ⓜ *Foggy Bottom/GWU* ✛ *1:C5.*

$
WINE BAR
✕ **Eno.** Start your night with wine and food pairings at this casual, cozy Georgetown hot spot—or even make it an evening in and of itself. While Eno offers wine by the bottle and glass, it's the wine-tasting flights of three 2.5-ounce pours where it really excels—after all, you feel better about yourself if you're learning while you drink. **Known for:** educational wine flights; the three Cs: charcuterie, cheese, and chocolate boards. Ⓢ *Average main: $14* ⊠ *2810 Pennsylvania Ave. NW, Georgetown* ☎ *202/295–2826* ⊕ *www.enowinerooms.com/hotspots/georgetown-d.c* ☉ *Closed Mon.* Ⓜ *Foggy Bottom/GWU* ✛ *1:C5.*

$$ AUSTRIAN 🍴 **Kafe Leopold.** As Euro trendy as it gets, Leopold has an all-day coffee and drinks bar, an architecturally hip dining space, and a chic patio complete with a mini-fountain. Food is pared-down Mitteleuropean; think olive-and-onion tarts, crisp schnitzel paired with arugula, and brussels sprouts with endives. **Known for:** hearty Austrian fare; arty crowd great for people-watching; great weekend brunch and daily breakfast served until 4. [$] *Average main: $20* ✉ *3315 Cady's Alley NW, Georgetown* ☎ *202/965–6005* 🌐 *www.kafeleopolds.com* ✣ *1:A5.*

$$ FRENCH 🍴 **La Chaumière.** A rustic and unpretentious atmosphere meets traditional French cuisine at this Georgetown stalwart with many devoted local fans. Dishes like the boudin blanc and pike dumplings baked in lobster sauce will warm you on the inside just like the large central stone fireplace does on the outside. **Known for:** French countryside dishes and ambience; cassoulet with duck confit, lamb stew, and sausage; great wine list with lots of French options. [$] *Average main: $26* ✉ *2813 M St. NW, Georgetown* ☎ *202/338–1784* 🌐 *www.lachaumieredc.com* 🕒 *Closed Sun.* [M] *Foggy Bottom/GWU* ✣ *1:C5.*

$$$$ AMERICAN 🍴 **1789 Restaurant.** This dining room with Early American paintings and a fireplace could easily be a room in the White House. But all the gentility of this 19th-century town-house restaurant is offset by the down-to-earth food on the menu, which changes daily. **Known for:** Szechuan-spiced lamb chops; historic upscale setting; several prix-fixe options. [$] *Average main: $85* ✉ *1226 36th St. NW, Georgetown* ☎ *202/965–1789* 🌐 *www.1789restaurant.com* 🕒 *No lunch* 👔 *Jacket required* ✣ *1:A5.*

$$ BELGIAN 🍴 **The Sovereign.** With two bars serving 50 beers on tap and another 350 in bottles, the Sovereign's devotion to suds is not in doubt. Food-wise, the menu focuses on traditional Belgian fare with some Dutch, French, and German flares as well, leading to tasty results like Dutch mussels, rabbit braised in beer, and slow-roasted pork belly. **Known for:** insane beer selection; rich northern European cuisine; friendly and informed staff. [$] *Average main: $24* ✉ *1206 Wisconsin Ave. NW, Georgetown* ☎ *202/774–5875* 🌐 *www.thesovereigndc.com* 🕒 *No lunch Mon.–Thurs.* [M] *Foggy Bottom/GWU* ✣ *1:B5.*

$$ JAPANESE 🍴 **Sushiko.** At the city's self-touted first raw-fish restaurant, the cuts are always ocean fresh, the cocktails fruity, and the presentations classic. Think blue crab topped with avocado and tuna crowned by jalapeño, while hot delicacies like melt-on-the-tongue fried tempura are always reliable. **Known for:** pioneer of the D.C. sushi scene; classic sushi presentations; bread pudding with green tea mousse for dessert. [$] *Average main: $24* ✉ *5455 Wisconsin Ave. NW, Chevy Chase* ☎ *301/961–1644* 🌐 *www.sushikorestaurants.com* [M] *Friendship Heights* ✣ *1:A2.*

DUPONT CIRCLE AND LOGAN CIRCLE

Before D.C.'s recent cultural renaissance, Dupont Circle and Logan Circle defied the city's staid, conservative reputation, turning into Washington's hip go-to neighborhoods at night. While much of the city's recent openings have shifted to other areas, these high-rent, liberal-minded neighborhoods still have art galleries, bookstores, and yoga studios that draw a mix of yuppies and activists. If possible, make reservations for sit-down meals, and expect crowds, especially on weekends.

DUPONT CIRCLE

$$ ✕ **Bistrot du Coin.** An instant hit in its Dupont Circle neighborhood,
FRENCH this moderately priced French bistro with a monumental zinc bar is noisy, crowded, and fun. The traditional bistro fare includes starter and entrée portions of six different mussels preparations, rightly dubbed the *moules festivales.* **Known for:** six varieties of mussels; fantastic steak frites; fun local hangout. $ *Average main: $24* ⊠ *1738 Connecticut Ave. NW, Dupont Circle* ☎ *202/234–6969* ⊕ *www.bistrotducoin.com* Ⓜ *Dupont Circle* ✛ *1:E3.*

$$ ✕ **DGS Delicatessen.** Your favorite Jewish grandma might be thrown for a
DELI loop by this precocious reboot of her staple dishes, but she will be won over by the traditional matzo ball soup (and, yes, it serves traditional Reubens, too). The younger set will also get a kick out of owners Nick and David Wiseman's take on favorite New York deli items, like the pastrami lo mein made with wheat noodles, for a bargain price during happy hour. **Known for:** rebooted Reubens—and traditional ones, too; chopped liver with cracklins. $ *Average main: $20* ⊠ *1317 Connecticut Ave. NW, Dupont Circle* ☎ *202/293–4400* ⊕ *www.dgsdelicatessen.com* Ⓜ *Dupont Circle* ✛ *1:F4.*

$$$ ✕ **Hank's Oyster Bar.** The watchword is simplicity at this chic take on
SEAFOOD the shellfish shacks of New England. A half-dozen oyster varieties are
Fodor'sChoice available daily on the half shell, both from the West Coast and local
★ Virginia waters, alongside another handful of daily fish specials, from bouillabaisse to grilled tuna, and a "meat-and-two" daily special for those who prefer turf to surf. **Known for:** oysters (of course!); lunchtime soup and sandwich specials. $ *Average main: $27* ⊠ *1624 Q St. NW, Dupont Circle* ☎ *202/462–4265* ⊕ *www.hanksdc.com* Ⓜ *Dupont Circle* ✛ *1:G4.*

$$ ✕ **Iron Gate.** One of the city's more romantic restaurants, Iron Gate
MEDITERRANEAN is located in the former carriageway and stable house of a Dupont Circle town house. Exposed brick walls, wood beams, and a fireplace compliment the upscale Italian and Greek fare, served either à la carte or via a tasting menu with optional wine pairings. **Known for:** eclectic dishes like cotechino sausage; romantic, cozy setting; creative cocktail menus. $ *Average main: $25* ⊠ *1734 N St. NW, Dupont Circle* ☎ *202/524–2502* ⊕ *www.irongaterestaurantdc.com* ☉ No lunch Mon. Ⓜ *Dupont Circle* ✛ *1:F5.*

$$$$ ✕ **Komi.** Johnny Monis, the young, energetic chef-owner of this small,
MEDITERRANEAN personal restaurant (just 14 tables), offers one of the most adventur-
Fodor'sChoice ous dining experiences in the city. The prix-fixe menu ususally comes
★ with 12 courses and showcases contemporary fare with a distinct

Mediterranean influence. **Known for:** always changing (and costly) prix-fixe menu; unique dishes that often incorporate dates, pita bread, and other Mediterranean staples; reservations that book up very quickly. [$] *Average main: $150* ✉ *1509 17th St. NW, Dupont Circle* ☎ *202/332–9200* 🌐 *www.komirestaurant.com* 🕓 *Closed Sun. and Mon. No lunch* [M] *Dupont Circle* ✥ *1:G4.*

$$ CAFÉ FAMILY 🍴 **Kramerbooks & Afterwords.** This popular bookstore-cum-café is a favorite neighborhood breakfast spot. There's a simple menu with a handful of special entrées, but many people drop in just for cappuccino and dessert. **Known for:** bustling bookstore café; late-night hours on weekends; brunch and breakfast menus. [$] *Average main: $21* ✉ *1517 Connecticut Ave. NW, Dupont Circle* ☎ *202/387–3825* 🌐 *www.kramers.com/cafe.html* [M] *Dupont Circle* ✥ *1:F4.*

$$$$ THAI Fodor's Choice ★ 🍴 **Little Serow.** This basement hideout next door to chef Johnny Monis's world-beating Komi gives the wunderkind chef a chance to cook Thai *his* way—which happens to be the northern Thai way. The ingredients are spicy, the presentations sometimes off-putting (what is a snakehead fish?), and the waiters can be sullen, but for sheer moxie and skill, the food is among the best in the city. **Known for:** innovative and spicy Thai dishes; strict no-substitutions or special-requests policy. [$] *Average main: $59* ✉ *1511 17th St. NW, Dupont Circle* 🌐 *www.littleserow.com* 💳 *No credit cards* 🕓 *No lunch. Closed Sun. and Mon.* [M] *Dupont Circle* ✥ *1:G4.*

$$$$ AMERICAN Fodor's Choice ★ 🍴 **Nora.** Chef and founder Nora Pouillon helped pioneer the sustainable-food revolution here, the first certified organic restaurant in the country. Settle into the sophisticated and attractive quilt-decorated dining room and enjoy dishes with seasonal ingredients that are out of this world. **Known for:** organic, well-balanced dishes; very vegetarian friendly; tasting menu available. [$] *Average main: $38* ✉ *2132 Florida Ave. NW, Dupont Circle* ☎ *202/462–5143* 🌐 *www.noras.com* 🕓 *Closed Sun. No lunch* [M] *Dupont Circle* ✥ *1:E3.*

$$$$ ITALIAN 🍴 **Obelisk.** You won't find the menu online or much buzz among locals, but this Italian stalwart has maintained a pull on special-occasion diners for three decades thanks in large part to its under-the-radar reputation. The five-course prix fixe, your only option, changes every day, combining traditional dishes with the innovations of founding chef Peter Pastan, also known for steering legendary pizzeria 2 Amys. **Known for:** intimate atmosphere perfect for special occasions; ever-changing prix-fixe menu; under-the-radar vibe. [$] *Average main: $83* ✉ *2029 P St. NW, Dupont Circle* ☎ *202/872–1180* 🌐 *www.obeliskdc.com* 🕓 *Closed Sun. and Mon. No lunch* [M] *Dupont Circle* ✥ *1:E4.*

$ ECLECTIC 🍴 **Sweetgreen.** When three Georgetown University graduates carved out a closet-size niche to sell freshly made salads and tart frozen yogurt a decade ago, no one in the city batted an eye. Since then, their empire has expanded to 20 D.C.-area locations—and many more locations all over the U.S.—while branching out into fresh juice and healthy soups that use all-local ingredients. **Known for:** build-your-own salads; nationwide chain with local origins; fresh juice bar. [$] *Average main: $10* ✉ *1512 Connecticut Ave. NW, Dupont Circle* ☎ *202/387–9338* 🌐 *www.sweetgreen.com* [M] *Dupont Circle* ✥ *1:E4.*

$$$ AMERICAN 🍴 **Tabard Inn.** Fading portraits and overstuffed furniture make the lobby lounge look like an antiques store, but this hotel restaurant's culinary sensibilities are thoroughly modern. The menu consistently offers interesting seafood and vegetarian options. **Known for:** cozy, historic setting; great brunch (complete with homemade doughnuts); scallops with seafood risotto. [$] *Average main: $30* ✉ *Hotel Tabard Inn, 1739 N St. NW, Dupont Circle* ☎ *202/331–8528* 🌐 *www.tabardinn.com* [M] *Dupont Circle* ✣ *1:F5.*

LOGAN CIRCLE

$$$ FRENCH 🍴 **Convival.** The shareable plates of new takes on traditional French dishes instantly made Convival a local favorite. Dishes like rainbow trout with roe atop snow peas or braised lamb with gnocchi will leave you raving. **Known for:** French plates meant for sharing; lots of local regulars; ambitious dishes like escargot in a blanket. [$] *Average main: $30* ✉ *801 O St. NW, Logan Circle* ☎ *202/525–2870* 🌐 *www.convivialdc.com* 🕒 *No lunch* [M] *Mt. Vernon Sq.* ✣ *2:D1.*

$$$ AMERICAN Fodor's Choice ★ 🍴 **The Dabney.** While many of D.C.'s standout restaurants earn their accolades for takes on cuisine from far-flung corners of the globe, at the Dabney, Virginia-born chef Jeremiah Langhorne draws rave reviews for his commitment to mid-Atlantic cuisine. Highlights at the farmhouse-inspired venue with a large hearth include whole lacquered quail stuffed with corn bread and a family-style serving of chicken and dumplings. **Known for:** local cuisine from a local chef; creative cocktails; low-key farmhouse vibe. [$] *Average main: $34* ✉ *122 Blagden Alley NW, Logan Circle* ☎ *202/450–1015* 🌐 *www.thedabney.com* 🕒 *Closed Mon.* [M] *Mt. Vernon Sq.* ✣ *2:C1.*

$$$ SPANISH Fodor's Choice ★ 🍴 **Estadio.** The name of this polished palace means "stadium," and its gorgeously baroque interior, which surrounds a high-wire open kitchen, makes a perfect stage for energetic and flavorful uses of top-notch ingredients. The menu, developed during research jaunts through Spain, is a master class in tapas, with smoky grilled scallions punched up by garlicky romesco sauce and tortilla Espanola smoother than any served in Barcelona. **Known for:** classic Spanish tapas with new flavors; boozy Slurpees. [$] *Average main: $28* ✉ *1520 14th St. NW, Logan Circle* ☎ *202/319–1404* 🌐 *www.estadio-dc.com* 🕒 *No lunch Mon.–Thurs.* [M] *U St./Cardozo* ✣ *1:H4.*

ADAMS MORGAN

In Adams Morgan legions of college-aged kids descend on 18th Street for abundant drink specials and dance clubs. Quaint ethnic cafés (Ethiopian, French, Italian) are bustling during evening hours. But as the night wears on the crowds gravitate to greasy spoons and "jumbo slice" pizza joints. The next culinary frontier lies just east along Columbia Road, where the immigrant community dines while young families flock to increasingly upscale bistros for refined takes on comfort-food favorites.

$ AFGHAN Fodor's Choice ★ 🍴 **Lapis.** The modern Afghan cuisine shines at this chic yet comfortable—and well-priced—Adams Morgan spot. Eight different varieties of kebabs (prepared via a secret recipe "known only to our mom and the NSA") are the stars of the menu, but you'll also want to try the dumplings and split-pea soup. **Known for:** different types of kebabs prepared with top-secret family recipe; carefully crafted cocktails; excellent bottomless brunch. [$] *Average main: $15* ✉ *1847 Columbia Rd. NW, Adams Morgan* ☎ *202/299–9630* 🌐 *www.lapisdc.com* ⏲ *No lunch* [M] *Dupont Circle* ✥ *1:E1.*

$$$ FRENCH 🍴 **Mintwood Place.** At this saloon-inspired venue, you're invited to dive into the French-inspired takes on American dishes, like an escargot hush puppy. The happy hour menu excels both in terms of value and flavor. **Known for:** French meets American cuisine; great happy hour deals; brunch menu that includes a creative flammekueche tart. [$] *Average main: $29* ✉ *1813 Columbia Rd. NW, Adams Morgan* ☎ *202/234–6732* 🌐 *www.mintwoodplace.com* ⏲ *Closed Mon. No lunch* ✥ *1:F1.*

$$ CONTEMPORARY 🍴 **Roofers Union.** The cavernous space that once hosted one of the capital's most notoriously crazy bars is now a symbol of the area's maturation, thanks to a slick makeover and classy comfort-food lineup. The hearty but well-designed fare includes four types of house-made sausage and a fried-chicken sandwich redolent of sriracha sauce that will rock a spice-lover's world. **Known for:** comfort food with great sausage options; hip, youthful vibe; excellent rooftop deck. [$] *Average main: $23* ✉ *2446 18th St. NW, Adams Morgan* ☎ *202/232–7663* 🌐 *www.roofersuniondc.com* ⏲ *No lunch* [M] *Woodley Park/Zoo* ✥ *1:F1.*

$ RAMEN 🍴 **Sakuramen.** Gourmet versions of Japanese ramen soup have become the latest trend to storm the city, and this hole-in-the-wall gem strikes the perfect balance between keep-it-simple affordability and adventurous flair. Embodying both of those traits in one bowl is the D.C. Miso, which pairs traditional fish cake and seaweed with a shot of Monterey Jack cheese. **Known for:** innovative ramen like the D.C. Miso; casual basement vibe; beef buns and crispy dumplings. [$] *Average main: $14* ✉ *2441 18th St. NW, Adams Morgan* ☎ *202/656–5285* 🌐 *www.sakuramen.net* 💳 *No credit cards* ⏲ *No lunch Mon.–Thurs.* ✥ *1:F1.*

$$ CONTEMPORARY Fodor's Choice ★ 🍴 **Tail Up Goat.** This instant favorite features cuisine influenced by the island of St. John, where one of the three founders was raised. Standouts on the carb-heavy menu—bread gets its own section—include cavatelli with a spicy pork-belly ragu and seaweed sourdough bread. **Known for:** lots and lots of carbs; constantly changing menu; small groups only (five people or less). [$] *Average main: $23* ✉ *1827 Adams Mill Rd. NW, Adams Morgan* ✥ *Entrance is on Lanier Pl. side of building* ☎ *202/986–9600* 🌐 *www.tailupgoat.com* ⏲ *No lunch* [M] *Woodley Park/Zoo* ✥ *1:F1.*

U STREET CORRIDOR

U Street links Shaw, centered near Howard University's campus, to Adams Morgan, and is known for indie rock clubs, edgy bars, and trendy restaurants. Although the urban hipster vibe is being threatened by skyrocketing rents and the intrusion of chain stores, you'll still find more tattoos and sneakers than pinstripes and pearls here.

$ ✕**Ben's Chili Bowl.** Long before U Street became hip, Ben's was serving
AMERICAN chili: chili on hot dogs, chili on Polish-style sausages, chili on burgers,
FAMILY and just plain chili. The shiny red-vinyl stools give the impression that
Fodor'sChoice little has changed since the 1950s, but don't be fooled—this favorite
★ of former President Obama has rocketed into the 21st century with
an iPhone app and an upscale Southern cuisine restaurant next door.
Known for: legendary half-smoke chili bowls; old-school vibe; South-
ern-style breakfast; cheese fries and milk shakes. $ *Average main: $7*
✉ *1213 U St. NW, U Street* ☎ *202/667–0909* ⊕ *www.benschilibowl.
com* Ⓜ *U St./Cardozo* ✛ *1:H2.*

$$ ✕**Cork.** This rustic, dimly lit wine bar brings chic cuisine to the city's
WINE BAR hippest neighborhood. The wine list features rare varietals—with a
Fodor'sChoice dozen still under $11 per glass, and even teetotalers will find much
★ to love among the menu's classic dishes. **Known for:** more than 50
wines by the glass; tight space means you're close to your fellow
diners; relaxing patio; bourbon pumpkin cheesecake. $ *Average
main: $24* ✉ *1720 14th St. NW, U Street* ☎ *202/265–2675* ⊕ *www.
corkdc.com* ⊘ *No lunch. Brunch on Sun. Closed Mon.* Ⓜ *U St./
Cardozo* ✛ *1:H3.*

$$$ ✕**Doi Moi.** The rise of foodie culture can leave adventurous diners
MODERN ASIAN feeling like they've turned over every culinary stone, but this pilgrim-
age into the southeast Asian unknown will wow even the most jaded
eater. Fried beef marinated in shark sriracha from Thailand and pork
ribs caramelized in a fish sauce from Vietnam are leading lights at
this white-tiled taste of the tropics. **Known for:** adventurous Asian
cuisine spanning several regions; bright and modern interior; special
vegetarian and gluten-free menus. $ *Average main: $27* ✉ *1800 14th
St. NW, U Street* ☎ *202/733–5131* ⊕ *www.doimoidc.com* ⊘ *No lunch*
Ⓜ *U St.* ✛ *1:H3.*

$ ✕**El Camino.** This California-style taco temple and its rockabilly charm
MEXICAN was one of the first reliable, quality restaurants in the Bloomingdale
neighborhood. Slide into a red velvet booth and try the organic local
chicken braised in Oaxacan-style mole or the eponymous burrito.
Known for: cheap à la carte tacos; chilaquiles for brunch; Mezcal cocktails. $ *Average main: $15* ✉ *108 Rhode Island Ave. NW, U Street*
☎ *202/847–0419* ⊕ *elcaminodc.com* ⊘ *No lunch Mon.–Thurs.* ▭ *No
credit cards* Ⓜ *Shaw/Howard U* ✛ *1:H2.*

$$ ✕**Hazel.** Asian-influenced medium-size plates like charcoal-grilled arctic
CHIU CHOW char and roasted cauliflower with cashews have made this Shaw spot
Fodor'sChoice one of the hottest openings in recent years. The zucchini bread (with
★ foie-gras mousse) is a recipe from the chef's grandmother, the restau-
rant's namesake. **Known for:** family-recipe zucchini bread; steak tartare
with egg yolk and tater tots; dim-sum brunch. $ *Average main: $25*
✉ *808 V St. NW, U Street* ☎ *202/847–4980* ⊕ *www.hazelrestaurant.
com* ⊘ *No lunch Mon.–Sat.* Ⓜ *U St./Cardozo* ✛ *1:H2.*

$$ ✕**Izakaya Seki.** Think of other Japanese restaurants in the city like Chi-
JAPANESE potle—and this is like a taste of authentic Tokyo in the District. The
only crowd-pleasing flourishes here are the freshness of the scallop
carpaccio and the perfect sear on the grilled yellowtail jaw, and that's
all adventurous foodies will need to make the most of a quiet evening at

this family-owned, off-the-beaten-path spot marked by little more than a red lantern outside the door. **Known for:** authentic, non-Americanized Japanese cuisine; only 40 seats and no reservations; small, adventurous plates like beef tongue. $ *Average main: $22* ⊠ *1117 V St. NW, Washington* ☎ *202/588–5841* ⊕ *www.sekidc.com* ☉ *Closed Mon. No lunch* Ⓜ *U St./Cardozo* ✛ *1:H2.*

$$$
AMERICAN
Fodor's Choice
★

✕ **Jack Rose Dining Saloon.** With 2,687 bottles of whiskey currently on the wall (your experience may vary), the food sometimes gets overshadowed here. But Southern-inspired dishes like roast marrow and crispy chicken skin bites, grilled quail with foie gras, and mushroom gnocchi make the menu much more than just something to accompany all the booze. **Known for:** small plates of modern Southern cuisine; fun rooftop tiki bar; immense selection of whiskeys. $ *Average main: $27* ⊠ *2007 18th St. NW, U Street* ☎ *202/588–7388* ⊕ *www.jackrosediningsaloon. com* ☉ *Closed Mon.* Ⓜ *U St./Cardozo* ✛ *1:F2.*

$$
GREEK

✕ **Kapnos.** Shareable Greek dishes—either small plates meant for nibbling or larger dishes for the table—are the allure of this happening spot from *Top Chef* alum Mike Isabella. Divided into cold, garden, ocean, and wood-roasted, you'll want to pick a few mezes to sample (suggestions: lamb tartare, falafel, charred octopus, or spiced baby goat). **Known for:** custom Greek meze for sharing; brunch menu with a Mediterranean focus; *Top Chef* alum in the kitchen. $ *Average main: $25* ⊠ *2201 14th St. NW, U Street* ☎ *202/234–5000* ⊕ *www.kapnosdc. com* ☉ *No lunch weekdays* Ⓜ *Shaw/Howard U* ✛ *1:H2.*

$$$
BRASSERIE
Fodor's Choice
★

✕ **Le Diplomate.** A faithful re-creation of the convivial Parisian bistro, the attention to detail makes a night here into more than just a meal. This excellent spot prizes quality above all, from graceful martinis and hand-stuffed cheese ravioli to succulent, textbook-worthy steak frites and roasted chicken. **Known for:** Parisian bistro vibe; juicy steak frites; popular brunch menu. $ *Average main: $30* ⊠ *1610 14th St. NW, U Street* ☎ *202/332–3333* ⊕ *www.lediplomatedc.com* ☉ *No lunch weekdays* ✛ *1:H4.*

$
SOUTHERN

✕ **Oohhs & Aahhs.** No-frills soul food is what you can find at this friendly eat-in/take-out place where the price is right and the food is delicious. Ultrarich macaroni and cheese, succulent baked chicken, and smoky-sweet short ribs just beg to be devoured. **Known for:** home-style soul cooking; mac and cheese, collard greens, and hummingbird cake; late night hours on the weekend. $ *Average main: $15* ⊠ *1005 U St. NW, U Street* ☎ *202/667–7142* ⊕ *www.oohhsnaahhs. com* Ⓜ *U St./Cardozo* ✛ *1:H2.*

$$
SEAFOOD

✕ **Pearl Dive Oyster Palace.** Chef Jeff Black does serve three kinds of po'boys, but that's about as working-class as it gets at this dazzlingly decorated homage to the bivalve. East and West Coast oysters come raw, with perfect dipping sauces—at a two-for-one price during happy hour—or warm in five irresistible guises, from bacon wrapped to crusted in cornmeal and sprinkled with sweet potato hash. **Known for:** three types of po'boys; upscale oysters (both raw and warm); steak options for non-oyster lovers; classy cocktails. $ *Average main: $24* ⊠ *1612 14th St. NW, U Street* ☎ *202/319–1612* ⊕ *www.pearldivedc. com* ☉ *No lunch Mon.–Thurs.* Ⓜ *U St./Cardozo* ✛ *1:H4.*

$$$
AMERICAN
Fodor's Choice
★

✕ **The Red Hen.** The cozy farmhouselike setting helped make the Red Hen a must-try for Italian-influenced takes on American dishes. If the name and giant hen on the facade have you thinking poultry, you'd be right to follow your instincts and order the pan-roasted half chicken with smoky bacon. **Known for:** farmhouse vibe; savvy wine list; pan-roasted half chicken; delicious pasta options. $ *Average main: $28* ✉ *1822 1st St. NW, U Street* ☎ *202/525–3021* ∰ *www.theredhendc.com* ☾ *No lunch* Ⓜ *Shaw/Howard U* ✛ *2:F1.*

$
WINE BAR
Fodor's Choice
★

✕ **Room 11.** You're invited to the coolest house party in the city, where deft hands in a tiny kitchen turn out urbane plates that go down like a designer outfit hidden on the sale rack. From the roasted mushroom risotto at dinner to the perfectly assembled breakfast sandwich on a biscuit for brunch, this small wonder has a dish for every mood. **Known for:** intimate (read: tiny) hip space; brunch-time biscuit sandwich; outdoor patio with heating lamps in winter. $ *Average main: $15* ✉ *3234 11th St. NW, U Street* ☎ *202/332–3234* ∰ *www.room11dc.com* ☾ *No lunch weekdays* Ⓜ *Columbia Heights* ✛ *1:H1.*

$
CAFÉ
Fodor's Choice
★

✕ **Taylor Gourmet.** Sandwiches crafted with attention to detail and fine ingredients are the hallmark of this Philadelphia-inspired classic. Taylor's substitution-friendly staff piles fresh roasted turkey, ham, chicken cutlets, and cold cuts beneath arugula, juicy roasted red peppers, and waves of provolone so finely aged it snaps on the palate. **Known for:** superb deli sandwiches; amazing cheesesteaks; hand-rolled meatballs, house-braised meat, and freshly made sauces. $ *Average main: $10* ✉ *1908 14th St. NW, U Street* ☎ *202/588–7117* ∰ *www.taylorgourmet. com* ▭ *No credit cards* Ⓜ *U St.* ✛ *1:H2.*

$
LAO
FAMILY

✕ **Thip Khao.** Chef Seng Luangrath's legendary Thai destination in suburban Virginia, Bangkok Golden, drew so many curious diners to its Laotian menu that she was inspired to find a home for it in D.C. proper. Now its quirky yet delicious offerings, from grilled banana leaves with red curry (*knap paa*) to grilled pork with lemongrass and ginger (*piing*), fill up diners on U Street. **Known for:** deep menu of authentic Laotian cuisine; minced-meat salads known as laab; bourbon and ginger cider drinks. $ *Average main: $16* ✉ *3462 14th St. NW, Washington* ☎ *202/387–5426* ∰ *thipkhao.com* ☾ *No lunch Mon.* Ⓜ *Columbia Heights* ✛ *2:B1.*

$$
LATIN AMERICAN

✕ **Tico.** One of Boston's celebrity chefs, Michael Schlow, scored prime real estate for this fast-paced parade of small Latin and South American plates with big personalities. The half-dozen seviches add witty touches like pressed watermelon and crispy rice, while the tacos thrill with inventive ingredients from shrimp to duck-skin "cracklings." **Known for:** fun takes on seviche; exciting (and tasty) vegetarian options; very small plates (so ordering several is a must). $ *Average main: $25* ✉ *1926 14th St. NW, U Street* ☎ *202/319–1400* ∰ *www.ticodc.com* ☾ *No lunch* Ⓜ *U St./Cardozo* ✛ *1:H2.*

$$
WINE BAR

✕ **Vinoteca.** This Euro-chic wine bar has one of the best patios in D.C. With a Tuscan vibe and a bocce court to match, the inviting outdoor plaza allows happy-hour revelers and casual diners to nosh on an abbreviated menu of smaller plates from the increasingly impressive kitchen, which turns out delicate house-made ricotta and octopus confit salad to go with a stellar kimchi burger. **Known for:** awesome outdoor dining with a bocce court; kimchi burger; steak and eggs poutine at brunch; huge wine list. [$] *Average main: $23* ✉ *1940 11th St. NW, U Street* ☎ *202/332–9463* 🌐 *www.vinotecadc.com* 🕑 *No lunch weekdays* [M] *U St./Cardozo* ✥ *1:H2.*

UPPER NORTHWEST

After the requisite cooing over the pandas and other cuddly creatures at the National Zoo, consider wandering around this popular neighborhood to observe locals eating, drinking, and playing. Many Hill staffers, journalists, and other inside-the-Beltway types live along this hilly stretch of Connecticut Avenue. Eateries and shops line the few blocks near each of the Red Line Metro stops. Restaurants in Cleveland Park range from tiny takeout spots to upscale restaurants where you stand a good chance of spying your favorite Sunday-morning talk-show guests at a nearby table. Ethnic dining is also abundant here, especially in Cleveland Park. Lined up along the stately stretch of modern row houses are diverse dining options ranging from Afghan to Thai.

$$$ FRENCH 🍴 **Bistrot Lepic.** Relaxed and upbeat, this small, crowded neighborhood bistro is French in every regard—starting with the flirty servers. Traditional bistro fare has been replaced with potato-crusted salmon served with spinach and butternut squash sauce, but some standards, like braised veal cheeks, remain. **Known for:** busy neighborhood bistro; all-French wine list; upstairs wine bar with small plates. [$] *Average main: $29* ✉ *1736 Wisconsin Ave. NW, Glover Park* ☎ *202/333–0111* 🌐 *www.bistrotlepic.com* 🕑 *No lunch weekends* [M] *Foggy Bottom* ✥ *1:A3.*

$$$ SEAFOOD 🍴 **BlackSalt.** Just beyond Georgetown in the residential neighborhood of Palisades, Black Salt is part fish market, part gossipy neighborhood hangout, part swanky restaurant. Fish offerings dominate, and vary from classics like oysters Rockefeller and fried Ipswich clams to more-offbeat fixings like cocoa-spiced big-eye tuna and a butterscotch *pot de crème* for dessert. **Known for:** fresh fish dishes; brioche French toast at one of the best brunches in D.C. [$] *Average main: $33* ✉ *4883 MacArthur Blvd., Upper Northwest* ☎ *202/342–9101* 🌐 *www.blacksaltrestaurant.com* 🕑 *No lunch Mon.–Sat.* ✥ *1:A2.*

$ PIZZA FAMILY 🍴 **Comic Ping Pong.** Pizza (and beer) in the front, Ping-Pong (and foosball) in the back make this pizza joint a neighborhood favorite for folks of all ages. While you can make your own pizza (including one with a gluten-free crust) from almost three dozen toppings, you'll be well served opting for one of the kitchen's specialty pizzas. **Known for:** make-your-own pizzas with dozens of toppings; Ping-Pong and foosball tables; sunrise pizza for brunch; the Yalie clam pizza. [$] *Average main: $12* ✉ *5037 Connecticut Ave. NW, Upper Northwest* ☎ *202/364–0404* 🌐 *www.cometpingpong.com* 🕑 *No lunch Mon.–Thurs.* [M] *Cleveland Park* ✥ *1:D1.*

$$$$ JAPANESE 🍴 **Makoto.** Leave your shoes at the door upon entering this Japanese *omakase* restaurant, where the chef's ever-changing menu showcases modern Japanese cooking. In the past, dishes in these multicourse meals have included tempura soft shell crabs, a pan-seared sea urchin with crispy rice cake, and pork in a cabbage roll. **Known for:** traditional

omakase restaurant; strict reservation policy; always changing, multicourse menus. $ *Average main: $70* ✉ *4822 MacArthur Blvd. NW, Upper Northwest* ☎ *202/298–6866* ⊕ *sakedokoromakoto.com* ⊗ *Closed Sun. and Mon. No lunch* ✛ *1:A2.*

$$$$ ✕ **Range.** Bryan Voltaggio has been a favorite son of area foodies ever
CONTEMPORARY since finishing second to his brother Michael on *Top Chef* in 2009, and this cavernous culinary collage of what he calls "classic and progressive techniques" packs the house with locals almost every night of the week. The open kitchen steps away from the Maryland–D.C. border epitomizes Voltaggio's easy-breezy approach to American standards, from charcuterie and a raw bar to six types of bread baked in-house. **Known for:** wood-grilled meats and wood-oven pizzas; *Top Chef* alum chef; high-end wine list. $ *Average main: $36* ✉ *5335 Wisconsin Ave. NW, Washington* ☎ *202/803–8020* ⊕ *www.voltrange.com* ⊗ *Closed Mon.* Ⓜ *Friendship Heights* ✛ *1:A1.*

$$$ ✕ **Ripple.** "Eat, drink, gather" is the motto of this warm and inventive
CONTEMPORARY tive neighborhood favorite for date nights at any age. Known for its attentive service and fun assortment of cheeses, the kitchen offers locally sourced new American fare in three courses. **Known for:** foie gras truffles; smart wine list; cozy neighborhood spot. $ *Average main: $31* ✉ *3417 Connecticut Ave. NW, Upper Northwest* ☎ *202/244–7995* ⊕ *www.rippledc.com* ⊗ *No lunch* Ⓜ *Cleveland Park* ✛ *1:D1.*

$$ ✕ **2 Amys.** Call it the Brando of D.C. pizzerias, because this Neapolitan
PIZZA sensation has played godfather to a number of throne-stealing wood
FAMILY ovens elsewhere in town since it opened more than a decade ago. Simple
Fodor's Choice recipes allow the ingredients to shine through and make the "wine bar"
★ menu of small Italian plates as exemplary as the pies. **Known for:** authentic Neapolitan wood-fired pizza with a chewy crust; tempting appetizers; pancetta happy hour on Saturday; family-friendly (read: noisy) atmosphere. $ *Average main: $20* ✉ *3715 Macomb St. NW, Upper Northwest* ☎ *202/885–5700* ⊕ *development.ginatolentino.com/2amys* ▭ *No credit cards* ⊗ *No lunch Mon.* Ⓜ *Cleveland Park* ✛ *1:A2.*

ARLINGTON AND NORTHERN VIRGINIA

$$$$ ✕ **Ashby Inn.** If there's a recipe for a perfect country inn restaurant,
AMERICAN chef Tom Whitaker and sommelier Stuart Brennen have it. Head an hour or so west of D.C., and your reward is extraordinary comfort food. **Known for:** intimate country inn dining; views of the Blue Ridge Mountains; prix-fixe menus with local ingredients. $ *Average main: $65* ✉ *692 Federal St., Paris* ☎ *540/592–3900* ⊕ *www.ashbyinn.com* ⊗ *Closed Mon. and Tues.* ✛ *1:A6.*

$$$$ ✕ **Inn at Little Washington.** A 90-minute drive from the District takes you
FRENCH past hills and farms to this English-style country manor, where the ser-
Fodor's Choice vice matches the setting. The three tasting menus come with wine pair-
★ ings, and each menu has a different theme: vegetarian, classic dishes, and contemporary cuisine. **Known for:** themed (and pricey) tasting menus; special occasion dining destination; old English manor vibe. $ *Average main: $218* ✉ *309 Middle St., Washington* ✛ *At Main St.* ☎ *540/675–3800* ⊕ *www.theinnatlittlewashington.com* ⊗ *No lunch* ✛ *2:A6.*

$ ⨉ **Kabob Palace.** The sign out front says parking is reserved for taxis,
PAKISTANI   but it's not so they can pick up passengers; rather so the drivers can
FAMILY   duck into this fast-casual restaurant for the area's top kebabs. Open
Fodor's Choice   24 hours a day, seven days a week, its chicken, lamb, and spicy beef
★   kebabs are cooked to perfection and best dipped in yogurt sauce and
chased with a bite of naan. **Known for:** authentic kebabs; crispy,
chewy naan; open 24/7. $ *Average main: $15* ⊠ *2315 S. Eads St.,
Arlington* ☎ *703/486–3535* ⊕ *www.kabobpalaceusa.com* Ⓜ *Crystal
City* ✛ *1:A6.*

$$$ ⨉ **2941 Restaurant.** Soaring ceilings, a woodsy lakeside location, and a
MODERN   koi pond make this one of the most striking dining rooms in the area.
AMERICAN   The playful cooking continually surprises, with plates like wild boar
Fodor's Choice   cannelloni and shiitake mushrooms, seafood matelote in a mussel
★   broth, and a rich peanut butter baked Alaska. **Known for:** romantic
date-night dining; peanut butter baked Alaska; gorgeous decor. $ *Av-
erage main: $35* ⊠ *2941 Fairview Park Dr., Falls Church* ☎ *703/270–
1500* ⊕ *www.2941.com* ◷ *No lunch Sat. Closed Sun.* ✛ *1:A6.*

WHERE TO EAT
AND STAY IN
WASHINGTON, D.C.

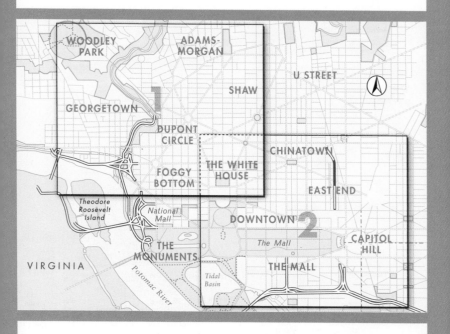

KEY	
□	Hotels
■	Restaurants
■	Restaurant in Hotel
M	Metro Station

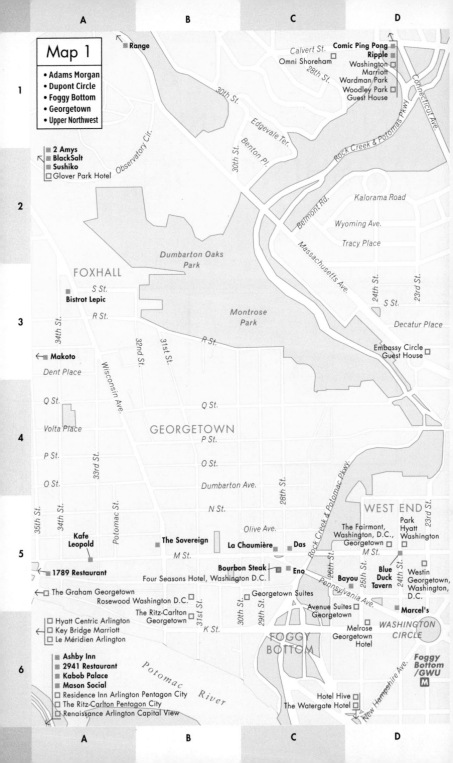

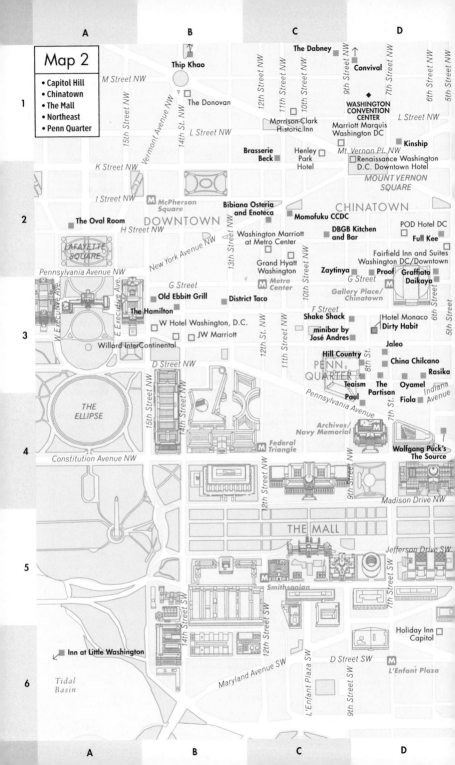

Map 2

- Capitol Hill
- Chinatown
- The Mall
- Northeast
- Penn Quarter

Thip Khao

M Street NW

The Donovan

The Dabney

Convival

L Street NW

WASHINGTON CONVENTION CENTER

Morrison-Clark Historic Inn

Marriott Marquis Washington DC

Kinship

Brasserie Beck

Henley Park Hotel

Renaissance Washington D.C. Downtown Hotel

Mt. Vernon Pl. NW

MOUNT VERNON SQUARE

K Street NW

I Street NW

McPherson Square

Bibiana Osteria and Enoteca

Momofuku CCDC

CHINATOWN

The Oval Room

DOWNTOWN

H Street NW

Washington Marriott at Metro Center

DBGB Kitchen and Bar

POD Hotel DC

Full Kee

New York Avenue NW

Grand Hyatt Washington

Fairfield Inn and Suites Washington DC/Downtown

Zaytinya

Proof

Graffiato

G Street

Metro Center

Daikaya

G Street

Gallery Place/ Chinatown

Old Ebbitt Grill

District Taco

F Street

Shake Shack

Hotel Monaco

The Hamilton

W Hotel Washington, D.C.

minibar by José Andres

Dirty Habit

Willard InterContinental

JW Marriott

JW Marriott

Jaleo

PENN QUARTER

China Chilcano

Rasika

D Street NW

Hill Country

Teaism

The Partisan

Oyamel

Paul

Fiola

Indiana Avenue

Pennsylvania Avenue

THE ELLIPSE

Archives/ Navy Memorial

Federal Triangle

Wolfgang Puck's The Source

Constitution Avenue NW

Madison Drive NW

THE MALL

Jefferson Drive SW

Smithsonian

Holiday Inn Capitol

Inn at Little Washington

D Street SW

L'Enfant Plaza

Tidal Basin

Maryland Avenue SW

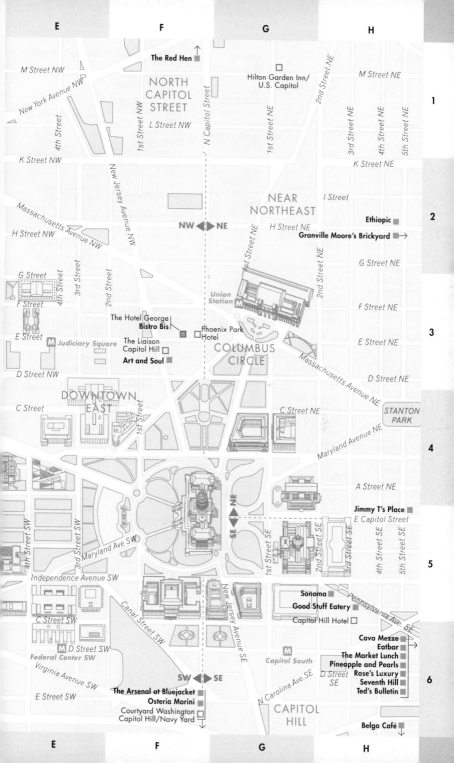

The Red Hen

NORTH CAPITOL STREET

M Street NW
New York Avenue NW
4th Street
1st Street NW
L Street NW
N Capitol Street
K Street NW

Hilton Garden Inn/ U.S. Capitol
M Street NE
1st Street NE
2nd Street NE
3rd Street NE
4th Street NE
5th Street NE
K Street NE

1

NEAR NORTHEAST

Massachusetts Avenue NW
New Jersey Avenue NW
H Street NW
I Street
H Street NE
1st Street NE
2nd Street NE
G Street NE

NW ◄►NE

Ethiopic
Granville Moore's Brickyard ■►

2

G Street
4th Street
3rd Street
2nd Street
F Street
E Street

Judiciary Square

The Hotel George
Bistro Bis
The Liaison Capitol Hill
Art and Soul
D Street NW

Union Station

Phoenix Park Hotel

COLUMBUS CIRCLE

Massachusetts Avenue NE

F Street NE
E Street NE
D Street NE

3

DOWNTOWN EAST

1st Street
C Street

C Street NE

Maryland Avenue NE

STANTON PARK

4

4th Street SW
3rd Street SW

A Street NE

Jimmy T's Place
E Capitol Street

NE ▲ SE

1st Street SE
2nd Street SE
3rd Street SE
4th Street SE
5th Street SE

5

Independence Avenue SW
Maryland Ave SW
Canal Street SW

Sonoma
Good Stuff Eatery
Capitol Hill Hotel

Pennsylvania Ave. SE

C Street SW

D Street SW
Federal Center SW
Virginia Avenue SW
E Street SW

New Jersey Avenue SE

Capitol South

N Carolina Ave. SE

D Street SE

Cava Mezze
Eatbar
The Market Lunch
Pineapple and Pearls
Rose's Luxury
Seventh Hill
Ted's Bulletin

6

SW ◄► SE

The Arsenal at Bluejacket
Osteria Morini
Courtyard Washington Capitol Hill/Navy Yard

CAPITOL HILL

Belga Café

E   F   G   H

Dining

1789 Restaurant, 1:A5
1905, 1:H2
2 Amys, 1:A2
2941 Restaurant, 1:A6
The Arsenal at Blue-jacket, 2:F6
Art and Soul, 2:F3
Ashby Inn, 1:A6
Bayou, 1:D5
Beau Thai, 1:H3
Belga Café, 2:H6
Ben's Chili Bowl, 1:H2
Bibiana Osteria and Enoteca, 2:C2
Bistro Bis, 2:F3
Bistro Français, 1:B5
Bistrot du Coin, 1:E3
Bistrot Lepic, 1:A3
Black Salt, 1:A2
Blue Duck Tavern, 1:D5
Bombay Club, 1:G6
Bourbon Steak, 1:C5
Brasserie Beck, 2:C2
Cava Mezze, 2:H6
Ceiba, 2:B3
China Chilcano, 2:D3
Comic Ping Pong, 1:D1
Convival, 1:D1
Cork, 1:H3
Dabney, 1:C1
Daikaya, 2:D3
Das, 1:C5
DBGB Kitchen & Bar, 2:C2
DGS Delicatessen, 1:F4
District Taco, 2:B3
Doi Moi, 1:H3
Eat Bar, 2:E6
El Camino, 1:H2
Eno, 1:C5
Equinox, 2:A2
Estadio, 1:H4
Ethiopic, 2:H2
Fiola, 2:D4
Full Kee, 2:D2
Good Stuff Eatery, 2:H5
Graffiato, 2:D3

Granville Moore's Brickyard, 2:H2
The Hamilton, 2:B3
Hank's Oyster Bar, 1:G4
Hazel, 1:H2
Hill Country, 2:D3
Inn at Little Washington, 2:A6
Iron Gate, 1:F5
Izakaya Seki, 1:H2
Jack Pase, 1:F2
Jaleo, 2:D3
Jimmy T's Place, 2:H5
Kabob, 1:H2
Kafe Leopold, 1:A5
Kapnos, 1:H2
Kaz Sushi Bistro, 1:F6
Kinship, 2:D1
Komi, 1:G4
Kramerbooks & After-words, 1:F4
La Cahaumière, 1:C5
Lapis, 1:E1
Le Diplomate, 1:H4
Little Serow, 1:G4
Makoto, 1:A2
Marcel's, 1:D6
The Market Lunch, 2:H6
Mason Social, 1:A6
minibar by José Andrés, 2:D3
Mintwood Place, 1:F1
Momofuku CCDC, 2:C2
Nooshi, 1:F5
Nora, 1:E3
Obelisk, 1:E4
Old Ebbitt Grill, 2:B3
Oohhs & Aahhs, 1:H2
Osteria Morini, 2:F6
Oyamel, 2:D3
The Oval Room, 2:A2
The Partisan, 2:D3
Paul, 2:D4
Pearl Dive Oyster Palace, 1:H4
Pineapple and Pearls, 2:H2
Proof, 2:D3
Range, 1:A1

Rasika, 2:D3
Rasika West End, 1:E5
Red Hen, 2:F1
Ripple, 1:D1
Room 11, 1:H1
Rose's Luxury, 2:H6
Sakuramen, 1:F1
Seventh Hill, 2:H6
Shake Shack, Sonoma, 2:H5
The Sovereign, 1:B5
Sushi-Ko, 1:A2
Sweetgreen, 1:E4
Tabard Inn, 1:F5
Tail Up Goat, 1:F1
Taylor Gourmet, 1:H2
Teaism, 2:D4
Ted's Bulletin, 2:H6
Thip Khao, 1:H1
Tico, 1:H2
Vinoteca, 1:H2
Water & Wall, 2:B6
Wolfgang Puck's The Source, 2:D4
Zaytinya, 2:D2

Lodging

Adam's Inn, 1:F1
Akwaaba DC, 1:G3
Avenue Suites George-town, 1:D6
Capital Hilton, 1:G6
Capitol Hill Hotel, 2:H6
Carlyle Dupont, 1:F3
The Churchill Hotel, 1:E3
Comfort Inn Downtown D.C., 1:H5
Courtyard Washington Capitol Hill/Navy Yard, 2:F6
Courtyard Washington, D.C./Dupont Circle, 1:E2
Donovan Hotel, 2:B1
The Dupont Circle Hotel, 1:F4
Embassy Circle Guest House, 1:D3
Embassy Row, 1:E4
Embassy Suites Washington, D.C., 1:E5

The Fairfax at Embassy Row, 1:E4
Fairfield Inn & Suites Washington DC/Down-town, 2:D2
The Fairmont, Washington, D.C., Georgetown, 1:D5
Four Seasons Hotel, Washington, D.C., 1:C5
Georgetown Suites, 1:C5
Glover Park Hotel, 1:A2
The Graham George-town, 1:A5
Grand Hyatt Washington, 2:C2
Hamilton Crowne Plaza, 1:H5
Hay-Adams Hotel, 1:G6
Henley Park Hotel, 2:C2
Hilton Garden Inn/U.S. Capitol, 1:H5
Holiday Inn Capitol, 2:D6
Homewood Suites by Hilton, Washington, 1:H5
The Hotel George, 2:F3
Hotel Hive, 1:D6
Hotel Lombardy, 1:E6
Hotel Madera, 1:E4
Hotel Monaco, 2:D3
Hyatt Centric Arlington, 1:A6
Hyatt Place Georgetown, 1:E5
The Jefferson, 1:G5
JW Marriott, 2:B3
Key Bridge Marriott, 1:A6
Le Méridien Arlington, 1:A6
The Liaison Capitol Hill, 2:F3
Loews Madison Hotel, 1:G5
Mansion on O Street, 1:E4
Marriott Marquis Washington D.C., 2:D1
Mason & Rook, 1:H4
The Mayflower, 1:F5
Melrose Georgetown Hotel, 1:D6

Morrison-Clark Historic Inn, 2:C1
The Normandy Hotel, 1:E2
Omni Shoreham Hotel, 1:C1
Palomar, Washington, D.C., 1:E4
Park Hyatt Washington, 1:D5
Phoenix Park Hotel, 2:F3
POD Hotel DC, 2:D2
The Quincy, 1:F5
Renaissance Arlington Capital View, 1:A6
Renaissance Washington, D.C., Downtown Hotel, 2:D2
Residence Inn Arlington Pentagon City, 1:A6
Residence Inn Washington, D.C./Dupont Circle, 1:E4
The Ritz-Carlton George-town, 1:B6
The Ritz-Carlton Penta-gon City, 1:A6
The Ritz-Carlton Washington, D.C., 1:E5
Rosewood, 1:B5
Rouge Hotel, 1:G4
Sofitel Washington, D.C. Lafayette Square, 1:H6
St. Gregory Luxury Hotel & Suites, 1:E5
The St. Regis Washington, D.C., 1:G6
Swann House, 1:F3
W Washington, D.C., 2:B3
Washington Hilton, 1:E2
Washington Marriott at Metro Center, 2:C2
Washington Marriott Wardman Park, 1:D1
Watergate Hotel, 1:D6
Westin Georgetown, Washington D.C., 1:D5
Willard InterContinental, 2:B3
Woodley Park Guest House, 1:D1

WHERE TO STAY

Updated by
Catherine
·Sharpe

The Capital City's hotel scene befits Washington's image as a world-class destination. With so much variety in lodging, the city has something for everyone, from historic properties to modern designer hotels to urban inns. You can pick your hotel based on the type of experience you set out to have when you arrive.

If you are seeking an experience steeped in pomp and circumstance consider one of the city's grand hotels: the Jefferson, the Hay-Adams, the Fairfax at Embassy Row, the Willard, the Mayflower, or the St. Regis, to name but a few. When you check in at any of these beautifully kept and storied properties, it is near impossible to forget the rich history that defines D.C.

If you prefer a more urban vibe, you have a variety of choices: from Hotel George, Hotel Monaco, the Watergate Hotel, and Topaz Hotel to contemporary inside-the-Beltway gems like the Palomar, Hotel Rouge, the W, and the Dupont Circle.

For a more traditional hotel experience consider checking into a first-rate chain located in strategic locations throughout the city and beyond.

Visitors in search of more intimate lodging may do well to cross the threshold at one of the city's many bed-and-breakfasts. The Swann House and Akwaaba DC offer exceptional, personalized service, art-filled guest rooms, and the pleasure of waking up to a home-cooked morning meal. Over the years, the Embassy Circle Guest House and the Woodley Park Guest House have been welcoming guests time and again for good reason.

PLANNING

RESERVATIONS

With more than 95,000 guest rooms available in the area, you can usually find a place to stay, but it's always prudent to reserve. Hotels fill up with conventioneers, politicians in transit, families, and—in the spring—school groups. Hotel rooms in D.C. can be particularly hard to come by in late March or early April during the Cherry Blossom Festival, and in May, when students at the many local colleges graduate. Late October's Marine Corps Marathon also increases demand for rooms. Never forget that when the time comes to celebrate the presidential inauguration every four years, rooms book up fast and prices increase.

FACILITIES

You can assume that all rooms have private baths, phones, TVs, and air-conditioning, unless otherwise indicated. Breakfast is noted when it is included in the rate, but it's not a typical perk at most Washington hotels, and one feature you may want to consider for a summertime visit is a pool, especially if you're traveling with kids.

WITH KIDS

From the free Smithsonian museums on the Mall to the cuddly pandas at the National Zoo, D.C. is a family-friendly town. Major convention hotels don't always cater to families, so we recommend looking Downtown, in Foggy Bottom, or in Upper Northwest; in the latter, many hotels offer special panda packages for the zoo bound. Also, the closer your hotel is to a Metro stop, the quicker you can get on the sightseeing trail. The Metro itself often ranks as a favorite attraction among the under-12 set. Consider a stay at an all-suites hotel, which will allow you to spread out and, if you prepare your meals in a kitchenette, keep costs down. It also gives the grown-ups the option of staying up past bedtime.

A number of well-known chains, including **Embassy Suites, Fairmont, Four Seasons, Ritz-Carlton,** and **St. Regis** offer special programs or packages for kids and—stars be praised—have babysitting services. **Holiday Inns** allow kids under 12 to eat free in their restaurants and several of the Kimpton properties offer family-friendly rooms complete with bunk beds and child-size bathrobes.

PARKING

Hotel parking fees in the city aren't cheap; daily rates can exceed $50. Street parking is free on Sunday and after 10 pm other nights. There are often far more cars searching than there are spaces available, particularly Downtown, in Georgetown, and in the upper Connecticut Avenue area.

During weekday rush hours, many streets are unavailable for parking; illegally parked cars are towed, and reclaiming a car is expensive and inconvenient. Read signs carefully; some are confusing, and the ticket writers are quick.

PRICES

If you're interested in visiting Washington at a calmer, less expensive time—and if you can stand semitropical weather—come in August, during the congressional recess. Rates also drop in late December and January, except around inaugurations. Weekend, off-season, and special rates, such as AAA and AARP discounts and online-only promotions, can make rooms more affordable. Hotels that cater to government workers and businesspeople, especially properties in the Virginia and Maryland suburbs, offer especially sizable discounts on weekends, even in busy tourist seasons. A little bit of research can pay off in big savings.

WHAT IT COSTS				
	$	$$	$$$	$$$$
FOR TWO PEOPLE	under $210	$210–$295	$296–$400	over $400

Prices are for a standard double room in high season, excluding room tax (14.5% in D.C., 7% in MD, and 6.5% plus one dollar in VA).

HOTEL REVIEWS

Listed alphabetically within neighborhoods. Use the coordinate (✛ 1:B2) at the end of each listing to locate a property on the Where to Eat and Stay map.

Hotel reviews have been shortened. For full information, visit Fodors.com.

THE WHITE HOUSE AREA

With the White House standing like a guard to the city's monumental core, this historic area exudes gravitas and stately visions, even though it also bristles with the same energy as D.C.'s vibrant Downtown. If your interests lie, however, in less commercial pursuits, or if you like to jog or even promenade, then the Mall stretches east and west past memorials and museums and lots of green space.

$$$$
HOTEL
Fodor's Choice
★

Hay-Adams Hotel. Given the elegant charm and refined style, with guest rooms decorated in a class above the rest, it's no wonder this impressive Washington landmark continues to earn international accolades for its guest experience. **Pros:** impeccable service; basically next door to the White House; complimentary bikes, helmets, locks, and cycling maps. **Cons:** expensive parking; no pool. **$** *Rooms from: $450* ⊠ *800 16th St. NW, White House area* ☎ *202/638–6600, 800/424–5054* ⊕ *www.hayadams.com* ▭ *No credit cards* ⇆ *145 rooms* ⦿ *No meals* Ⓜ *McPherson Sq. or Farragut N* ✛ *1:G6.*

$$$
HOTEL
Fodor's Choice
★

Sofitel Washington, D.C. Lafayette Square. Only a minute's walk from the White House, the French luxury chain could not have landed a better location, and its caring, multilingual staff offers a warm welcome and great service. **Pros:** prestigious location; highly rated restaurant; lovely rooms. **Cons:** lobby on the small side; expensive parking. **$** *Rooms from: $360* ⊠ *806 15th St. NW, White House area* ☎ *202/730–8800* ⊕ *www.sofitel.com* ▭ *No credit cards* ⇆ *237 rooms* ⦿ *No meals* Ⓜ *McPherson Sq.* ✛ *1:H6.*

WHERE SHOULD I STAY?

	Neighborhood Vibe	Pros	Cons
The White House Area	Pleasant residential and office area along Pennsylvania Avenue. Stately early-20th-century buildings.	Safe area; close to Downtown's commercial sites and to halls of government, and the Mall.	Parking is always difficult and lots of traffic; older hotels with few budget rates.
Foggy Bottom	Bustling with college students most of the year. Its 18th- and 19th-century homes make for pleasant views.	Safe area; walking distance to Georgetown and the Kennedy Center; good Metro access.	Somewhat removed from other areas of city; paltry dining options.
Capitol Hill and Northeast D.C.	Charming residential blocks of Victorian row houses on Capitol Hill populated by members of Congress and their staffers.	Convenient to Union Station and Capitol. Stylish (if not cheap) hotels. Fine assortment of restaurants and shops.	Some streets iffy at night; parking takes some work; hotels are pricey. Blocks around Capitol and Union Station are chock-full of tourists.
Downtown	A vibrant, bustling, modern mix of commercial and residential properties, packed during the day and rowdy in places at night.	Right in the heart of the Metro system; easy access to the White House. Large selection of hotels, shops, and restaurants.	Crowded; busy; daytime street parking near impossible.
Georgetown	Wealthy neighborhood bordered by the Potomac and a world-class university. Filled with students, upscale shops, and eateries.	Safe area. Historic charm on every tree-lined street. Wonderful walking paths along river.	Crowded; no nearby Metro access; lots of traffic. Almost no parking. Lodging options tend to be expensive.
Dupont Circle and Logan Circle	Cosmopolitan, lively neighborhood filled with bars and restaurants; beautiful city sights.	Plenty of modern hotels; easy Metro access; good selection of bars and restaurants.	Few budget hotel options; very limited street parking; crowded in summer months.
Adams Morgan	The center of late-night activity; eclectic and down-to-earth; languages galore.	Fabulous selection of ethnic bars and restaurants; vibrant, hip nightlife.	Few lodging options; 10-minute walk to Metro; very hard to park.
Upper Northwest	A pleasant residential neighborhood with a lively strip of good restaurants.	Safe, quiet; easy walk to zoo, Metro, restaurants; street parking easier than Downtown.	A long ride to attractions other than the zoo; feels like an inner suburb. Few new hotels.

$$$$ **W Washington, D.C.** It's hip, sleek, very cool, and just steps from the
HOTEL   White House. **Pros:** trendy ambience; individualized and attentive ser-
Fodor'sChoice   vice; popular rooftop bar. **Cons:** pricey; might be too modern for some;
★   no pool. $ *Rooms from: $599* ⊠ *515 15th St. NW, White House area*
☎ *202/661–2400* ⊕ *www.starwoodhotels.com/whotels* 🛏 *349 rooms*
🍴 *No meals* Ⓜ *McPherson Sq.* ✛ *2:B3.*

$$$
HOTEL
FAMILY
Fodor's Choice
★

Willard InterContinental. Favored by American presidents and other news makers, this Washington landmark offers superb service, a wealth of amenities, and guest rooms filled with period detail and Federal-style furniture. **Pros:** lots of history; great location two blocks from the White House; impeccable service. **Cons:** expensive valet parking; no pool. *§ Rooms from: $399 ⊠ 1401 Pennsylvania Ave. NW, White House area ☎ 202/628–9100, 800/827–1747 ⊕ www.washington.intercontinental. com ⇨ 376 rooms ⊙ No meals M Metro Center ✦ 2:B3.*

FOGGY BOTTOM

With the Kennedy Center for the Performing Arts anchoring its southwestern side and the George Washington University campus to the north, this D.C. community is hopping with youth, even though most of its residents are longtime Washingtonians and most of its homes hearken back to the 18th and 19th centuries. Additionally, nothing beats the early-morning views of the Potomac River, where sculls and shells race along the surface as crews prepare for upcoming races.

$$$
HOTEL
FAMILY

Avenue Suites Georgetown. Luxurious and practical at the same time, this is a great choice for families and groups because all the suites have separate bedrooms and full kitchens, and some have views of the city and the Potomac River. **Pros:** service oriented; complimentary Saturday-morning yoga; "Stock the Fridge" service with Trader Joe's. **Cons:** a long walk away from the Mall (but close to Georgetown); expensive valet parking. *§ Rooms from: $296 ⊠ 2500 Pennsylvania Ave. NW, Foggy Bottom ☎ 202/333–8060 ⊕ www.avenuesuites.com ⇨ 124 rooms ⊙ No meals M GWU/Foggy Bottom ✦ 1:D6.*

$$$
HOTEL
FAMILY

Embassy Suites Washington, D.C. All accommodations at this convenient hotel within walking distance of Georgetown and Dupont Circle have a living room and bedroom and surround an atrium filled with comfortable seating areas and the hotel's dining options. **Pros:** family-friendly; reception with complimentary drinks and apps every night; pool to keep the little ones—and sweaty tourists—happy. **Cons:** museums not in walking distance; four blocks from Metro; expensive parking (not valet). *§ Rooms from: $319 ⊠ 1250 22nd St. NW, Foggy Bottom ☎ 202/857–3388, 800/362–2779 ⊕ www.embassysuites.com ⇨ 318 rooms ⊙ Breakfast M Foggy Bottom/GWU or Dupont Circle ✦ 1:E5.*

$$$
HOTEL
Fodor's Choice
★

The Fairmont, Washington, D.C., Georgetown. Great for exploring Georgetown, this hotel centers on an elegant central courtyard and gardens, overlooked by the large glassed-in lobby and about a third of the bright, spacious rooms. **Pros:** fitness fanatics will love the gym and 50-foot indoor pool; great no-charge pet program includes homemade treats for dog; tasty food options on-site. **Cons:** expensive parking; far from most major attractions. *§ Rooms from: $309 ⊠ 2401 M St. NW, Foggy Bottom ☎ 202/429–2400, 866/540–4505 ⊕ www.fairmont.com ⇨ 445 rooms ⊙ No meals M Foggy Bottom/GWU ✦ 1:D5.*

$$
HOTEL

Hotel Hive. Hip and trendy, D.C.'s first microhotel is designed for travelers who care more about exploring and socializing than spending a lot of time in their room. **Pros:** great prices; on-site restaurant offers all-day dining; plenty of amenities like free Wi-Fi, Bluetooth music, and individual thermostats. **Cons:** pod concept not for everyone; rooms on lower floors are noisy; very, very small rooms. $ *Rooms from: $239* ✉ *2224 F St. NW, Foggy Bottom* ☏ *202/849–8499* ⊕ *www.hotelhive. com* ➥ *83 rooms* ⦿ *No meals* ✛ *1:D6.*

$$$
HOTEL

🛏 **Hotel Lombardy.** This romantic spot, three blocks from the White House and Metro, is ideal for couples seeking a peaceful retreat. **Pros:** homey rooms; beautiful lounge; complimentary Wi-Fi. **Cons:** old-fashioned decor; expensive valet parking; on busy street. $ *Rooms from: $300* ✉ *2019 Pennsylvania Ave. NW, Foggy Bottom* ☏ *202/828–2600* ⊕ *www.hotellombardy.com* ➥ *161 rooms* ⦿ *No meals* Ⓜ *Foggy Bottom/GWU* ✛ *1:E6.*

$$$
HOTEL

🛏 **Hyatt Place Washington DC/Georgetown/West End.** Families and business travelers will appreciate this modern hotel conveniently located in the West End neighborhood just a few blocks from the Foggy Bottom Metro. **Pros:** complimentary daily breakfast buffet; fitness center and heated indoor pool; free Wi-Fi. **Cons:** decor is not very distinctive; expensive valet parking. $ *Rooms from: $382* ✉ *2121 M St. NW, Foggy Bottom* ☏ *202/838–2222* ⊕ *www.washingtondcgeorgetown. place.hyatt.com* ➥ *168 rooms* ⦿ *Breakfast* Ⓜ *Foggy Bottom* ✛ *1:E5.*

$$$$
HOTEL
FAMILY
Fodor's Choice
★

🛏 **Park Hyatt Washington.** Understated elegance and refined service can be found at this soothing city getaway, where the guest rooms are a minimalist tribute to the American experience and feature walnut floors, hard-covered books, and folk-art accent pieces. **Pros:** spacious and luxurious rooms; in-house restaurant one of the best in the city; beautiful indoor saltwater pool. **Cons:** expensive valet parking; 10-minute walk to Foggy Bottom Metro. $ *Rooms from: $629* ✉ *1201 24th St. NW, Foggy Bottom* ☏ *202/789–1234* ⊕ *www.washingtondc.park.hyatt.com* ➥ *216 rooms* ⦿ *No meals* Ⓜ *Foggy Bottom* ✛ *1:D5.*

$$$$
HOTEL
Fodor's Choice
★

🛏 **The Ritz-Carlton Washington, D.C.** Luxury oozes from every polished marble surface at one of Washington's most upscale hostelries, and personalized service makes you feel pampered. **Pros:** attentive service; convenient to several parts of town; attached to fabulous health club, spa, and pool. **Cons:** pricey room rates especially during peak times; expensive valet parking. $ *Rooms from: $430* ✉ *1150 22nd St. NW, Foggy Bottom* ☏ *202/835–0500, 800/241–3333* ⊕ *www.ritzcarlton. com* ➥ *299 rooms* ⦿ *No meals* Ⓜ *Foggy Bottom/GWU* ✛ *1:E5.*

$$
HOTEL

🛏 **St. Gregory Hotel & Suites.** This sophisticated and very chic boutique hotel offers the ideal accommodations for business and leisure travelers, thanks to the rooms that feature fully stocked kitchens and sofa beds. **Pros:** big rooms; central location near business district of K Street; 24-hour fitness center. **Cons:** far from museums; expensive valet parking; area is quiet at night. $ *Rooms from: $269* ✉ *2033 M St. NW, Foggy Bottom* ☏ *202/530–3600, 800/829–5034* ⊕ *www. stgregoryhotelwdc.com* ➥ *155 rooms* ⦿ *No meals* Ⓜ *Foggy Bottom or Farragut N* ✛ *1:E5.*

$$$$
HOTEL
Fodor's Choice
★

🛏 **The Watergate Hotel.** Beautifully situated along the Potomac River, the legendary Watergate simply oozes sophistication and glamour after an extensive renovation, embracing its infamous past while at the same time celebrating its midcentury modernism. **Pros:** beautiful mosaic-tiled saltwater pool; fun, cheeky historical touches; close to Foggy Bottom

Metro; gorgeously designed bars and restaurant with excellent menus. **Cons:** some rooms are small; elevators are a bit complicated to use; 1960s style not for everyone. [$] *Rooms from: $450* ✉ *2650 Virginia Ave. NW, Foggy Bottom* ☎ *202/827–1600* 🌐 *www.thewatergatehotel.com* 🛏 *336 rooms* 🍴 *No meals* [M] *Foggy Bottom/GWU* ✣ 1:D6.

$$$ HOTEL FAMILY 🏨 **Westin Georgetown, Washington D.C.** Although not truly in Georgetown (but it's nearby), this Westin is in a busy West End location. **Pros:** quiet neighborhood; comfortable rooms; outdoor pool open seasonally. **Cons:** 10-minute walk to Metro; a bit out of the way for sightseeing; expensive parking. [$] *Rooms from: $400* ✉ *2350 M St. NW, Foggy Bottom* ☎ *202/429–0100* 🌐 *www.westingeorgetown.com* 🛏 *267 rooms, 6 suites* 🍴 *No meals* [M] *Foggy Bottom* ✣ 1:D5.

CAPITOL HILL AND NORTHEAST D.C.

To be sure, politics and commerce, like oil and water, don't mix, but they sure make a great neighborhood. With the dome of the Capitol hovering above and the bustle of Eastern Market teeming below, this District neighborhood is guaranteed to keep you entertained. Plus, Folger Shakespeare is but a walk away from the dome. If that's not enough, then head north for an edgy evening along the H Street Corridor with its bars and Atlas Performing Arts Center.

$$$ HOTEL FAMILY 🏨 **Capitol Hill Hotel.** A great choice if you want to stay on the Hill and need some extra room to spread out: all Federalist-chic-style units are suites, with kitchenettes, large work desks, flat-screen TVs, and spacious closets. **Pros:** close to Metro; complimentary bikes, helmets, and locks; eco-friendly. **Cons:** expensive valet parking; hotel is spread out in two buildings, which can be inconvenient. [$] *Rooms from: $350* ✉ *200 C St. SE, Capitol Hill* ☎ *202/543–6000* 🌐 *www.capitolhillhotel-dc.com* 🛏 *153 suites* 🍴 *Breakfast* [M] *Capitol S* ✣ 2:H6.

$ HOTEL 🏨 **Courtyard Washington Capitol Hill/Navy Yard.** Located just a block from a Metro station and within walking distance to Nationals Park, this is a smart choice for budget-savvy travelers. **Pros:** good value; popular bar; fitness center and heated indoor pool. **Cons:** popular with groups, so some nights may be noisy; neighborhood construction; parking in nearby garage is expensive. [$] *Rooms from: $200* ✉ *140 L St. SE, Navy Yard, D.C. Waterfront* ☎ *202/479–0027* 🌐 *www.marriott.com/hotels/travel/wasny-courtyard-washington-capitol-hill-navy-yard* 🛏 *104 rooms* 🍴 *No meals* [M] *Navy Yard* ✣ 2:F6.

$$$ HOTEL 🏨 **Hilton Garden Inn/U.S. Capitol.** Just a block away from a Metro stop, this hotel is convenient for getting around the city. **Pros:** great views; indoor pool; free Wi-Fi and printing. **Cons:** can be noisy at night; not in the center of town; no self-parking, and valet parking is pricey. [$] *Rooms from: $340* ✉ *1225 1st St. NE, Capitol Hill* ☎ *202/408–4870* 🌐 *www.hiltongardeninn.com* 🛏 *204 rooms* 🍴 *No meals* [M] *Noma/Gallaudet U/New York Ave.* ✣ 2:G1.

$ HOTEL FAMILY 🏨 **Holiday Inn Capitol.** One block from the National Air and Space Museum, this family-friendly hotel is in a great location for those bound for the Smithsonian museums, and, with Old Towne Trolley Tours stopping here, getting around town is a snap. **Pros:** rooftop pool and large deck area; kids stay (and eat) for free. **Cons:** limited dining options nearby; not much going on in the neighborhood at night. [$] *Rooms from: $200* ✉ *550 C St. SW, Capitol Hill* ☎ *202/479–4000* 🌐 *www.hicapitoldc.com* 🛏 *542 rooms* 🍴 *No meals* [M] *L'Enfant Plaza* ✛ 2:D6.

$$$ HOTEL Fodor's Choice ★ 🏨 **The Hotel George.** We cannot tell a lie—D.C.'s first contemporary boutique hotel is still one of its best, and the public areas and stylishly soothing guest quarters still excel at providing a fun and funky alternative to cookie-cutter chains. **Pros:** close to Union Station; complimentary wine hour nightly; popular in-house restaurant. **Cons:** small closets; some reports of street noise; ultramodern feel not everyone's cup of tea. [$] *Rooms from: $329* ✉ *15 E St. NW, Capitol Hill* ☎ *202/347–4200, 800/576–8331* 🌐 *www.hotelgeorge.com* 🛏 *140 rooms* 🍴 *No meals* [M] *Union Station* ✛ 2:F3.

4

$$$ HOTEL 🏨 **The Liaison Capitol Hill.** If the city's most stately buildings weren't steps away, you could easily think you had checked into a sleek Manhattan hotel, with a trendy buzz and guest rooms defined by modern chic. **Pros:** fantastic rooftop pool and deck open seasonally; pet friendly; 24-hour fitness center. **Cons:** can be noisy; no great room views; expensive parking. [$] *Rooms from: $319* ✉ *415 New Jersey Ave. NW, Capitol Hill* ☎ *202/638–1616, 888/513–7445* 🌐 *www.jdvhotels.com/hotels/washington-dc/washington-dc-hotels/the-liaison-capitol-hill-dc* 🛏 *340 rooms* 🍴 *No meals* [M] *Union Station* ✛ 2:F3.

$$$ HOTEL 🏨 **Phoenix Park Hotel.** If you prefer to be near the Hill but not in a convention hotel, the small but beautifully appointed and comfortable guest rooms in this European-style inn across the street from Union Station may fit the bill. **Pros:** comfy beds with good linens; friendly service; free Wi-Fi. **Cons:** no swimming pool; small rooms; some rooms are noisy. [$] *Rooms from: $299* ✉ *520 N. Capitol St. NW, Capitol Hill* ☎ *202/638–6900, 855/371–6824* 🌐 *www.phoenixparkhotel.com* 🛏 *149 rooms* 🍴 *No meals* [M] *Union Station* ✛ 2:F3.

DOWNTOWN

For those who have not visited Washington for a decade or so, throw away your expectations. Downtown rocks with energy and excitement. Whether you want theater—from the latest musical to the hardest-hitting drama—clubs, restaurants, or museums, this revitalized D.C. neighborhood, with its proximity to the Mall, is the place to settle in for your stay.

$$$ HOTEL 🏨 **Capital Hilton.** The choice of many celebrities and dignitaries since it opened in 1943, the Hilton has modern perks like a health club and spa and is well located for shopping and eating out. **Pros:** nice guest rooms; desirable location; great gym, however, there's a daily fee unless you're a silver, gold, or diamond Hilton Honors member. **Cons:** expensive valet parking; reports of street noise; fee for Wi-Fi. [$] *Rooms from: $400* ✉ *1001 16th St. NW, Downtown* ☎ *202/393–1000* 🌐 *www.capital.hilton.com* 🛏 *576 rooms* 🍴 *No meals* [M] *Farragut N* ✛ 1:G6.

$$$ HOTEL 🏨 **Comfort Inn Downtown D.C/Convention Center.** There's nothing fancy at this hotel and rooms tend to be on the small side, but the location, price, and daily hot breakfast buffet all add up to a good value. **Pros:** fresh afternoon cookies and popcorn and all-day coffee/tea; pleasant

staff; excellent hot breakfast. **Cons:** some street noise at night; a bit out of the way; valet parking is $30/day. [$] *Rooms from: $339* ✉ *1201 13th St. NW, Downtown* ☎ *202/682–5300* 🌐 *www.dcdowntownhotel.com* 🛏 *100 rooms* 🍴 *Breakfast* [M] *Mt. Vernon Sq. 7th St.* ✥ 1:H5.

$$$ HOTEL 🏨 **The Donovan.** You won't find anything remotely close to a colonial reproduction at this Kimpton property amid the leather canopy beds, slick furniture, and spiral showers—perfect if you're seeking an out-of-the-box-style lodging. **Pros:** evening wine hour; hip rooftop pool; close to the White House. **Cons:** smallish rooms; 10-minute walk to Metro. [$] *Rooms from: $380* ✉ *1155 14th St. NW, Downtown* ☎ *202/737–1200, 888/550–0012* 🌐 *www.donovanhoteldc.com* 🛏 *210 rooms* 🍴 *No meals* [M] *McPherson Sq.* ✥ 2:B1.

$$$ HOTEL 🏨 **Grand Hyatt Washington.** A city within the city is what greets you as you step inside the Hyatt's doors and gaze upward to the balconies overlooking the blue lagoon and the many conveniences within the atrium. **Pros:** great location for sightseeing and shopping; often has weekend deals; nice gym and indoor pool. **Cons:** often filled with conventioneers; chain-hotel feel. [$] *Rooms from: $319* ✉ *1000 H St. NW, Downtown* ☎ *202/582–1234, 800/233–1234* 🌐 *www.grandwashington.hyatt.com* 🛏 *897 rooms* 🍴 *No meals* [M] *Metro Center* ✥ 2:C2.

$$$$ HOTEL 🏨 **Hamilton Crowne Plaza.** A short walk from the White House and the Mall, this appealing art-deco hotel, on the National Register of Historic Places, is a good choice for visitors doing the sights, as well as business guests who come for top-notch meeting rooms and the nearby Convention Center. **Pros:** central location near White House; well-equipped fitness center; personal service. **Cons:** some street noise; small rooms; expensive valet parking. [$] *Rooms from: $440* ✉ *1001 14th St. NW, Downtown* ☎ *202/682–0111* 🌐 *www.hamiltonhoteldc.com* 🛏 *318 rooms* 🍴 *No meals* [M] *McPherson Sq.* ✥ 1:H5.

$$ HOTEL 🏨 **Henley Park Hotel.** A Tudor-style building adorned with gargoyles, this National Historic Trust property has the cozy feel of an English country house, and the atmosphere extends to charming rooms that were once the choice of senators and notables from Washington society. **Pros:** centrally located; historic building; welcoming staff. **Cons:** some rooms are small with very tiny bathrooms; rooms can be noisy and not all have views; expensive valet parking. [$] *Rooms from: $250* ✉ *926 Massachusetts Ave. NW, Downtown* ☎ *202/638–5200, 800/222–8474* 🌐 *www.henleypark.com* 🛏 *96 rooms* 🍴 *No meals* [M] *Mt. Vernon Sq.* ✥ 2:C2.

$$$ HOTEL Fodor's Choice ★ 🏨 **Hotel Monaco.** Elegance and whimsy are in perfect harmony at this popular boutique Kimpton hotel—Washington's first all-marble building—in the heart of the Penn Quarter. **Pros:** near great restaurants and shops; all the Kimpton extras like a nightly wine hour; amazing design throughout; historic charm. **Cons:** noisy part of town; no pool; expensive valet parking. [$] *Rooms from: $380* ✉ *700 F St. NW, Downtown* ☎ *202/628–7177, 800/649–1202* 🌐 *www.monaco-dc.com* 🛏 *183 rooms* 🍴 *No meals* [M] *Gallery Pl./Chinatown* ✥ 2:D3.

$$$$ HOTEL Fodor's Choice ★ 🏨 **The Jefferson.** Every inch of this 1923 beaux arts landmark exudes refined elegance, from the intimate seating areas that take the place of a traditional check-in counter to the delicate blooms and glass atrium at the entryway to Plume, the fine-dining restaurant. **Pros:** exquisite historic

hotel; impeccable service; prestigious location; adorable dog mascot to greet you. **Cons:** expensive; some rooms have views of other buildings. $ *Rooms from: $600* ✉ *1200 16th St. NW, Downtown* ☎ *202/448–2300* ⊕ *www.jeffersondc.com* ↩ *119 rooms* ⏍ *No meals* Ⓜ *Farragut N* ✛ *1:G5.*

$$$$
HOTEL
🖼 **JW Marriott.** From the location near the White House to the views from the top floors, it's hard to forget you are in the nation's capital when you stay in one of the beautifully furnished rooms here. **Pros:** in the heart of town; lovely rooms with a luxurious, traditional feel; good views from top floors; great restaurants within walking distance. **Cons:** very busy; charge for in-room Wi-Fi; pricey in-house restaurants. $ *Rooms from: $449* ✉ *1331 Pennsylvania Ave. NW, Downtown* ☎ *202/393–2000, 800/393–2503* ⊕ *www.jwmarriottdc.com* ↩ *772 rooms* ⏍ *No meals* Ⓜ *Metro Center* ✛ *2:B3.*

$$$$
HOTEL
🖼 **Loews Madison Hotel.** The signatures of presidents, prime ministers, sultans, and kings fill the guest register at this classic Washington address, noted for polite service and stylish comfort. **Pros:** central location; pretty guest rooms with plush furnishings and linens; great restaurant. **Cons:** 20-minute walk from the Mall; many rooms are a bit dark with no views. $ *Rooms from: $469* ✉ *1177 15th St. NW, Downtown* ☎ *202/862–1600, 800/424–8577* ⊕ *www.loewshotels.com/madison/* ↩ *356 rooms* ⏍ *No meals* Ⓜ *McPherson Sq.* ✛ *1:G5.*

$$$
HOTEL
🖼 **Marriott Marquis Washington, D.C.** This eco-friendly hotel, directly adjacent to the Washington Convention Center, spans an entire city block, and is capped with an enormous atrium skylight that accentuates the dramatic lobby sculpture. **Pros:** location near Metro; nicely designed building; within walking distance of great restaurants. **Cons:** rooms overlooking atrium can be noisy; fee for in-room Wi-Fi. $ *Rooms from: $389* ✉ *901 Massachusetts Ave. NW, Downtown* ☎ *202/824–9200* ⊕ *www.marriott.com* ↩ *1,224 rooms* ⏍ *No meals* Ⓜ *Mt. Vernon Sq./7th St.-Convention Center* ✛ *2:C1.*

$$$
HOTEL
FAMILY
Fodor's Choice
★
🖼 **The Mayflower Hotel, Autograph Collection.** With its magnificent block-long lobby filled with antique crystal chandeliers, layers of gold trim, and gilded columns, there's little wonder that this luxurious landmark has hosted presidential balls since its opening in 1925, as well as historic news conferences and even, for a short time, the Chinese Embassy. **Pros:** historic 1925 building; near dozens of restaurants; a few steps from Metro; the setting of plenty of political history and scandal. **Cons:** rooms vary greatly in size; expensive parking and pet fees; charge for in-room Wi-Fi unless you're a Marriott rewards member. $ *Rooms from: $370* ✉ *1127 Connecticut Ave. NW, Downtown* ☎ *202/347–3000, 800/228–7697* ⊕ *www.marriott.com/hotels/travel/wasak-the-mayflower-hotel-autograph-collection* ↩ *731 rooms* ⏍ *No meals* Ⓜ *Farragut N* ✛ *1:F5.*

$$
HOTEL
Fodor's Choice
★
🖼 **Morrison-Clark Historic Inn.** A fascinating history makes these beautiful 1864 Victorian town houses an interesting as well as a comfortable and well-located choice. **Pros:** charming alternative to cookie-cutter hotels; historic feel throughout; near Convention Center. **Cons:** some street noise; room size and style vary considerably. $ *Rooms from: $249* ✉ *1015 L St. NW, Downtown* ☎ *202/898–1200, 800/332–7898* ⊕ *www.morrison-clark.com* ↩ *114 rooms* ⏍ *No meals* Ⓜ *Metro Center* ✛ *2:C1.*

$$$$ HOTEL 🏨 **The St. Regis Washington, D.C.** Just two blocks from the White House, this gorgeous 1926 Italian Renaissance–style landmark attracts a business and diplomatic crowd. **Pros:** close to White House; historic property; exceptional service. **Cons:** most rooms don't have great views; very expensive; some rooms noisy and in need of upgrading. [$] *Rooms from: $625* ✉ *923 16th St. NW, Downtown* ☎ *202/638–2626* 🌐 *www.stregiswashingtondc.com* 🛏 *172 rooms* 🍴 *No meals* [M] *Farragut N or McPherson Sq.* ✥ 1:G6.

$$$ HOTEL 🏨 **Washington Marriott at Metro Center.** The big-chain feel is offset by a good location just steps away from the monuments and museums; attractive, comfortable guest rooms; and an indoor pool and health club. **Pros:** great location; Starbucks on property with outdoor patio. **Cons:** generic decor; charge for in-room Wi-Fi. [$] *Rooms from: $379* ✉ *775 12th St. NW, Downtown* ☎ *202/737–2200, 800/393–2100* 🌐 *www.marriott.com/wasmc* 🛏 *459 rooms* 🍴 *No meals* [M] *Metro Center* ✥ 2:C2.

CHINATOWN

This is by far one of D.C.'s most vibrant commercial neighborhoods, with a seemingly endless variety of local and national chains offering not only the best in Asian cuisine but also African, Mediterranean, and pub food. The Verizon Center offers visitors an array of entertainment, and the nationally recognized Shakespeare Theatre Company presents audiences with the best in classical fare.

$$$ HOTEL 🏨 **Fairfield Inn & Suites Washington DC/Downtown.** Bold, contemporary design provides a soothing retreat in a busy part of town, near many of the top attractions like the Verizon Center, the National Portrait Gallery, and the Mall. **Pros:** complimentary hot breakfast buffet; lots of restaurants, entertainment, and attractions nearby; authentic Irish pub on-site. **Cons:** some complaints about street noise; small gym; part of town not for everyone. [$] *Rooms from: $339* ✉ *500 H St. NW, Chinatown* ☎ *202/289–5959* 🌐 *www.marriott.com* 🛏 *198 rooms* 🍴 *No meals* [M] *Gallery Pl./Chinatown* ✥ 2:D2.

$$ HOTEL 🏨 **POD Hotel DC.** If you're the type of traveler who doesn't spend a lot of time in your room because you'd rather be actually seeing the city, check out Pod Hotel in the Penn Quarter area of the city. **Pros:** affordable for this part of the city; on-site restaurant and rooftop lounge. **Cons:** very small rooms, but that's the point; not many amenities. [$] *Rooms from: $249* ✉ *627 H St. NW, Chinatown* ☎ *202/847–4444* 🌐 *www.thepodhotel.com* 🛏 *245 rooms* 🍴 *No meals* [M] *Gallery Pl./Chinatown* ✥ 2:D2.

$$$ HOTEL 🏨 **Renaissance Washington, D.C. Downtown Hotel.** Large rooms with views, extensive business services, such touches as fine linens, and a lavish fitness center and spa elevate this chain hotel into the luxury realm. **Pros:** convenient to Convention Center; near Metro; nice lobby and rooftop terrace; great fitness center and spa. **Cons:** convention crowds; chain-hotel feel; expensive parking. [$] *Rooms from: $379* ✉ *999 9th St. NW, Chinatown* ☎ *202/898–9000, 800/228–9898* 🌐 *www.marriott.com* 🛏 *794 rooms, 13 suites* 🍴 *No meals* [M] *Gallery Pl./Chinatown* ✥ 2:D2.

GEORGETOWN

Even to other native Washingtonians, this high-end neighborhood—home to Washington's elite—is a tourist destination in itself. Historic homes on quiet streets with plenty of trees and a canal make this area ideal for strolling. M Street and Wisconsin Avenue restaurants and shops also make it the hottest spot in town for those with money to burn. Georgetown University students keep this area bustling into the early hours.

$$$$ HOTEL FAMILY Fodor's Choice ★ **Four Seasons Hotel, Washington, D.C.** An army of valets, doormen, and bellhops, plus a wealth of amenities, make one of Washington's leading hotels a favorite with celebrities, hotel connoisseurs, and families. **Pros:** edge of Georgetown makes for a fabulous location; lap-of-luxury feel; impeccable service; excellent fitness center and spa; gorgeous saltwater lap pool. **Cons:** astronomically expensive; challenging street parking; far from Metro. [$] *Rooms from: $795* ✉ *2800 Pennsylvania Ave. NW, Georgetown* ☎ *202/342–0444, 800/332–3442* 🌐 *www.fourseasons.com/washington* 🛏 *164 rooms, 58 suites* 🍴 *No meals* [M] *Foggy Bottom* ✥ 1:C5.

$$$ HOTEL FAMILY **Georgetown Suites.** If you're looking for plenty of space in a top location, these suites vary in size, but all come with fully equipped kitchens and separate sitting rooms, and offer a welcome break from standard hotel rooms. **Pros:** spacious suites; good choice for a family that wants to spread out; laundry facilities; lobby and most rooms have recently been renovated. **Cons:** limited underground garage parking is $35/night; no pool. [$] *Rooms from: $355* ✉ *1111 30th St. NW, Georgetown* ☎ *202/298–7800, 800/348–7203* 🌐 *www.georgetownsuites.com* 🛏 *221 suites* 🍴 *Breakfast* [M] *Foggy Bottom/GWU* ✥ 1:C5.

$$$ HOTEL **The Graham Georgetown.** Alexander Graham Bell, the inventor who once lived in Georgetown, would be honored to lend his name to this stylish property with panoramic views of the Kennedy Center, Washington Monument, and Rosslyn skyline. **Pros:** great Georgetown location; quiet and extremely attractive surroundings; nice water and city views; free Wi-Fi; business center open 24 hours and provides free wireless printing. **Cons:** expensive parking; no pool; small fitness room. [$] *Rooms from: $389* ✉ *1075 Thomas Jefferson St. NW, Georgetown* ☎ *855/341–1292* 🌐 *www.thegrahamgeorgetown.com* 🛏 *27 rooms, 30 suites* 🍴 *No meals* [M] *Foggy Bottom/GWU* ✥ 1:A5.

$$$ HOTEL FAMILY **Melrose Georgetown Hotel.** Gracious, traditional rooms done in a soothing palette of creams and grays with splashes of green, blue, and red all have oversize bathrooms, and many have pullout sofa beds, making this boutique hotel a good choice for families. **Pros:** good alternative to chain hotels; nice fitness center; location; walk to dining and shopping; in-room mini-refrigerators. **Cons:** street noise; no pool; expensive valet parking; fee for in-room Wi-Fi. [$] *Rooms from: $349* ✉ *2430 Pennsylvania Ave. NW, Georgetown* ☎ *202/955–6400, 800/635–7673* 🌐 *www.melrosehoteldc.com* 🛏 *203 rooms, 37 suites* 🍴 *No meals* [M] *Foggy Bottom* ✥ 1:D6.

$$$$ HOTEL Fodor's Choice ★ **The Ritz-Carlton Georgetown.** Once an incinerator dating from the 1920s, this building still topped with a smokestack might seem the most unlikely of places for upscale lodgings, but settle into one of the large and chicly designed guest rooms (upper-level suites overlook the river) and you'll agree the concept works. **Pros:** quiet; steps away from

HOT HOTEL BARS AND LOUNGES

Some of the most iconic examples of power bars, where inside-the-Beltway decision makers talk shop and rub elbows, are housed in many of this town's historic hotels. So grab a snifter of single malt and begin your people-watching at these classic D.C. hotel bars.

Quill at **the Jefferson** is a hidden gem with live piano music, an outdoor terrace, and cocktail menus that change monthly. Ask for a basic drink and the bartenders will add their creative touches to your handcrafted cocktail, all while providing great service. Plus the nibbles of olives and nuts are simply divine.

The **Off the Record** bar at the **Hay-Adams** advertises itself as the place to be seen and not heard. Being just steps from the White House, that couldn't be more true. Tucked away in the historic hotel's basement, you really never know who you might run into here.

Although they don't boast the same old-world dark wood and red-leather charm of the bars at the historic hotels, the **Dirty Habit** at the decidedly more modern **Hotel Monaco** and **P.O.V.** on the roof of the **W Hotel** hold their own as stops on the see-and-be-seen hotel bar scene.

restaurants and shopping; polished service; good spa and fitness center; complimentary morning newspaper delivery; 24-hour room service; free in-room Wi-Fi; movie theaters located in the property complex. **Cons:** far from the Metro; very expensive; expensive parking. [$] *Rooms from: $685* ✉ *3100 South St. NW, Georgetown* ☎ *202/912–4200* 🌐 *www.ritzcarlton.com/hotels/georgetown* 🛏 *54 rooms, 32 suites* 🍴 *No meals* [M] *Foggy Bottom/GWU* ✣ 1:B6.

$$$$ HOTEL Fodor's Choice ★ 🏨 **Rosewood Washington D.C.** One of the most expensive hotels in town comes with superlative standards, and the pampering begins even before you arrive—a personal assistant will make arrangements for tickets, tours, transportation, personal shopping, behind-the-scenes access to events, or anything else you may need. **Pros:** unparalleled service; sumptuous guest rooms and public areas; prime Georgetown location. **Cons:** expensive; far from Metro and Mall. [$] *Rooms from: $695* ✉ *1050 31st St. NW, Georgetown* ☎ *202/617–2400* 🌐 *www.rosewoodhotels.com/en/washington-dc* 🛏 *61 rooms* 🍴 *No meals* [M] *Foggy Bottom/GWU* ✣ 1:B5.

DUPONT CIRCLE AND LOGAN CIRCLE

Around the Dupont traffic circle spins everything that makes D.C. what it is: embassies from all over the world with their ethnically diverse communities, and a vibrant Connecticut Avenue and 14th Street with their panoply of restaurants, bars, and shops. Add to that an assortment of theaters, museums, and galleries—seemingly on every block—and this rich Washington neighborhood has something for everyone. And, of course, the Circle is also known for its fabulously eclectic gatherings of people. The upwardly mobile Logan Circle area includes a historic district with some fine buildings, plus shops, galleries, and nightlife.

$$ B&B/INN **Akwaaba DC.** If your perfect vacation includes having a good book, warm fire, and soft bed, then this charming bed-and-breakfast is your dream come true. **Pros:** lovely neighborhood location; rooms and decor that celebrate African American literature; well-kept historic home. **Cons:** smallish bathrooms; older building; some noise in street-facing rooms. [$] *Rooms from: $285* ✉ *1708 16th St. NW, Dupont Circle* ☎ *877/893–3233* 🌐 *www.akwaaba.com* 🛏 *7 rooms, 1 apartment* 🍴 *Breakfast* [M] *Dupont Circle* ⊕ 1:G3.

$$$ HOTEL FAMILY **Carlyle Hotel Dupont Circle.** Tucked away on a quiet tree-lined street, this stylish Kimpton property makes for a comfortable and convenient base for exploring the city. **Pros:** all the Kimpton amenities, like hosted evening wine hour and complimentary bikes; in-room yoga mats and robes; sophisticated bar and restaurant. **Cons:** rooms can be noisy; no business center. [$] *Rooms from: $339* ✉ *1731 New Hampshire Ave. NW, Dupont Circle* ☎ *202/234–3200* 🌐 *www.carlylehoteldc.com* 🛏 *198 rooms* 🍴 *No meals* [M] *Dupont Circle* ⊕ 1:F3.

$$$ HOTEL Fodor's Choice ★ **The Dupont Circle Hotel.** With its contemporary furniture, sleek color scheme, and clean lines, the Dupont pulls off *Mad Men* chic without so much as a hint of kitsch. **Pros:** right on Dupont Circle; free Wi-Fi; fitness center. **Cons:** traffic and noise on Dupont Circle; some guest rooms are on the small side; limited closet space. [$] *Rooms from: $385* ✉ *1500 New Hampshire Ave. NW, Dupont Circle* ☎ *202/483–6000, 800/423–6953* 🌐 *www.doylecollection.com/dupont* 🛏 *342 rooms* 🍴 *No meals* [M] *Dupont Circle* ⊕ 1:F4.

$$$ B&B/INN Fodor's Choice ★ **Embassy Circle Guest House.** Owners Laura and Raymond Saba have lovingly restored this former embassy, transforming it into a warm and friendly home away from home. **Pros:** lovely hosts; personal service; good location; complimentary all-day coffee and tea, plus afternoon treats. **Cons:** too intimate for some; two-night minimum and $35 booking fee; no television on premises. [$] *Rooms from: $330* ✉ *2224 R St. NW, Dupont Circle* ☎ *202/232–7744, 877/232–7744* 🌐 *www.dcinns.com* 🛏 *11 rooms* 🍴 *Breakfast* [M] *Dupont Circle* ⊕ 1:D3.

$$$ HOTEL **The Embassy Row Hotel.** Just steps from Dupont Circle, this modern boutique hotel attracts a young, hip crowd. **Pros:** fun bar with games and stunning art; awesome views in a lot of rooms; great rooftop bar and pool; daily food and drink tastings. **Cons:** expensive valet parking; hotel style/experience not for everyone. [$] *Rooms from: $299* ✉ *2015 Massachusetts Ave. NW, Dupont Circle* ☎ *202/265–1600* 🌐 *www.destinationhotels.com/hotels-and-resorts/the-embassy-row-hotel* 🛏 *231 rooms* 🍴 *No meals* [M] *Dupont Circle* ⊕ 1:E4.

$$$ HOTEL **The Fairfax at Embassy Row.** Light-filled hallways, invitingly bright guest rooms, soft bed linens, marble baths, and impeccable service make this hotel, formerly Al Gore's childhood home, a bastion of comfort. **Pros:** historic hotel; large rooms; great location. **Cons:** expensive valet parking; fee for in-room Wi-Fi. [$] *Rooms from: $329* ✉ *2100 Massachusetts Ave. NW, Dupont Circle* ☎ *202/293–2100, 888/625–5144* 🌐 *www.fairfaxwashingtondc.com* 🛏 *279 rooms* 🍴 *No meals* [M] *Dupont Circle* ⊕ 1:E4.

$$$$ HOTEL FAMILY **Homewood Suites by Hilton, Washington.** Suites with kitchens, a free grocery-shopping service, and complimentary hot breakfast buffet daily make this a popular choice for tourists, but the large family-room-style

lobby may well also be abuzz with people in suits preparing presentations. **Pros:** roomy suites; evening social Monday through Thursday; great for cooking in your room. **Cons:** difficult street parking; 10 minutes to Metro. ⓈＲooms from: $429 ⊠ 1475 Massachusetts Ave. NW, Logan Circle ☎ 202/265–8000 ⊕ www.homewoodsuites.com ⤳ 175 suites Ⓞ Breakfast Ⓜ McPherson Sq. ✛ 1:H5.

$$$ ⛫ **Hotel Madera.** Located just south of vibrant Dupont Circle, this sophis-
HOTEL ticated and art-focused Kimpton hotel provides the perfect respite after an evening restaurant and club hopping along P Street and Connecticut Avenue. **Pros:** fun place to stay thanks to nightly wine hour and other amenities; convenient to Metro, restaurants, and bars; friendly staff. **Cons:** no pool or gym on-site; small bathrooms. Ⓢ Rooms from: $379 ⊠ 1310 New Hampshire Ave. NW, Dupont Circle ☎ 202/296–7600, 800/430–1202 ⊕ www.hotelmadera.com ⤳ 82 rooms ⓄＮo meals Ⓜ Dupont Circle ✛ 1:E4.

$$$ ⛫ **Mansion on O Street.** Rock 'n' roll palace meets urban thrift shop in this
HOTEL unique guesthouse, a scramble of five connected town houses crammed with art, kitsch, and everything in between—it's the most unusual sleep in town. **Pros:** one-of-a-kind setup and decor; serious about privacy; glamorous common areas (and secret doorways!). **Cons:** layout makes for many dark rooms; eccentric staff and service. Ⓢ Rooms from: $350 ⊠ 2020 O St. NW, Dupont Circle ☎ 202/496–2020 ⊕ www.omansion. com ⤳ 29 rooms ⓄＢreakfast Ⓜ Dupont Circle ✛ 1:E4.

$$$ ⛫ **Mason & Rook.** A nod to the secret society of Freemasonry and the
HOTEL game of chess, this stylish Kimpton hotel has spacious rooms designed in rich shades of browns and grays, featuring large flat-screen TVs, plush bedding, and Bluetooth speakers. **Pros:** chic rooftop pool and lounge open seasonally; excellent service; complimentary bikes and nightly wine hour; fun and clever decor. **Cons:** a walk to the Metro; low ceilings. Ⓢ Rooms from: $399 ⊠ 1430 Rhode Island Ave. NW, Logan Circle ☎ 202/462–9001, 866/508–0658 ⊕ www.masonandrookhotel. com ⤳ 178 rooms ⓄＮo meals Ⓜ McPherson Sq. ✛ 1:H4.

$$$ ⛫ **Palomar, Washington, D.C.** Aside from the hard-to-beat location, these
HOTEL modern rooms are some of the largest in town and are decorated with
Fodor'sChoice cool abstract art, accessories in rich jewel tones, and plush purple-and-
★ fuchsia furnishings. **Pros:** huge rooms; awesome outdoor pool; classic Kimpton decor, service, and amenities. **Cons:** busy public areas get crowded; expensive valet parking. Ⓢ Rooms from: $359 ⊠ 2121 P St. NW, Dupont Circle ☎ 202/448–1800 ⊕ www.hotelpalomar-dc.com ⤳ 335 rooms ⓄＮo meals Ⓜ Dupont Circle ✛ 1:E4.

$$$$ ⛫ **Residence Inn Washington, D.C./Dupont Circle.** It's remarkable that a com-
HOTEL mercial chain can feel so cozy—kitchens come stocked with everything
FAMILY you need, and sleeper sofas are an added bonus for families looking for more room to spread out. **Pros:** free hot breakfast daily; two blocks from Metro. **Cons:** small gym; no pool. Ⓢ Rooms from: $449 ⊠ 2120 P St. NW, Dupont Circle ☎ 202/466–6800, 800/331–3131 ⊕ www.marriott. com/wasri ⤳ 107 suites ⓄＢreakfast Ⓜ Dupont Circle ✛ 1:E4.

$$$ ⛫ **Rouge Hotel.** You'll be seeing red and loving it; rooms at this Kimpton
HOTEL are a sleek postmodern tribute to the color, from the red platform beds
FAMILY to the red velvet curtains, offset with chic accent pieces and sumptuous

leather cream furniture. **Pros:** gay-friendly vibe; good location near two Metro stations; all the classic Kimpton style and amenities. **Cons:** the scene is not for everyone; decor might be a little too bold for some. [$] *Rooms from: $339* ✉ *1315 16th St. NW, Dupont Circle* ☎ *202/232–8000, 800/738–1202* 🌐 *www.rougehotel.com* 🛏 *137 rooms* 🍴 *No meals* [M] *Dupont Circle* ✣ 1:G4.

$$ B&B/INN Fodor's Choice ★ 🏨 **Swann House.** You'll be hard-pressed to find a more charming inn or hosts more delightful than innkeeper Isabelle Hauswald and her staff. **Pros:** perfect location; lavish rooms; fireplaces in winter in some rooms, a pool in summer; lovely hot breakfast buffet and afternoon refreshments. **Cons:** intimate atmosphere not for everyone; less expensive rooms are small; children under the age of 12 not allowed. [$] *Rooms from: $265* ✉ *1808 New Hampshire Ave. NW, Dupont Circle* ☎ *202/265–4414* 🌐 *www.swannhouse.com* 🛏 *12 rooms* 🍴 *Breakfast* [M] *Dupont Circle* ✣ 1:F3.

ADAMS MORGAN

This thriving multiethnic community is the place to be for a fabulous assortment of aromas, languages, tastes, and late-night entertainments. A short walk from a nearby hotel or Metro stop gives you salsa, hip-hop, jazz, or the latest in experimental performance art. Its neighborhoods of 19th- and early-20th-century homes and row houses and its proximity to Rock Creek Park provide this bustling area with a tranquil shell.

$ B&B/INN 🏨 **Adam's Inn.** Live like a local at this cozy, Victorian-style bed-and-breakfast spreading through three residential town houses near Adams Morgan, the zoo, and Dupont Circle. **Pros:** affordable rates; near Metro; lively neighborhood; backyard garden is a Certified Wildlife Habitat by the National Wildlife Federation. **Cons:** tight parking; some shared baths; steps to climb; some guests complain of noise between rooms. [$] *Rooms from: $174* ✉ *1746 Lanier Pl. NW, Woodley Park, Adams Morgan* ☎ *202/745–3600, 800/578–6807* 🌐 *www.adamsinn.com* 🛏 *27 rooms* 🍴 *Breakfast* [M] *Woodley Park/Zoo* ✣ 1:F1.

$$ HOTEL 🏨 **Churchill Hotel Near Embassy Row.** One of the Historic Hotels of America, this beaux arts landmark built in 1906 has spacious guest rooms that are comfortable and elegant, include small work and sitting areas, and many have excellent views. **Pros:** good-sized rooms; relaxed and quiet; comfortable walking distance to Adams Morgan and northern Dupont Circle. **Cons:** older building; some rooms very small; limited room service hours. [$] *Rooms from: $289* ✉ *1914 Connecticut Ave. NW, Adams Morgan* ☎ *202/797–2000, 800/424–2464* 🌐 *www.thechurchillhotel.com* 🛏 *91 rooms, 82 suites* 🍴 *No meals* [M] *Dupont Circle* ✣ 1:E3.

$$$ HOTEL 🏨 **Courtyard Washington, D.C./Dupont Circle.** The standard Courtyard amenities come with a big plus here; some of the south-facing rooms on higher floors enjoy fantastic panoramic views of the city that take in the Washington Monument and other historic landmarks through the floor-to-ceiling windows. **Pros:** amazing views from some rooms; good location for restaurants and shopping; friendly, helpful staff. **Cons:** a busy location on Connecticut Avenue; chain-hotel feel with few unique

touches; expensive valet parking. $ *Rooms from: $300* ✉ *1900 Connecticut Ave. NW, Adams Morgan* ☎ *202/332–9300* ⊕ *www.marriott. com* ☞ *148 rooms* ⦿ *Breakfast* Ⓜ *Dupont Circle* ✛ *1:E2.*

$$$
HOTEL
▣ **The Normandy Hotel.** On a quiet street in the embassy area of Connecticut Avenue stands this small Irish chain hotel. **Pros:** quiet location; coffee and tea served in garden room every afternoon; complimentary access to nearby fitness center and spa. **Cons:** smallish rooms; no room service; no restaurant. $ *Rooms from: $309* ✉ *2118 Wyoming Ave. NW, Adams Morgan* ☎ *202/483–1350, 800/424–3729* ⊕ *www.the-normandydc.com* ☞ *75 rooms* ⦿ *No meals* Ⓜ *Dupont Circle* ✛ *1:E2.*

$$$
HOTEL
▣ **Washington Hilton.** Yes, it's a fairly large hotel and can be busy at times, but this historic 1965 hotel, at the intersection of Dupont Circle, Adams Morgan, and U and 14th Streets, has a great location and is a perfect spot to unwind after a day of business or seeing the sights. **Pros:** great lobby; plenty of services; lots of restaurants and shops within walking distance. **Cons:** corporate feel; busy; noisy location; fee for Wi-Fi. $ *Rooms from: $348* ✉ *1919 Connecticut Ave. NW, Adams Morgan* ☎ *202/328–2080* ⊕ *www.washington.hilton.com* ☞ *1,117 rooms* ⦿ *No meals* Ⓜ *Dupont Circle* ✛ *1:E2.*

UPPER NORTHWEST

Whether you travel north through Rock Creek Park on a scenic jaunt, or head up Connecticut Avenue past the National Zoo, or take Wisconsin Avenue starting at the Washington National Cathedral, you see a diverse collection of prosperous neighborhoods with single-family homes, apartment high-rises, and shopping districts. These Upper Northwest communities won't have as many museums or as much history as the other parts of D.C., but they still have plenty of sights, movie theaters, and minimalls.

$$
HOTEL
▣ **Glover Park Hotel.** In the heart of Embassy Row is this Kimpton hotel and its beautifully decorated rooms with lovely views of the city. **Pros:** classic Kimpton service, charm, and extras; spacious rooms; close to Dumbarton Oaks and Washington Cathedral; great Italian restaurant. **Cons:** distance from Metro and Downtown; valet parking is $35 per day. $ *Rooms from: $289* ✉ *2505 Wisconsin Ave. NW, Glover Park, Upper Northwest* ☎ *202/337–9700* ⊕ *www.gloverparkhotel.com* ☞ *150 rooms* ⦿ *No meals* Ⓜ *Woodley Park* ✛ *1:A2.*

$$$$
HOTEL
FAMILY
Fodor'sChoice
★
▣ **Omni Shoreham Hotel.** Since its opening in 1930, this elegant landmark overlooking Rock Creek Park, a Historic Hotel of America, has welcomed heads of state, U.S. politicians, and celebs like the Beatles, Judy Garland, and Bob Hope. **Pros:** historic property with gorgeous grounds; great pool and sundeck; good views from many rooms; walking/jogging trails through Rock Creek Park. **Cons:** not near major sights; noisy at times; extremely large. $ *Rooms from: $409* ✉ *2500 Calvert St. NW, Woodley Park, Upper Northwest* ☎ *202/234–0700, 800/834–6664* ⊕ *www.omni-hotels.com* ☞ *834 rooms* ⦿ *No meals* Ⓜ *Woodley Park/Zoo* ✛ *1:C1.*

$$$
HOTEL
FAMILY
▣ **Washington Marriott Wardman Park.** In a pleasant neighborhood, this is a good choice for families—kids will love the outdoor pool and the proximity to the pandas at the zoo—and is popular with groups. **Pros:**

right next to Metro stop; light-filled sundeck and pool; pretty residential neighborhood with lots of restaurants. **Cons:** busy and hectic public areas; massive size; fee for in-room Wi-Fi. [$] *Rooms from: $379* ✉ *2660 Woodley Rd. NW, Woodley Park, Upper Northwest* ☎ *202/328–2000, 800/228–9290* 🌐 *www.marriott.com* 🛏 *1,152 rooms* 🍴 *No meals* [M] *Woodley Park/Zoo* ✥ 1:D1.

$$ B&B/INN Fodor's Choice ★ 🏨 **Woodley Park Guest House.** Experience the height of hospitality at this charming bed-and-breakfast on a quiet residential street near the zoo. **Pros:** close to Metro; excellent breakfast; friendly and welcoming hosts. **Cons:** some shared baths; limited privacy; no television. [$] *Rooms from: $260* ✉ *2647 Woodley Rd. NW, Woodley Park, Upper Northwest* ☎ *202/667–0218, 866/667–0218* 🌐 *www.dcinns.com* 🛏 *15 rooms* 🍴 *Breakfast* [M] *Woodley Park/Zoo* ✥ 1:D1.

4

ARLINGTON AND NORTHERN VIRGINIA

Across the Potomac, with excellent Metro access and views of D.C., you'll find Arlington County, one of the largest areas in the Washington metro area. Its neighborhoods include Pentagon City with its three popular malls: Pentagon Row, Fashion Centre, and Pentagon Centre; Crystal City with its underground network of corridors linking offices and shops to high-rise apartments; Ballston, home to the Washington Capitals National Hockey League training facility; and Rosslyn, a former ferry landing turned transportation hub for rail, car, and bike. These thriving communities might not offer as much as D.C. proper, but they have everything the weary traveler might need in terms of accommodations, cuisine, and entertainment, often at a more affordable price point.

$$ HOTEL 🏨 **Hyatt Centric Arlington.** If you're feeling energetic, it's just a five-minute walk to Georgetown over Key Bridge from this solid over-the-Potomac choice, but if energy is lacking, the hotel is just across from the Rosslyn Metro station. **Pros:** across from Metro; runners/walkers can receive trail maps and GPS watches; nice-sized rooms. **Cons:** dull neighborhood; not great for kids; not close to any major sights. [$] *Rooms from: $279* ✉ *1325 Wilson Blvd., Rosslyn* ☎ *703/525–1234, 800/908–4790* 🌐 *www.arlington.centric.hyatt.com* 🛏 *318 rooms* 🍴 *No meals* [M] *Rossyln* ✥ 1:A6.

$$ HOTEL 🏨 **Key Bridge Marriott.** Camera-ready views and proximity to Georgetown, which is just across Key Bridge, may help you overlook the '60s style and small rooms here. **Pros:** near the Metro; nice indoor-outdoor pool; Georgetown and monument views. **Cons:** area is dull at night; chain-hotel ambience; fee for in-room Wi-Fi. [$] *Rooms from: $279* ✉ *1401 Lee Hwy., Rosslyn* ☎ *703/524–6400, 800/228–9290* 🌐 *www.marriott.com* 🛏 *571 rooms* 🍴 *No meals* [M] *Rosslyn* ✥ 1:A6.

$$ HOTEL 🏨 **Le Méridien Arlington.** This modern gem, just over the bridge from Georgetown and steps from the Metro, offers stylish and comfortable rooms, many with great views of the Potomac River. **Pros:** convenient to Metro and Arlington Cemetery; nice artwork throughout; great views of the skyline. **Cons:** unhip location; fee for in-room Wi-Fi unless you're an SPG member; some rooms are small. [$] *Rooms from: $293* ✉ *1121 N. 19th St., Rosslyn* ☎ *703/351–9170* 🌐 *www.starwoodhotels.com* 🛏 *154 rooms* 🍴 *No meals* [M] *Rosslyn* ✥ 1:A6.

$$$ HOTEL **Renaissance Arlington Capital View Hotel.** Spacious rooms, excellent service, and a tasty contemporary Italian restaurant all add up to an excellent hotel choice outside the city. **Pros:** nice-sized fitness center and heated indoor pool; stunning lobby with dramatic artwork; delightful coffee shop. **Cons:** fee for in-room Wi-Fi; noise from trains on one side of hotel; a bit of a walk to restaurants. [$] *Rooms from: $379* ✉ *2800 Potomac Ave., Arlington* ☎ *703/413–1300, 888/236–2427* 🌐 *www.marriott.com/hotels/travel/waspy-renaissance-arlington-capital-view-hotel* 🛏 *300 rooms* 🍴 *No meals* [M] *Crystal City or Ronald Reagan Washington National Airport* ✥ 1:A6.

$$$ HOTEL FAMILY Fodor's Choice ★ **Residence Inn Arlington Pentagon City.** The view across the Potomac of the D.C. skyline and the monuments is magnificent from these suites in a high-rise adjacent to the Pentagon and two blocks from the Fashion Centre at Pentagon City. **Pros:** indoor pool and fitness center; lovely public areas; airport shuttle to/from Ronald Reagan Washington National. **Cons:** parking fee of $29 per day; neighborhood dead at night. [$] *Rooms from: $349* ✉ *550 Army Navy Dr., Arlington* ☎ *703/413–6630, 800/331–3131* 🌐 *www.marriott.com/hotels/travel/waspt-residence-inn-arlington-pentagon-city* 🛏 *299 suites* 🍴 *Breakfast* [M] *Pentagon City* ✥ 1:A6.

$$$$ HOTEL FAMILY **The Ritz-Carlton Pentagon City.** The feel is more contemporary and casually chic than generally associated with this luxury chain, and it's convenient for both downtown D.C. and Ronald Reagan Washington National Airport. **Pros:** indoor walk to Metro; connected to shops and restaurants; welcome amenity kit for children. **Cons:** daily fee for Wi-Fi; less luxurious than other Ritz properties; expensive, given the location. [$] *Rooms from: $419* ✉ *1250 S. Hayes St., Arlington* ☎ *703/415–5000, 800/241–3333* 🌐 *www.ritzcarlton.com/PentagonCity* 🛏 *366 rooms* 🍴 *No meals* [M] *Pentagon City* ✥ 1:A6.

5

NIGHTLIFE

Updated by
Doug Rule

From buttoned-down political appointees who've just arrived to laid-back folks who've lived here their whole lives, Washingtonians are always looking for a place to relax. And they have plenty of options when they head out for a night on the town. Most places are clustered in several key neighborhoods, making a night of barhopping relatively easy.

Georgetown's bars, nightclubs, and restaurants radiate from the intersection of Wisconsin and M Streets, attracting crowds that include older adults and college students. Many restaurants here turn into bars after the dinner crowd leaves. Georgetown is one of the safest neighborhoods in D.C., with a large police presence on weekends.

Those seeking a younger and less inhibited nightlife may prefer the 18th Street strip in Adams Morgan, between Columbia Road and Florida Avenue, which offers a wide variety of places for dancing, drinking, and eating. The best part of Adams Morgan is that there are so many bars and clubs around 18th Street that if you don't like one, there's another next door. AdMo, as it's affectionately called, is best known for its bars, but there are some restaurants that make the strip worth the trip for those in search of a good meal.

The U Street Corridor (U Street NW between 9th and 17th Streets NW), historically D.C.'s hippest neighborhood and a regular stop for jazz greats, has undergone a revival and is now the hottest spot in town, with bars that appeal to all types. Down 14th Street NW you will also find new bars and restaurants spilling revelers out on the street on weekends. Wine bars, dive bars, hipster bars, gastropubs, and dance clubs make for a full night out. Other hot spots include Capitol Hill, Downtown, and the city's most-up-and-coming area, Shaw. The stretch of Pennsylvania Avenue SE between 2nd and 4th Streets has a half-dozen bars. Thanks to massive redevelopment, Penn Quarter/Chinatown is burgeoning with new bars and music venues orbiting the Verizon Center and Gallery Place. The newest center of gravity for D.C. nightlife is the H Street Corridor, still tricky to get to, but home to some of the city's most dynamic venues.

PLANNING

DRESS CODE

Despite how formally they might have to dress during the week, on the weekend Washingtonians really let their hair down. Although many of the high-end clubs require you to "dress to impress," including dress shoes for men, most bars and pubs are slightly more casual. This is especially true during the summer, when shorts can be considered acceptable on an oppressively humid night.

HOURS

Last call in D.C. is 2 am on weekends, and most bars and clubs close by 3 am on the weekend and between midnight and 2 am during the week. The exceptions are after-hours dance clubs and bars with kitchens that stay open late.

NIGHTLIFE INFORMATION

To survey the local scene, consult Friday's "Weekend" section in the *Washington Post* and the free weekly *Washington CityPaper*. A terrific website (with an accompanying cell-phone app) for local happenings is the *Post*'s Going Out Guide (⊕ *www.washingtonpost.com/gog*). The free publications *Metro Weekly* and *Washington Blade* offer insights on LGBT nightlife. Local blog DCist (⊕ *www.dcist.com*) posts daily on D.C. events. It's a good idea to call clubs ahead of time, as last week's punk-rock party might be this week's merengue marathon.

Contacts D.C. Blues Society. ⊕ www.dcblues.org. **Folklore Society of Greater Washington.** ☎ 202/546–2228 ⊕ www.fsgw.org.

WHITE HOUSE AREA AND FOGGY BOTTOM

The area near the White House and Foggy Bottom once offered a less frantic nightlife environment as the city center emptied out during the weekends. Today, some interesting clubs and restaurants have reenergized the area. Many are near—or in—major hotels, making the area more attractive to the going-out crowd.

WHITE HOUSE AREA

BARS AND LOUNGES

The Hamilton. From the street, it looks like a swanky downtown D.C. restaurant with a high-ceilinged power bar to match. The magic really happens, however, with live shows in The Hamilton's cavernous basement space. Care in equal parts has focused on acoustics, comfort, and tiered seating that makes it hard to find a bad seat. There is secondary space above the bar-restaurant where the venue regularly hosts more intimate acts and "Free Late Night Music in the Loft."✉ *600 14th St. NW, White House area* ☎ *202/787–1000* ⊕ *live.thehamiltondc. com* Ⓜ *Metro Center.*

P.O.V. For decades, the perfect way to end a night out in Washington was a trip up to the Sky Tavern on the Hotel Washington's 11th-floor rooftop. The W Hotel has replaced the Hotel Washington, and the Sky Tavern has been reincarnated as P.O.V. ("Point of View"), a trendy indoor lounge and outdoor terrace offering a tremendous view over D.C.'s low skyline. Enjoy the unique view of the Washington Monument and the White House while enjoying a pan-Mediterranean menu of cocktails, appetizers, and small plates. While the view here is no secret, meaning waits are common, P.O.V. does take reservations. Popping by in the late afternoon may be a more relaxed option. ■TIP→ After 5 pm, the venue only allows 21 and older. ⊠ *515 15 St. NW, White House area* ☎ *202/661–2400* ⊕ *www.povrooftop.com* Ⓜ *McPherson Sq.*

FOGGY BOTTOM

DANCE CLUBS

Eden. This four-floor hot spot near the White House attracts Washington celebrities, foreign visitors, and the sophisticated elite. The club hosts a variety of local and big-name DJs and is famous for its rooftop deck, attracting big crowds in the summer. Bottle service is available. ⊠ *1716 I St. NW, Foggy Bottom* ☎ *202/785–0270* ⊕ *www.edendc.com* Ⓜ *Farragut W.*

CAPITOL HILL AND NORTHEAST D.C.

Seemingly overnight, Capitol Hill has become a hot location. Great new restaurants and bars match time-tested steadies, allowing nighttime crowds to enjoy food from celebrity chefs and then dance away the night or relax in a casual dive bar. A four-block area in the H Street Corridor, known as the Atlas District, is home to some great music venues and plenty of D.C.'s new hipster bars. Keep in mind, though, that the H Street area is not easily accessed by public transport, so be ready to take a cab.

Northeast's industrial environment can be intimidating, and caution is warranted for safety reasons. Make use of the premium parking—for about $20—that will put you close to the entrance. Even parking a few blocks away on neighborhood streets is risky at night. Taxis are another good option.

CAPITOL HILL

BARS AND LOUNGES

Dubliner. A short walk from Union Station and Capitol Hill, this Washington institution offers cozy paneled rooms, rich pints of Guinness, and other authentic fare. It's especially popular with Hill staffers and Georgetown law students. While offering live Irish music seven nights a week, this charming spot never charges a cover, save for St. Patrick's Day. ⊠ *4 F St. NW, Capitol Hill* ☎ *202/737–3773* ⊕ *www.dublinerdc.com* Ⓜ *Union Station.*

FIVE GREAT NIGHTLIFE EXPERIENCES

9:30 Club: The best live music venue in D.C., the club showcases new and legendary performers from across the nation.

The Birchmere: Known for bluegrass, the club offers a variety of genres, with something for everybody—from Kelly Willis to Aaron Neville to Tom Rush and Jerry Jeff Walker.

Blues Alley: D.C.'s classiest jazz club is the place to enjoy outstanding performers and Cajun food in an intimate setting.

P.O.V: At the top of the W Hotel, the picture-perfect views are matched by the expert cocktails.

Rock and Roll Hotel: Experience the H Street Corridor with locals in the know, while enjoying indie acts and a great dance party.

MUSIC CLUBS

Mr. Henry's. Opened in 1966, this laid-back club is the last holdout of a once-thriving live-music scene on Capitol Hill. Roberta Flack got her start in the upstairs performance space, where a dozen or so tables are scattered around the wood-paneled room. There's never a cover. ⊠ *601 Pennsylvania Ave. SE, Capitol Hill* ☎ *202/546–8412* ⊕ *www. mrhenrysdc.com* Ⓜ *Eastern Market.*

NORTHEAST D.C.

BARS AND LOUNGES

Biergartenhaus. Step off H Street and into a boisterous bit of Bavaria. There might be football on TV, but that's not enough to break the spell of a place so genuinely Germanic. With about a dozen drafts on offer, along with other authentic specialties—apfel schnapps?—and a full bar, there's something for everyone, including a variety of spaces. Get cozy inside, or head for the courtyard, heated in winter. In pleasant weather, the second-story terrace also packs them in. ⊠ *1355 H St. NE, Northeast* ☎ *202/388–4085* ⊕ *www.biergartenhaus.com.*

Granville Moore's. Beer and mussels: the appeal is that simple, and they're that satisfying. The Belgian-themed gastropub has its own "beverage director" and one of the largest selections of beer, from pilsners to Flemish reds, in Washington. Offerings in this cozy spot go beyond mussels, and the executive-chef Teddy Folkman has been featured on the Food Network—and is also a "culinary ambassador" for the New York brewery Ommegang. The narrow, rustic bars on two floors attract more than a dinner crowd. ⊠ *1238 H St. NE, Northeast* ☎ *202/399–2546* ⊕ *www.granvillemoores.com* Ⓜ *Union Station.*

H Street Country Club. The only D.C. bar to offer indoor miniature golf, Big Buck Hunter, and skeeball has a friendly, laid-back vibe. Margaritas, fish tacos, and an impressive tequila list round out the fun mix at this popular nightspot. Big-screen sports line the walls downstairs, but you can usually catch a breath of fresh air on the roof deck. ⊠ *1335 H St. NE, Northeast* ☎ *202/399–4722* ⊕ *www.hstcountryclub.com* Ⓜ *Union Station.*

MUSIC CLUBS

Echostage. This sprawling complex of more than 30,000 square feet in Northeast D.C. effectively re-creates the vibe of an otherwise bygone era in D.C. of mega-nightclubs in retrofitted warehouses in derelict neighborhoods. With unobstructed sight lines to the stage and a German-imported sound system (the first of its kind on the East Coast), it's the place for club kids to dance to the biggest names in E.D.M., from Calvin Harris to David Guetta to Tiesto. It's also the place to see taste-making dance and synth-pop acts such as Disclosure, Empire of the Sun, and Chvrches. ■TIP➔ With no Metro stops nearby, driving or taking a cab/Uber is required. ✉ 2135 Queens Chapel Rd. NE, Northeast ☎ 202/503–2330 ⊕ www.echostage.com.

Fodor'sChoice **Rock and Roll Hotel.** A former funeral home hosts some of the nation's ★ best indie acts. Live bands are in the main room and DJs spin on the second floor, called the Hotel Bar, hosting some of the most enthusiastic dance parties in town—and the dance floor can get very crowded. The rooftop bar is festive, too. Notable acts include A Place to Bury Strangers, Lost in the Trees, Dead Kennedys, and Emily King. It's a 15-block walk (or a quick ride on the still-in-beta-testing DC Streetcar) from the Union Station Metro, though it's probably best to take a taxi or Uber in this still up-and-coming area. ✉ 1353 H St. NE, Northeast ☎ 202/388–7625 ⊕ www.rockandrollhoteldc. com Ⓜ Union Station.

DOWNTOWN

You'll find plenty of bars and lounges in the Downtown area, which has been wonderfully revitalized, compared to years past. Development around Chinatown and the Verizon Center has turned this into a lively neighborhood, especially when there's a sports or musical event at the arena. A few blocks south, the formerly quiet Penn Quarter is seeing larger evening crowds, thanks to the opening of several terrific new restaurants, cafés, bars, and a world-class theater scene. Conveniently, especially if you plan to imbibe, you can easily get to Downtown on the Metro, exiting at the Archives/Navy Memorial/Penn Quarter station (Green and Yellow lines) or at the Gallery Place/Chinatown stop (Green, Yellow, and Red lines).

BARS AND LOUNGES

Barmini. Only a small plaque on a bland concrete wall in a nondescript block of Penn Quarter identifies one of Washington's most sophisticated experiences. Step inside to see José Andrés's cocktail lab for his acclaimed chain of restaurants that looks the part, with white-on-white furnishings and mixologists in lab attire often seen pouring smoking libations out of beakers. A metal notebook features a menu of more than 100 alcohol-centered liquid experiments, grouped by spirit. Make it a show with drinks such as the tequila-based Cedar and Agave, in which a glass and block of ice are infused with the smell of burning wood, table-side, or the Floral Cloud, a fruity gin-based beverage delivered in a hibiscus haze. Soak up the chemical reactions with snacks such as savory miniwaffles. Behind the bar you can peer through a framed glass window to see a handful of foodies at the sister minibar taking a similarly science-inspired culinary tour. ⊠ *501 9th St. NW, Penn Quarter* ☎ *202/393–4451* ⊕ *www.minibarbyjoseandres. com/barmini* Ⓜ *Archives.*

The Dignitary. Inside the shell of an art deco–inspired edifice that once housed a labor union is one of the newest and most comfortably elegant bars in D.C., the corner spot of the new Marriott Marquis. Deeper inside the hotel you'll find a bustling lobby bar as well as a large, noisy sports bar with 48 beers on tap. But the Dignitary attracts a more refined crowd with its focus on more than 50 types of bourbons and ryes poured by a crew of bartenders as experienced as they are friendly. Also features an outdoor patio in the warmer months. ⊠ *901 Massachusetts Ave. NW, Downtown* ☎ *202/824–9681* ⊕ *www. marriott.com/hotels/hotel-information/restaurant/wasco-marriott- marquis-washington-dc* Ⓜ *Mt. Vernon Sq.*

COMEDY CLUBS

Fodor'sChoice

★

Capitol Steps. Putting the "mock" in democracy, the musical political satire of this group—many of whom are current or former Hill staffers—is presented in the amphitheater of the Ronald Reagan Building every Friday and Saturday at 7:30 pm and occasionally at other spots around town. This Washington classic is fun for the whole family, no matter on which side of the aisle you sit. Tickets are available through Ticketmaster and online. ⊠ *Ronald Reagan Bldg. and International Trade Center, 1300 Pennsylvania Ave. NW, Downtown* ☎ *703/683– 8330* ⊕ *www.capsteps.com* Ⓜ *Federal Triangle.*

DC Improv. Having just passed its 25th anniversary, the Improv is D.C.'s main spot for comedy, offering a steady menu of well-known and promising stand-up headliners—recent acts have included Judah Friedlander—as well as a bevy of funny amateurs. There's a two-item minimum from a full food and drink menu. ⊠ *1140 Connecticut Ave. NW, Downtown* ☎ *202/296–7008* ⊕ *www.dcimprov.com* Ⓜ *Farragut N.*

DANCE CLUBS

The Park at Fourteenth. A high-end crowd includes visiting basketball players and R&B stars, who dance on four levels. The fancy and formal dress code is strictly enforced by the bouncers. You can arrange in advance to get a table or brave the long lines that develop later in the night. ⊠ *920 14th St. NW, Downtown* ☎ *202/737–7275* ⊕ *www. park14.com* Ⓜ *McPherson Sq.*

5

GEORGETOWN

Due to its proximity to the university, weekends (and even weeknights) are a happening affair in Georgetown. A number of bars serve as restaurants by day, until the college and intern crowds take over at night. Although most venues here tend to attract a younger set, the neighborhood still offers many options for patrons over thirty, such as the legendary Blues Alley. There's little parking here, and no easy Metro access, so if you're not staying nearby your best bet is a taxi. In late spring and summer, head to the Washington Harbour for drinks and a riverside stroll.

BARS AND LOUNGES

Degrees. Hidden away inside the Ritz-Carlton hotel, in what was once the Georgetown Incinerator, this modern bar exudes elegance from all corners and is a breath of fresh air in the neighborhood's rather monotone scene. There's an extensive wine and cocktail selection behind the black granite bar and a hip, well-dressed set of patrons in front of it. If there's too much attitude in the bar, head out to the hotel's lovely lobby and sit by the fireplace. This is a perfect premovie, postdate, mid-shopping stop. ⊠ *Ritz-Carlton, 3100 South St. NW, Georgetown* ☎ *202/912-4100* ⊕ *www.ritzcarlton.com.*

J Paul's. Located in a historic building that's more than 100 years old, this neighborhood saloon is a festive place to go for a beer and a game. The menu is extensive, but stick to the great hamburgers and seafood dishes. J Paul's attracts a diverse crowd from students to lobbyists to politicians. ⊠ *3218 M St. NW, Georgetown* ☎ *202/333-3450* ⊕ *www.jpaulsdc.com.*

Nick's Riverside Grille. This perch on the Georgetown waterfront affords a great view of the Potomac and, in winter, the ice-skating rink. When the weather's nice, crowds of college students flock to the outdoor tables. The food is fine but the draw is location, location, location. ⊠ *3050 K St. NW, Georgetown* ☎ *202/342-3535* ⊕ *www.nicksriversidegrill.com.*

The Tombs. Visitors to Georgetown University looking for a pint or some pub grub head down the stairs below 1789 restaurant to this traditional, half-century-old collegiate watering hole adorned with rowing paraphernalia and steeped in charming Georgetown boosterism. One block from the main gate, it's the closest bar to campus so it gets crowded with students at night. ⊠ *1226 36th St. NW, Georgetown* ☎ *202/337-6668* ⊕ *www.tombs.com.*

Tony and Joe's. Right on Georgetown's waterfront, this seafood restaurant has a large outdoor patio where you can enjoy a drink alfresco on a spring or summer evening. The cocktails are a little pricey, but you can't beat the view of the Potomac River and Kennedy Center at night. ⊠ *3000 K St. NW, Georgetown* ☎ *202/944-4545* ⊕ *www.tonyandjoes.com.*

MUSIC CLUBS

Fodor'sChoice
★
Blues Alley. Head here for a classy evening in an intimate setting, complete with great blues, jazz, and R&B music from well-known performers such as Mose Allison and Wynton Marsalis and outstanding

New Orleans–style grub. Expect to pay a cover charge as well as a food or drink minimum. ■ TIP→ **You can come for just the show, but those who enjoy a meal get better seats.** ✉ *1073 Wisconsin Ave. NW, near M St., Georgetown* ☎ *202/337–4141* ⊕ *www.bluesalley. com* Ⓜ *Foggy Bottom.*

DUPONT CIRCLE AND LOGAN CIRCLE

Dupont Circle is a long-standing weekend hot spot, with numerous bars and lounges for all ages and preferences. Home to some legendary classics, like Russia House and Kramerbooks & Afterwords, the expansion toward Logan Circle has introduced new favorites like ChurchKey. P Street, especially between 17th and 14th Streets, is Washington's answer to San Francisco's Castro Street, and remains the vibrant focal point of the city's gay and lesbian nightlife scene. The Dupont Circle Metro (Red Line) is the western jumping-off point, while the Shaw/Howard University and Mount Vernon Square/7th Street/Convention Center stops (Green and Yellow lines) cover the east.

DUPONT CIRCLE

BARS AND LOUNGES

Board Room. "Put down your smart phone and interact!" is the motto at this pub with 20-plus beers on tap, a full bar, and a huge choice of board games to rent, from tried-and-true classics to vintage oddities. To enhance the fun, you can bring in your own food or have it delivered. Kids welcome on occasion, but the rule is 21 and older. Reservations are accepted. ✉ *1737 Connecticut Ave. NW, Dupont Circle* ☎ *202/518–7666* ⊕ *www.boardroomdc.com* Ⓜ *Dupont Circle.*

Fodor'sChoice
★
Eighteenth Street Lounge. This multilevel space's division into an array of sofa-filled rooms makes an evening at this home away from home for Washington's hipper globalists seem like a chill house party. Jazz musicians often entertain on the top floor of the former mansion, and the luxe back deck, complete with hanging chandeliers, provides summer visitors with two extra bars and a fresh-air dance floor. Fans of ambient house music flock here as it's the home of the ESL record label and the renowned musical duo Thievery Corporation. ■ TIP→ **The dress code here is strictly enforced by the doorman: no khakis, baseball caps, sneakers, or light-color jeans. For men: no shorts or open-toe shoes.** ✉ *1212 18th St. NW, Dupont Circle* ☎ *202/466–3922* ⊕ *www.eighteenthstreetlounge.com* Ⓜ *Dupont Circle.*

Hank's Oyster Bar. A small, sleek, and unpretentious nautical-themed bar offers a half-price raw bar after 10 pm every night of the week, here and at its locations on Capitol Hill and Old Town Alexandria. The bartenders are friendly, giving you tastes of different wines or drinks to try, along with recommendations on the daily catch and other food options, including one of the best lobster rolls around. ✉ *1624 Q St. NW, Dupont Circle* ☎ *202/462–4265* ⊕ *www.hanksoysterbar.com* Ⓜ *Dupont Circle.*

GAY BARS IN DUPONT

Dupont's gay scene—or what's left of it, as the community has spread out throughout the city—is concentrated mainly on 17th Street. A variety of gay-friendly, lively, and offbeat bars and restaurants stretch between P and R Streets, many with outdoor seating. JR's Bar & Grill and Cobalt are favorites. D.I.K. Bar is the place to be on Tuesday, Friday, and Saturday for the always-popular karaoke nights. On the Tuesday before Halloween, the bar hosts the annual High Heel Drag Race down 17th Street; elaborately costumed drag queens and other revelers strut their stuff along the route from Church to R streets and then race to the finish line.

JR's Bar & Grill. A popular institution on the 17th Street strip packs in a mostly male, mostly professional gay crowd. Various nights offer show-tunes singalongs, trivia contests, and the like. For the "Sunday Funday" daylong happy hour or anytime the federal government shuts down, expect a festive, wall-to-wall crowd in this narrow, window-lined space. ⊠ *1519 17th St. NW, Dupont Circle* ☎ *202/328–0090* ⊕ *www. jrsbar-dc.com* Ⓜ *Dupont Circle.*

Quill. At this *Mad Men* flashback fantasy bar tucked inside the Jefferson Hotel, the drinks are stiff and complicated, while the mood is a quiet celebration of all things civilized. The dimly lit, two-room, wood-paneled, art deco space provides an intimate atmosphere made even more welcoming by the friendly and expert service of the bartenders. A pianist quietly serenades patrons throughout the evening. Pricey, but worth it. ⊠ *1200 16th St. NW, Dupont Circle* ☎ *202/448–2300* ⊕ *www. jeffersondc.com/dining/quill* Ⓜ *Farragut N.*

Russia House Restaurant and Lounge. Transport yourself by sampling vodka flights from an entire menu devoted to Russia's signature spirit. The brooding vibe, bizarre old-world charm, and authentic food might feel kitschy until you see real Eastern European revelers dancing it up late at night in one of the lounges (there are four floors, though they are not all open all the time). While the DJ reigns supreme Saturday night, the live music in the lounge may be preferable for Tatar-esque tippling. ⊠ *1800 Connecticut Ave. NW, Dupont Circle* ☎ *202/234–9433* ⊕ *www.russiahouselounge.com* Ⓜ *Dupont Circle.*

St. Arnold's Mussel Bar on Jefferson. This cozy space in the heart of Dupont is named after the patron saint of brewing, and it's certainly blessed with its choice of hard-to-find Belgian beers. The Belgian theme continues in the menu, and mussels (available in essentially half-price pots during happy hour) are prepared in numerous ways. It all makes for a casual evening out or a comfortable happy-hour spot, and the wood-lined basement is sure to transport you to the old world. Additional location in Cleveland Park. ⊠ *1827 Jefferson Pl. NW, Dupont Circle* ☎ *202/833–1321* ⊕ *www.starnoldsmusselbar. com* Ⓜ *Dupont Circle.*

DANCE CLUBS

Cafe Citron. Mojitos are the specialty at this Latin bar and dance club, with no less than eight varieties available, from the standard to a spicy ginger mojito. The club's DJs play mostly salsa, merengue, bachata, and Latin rock, though pumping Euro-dance and techno often sneak their way into the mix. The festivities start every weekday at 4 pm with the bar's popular "Hora Feliz" happy hour prices on pitchers and South of the Border–style appetizers. With two floors to get your groove on, Citron encourages revelers to dance on the tables and take a whirl at the bongos. The sign above the bar sets the tone: "Be Nice Or Go Away." Free salsa lessons offered weekly. ✉ *1343 Connecticut Ave. NW, Dupont Circle* ☎ *202/530–8844* ⊕ *www.cafecitrondc.com* Ⓜ *Dupont Circle.*

Cobalt. Popular among the gay and lesbian crowd, this venue anchors the 17th Street strip with three distinct floors: the bottom floor is the Level One restaurant, home to a popular weekend brunch with bottomless mimosas and Bloody Marys. The chic 30 Degrees lounge occupies the second level, and above that is the booming dance club Cobalt. The weekends get wild Friday and Saturday when the club presents popular DJs, both local and national, and drag shows with well-known illusionists. ✉ *1639 R St. NW, Dupont Circle* ☎ *202/232–4416* ⊕ *www. cobaltdc.com* Ⓜ *Dupont Circle.*

LOGAN CIRCLE

BARS AND LOUNGES

ChurchKey. There's an astounding selection of beers at ChurchKey—555 varieties from more than 30 countries, including 50 beers on tap and exclusive draft and cask ales. If you have trouble making a choice, bartenders will offer you 4-ounce tasters. The urban-vintage vibe balances unassuming and pretentious in pretty much equal measure, reflected in a menu that ranges from tater tots through a Caesar salad with fried boquerones to flatbread options including "Margherita" and "Duck Confit." ✉ *1337 14th St. NW, Logan Circle* ☎ *202/567–2576* ⊕ *www. churchkeydc.com* Ⓜ *McPherson Sq.*

El Centro D.F. A sunny spot—whatever the weather—on D.C.'s 14th Street, this Richard Sandoval outpost celebrates tequila with a ridiculously expansive selection and an expert staff to guide you, particularly in crafting a personalized flight. The real draw, however, is the roof deck, where the young and boisterous keep the fiesta going. Great nightly happy hour. ✉ *1819 14th St. NW, Logan Circle* ☎ *202/328– 3131* ⊕ *www.richardsandoval.com/elcentrodf* Ⓜ *U St./Cardozo.*

Number Nine. The heart of Logan Circle nightlife is a predominantly male gay bar attracting guests of all ages. The downstairs lounge offers plush banquettes and street views, while big-screen viewing is offered upstairs at the "9 1/2" video bar. The daily happy hour (5 pm–9 pm) offers two-for-one drinks. At any time this is a great place for a cocktail and some good conversation in a bustling neighborhood that includes, a block away on 14th Street, Trade, which is another popular, no-frills gay bar from the same owners as Number Nine. ✉ *1435 P St. NW, Logan Circle* ☎ *202/986–0999* ⊕ *www.numberninedc.com* Ⓜ *Dupont Circle.*

MUSIC CLUBS

New Vegas Lounge. The New Vegas Lounge may be a vestige from a grittier, less affluent era, but the Logan Circle club is in its fifth decade of offering live blues every weekend. Vegas Lounge is run by the wife and sons of its late founder, known as Dr. Blues. Friday- and Saturday-night performances by the house ensemble the Out of Town Blues Band attract an eclectic crowd, from veteran blues fans to newer residents who don't know from Muddy Waters—drawn to the club out of sheer curiosity, or because it's a refreshing cultural and historical diversion in the neighborhood. After all, even in a now-tony neighborhood such as Logan Circle, people still get the blues. ✉ 1415 P St. NW, Logan Circle ☎ 202/483–3971 ⊕ www.newvegasloungedc.com Ⓜ Dupont Circle.

ADAMS MORGAN

Adams Morgan is Washington's version (albeit much smaller) of New Orleans's French Quarter. The streets are jammed on the weekends with people of all ages and descriptions. Bars and restaurants of all types line the streets, making it easy to find one that will suit your tastes. Be prepared for crowds on the weekends and a much tamer vibe on weeknights. Getting there is easy, with four nearby Metro stops: Woodley Park/Adams Morgan (Red Line), Dupont Circle (Red Line), Columbia Heights (Green and Yellow lines), and U Street/Cardozo (Green and Yellow lines). Taxis also are easy to find, except after last call when the crowds pour out of bars.

BARS AND LOUNGES

Bourbon. A more mature Southern-tinged drinking and dining experience diverges from the typical Adams Morgan scene. Though you can dance on the second floor into the wee hours Friday and Saturday, earlier in the evening you'll find interesting whiskey, scotch, and bourbon options coupled with Southern goodies like barbecue chicken salads, grits, and mac and cheese. It's casual, sometimes crowded, and the outdoor porch in summer is a welcome respite from the 18th Street crowd. ✉ 2321 18th St. NW, Adams Morgan ☎ 202/332–0800 ⊕ www.bourbondc.com Ⓜ Adams Morgan/Woodley Park.

L'Enfant Cafe. This French-flavored café boasts the most sidewalk seating in Adams Morgan, superb for watching the world go by at the intersection where Adams Morgan meets Dupont Circle. Inside, things get very intimate with a corner transformed on occasion to offer cabaret. The mood is downright bacchanalian, however, during Saturday's "La Boum" brunch that gets the nightlife started long before the sun goes down and has D.C.'s bohemian set clamoring to get in, making reservations mandatory. Dancing on the bar during La Boum with a sparkler in one hand and a tambourine in the other is optional—but hardly discouraged. The event is so popular, it spawned a weekly Saturday night offshoot, La Boum Boum Room, "A Pansexual Paradise" where reservations are also required. ✉ 2000 18th St. NW, Adams Morgan ☎ 202/319–1800 ⊕ www.lenfantcafe.com Ⓜ Dupont Circle.

Madam's Organ. Neon lights behind the bar, walls covered in kitsch, and works from local artists add to the gritty feel of three levels that play host to an eclectic clientele that listens to live music performed every night (open-mike night is Tuesday) and soaks up rays on the roof deck by day. This is a place that's hard not to like. ⊠ *2461 18th St. NW, Adams Morgan* ☎ *202/667–5370* ⊕ *www.madamsorgan.com* Ⓜ *Woodley Park/Zoo.*

Tryst. Bohemian and unpretentious, this coffeehouse-bar serves fancy sandwiches and exotic coffee creations. Comfy chairs and couches fill the big open space, where you can sit for hours sipping a cup of tea— or a martini—while chatting or clacking away at your laptop. Some of D.C.'s many bloggers make this their home base during the day, and the management has no problem letting people relax for an hour or two—or eight. Tryst is best in the warm months, when the front windows swing open and the temperature matches the temperament. ⊠ *2459 18th St. NW, Adams Morgan* ☎ *202/232–5500* ⊕ *www.trystdc. com* Ⓜ *Woodley Park/Zoo.*

DANCE CLUBS

Habana Village. No matter what the temperature is outside, it's always balmy inside this unpretentious Cuban oasis. The tiny dance floors are packed nightly with couples moving to the latest live salsa and merengue music, and this is one of the only places in D.C. where you'll find older men twirling young women across the dance floor. When it's time to cool down, you can head to one of several lounges and sip the house specialty: a mojito garnished with sugarcane. ⊠ *1834 Columbia Rd. NW, Adams Morgan* ☎ *202/462–6310* ⊕ *www.habanavillage.com* Ⓜ *Woodley Park/Zoo.*

MUSIC CLUBS

Columbia Station. An unpretentious retreat on the 18th Street strip attracts a diverse crowd, many of whom were pulled in off the street by the good vibes emanating from this place. Amber lights and morphed musical instruments adorn the walls, and high-quality live local jazz and blues fills the air. The large, open windows up front keep the place cool—much like the music—in summer months. Reservations are available, though the tunes, and not the mediocre food, are the real draw. ⊠ *2325 18th St. NW, Adams Morgan* ☎ *202/462–6040* ⊕ *www.columbiastationdc.com* Ⓜ *Woodley Park/Zoo.*

U STREET CORRIDOR

Decades ago, the U Street Corridor was famous as D.C.'s Black Broadway. After many dormant years, today the neighborhood has come roaring back with a lively bar, club, and music scene that's expanding both north and south along 14th Street. The U Street Corridor is easily accessible from the U Street/Cardozo Metro stop, on the Green and Yellow lines. Taxis also are easy to find.

In the last couple of years nearby Shaw has become the most revitalized downtown neighborhood in the capital. But any night out in Shaw almost by default includes spending time in the U Street Corridor to the north and west—especially because some destinations, like the Howard Theatre and the 9:30 Club, straddle both increasingly diverse urban neighborhoods. Shaw is centered on 7th Street, with Howard University and Hospital to the north and the Washington Convention Center at the very southern edge.

BARS AND LOUNGES

A&D Neighborhood Bar. From the street, A&D is camouflaged with a front window brimming with houseplants and an old bicycle. Don't be fooled. Inside, you'll find a friendly bar serving a young, fashionably relaxed crowd some of the best cocktails in town. (Be sure to try the namesake cocktail, a tangy and tart twist on a dirty martini with gin instead of vermouth and a juice blend made in-house from olives, cornichons, and pickled onions.) Happy hour starts off mellow, but the place is often jumping in the later hours. And while other trendy spots are still offering the game on TV, A&D's only sports action is the foosball table in the back room. If you're hungry, and want more than the few variations on bar staples and snacks (from "potato chips poutine" to chicken potpie), bring in a sandwich from the bar's sister gourmet Sundevich in the adjacent alley. Closed Sunday. ⊠ *1314 9th St. NW, Shaw* ☎ *202/290–1804* ⊕ *www.andbardc.com* Ⓜ *Mt. Vernon Sq./Convention Center.*

Black Jack. A red-velvet, almost vaudeville-like interior around the bar offers a saucy experience upstairs from the highly rated Pearl Dive Oyster Palace. In the back, you'll find a bocce court surrounded by stadium-style seats so onlookers can recline, imbibe, and cheer simultaneously. Though the most exquisite cocktail confections can be pricey, there's also an impressive beer lineup and a worthwhile menu ranging from mussels to pizza. ⊠ *1612 14th St. NW, Logan Circle* ☎ *202/319–1612* ⊕ *www.blackjackdc.com* Ⓜ *U St./Cardozo.*

Fodor'sChoice ★   **The Brixton.** An English pub with an upscale D.C. twist offers three levels of fun in the heart of the U Street bustle. The menu is inspired by the Commonwealth's reach, including Indian, some Caribbean spice, and outstanding English, right down to the fish-and-chips. The sprawling roof deck changes pace with two bars, great views, and weekend DJs. In between, the second floor is wide open. Brixton also offers trivia contests and comedians. ⊠ *901 U St. NW, U Street* ☎ *202/560–5045* ⊕ *www.brixtondc.com* Ⓜ *U. St./Cardozo.*

Busboys and Poets. Part eatery, part bookstore, and part event space, this popular local hangout draws a diverse crowd and hosts a wide range of entertainment, from poetry open mikes to music to guest authors and activist speakers. The name is an homage to Langston Hughes, who worked as a busboy in D.C. before becoming a famous poet. This original location is open until 2 am on weekends—there's another downtown (at 1025 5th Street NW), as well as outposts in upper D.C., Maryland, and Virginia. ⊠ *2021 14th St. NW, U Street* ☎ *202/387–7638* ⊕ *www.busboysandpoets.com* Ⓜ *U St./Cardozo.*

Café Saint-Ex. Named for Antoine de Saint-Exupéry, French pilot and author of *The Little Prince,* this bi-level bar has a split personality. The upstairs brasserie has pressed-tin ceilings and a propeller hanging over the polished wooden bar. Downstairs is the Gate 54 nightclub, designed to resemble an airplane hangar, with dropped corrugated-metal ceilings and backlit aerial photographs. The downstairs DJs draw a fairly young crowd, while the upstairs menu attracts a more subdued clientele for dinner. ⊠ *1847 14th St. NW, U Street* ☎ *202/265–7839* ⊕ *www. saint-ex.com* Ⓜ *U St./Cardozo.*

Chi-Cha Lounge. Groups of young professionals relax on sofas and armchairs in this hip hangout modeled after an Ecuadorian hacienda, while Latin jazz mingles with pop music in the background and old movies run silently behind the bar. The place gets packed on weekends, so come early to get a coveted sofa along the back wall. Down the tasty tapas as you enjoy the namesake drink—think sangria with a bigger kick. Or try a hookah filled with a range of flavored tobaccos, from apple to watermelon. A dress-to-impress dress code is strictly enforced. ⊠ *1624 U St. NW, U Street* ☎ *202/234–8400* ⊕ *www.chicha-loungedc.com* Ⓜ *U St./Cardozo.*

Fodor's Choice ★ **Columbia Room.** Derek Brown's two-time James Beard–nominated ode to the American cocktail is located in downtown D.C.'s hippest 'hood for gourmands. Off Blagden Alley and up a flight of stairs you'll find a secluded outdoor Punch Garden. Deep inside comes the special-occasion, reservations-only Tasting Room, where a dozen or so cocktail connoisseurs can enjoy snacks and drinks in three- and five-course prix-fixe rounds. The main room, Spirits Library, is an intimate, romantic space, with a wall of books (and booze) and comfy, high-end furniture. You can't go wrong with the à la carte drink menu, full of creative, well-crafted spins on old fashioneds and highballs, among other themed concoctions. ⊠ *124 Blagden Alley NW, Shaw* ☎ *202/316–9396* ⊕ *www. columbiaroomdc.com* Ⓜ *Mt. Vernon Sq.*

Fodor's Choice ★ **Cork Wine Bar.** On weekends, the crowds can spill onto 14th Street—but one of the best wine bars in D.C. is worth the wait. An outstanding wine list (mainly French and Italian) is matched with delectable small plates (especially notable are the avocado-pistachio bread and goat-cheese cheesecake with berries). ⊠ *1720 14th St. NW, U Street* ☎ *202/265–2675* ⊕ *www.corkdc.com* Ⓜ *U St./Cardozo.*

Dacha Beer Garden. Set off by a three-story mural of Elizabeth Taylor, Dacha has become the go-to outdoor drinking venue in midtown D.C., with lines of people (and their dogs) waiting to get in most evenings anytime of year whenever the weather isn't bitterly cold or inclement. (A windscreen wall and heaters further help keep patrons toasty during the winter.) The beer garden serves drafts of craft beers from Germany, Belgium, and the U.S. as well as Bavarian-inspired nosh, while the adjoining café serves hot coffee and bagels and sandwiches during the day. ⊠ *1600 7th St. NW, Shaw* ☎ *202/350–9888* ⊕ *www. dachadc.com* Ⓜ *Shaw.*

Marvin. Young crowds cram in on the weekend, but even if that's not your scene this trendsetter, an homage to native son Marvin Gaye, is still worth a visit. The excellent gastropub—moules and frites, shrimp and grits—and a chill lower level offer a respite from the dance floors above. The outdoor back porch (heated in chillier months) provides an additional outlet for the partying masses. ✉ *2007 14th St. NW, U Street* ☎ *202/797-7171* ⊕ *www.marvindc.com* Ⓜ *U St./Cardozo.*

Nellie's Sports Bar. This popular sports bar with a gay following makes everyone feel welcome. Catch the games on multiple screens, or try your luck with "drag bingo" or trivia games. Spaces in this eclectic two-story venue range from roof deck to cozy pub room to a dining area serving all-American pub grub meets Venezuelan specialties—from empanadas to arepas. And every weekend brings a reservations-required brunch buffet with drag queens as servers and, of course, performers. ✉ *900 U St. NW, U Street* ☎ *202/332-6355* ⊕ *www.nelliessportsbar. com* Ⓜ *U St./Cardozo.*

The Saloon. A classic watering hole has no TVs, no light beer, and no martinis. What you can find are locals engaged in conversation—a stated goal of the owner—and some of the world's best beers, including the rare Urbock 23, an Austrian brew that is rated one of the tastiest and strongest in the world, with 9.6% alcohol content (limit one per customer). The Saloon also offers a broader bar menu, too. ✉ *1207 U St. NW, U Street* ☎ *202/462-2640* Ⓜ *U St./Cardozo.*

Satellite Room. Pre- and postconcert patrons of the adjacent 9:30 Club can enjoy boozy, vaguely Mexican milk shakes: think avocado with tequila, a more traditional chocolate with Kahlúa, or "Cinnamon Toast Punch"—all of which taste better than they sound. Delicious, albeit greasy, American-inspired fare is also on offer, including a series of burgers named after famous D.C.-native rock and pop stars, including Dave Grohl, Henry Rollins, Joan Jett, and Chuck Brown. A walled-off patio and dark, hip vibe can provide the perfect complement to a musical night out. ✉ *2047 9th St. NW, U Street* ☎ *202/506-2496* ⊕ *www. satellitedc.com* Ⓜ *U St./Cardozo.*

Southern Efficiency. This narrow whiskey bar's name is drawn from a famous JFK quote about the Southern flavor of the capital city. Southern Efficiency offers a selection of premium whiskeys and always has a couple of bourbon-based concoctions on draft, plus other libations from D.C. and places South. Also served are some food staples its owner Derek Brown loved during college in Charleston, South Carolina: Parker House rolls, shrimp paste, a lamb patty melt, and bourbon balls for dessert. Sit in the window and watch as passersby hustle to the Metro or to the Howard Theatre around the corner, or take a seat at the long beige-color bar, furnished to resemble a Southern lunch counter. From Thanksgiving to New Year's the bar and the connecting restaurants Eat The Rich and Mockingbird Hill are fully given over to a wildly popular Miracle on 7th Street pop-up with holiday-themed cocktails and decor. ✉ *1841 7th St. NW, Washington* ☎ *202/316-9396* ⊕ *www.whiskeyhome.com* Ⓜ *Shaw.*

Fodor's Choice
★
2 Birds, 1 Stone. In a barely marked underground spot just off the city's hottest strip you'll find this hip cocktail bar, serving an ever-changing menu of bold cocktails, both classic and experimental, featuring carefully chosen liquors mixed with house-made juices and sodas. Nibbles can be ordered from a small bar menu that overlaps with, and comes from the kitchen of, the acclaimed, adjoining pan-Asian restaurant Doi Moi. Unless you don't mind waiting and standing in an overcrowded space, opt to go midweek, or soon after the bar opens at 6 pm on weekends. ⊠ *1800 14th St. NW, Washington* ✚ *Entrance on S St.* ☎ *202/733–5131* ⊕ *2birds1stonedc.com* Ⓜ *U St./Cardozo.*

U Street Music Hall. This basement dance hall boasts one of the best sound systems in the city and features both DJs and live acts playing indie rock, dance, and electro music. The diverse crowd can feature young hipsters here for the bands early evening followed by club kids when DJs take over. Check the website to plan your visit accordingly. ⊠ *1115 U St. NW, U Street* ☎ *202/588–1880* ⊕ *www.ustreetmusichall. com* Ⓜ *U St./Cardozo.*

Vinoteca. The sophisticated set flocks here for a solid list of around 100 wines, a menu of delicious small bites, and weekend brunches. There's a daily happy hour (5–7 pm), and the flights of wine to sample are attractively priced. On Sunday nights there are live flamenco performances. In good weather you can dine on the front patio, and out back there's a large bar and a bocce court. Vinoteca also offers wine classes for small groups in the private rooms upstairs. ⊠ *1940 11th St. NW, U Street* ☎ *202/332–9463* ⊕ *www.vinotecadc. com* Ⓜ *U St./Cardozo.*

DANCE CLUBS

Fodor's Choice
★
Flash. The decline of megaclubs in D.C. has coincided with a rise in more intimate and inviting venues for those serious about dancing. This photography-themed jewel is near the Howard Theatre that replaced a pawnshop—a telling sign of this changing neighborhood. An operational photo booth is an entry point to the main upstairs dance floor, which envelopes you in walls lined with 10,000 LED lights and a best-in-the-business Funktion One sound system. Pioneering underground DJs—Carl Craig, Chus & Ceballos—move their flocks of a couple hundred fans while intermittently flashing them from the rigged 24 parabolic reflectors behind them. ⊠ *645 Florida Ave. NW, Washington* ☎ *202/827–8791* ⊕ *www.flashdc.com* Ⓜ *Shaw.*

Local 16. When they have to remove all the chairs in the joint to make more room for dancing, you know you've picked a good spot. Locals and out-of-towners alike pack in on weekends to enjoy the joyful pop music, multiple dance rooms, and the outdoor-deck bar perched one story above 16th Street. Luxe couches, chandeliers, vintage pieces, and winding staircases enhance the atmosphere of a Victorian house party with a modern twist. Outstanding $5 happy hour. ⊠ *1602 U St. NW, U Street* ☎ *202/265–2828* ⊕ *www.localsixteen.com* Ⓜ *U St./Cardozo.*

Town Danceboutique. Two nights of drag shows, international DJs, go-go boys, and a "chill-out room" keep the crowds coming to this U Street corridor party place, which also has one of the hippest outdoor patios, enhancing warm-weather fun. Expect lines, but not too much attitude and a festive, mixed-age crowd—particularly on Friday nights, when DC Bear Crue hosts "the nation's largest weekly bear event" at happy hour. Regular hours are Friday and Saturday, but some weeks see special events on other nights. ⊠ *2009 8th St. NW, U Street* ☏ *202/234–8696* ⊕ *www.towndc.com* Ⓜ *U St./Cardozo.*

MUSIC CLUBS

JAZZ AND BLUES

Twins Jazz. For nearly three decades, twin sisters Kelly and Maze Tesfaye have been offering great jazz, featuring some of D.C.'s strongest straight-ahead jazz players, as well as groups from as far away as New York. The food is nothing to write home about, but it's easy to meet the nightly minimum with drinks. Connections with local universities bring in new and experimental talent. ⊠ *1344 U St. NW, U Street* ☏ *202/234–0072* ⊕ *www.twinsjazz.com* Ⓜ *U St./Cardozo.*

ROCK AND POP

Fodor'sChoice ★

Black Cat. Way before its stretch of 14th Street became the trendiest few blocks in town, the Black Cat was a destination for alternative music and quirky nostalgic dance parties—chiefly ever-popular ironic "duels" between pop acts (e.g., "The Cure vs. The Smiths," "Divas Dance Party"). But in addition to D.C.'s most popular bands and indie-rock favorites such as the Dandy Warhols, the Ravonettes, and Ex Hex, the Black Cat also regularly offers edgy burlesque and comedy. The postpunk crowd whiles away the time in the ground floor's Red Room, a side bar with pool tables, an eclectic jukebox, and no cover charge. The club is also home to Food for Thought, a legendary vegetarian café. ⊠ *1811 14th St. NW, U Street* ☏ *202/667–4490* ⊕ *www.blackcatdc. com* Ⓜ *U St./Cardozo.*

DC9. With live music most days of the week, this small two-story rock club with an upper deck hosts fledgling indie bands and the occasional nationally known act. There's a narrow bar on the ground floor, a sizable concert space on the second floor, and an enclosed roof deck on top. DJs take the controls for weekend night dance parties. ⊠ *1940 9th St. NW, U Street* ☏ *202/483–5000* ⊕ *www.dcnine. com* Ⓜ *U St./Cardozo.*

Fodor'sChoice ★

9:30 Club. Consistently ranked as one of the best concert venues in the country, the 9:30 Club is also a favorite of many rock acts due to warm receptions from crowds and a doting staff. The best indie and up-and-coming performers are the main attraction, though every now and then a bigger act such as Justin Timberlake or Loretta Lynn stops by to soak up the vibe of this large but cozy space wrapped by balconies on three sides. Recent acts have included critical darlings the Punch Brothers, Kasey Chambers, San Fermin, and Disclosure, as well as groups with a long history, such as George Clinton, OAR, and hometown favorites Thievery Corporation and

Animal Collective. Bands and singers occasionally make way for DJ-fueled dance parties late on weekend nights. ■TIP➜ For the best view, arrive at least an hour before the doors open, typically at 8:30. ✉ *815 V St. NW, U Street* ☎ *202/265–0930* ⊕ *www.930.com* Ⓜ *U St./Cardozo.*

Velvet Lounge. Squeeze up the narrow stairway and check out the eclectic local and national bands that play at this unassuming, tiny neighborhood joint. In addition to performers ranging from indie mainstays to critically touted up-and-comers, the venue regularly hosts comedy and variety shows. ✉ *915 U St. NW, U Street* ☎ *202/462–3213* ⊕ *www. velvetloungedc.com* Ⓜ *U St./Cardozo.*

ARLINGTON AND NORTHERN VIRGINIA

Just across the Potomac, Arlington and Alexandria boast some topnotch bars and lounges—with considerably more parking and less hectic traffic than D.C. Also accessible by the Metro, revitalized Ballston and Clarendon are interesting and enjoyable places, though more laid-back, even quiet, to visit at night.

BARS AND LOUNGES

Carpool. "Andy Warhol meets General Motors" is how one magazine described this former garage turned bar. Enjoy a brew and standard bar fare, from Caesars to sliders. Amenities include eight pool tables, as well as skeeball, shuffleboard, and darts. Carpool also boasts more sports screens than you can shake a foam finger at. Fun and games aside, keep in mind it's 21 and older after 4 pm. ✉ *4000 Fairfax Dr., Arlington* ☎ *703/532–7665* ⊕ *www.gocarpool.com* Ⓜ *Ballston.*

Fishmarket. There's something different in just about every section of this multilevel, multiroom space, though the nightlife centers on the sports-focused Anchor Bar. The thirty- and fortysomething crowd watching local televised games is boisterous. If you really like beer, order a "Schooner" size; at 32 ounces, it's a glass big enough to put your face in. Or make it an innocent night out at their adjacent Pop's Old Fashioned Ice Cream Co. ✉ *105 King St., Old Town* ☎ *703/836–5676* ⊕ *www.fishmarketva.com* Ⓜ *King St.*

PX. Reservations are accepted for this swanky, small speakeasy featuring artisanal libations by Todd Thrasher, but if the blue light is lit that's the sign they've got room for some walk-ins. It's hard to say what's the best part—the intimate setting, the attentive service, or the otherworldly drinks. PX asks its patrons to dress up—no baseball caps, T-shirts or jeans—and to refrain from wearing anything that shows too much skin, from tank tops to shorts and flip-flops. ✉ *728 King St., Old Town* ☎ *703/299–8385* ⊕ *www.barpx.com* Ⓜ *King St.*

State Theatre. This is the place to go to see concerts by aging hit makers from the past such as the Smithereens or tribute bands to the likes of Led Zeppelin, Pink Floyd, and Bon Jovi. You have the choice of sitting or standing in this renovated movie theater, which is about 10 miles south of D.C. The popular 1980s retro dance parties, featuring the Leg-warmers tribute band, draw locals who like to dress the part. ⊠ *220 N. Washington St., Falls Church* ☎ *703/237–0300* ⊕ *www.thestatetheatre. com* Ⓜ *E. Falls Church*.

MUSIC CLUBS

Fodor'sChoice   **The Birchmere.** A legend in the D.C. area, the Birchmere is one of the
★   best places outside the Blue Ridge Mountains to hear acoustic folk, country, and bluegrass. Enthusiastic crowds regularly enjoy table-side service while taking in performances by artists such as Judy Collins, Don McLean, Bela Fleck, and Emmylou Harris. But the club is also a draw for some of the country's best jazz and R&B artists (Rachelle Farrell, Sheila E., Angie Stone). ⊠ *3701 Mt. Vernon Ave., Alexandria* ☎ *703/549–7500* ⊕ *www.birchmere.com*.

PERFORMING
ARTS

Updated
by Robert
Michael Oliver
Whether you're looking for theater, jazz, dance, cinema, cabaret, comedy, or something classical, Washington, D.C., has some of the most exciting and thought-provoking entertainment in the country. Since the opening of the John F. Kennedy Center for the Performing Arts in 1971, the city's performing arts culture has grown steadily. Washington now hosts the third-largest theater scene in the country, as well as a rich offering of nightly music opportunities featuring local, national, and international talent, and so much more. No city outshines the District on the magnificence and variety of its arts venues.

Diverse theaters offer everything from Rodgers and Hammerstein to experimental fare. The Kennedy Center and the historic National Theatre bring in primarily big-time touring shows, but the 65-year-old Arena Stage offers the best in regional theater. Meanwhile, relative newcomers like the Studio Theatre, Woolly Mammoth, and northern Virginia's Signature Theatre offer a palette of performances as varied as any in the country.

The city also has its share of every kind of music imaginable, from classical quartets to the most current EDM sensation. With venues ranging from DAR Constitution Hall to the Verizon Center near D.C.'s Chinatown to northern Virginia's Birchmere Music Hall, music can be found wherever you are, both in the city and its many suburbs.

Those looking for cinema can catch unusual foreign fare, rare documentaries, independent features, and classics. As for dance, Washington has more than enough options for ballet, modern dance, and more.

PLANNING

TICKETS

Tickets to most events are available by calling or visiting the venue's box office and website or through the following ticket agencies:

Contacts Ticketmaster. ☎ *800/745–3000, 866/448–7849,* ⊕ *www.ticketmaster.com.* **Ticketplace.** ⊕ *www.ticketplace.org.* **Tickets.com.** ☎ *800/955–5566* ⊕ *www.tickets.com.*

EVENTS INFORMATION

For information on events in D.C., the best listings are found at the *Washington Post Going Out Guide* (⊕ *www.washingtonpost.com/gog*) and the free weekly *Washington CityPaper* (⊕ *www.washingtoncitypaper.com*). Other events listings are found in the daily "Guide to the Lively Arts" and the Friday "Weekend" sections in the *Washington Post,* and the "City Lights" section in the monthly *Washingtonian* magazine. For theater and other arts activities, you can also check out Theatre Washington (⊕ *www.theatrewashington.org*), which keeps a weekly listing of theatrical performances, and the Culture Capital (⊕ *www.culturecapital.com*). DCMetroTheaterArts (⊕ *www.dcmetrotheaterarts.com*), the MD Theatre Guide (⊕ *www.mdtheatreguide.com*), and DC Theatre Scene (⊕ *www.dctheatrescene.com*) also post daily on D.C. events.

WHITE HOUSE AREA

Surrounding the president's home and the nation's monumental core is a wealth of concerts, films, music, and dance, not to mention galleries of the world's most famous art and relics displayed in the Smithsonian Institution's many exhibits. The best part of all, many of these treasures are free and open to the public.

MAJOR VENUES

DAR Constitution Hall. Acts ranging from Steve Harvey to Louis CK to B.B. King perform at this 3,700-seat venue, one of Washington's grand old halls. It's well worth a visit for both the excellent performers it attracts as well as its awesome architecture and acoustics. ⊠ *1776 D St. NW, White House area* ☎ *202/628–4780* ⊕ *www.dar.org/constitution-hall* Ⓜ *Farragut W.*

National Gallery of Art. On Fridays from 5 to 9 pm from Memorial Day through Labor Day, local jazz groups perform to packed crowds in the Pavilion Café at the Sculpture Garden. Listeners dip their feet in the fountain, sip sangria, and let the week wash away. From October to June free concerts by the National Gallery Orchestra and performances by visiting recitalists and ensembles are held in the West Building's West Garden Court on Sunday nights. Entry is first come, first served, with doors opening at 6 pm and concerts starting at 6:30 pm. On Wednesdays, free midday performances of classical music begin around noon. Also be sure to check out their film series. ⊠ *6th St. and Constitution Ave. NW, White House area* ☎ *202/842–6941* ⊕ *www.nga.gov* Ⓜ *Archives/Navy Memorial.*

Fodor's Choice ★ **Smithsonian Institution.** Throughout the year the Smithsonian Associates sponsor programs that offer everything from a cappella groups
to Cajun zydeco bands; all events require tickets and locations vary.
For an especially memorable musical experience, catch a performance
of the Smithsonian Jazz Masterworks Orchestra in residence at the
National Museum of American History. Children and adults will enjoy
the two IMAX theaters, at the Museum of Natural History and at the
Air and Space Museum. The Smithsonian's annual summer Folklife
Festival, held on the Mall, highlights the cuisine, crafts, and day-to-day
life of several different cultures. ⊠ *1000 Jefferson Dr. SW, The Mall*
🕾 *202/357–2700, 202/633–1000 recording, 202/357–3030 Smithsonian Associates* ⊕ *www.si.edu* Ⓜ *Smithsonian.*

FILM

National Archives. Historical films, usually documentaries, are shown
here regularly. Screenings range from Robert Flaherty's 1942 cover-
age of the plight of migrant workers to archival footage of Charles
Lindbergh's solo flight from New York to Paris. After catching a
documentary, stroll by and inspect the Constitution in this solemn
and impressive venue. ⊠ *Constitution Ave. between 7th and 9th Sts.
NW, The Mall* 🕾 *202/501–5000* ⊕ *www.archives.gov* Ⓜ *Archives/
Navy Memorial.*

National Gallery of Art, East Building. Free classic and international films,
from Steven Spielberg's first feature-length film, *Duel*, to Béla Tarr's
Macbeth that was filmed inside a Budapest castle, are usually shown in
this museum's large auditorium each weekend. Sometimes films complement the exhibits. For more information about the specific films, pick
up a film calendar at the museum or go online. ⊠ *Constitution Ave.
between 3rd and 4th Sts. NW, The Mall* 🕾 *202/842–6799* ⊕ *www.nga.
gov* Ⓜ *Archives/Navy Memorial.*

PERFORMANCE SERIES

Armed Forces Concert Series. In a Washington tradition, bands from the
four branches of the armed services perform June to August on Monday, Tuesday, Wednesday, and Friday evenings on the west steps of
the U.S. Capitol. Concerts usually include marches, patriotic numbers,
and some classical music. Other performances take place at 8 pm from
June to August, on Tuesday, Thursday, Friday, and Sunday nights at
various locations throughout the metro area. ⊠ *U.S. Capitol, Capitol
Hill* 🕾 *202/767–5658 Air Force, 703/696–3718 Army, 202/433–4011
Marines, 202/433–2525 Navy* Ⓜ *Capitol S.*

Screen on the Green. Every July and August, since 1999, this weekly
series of classic films turns the Mall into an open-air cinema. People
arrive as early as 5 pm to picnic, socialize, and reserve a spot. The
show starts at dusk. ⊠ *The Mall at 7th St., The Mall* 🕾 *877/262–5866*
Ⓜ *Smithsonian.*

FOGGY BOTTOM

South of Downtown D.C. and north of Georgetown, Foggy Bottom is home to the John F. Kennedy Center for the Performing Arts and George Washington University's Lisner Auditorium—two great venues for the performing arts. Both facilities present drama, dance, and music, offering a platform for some of the most famous American and international performers. Hungry and thirsty visitors to the Kennedy Center can dine and drink at the Roof Top Terrace Restaurant and Bar.

MAJOR VENUES

Fodor'sChoice
★ **John F. Kennedy Center for the Performing Arts.** On the bank of the Potomac River, the gem of the Washington, D.C., performing arts scene is home to the National Symphony Orchestra, the Suzanne Farrell Ballet, and the Washington National Opera. The best out-of-town acts perform at one of three performance spaces—the Concert Hall, the Opera House, or the Eisenhower Theater. An eclectic range of performances is staged at the center's smaller venues, which showcase chamber groups, experimental works, cabaret-style performances, and the KC Jazz Club. But that's not all. On the Millennium Stage in the center's Grand Foyer, you can catch free performances almost any day at 6 pm. Finally, each year in March the Center presents an international theater and performance festival; recent festivals have featured Norway, China, Australia, and South Africa. ■TIP➜ **On performance days, a free shuttle bus runs between the Center and the Foggy Bottom/GWU Metro stop.** ✉ *New Hampshire Ave. and Rock Creek Pkwy. NW, Foggy Bottom* ☎ *202/467–4600, 800/444–1324* ⊕ *www.kennedy-center.org* Ⓜ *Foggy Bottom/GWU.*

Lisner Auditorium. A 1,500-seat theater on the campus of George Washington University hosts pop, classical, and choral music shows, modern dance performances, and musical theater, attracting students and outsiders alike. ✉ *730 21st St. NW, Foggy Bottom* ☎ *202/994–6800* ⊕ *www.lisner.org* Ⓜ *Foggy Bottom/GWU.*

DANCE

Suzanne Farrell Ballet. Founded in 2000, this dance company, which began as an educational program at the Kennedy Center, has grown into an internationally recognized troupe with more than 50 ballets in its repertoire. The company's Balanchine Preservation Initiative is committed to carrying forth the legacy of George Balanchine, the famous Bolshoi choreographer and innovator. ✉ *John F. Kennedy Center for the Performing Arts, 2700 F St. NW, Foggy Bottom* ⊕ *www.kennedy-center.org* Ⓜ *Foggy Bottom.*

Washington Ballet. The company's classical and contemporary dances are performed from September through May, with works by such choreographers as George Balanchine, Choo-San Goh, and artistic director Septime Webre. The main shows are mounted at the Kennedy Center and at THEARC in Southeast D.C. Each December the company also performs *The Nutcracker* at the Warner Theatre. ✉ *3515 Wisconsin Ave. NW, Woodley Park* ☎ *202/362–3606* ⊕ *www.washingtonballet.org.*

6

CLOSE UP

Five Great Arts Experiences

■ **Arena Stage:** Housed in the audience-friendly Mead Center for American Theatre, Arena Stage offers innovative new American plays as well as classic plays and musicals.

■ **John F. Kennedy Center for the Performing Arts:** The gem of the D.C. arts scene, this is the one performance venue you might take with you if you were stranded on a desert island.

■ **Shakespeare Theatre:** Among the top Shakespeare companies in the world, this troupe excels at both classical and contemporary interpretations.

■ **Studio Theatre:** With its four intimate theaters and its hip urban locale, this 14th Street landmark provides the best in contemporary dramas and comedies.

■ **Woolly Mammoth:** This remarkable theater company stages some of the most creative and entertaining new plays from the nation's best playwrights.

MUSIC

CHORAL MUSIC

Choral Arts Society of Washington. From fall to late spring, this 200-voice choir performs a musical array, ranging from classical to tango to Broadway hits, at the Kennedy Center Concert Hall and other venues. Three Christmas sing-alongs are also scheduled each December, and in January or February there's a popular tribute to Martin Luther King Jr. ⊠ *5225 Wisconsin Ave. NW, Friendship Heights, Suite 603, Foggy Bottom* ☎ *202/244–3669* ⊕ *www.choralarts.org* Ⓜ *Friendship Heights.*

OPERA

Washington National Opera. Founded in 1956, the Washington National Opera presents a variety of classical works each year at the Kennedy Center Opera House. The operas are performed in their original languages with English supertitles. In 2012 the WNO created the New American Opera Initiative, which produces three new 20-minute operas in the fall and an hour-long opera in the spring. The WNO also started the Young Artists Program in 2002 under the leadership of Plácido Domingo. These emerging international talents perform throughout the year. ⊠ *John F. Kennedy Center for the Performing Arts, New Hampshire Ave. and Rock Creek Pkwy. NW, Foggy Bottom* ☎ *202/295–2400, 800/876–7372* ⊕ *www.kennedy-center.org/wno.*

ORCHESTRA

National Symphony Orchestra. Under the leadership of music director Gianandrea Noseda, the orchestra performs classic works by composers such as Verdi, Handel, and Rossini in the Kennedy Center Concert Hall. In summer the orchestra performs at Wolf Trap and gives free concerts at Rock Creek Park's Carter Barron Amphitheatre. On Memorial and Labor Day weekends and on July 4, the NSO performs on the West Lawn of the Capitol. ⊠ *John F. Kennedy Center for the Performing Arts, New Hampshire Ave. and Rock Creek Pkwy. NW, Foggy Bottom* ☎ *202/467–4600* ⊕ *www.kennedy-center.org/nso* Ⓜ *Foggy Bottom.*

PERFORMANCE SERIES

Washington Performing Arts Society. One of the city's oldest arts organizations stages high-quality classical music, jazz, gospel, world music, modern dance, and performance art in major venues around the city. Past artists include the Alvin Ailey American Dance Theater, Yo-Yo Ma, The Chieftains, Herbie Hancock, and Savion Glover. ⊠ *2000 L St. NW, Suite 510, Foggy Bottom* ☎ *202/785–9727* ⊕ *www.wpas.org.*

CAPITOL HILL AND NORTHEAST D.C.

The arts scene in Capitol Hill and Northeast D.C. has blossomed in recent years with the opening of several performance venues and the explosion of restaurants, bars, and stages along the emerging H Street Corridor. Leading the charge is the Atlas Performing Arts Center, at the cutting edge of dance, music, and drama. For classical drama, you will discover great performances and an intimate atmosphere at the Folger Theatre near the Capitol.

MAJOR VENUES

Atlas Performing Arts Center. Known as the "People's Kennedy Center," this performance venue occupies a restored historic movie theater in one of Washington's up-and-coming neighborhoods. The Atlas's four theaters and three dance studios house a diverse group of resident arts organizations, including the Mosaic Theater Company of D.C., the Joy of Motion Dance Center, and the Capital City Symphony. Street parking can be difficult, but you can now take the DC Streetcar here from the Metro stop at Union Station. ⊠ *1333 H St. NE, Northeast* ☎ *202/399–7993* ⊕ *www.atlasarts.org* Ⓜ *Union Station.*

DANCE

Dance Place. This studio theater showcases an eclectic array of local, national, and international dance and performance art talent in an assortment of modern and ethnic shows; performances take place most weekends. It also conducts drop-in dance classes daily. The company is located in Northeast Washington, quite close to the Metro and Monroe Market with its Arts Walk. ⊠ *3225 8th St. NE, Northeast* ☎ *202/269–1600* ⊕ *www.danceplace.org* Ⓜ *Catholic U.*

Joy of Motion. Resident companies include El Teatro de Danza Contemporanea El Salvador, Furia Flamenca, and Silk Road Dance Company (traditional Middle Eastern and Central Asian), among others. They offer drop-in classes in three locations: the Atlas Performing Arts Center; the studio's Jack Guidone Theatre in Upper Northwest; and in Bethesda, Maryland. There are weekly performances. ⊠ *5207 Wisconsin Ave. NW, Northeast* ☎ *202/362–3042* ⊕ *www.joyofmotion.org* Ⓜ *Friendship Heights.*

MUSIC

CHAMBER MUSIC

Coolidge Auditorium at the Library of Congress. Since its first concert, in 1925, the Coolidge has hosted most of the 20th and 21st century's' greatest performers and composers, including Copland and Stravinsky. Today, the theater draws musicians from all genres, including classical, jazz, and gospel, and the hall continues to wow audiences with its near-perfect acoustics and sight lines. Concert tickets are free, but must be ordered in advance through Ticketmaster. ■TIP➜ **Because of the Library's security procedures, patrons are urged to arrive 30 minutes before the start of each event.** ✉ *Library of Congress, Jefferson Bldg., 101 Independence Ave. SE, Capitol Hill* ☎ *800/551–7328* ⊕ *www.loc. gov* Ⓜ *Capitol S.*

Folger Shakespeare Library. The library's internationally acclaimed resident chamber music ensemble, the Folger Consort, regularly presents medieval, Renaissance, and baroque pieces performed on period instruments. The season runs from October to May. ✉ *201 E. Capitol St. SE, Capitol Hill* ☎ *202/544–7077* ⊕ *www.folger.edu* Ⓜ *Union Station/Capitol S.*

CHORAL MUSIC

Basilica of the National Shrine of the Immaculate Conception. Choral and church groups occasionally perform at the largest Catholic church in the Americas, and every summer, recitals featuring the massive pipe organ are offered. While you are there, be sure to go down to the crypt to experience the mysteries of the world's many Madonnas. See the website for times and visiting performers. ✉ *400 Michigan Ave. NE, Northeast* ☎ *202/526–8300* ⊕ *www.nationalshrine.com* Ⓜ *Brookland/CUA.*

THEATER AND PERFORMANCE ART

Fodor's Choice
★
Arena Stage. The first regional theater company to win a Tony Award performs innovative American theater, reviving such classic plays as *Oklahoma* and also showcasing the country's best new playwrights. The architecturally magnificent Mead Center for American Theatre houses three stages and, after the Kennedy Center, is the second-largest performing arts complex in Washington. Near the waterfront neighborhood in Southwest D.C., the Mead Center features the Fichandler Stage, a theater-in-the-round seating 680; the Kreeger Theater, a modified thrust seating 514; and the Kogod Cradle, a 200-seat black-box theater for new or experimental productions. ■TIP➜ **Inside the Mead, the Catwalk Café serves meals inspired by the shows playing that evening.** ✉ *1101 6th St. SW, Southwest* ☎ *202/554–9066* ⊕ *www.arenastage.org* Ⓜ *Waterfront/SEU.*

Capital Fringe Festival. Since its founding in 2005, the Capital Fringe Festival has grown each year, and currently offers no fewer than 125 productions over a three-week period in July. Local and national performers display the strange, the political, the surreal, and the avant-garde to eclectic crowds at all times of the day in venues throughout the city. With tickets around $17, this is an affordable theater experience. ■TIP➜ **Don't forget your Fringe Button, a pin that grants the**

holder access to all festival events and benefits from local retailers. Be ready to party at the Fringe Arts Bar, where performers, musicians, and patrons rock into the wee hours. ✉ *1358 Florida Ave. NE, Downtown* ☎ *866/811–4111* ⊕ *www.capfringe.org.*

Fodor'sChoice
★
Folger Theatre. The theater at the Folger Shakespeare Library, an intimate 250-seat re-creation of the inn-yard theaters of Shakespeare's time, hosts three to four productions each year of Shakespearean or Shakespeare-influenced works. Although the stage is a throwback, the sharp acting and inspired direction consistently challenge and delight audiences. ✉ *Folger Shakespeare Library, 201 E. Capitol St. SE, Capitol Hill* ☎ *202/544–7077* ⊕ *www.folger.edu* Ⓜ *Union Station/Capitol S.*

Rorschach Theatre. This company's intimate and passionate performances on the stages of H Street's Atlas Performing Arts Center are some of the most offbeat plays in Washington. The company offers lesser-known works by such playwrights as Fengar Gael, Jennifer Maisel, and José Rivera, as well as imaginative revivals of classics like Thornton Wilder's *The Skin of our Teeth.* ✉ *1333 H St. NE, Northeast* ☎ *202/452–5538* ⊕ *www.rorschachtheatre.com* Ⓜ *Union Station.*

6

DOWNTOWN

Several of Washington's most prestigious performance centers can be found in Downtown D.C. Woolly Mammoth Theater, the Shakespeare Theatre's Sidney Harmon Hall, and other venues are surrounded by a bustling nightlife where visitors have their choice of cuisines and after-performance conversation. You'll also be entertained by a host of street performers and musicians.

MAJOR VENUES

Verizon Center. In addition to being the home of the Washington Capitals hockey and Washington Wizards basketball teams, this 19,000-seat arena also plays host to D.C.'s biggest concerts and other major events. Drivers need to park in one of the many underground garages close by, but there are several convenient Metro lines, too. During warmer months be sure to check out the frequent street concerts on the intersections surrounding the Center. ✉ *601 F St. NW, Chinatown* ☎ *202/661–5000* ⊕ *www.verizoncenter.com* Ⓜ *Gallery Pl./Chinatown.*

FILM

Fodor'sChoice
★
Landmark's E Street Cinema. Specializing in independent, foreign, and documentary films, this theater has been warmly welcomed by D.C. movie lovers both for its selection and its state-of-the-art facilities. The *Washington Post* has often declared it D.C.'s best movie theater in its annual assessments. Its concession stand is fabulous and it is also one of the few movie theaters in the city that serve alcohol. ✉ *555 11th St. NW, Downtown* ☎ *202/452–7672* ⊕ *www.landmarktheatres.com* Ⓜ *Metro Center.*

READINGS AND LECTURES

National Academy of Sciences. In collaboration with various local professional theaters, the NAS offers a staged reading series of science-themed plays, and on the third Thursday of the month, the DASER (D.C. Art Science Evening Rendezvous) Salons focus on the fusion of culture and science. Events are free to the public but be sure to go online and register in advance. ✉ *2100 C St. NW, Downtown* ☎ *202/334–2436* ⊕ *www. nationalacademies.org/arts* Ⓜ *Foggy Bottom/GWU.*

THEATER AND PERFORMANCE ART

FAMILY **Ford's Theatre.** Looking much as it did before President Lincoln was shot at a performance of *Our American Cousin,* Ford's hosts musicals as well as dramas with historical connections, and stages *A Christmas Carol* every year. The historic theater is now maintained by the National Park Service. Tours of the theater and accompanying museum are available for free, but timed entry tickets are required. ✉ *511 10th St. NW, Downtown* ☎ *202/426–6925* ⊕ *www.fordstheatre.org* Ⓜ *Metro Center.*

FAMILY **National Theatre.** Though rebuilt several times, the National Theatre has operated in the same location since 1835. It now hosts touring Broadway shows, from classics like *Porgy and Bess* and *Chicago,* to contemporary punk like *American Idiot.* ∎**TIP**➜ **From September through April, look for free children's shows Saturday mornings and free Monday night shows that may include Asian dance, performance art, and a cappella cabarets.** ✉ *1321 Pennsylvania Ave. NW, Downtown* ☎ *800/447–7400* ⊕ *thenationaldc.org* Ⓜ *Metro Center.*

Fodor'sChoice **Shakespeare Theatre.** This acclaimed troupe crafts fantastically staged
★ and acted performances of works by Shakespeare and other significant playwrights, offering traditional renditions but also some with a modern twist. Complementing the stage in the Lansburgh Theatre is Sidney Harman Hall, which provides a state-of-the-art, midsize venue for an outstanding variety of performances, from Shakespeare's *Much Ado About Nothing* to Racine's tragic *Phèdre* for visiting companies like South Africa's Baxter Theatre and its production of *Mies Julie.* For two weeks in the summer the group performs Shakespeare for free at Sidney Harmon Hall. ✉ *450 7th St. NW, Downtown* ☎ *202/547–1122* ⊕ *shakespearetheatre.org* Ⓜ *Gallery Pl./Chinatown or Archives/ Navy Memorial.*

Sixth & I Historic Synagogue. Known for its author readings and its comedy, with guests ranging from comedian Tina Fey to Nancy Pelosi, the Sixth & I Historic Synagogue has been named one of the most vibrant congregations in the nation. The intimate space, founded in 1852, hosts religious events as well. ✉ *600 I St. NW, Chinatown* ☎ *202/408–3100* ⊕ *www.sixthandi.org* Ⓜ *Gallery Pl./Chinatown.*

Warner Theatre. One of Washington's grand theaters, the Warner hosts Broadway road shows, dance recitals, high-profile pop-music acts, and comedians in a majestic art deco performance space. ✉ *513 13th St. NW, Downtown* ☎ *202/783–4000* ⊕ *warnertheatredc.com* Ⓜ *Metro Center.*

Fodor's Choice
★ **Woolly Mammoth.** Unusual cutting-edge shows with solid acting have earned this company top reviews and 35 Helen Hayes Awards. The theater performs works for a decidedly urban audience that challenge the status quo. In recent years, they have welcomed Chicago's The Second City for an annual political comedy show as well as the works of Mike Daisey, the author of *The Agony and Ecstasy of Steve Jobs*. The troupe's talent is accentuated by its modern 265-seat theater in bustling Downtown D.C. The Woollies also create a unique lobby experience for each show; bring your iPhone and share the experience. ✉ *641 D St. NW, Downtown* ☎ *202/393–3939* ⊕ *www.woollymammoth.net* Ⓜ *Gallery Pl./Chinatown or Archives/Navy Memorial.*

GEORGETOWN

Georgetown entertainment goes far beyond barhopping on a Saturday night. Smaller drama groups stage productions in several of Georgetown's larger churches; check local publications for the latest offerings.

MUSIC

CHAMBER MUSIC
Dumbarton Concerts. A fixture in Georgetown since 1772 (in its current location since 1850), Dumbarton United Methodist Church sponsors a concert series that has been host to such musicians as the American Chamber Players, the St. Petersburg String Quartet, and the Thibaud String Trio. ■ TIP➔ Before or after a performance, take a stroll through the nearby Dumbarton Oaks estate and park. ✉ *Dumbarton United Methodist Church, 3133 Dumbarton Ave. NW, Georgetown* ☎ *202/965–2000* ⊕ *dumbartonconcerts.org* Ⓜ *Foggy Bottom.*

DUPONT CIRCLE AND LOGAN CIRCLE

Dupont Circle's reputation has grown in recent years as a place for good drama, with the Studio Theatre offering outstanding productions from new writers and some of Europe and America's best-known playwrights. Talented troupes in unique venues are sprinkled throughout the neighborhood, including the Keegan Theatre on Church Street and Washington Stage Guild at the Undercroft Theatre. But a little-known secret is that free concerts are offered at the Phillips Collection.

MAJOR VENUES

D.C. Jewish Community Center. The Washington Jewish Music Festival and the Washington Jewish Film Festival are hosted here, along with periodic musical performances by a diverse group of performers. The JCC is also the home of Theatre J. ✉ *1529 16th St. NW, Dupont Circle* ☎ *202/518–9400* ⊕ *www.washingtondcjcc.org* Ⓜ *Dupont Circle.*

6

FILM

Filmfest DC. Now entering its 29th year, this annual citywide festival of international cinema (officially known as the D.C. International Film Festival) takes place in April or early May at venues throughout Washington. ⊠ *1700 14th St. NW, Logan Circle* ☎ *202/274–5782* ⊕ *www. filmfestdc.org* Ⓜ *U St./Cardozo.*

National Geographic Society. Documentary films with a scientific, geographic, or anthropological focus are shown regularly at National Geographic's Grosvenor Auditorium. An easy walk from Dupont Circle, "NatGeo" also hosts speakers, concerts, and photography exhibits year-round. Be sure to check out their 3-D films. ⊠ *1145 17th St. NW, Dupont Circle* ☎ *202/857–7700* ⊕ *events.nationalgeographic.com/ events* Ⓜ *Farragut N.*

MUSIC

CHAMBER MUSIC

Phillips Collection. Duncan Phillips's mansion is more than an art museum. On Sunday afternoon from October through May, chamber groups from around the world perform in the long, dark-paneled Music Room. Plus, on the first Thursday of the month, from 5 to 8:30 pm, the museum offers Phillips After 5, a lively mix of jazz performances, food and drink, gallery talks, films, and more. The free Sunday concerts begin at 4 pm; arrive early for decent seats. ⊠ *1600 21st St. NW, Dupont Circle* ☎ *202/387–2151* ⊕ *www.phillipscollec-tion.org* Ⓜ *Dupont Circle.*

THEATER AND PERFORMANCE ART

The Keegan Theatre. This newly renovated historic 115-seat black-box theater offers a rich variety of contemporary Irish and American plays and musicals. ⊠ *1742 Church St. NW, Dupont Circle* ☎ *703/892–0202* ⊕ *keegantheatre.com* Ⓜ *Dupont Circle.*

Fodor'sChoice ★ **Studio Theatre.** One of the busiest groups in the city, this multifaceted theater company produces an eclectic season of contemporary European and offbeat American plays in four spaces: the original Mead and Milton theaters, the newer 200-seat Metheny Theatre, and the experimental Stage 4. The theater is part of Washington's energetic 14th Street Corridor. ⊠ *1501 14th St. NW, Dupont Circle* ☎ *202/332–3300* ⊕ *www. studiotheatre.org* Ⓜ *Dupont Circle.*

Theater J. One of the country's most distinguished Jewish performance venues offers an ambitious range of programming that includes work by noted playwrights, directors, designers, and actors. Past performances have included one-person shows featuring Sarah Bernhard and Judy Gold as well as more edgy political pieces. Performances take place in the Aaron and Cecile Goldman Theater at the D.C. Jewish Community Center. ⊠ *1529 16th St. NW, Dupont Circle* ☎ *202/518–9400* ⊕ *www. theaterj.org* Ⓜ *Dupont Circle.*

Washington Stage Guild. This company performs neglected classics as well as contemporary literary plays in the Undercroft Theatre of Mount Vernon Place United Methodist Church. In recent years they have offered lesser-known works by Oscar Wilde and George Bernard Shaw. Contemporary plays such as *Tryst* by Karoline Leach and David Marshall Grant's *Pen* are also offered. ✉ *900 Massachusetts Ave. NW, Logan Circle* ☎ *240/582–0050* ⊕ *www.stageguild.org* Ⓜ *Dupont Circle.*

ADAMS MORGAN

Adams Morgan has long been the hub of the city's best avant-garde performances, primarily offered by the District of Columbia Arts Center. You can enjoy an incredible meal at one of many nearby ethnic restaurants, see a performance at the Gala Hispanic Theatre, and then head to one of the neighborhood's colorful bars after the show.

THEATER AND PERFORMANCE ART

District of Columbia Arts Center. Known by area artists as DCAC, this cross-genre space shows changing exhibits in its gallery and presents avant-garde performance art, improv, and experimental plays in its tiny, funky black-box theater. DCAC is the home of Washington's oldest experimental theater group, Theatre Du Jour. ✉ *2438 18th St. NW, Adams Morgan* ☎ *202/462–7833* ⊕ *www.dcartscenter.org* Ⓜ *Woodley Park.*

Gala Hispanic Theatre. This company attracts outstanding Hispanic actors from around the world, performing works by such leading dramatists as Federico García Lorca and Mario Vargas Llosa. Plays are presented in English or in Spanish with projected subtitles. The company performs in the Tivoli Theatre in Columbia Heights, a hot spot for Latino culture and cuisine. ✉ *Tivoli Sq., 3333 14th St. NW and Park Rd., Columbia Heights, Adams Morgan* ☎ *202/234–7174* ⊕ *www.galatheatre.org* Ⓜ *Columbia Heights.*

U STREET CORRIDOR

The U Street Corridor is enjoying a renaissance and is starting to reclaim its former title of Washington's "Black Broadway." The Howard Theatre offers great productions from diverse sources while the Lincoln Theatre offers music from the best in country, reggae, pop, and more. Try some of the smaller venues in this neighborhood for original and compelling performances.

MAJOR VENUES

Fodor's Choice ★ **The Howard Theatre.** What was once was "the largest colored theatre in the world" is operating again in the heart of Washington's historic "Black Broadway." The Howard now hosts a regular array of music acts from Kid Creole & The Coconuts to Ginger Baker's Jazz Confusion to the Harlem Gospel Choir. ✉ *620 T St. NW, U Street* ☎ *202/803–2899* ⊕ *thehowardtheatre.com* Ⓜ *Shaw/Howard U.*

MUSIC

The In Series. Trademark cabaret, experimental chamber opera, and Spanish musical theater (also known as zarzuela) are among the hallmarks of this nonprofit company founded in 1982, which performs at Source and Gala theaters and other venues around the city. ⊠ *1835 14th St. NW, U Street* ☎ *202/204–7763* ⊕ *www.inseries.org.*

Lincoln Theatre. Once the host of such notable black performers as Cab Calloway, Lena Horne, and Duke Ellington, the 1,250-seat 1920s-inspired Lincoln is part of the lively U Street Corridor. Today, it presents contemporary musical performers such as Jennifer Nettles, Billy Idol, and Stephen "Ragga" Marley. ⊠ *1215 U St. NW, U Street* ☎ *202/328–6000* ⊕ *www.thelincolndc.com* Ⓜ *U St./Cardozo.*

UPPER NORTHWEST

Summer is when the performing arts come alive in Upper Northwest D.C. One of the city's gems is Carter Barron, an outdoor amphitheater in Rock Creek Park that offers a variety of musical and cinema events during August. Other venues include the refurbished Avalon Theatre, which features outstanding documentaries and hard-to-find independent films. Some of the biggest blockbuster films are presented at the historic Loews Cineplex Uptown, which has the largest film screen in town.

FILM

AMC Loews Uptown 1. This is a true movie palace, with art-deco flourishes; a wonderful balcony; and—in two happy concessions to modernity—crystal clear Dolby sound and a Christie Dual-Projector 3-D system. The theater boasts the town's largest movie screen, almost three times the size of a standard screen with triple the effect. ⊠ *3426 Connecticut Ave. NW, Cleveland Park, Upper Northwest* ☎ *202/966–5400* ⊕ *www.amctheatres.com/uptown1* Ⓜ *Cleveland Park.*

FAMILY **Avalon Theatre.** This classic movie house from 1923 is D.C.'s only nonprofit film center. The theater offers a wide array of studio films and independent and foreign films, plus monthly showcases of the best in French, Israeli, Czech, and Greek cinema. The theater also offers programming for families and children. ⊠ *5612 Connecticut Ave. NW, Upper Northwest* ☎ *202/966–6000 info line, 202/966–3464 box office* ⊕ *www.theavalon.org* Ⓜ *Friendship Heights.*

MUSIC

CHORAL MUSIC
Washington National Cathedral. Concerts and recitals by visiting musicians augment the choral and church groups that frequently perform in this breathtaking cathedral. Organ recitals on the massive pipe organ are offered every Sunday afternoon and the choir sings Evensong most weekdays around 5:30. Admission is frequently free. ⊠ *Massachusetts*

and Wisconsin Aves. NW, Cathedral Heights, Upper Northwest ✛ From Tenleytown Metro station, take any 30 series bus south ☎ *202/537–6207* ⊕ *www.nationalcathedral.org* Ⓜ *Tenleytown.*

PERFORMANCE SERIES

Carter Barron Amphitheatre. This 3,750-seat outdoor theater in the middle of Washington's historic Rock Creek Park used to host a variety of pop, jazz, gospel, and rhythm-and-blues artists such as Chick Corea and Nancy Wilson throughout the summer. Government spending cuts mean the schedule is currently limited to weekends in August and September, but the event is still free and the venue magnificent. ⊠ *Rock Creek Park, 4850 Colorado Ave. NW, Upper Northwest* ☎ *202/426–0486* ⊕ *www.nps.gov/rocr/index.htm* Ⓜ *Van Ness.*

ARLINGTON AND NORTHERN VIRGINIA

Suburban Virginia is home to a number of outstanding performance venues offering Shakespeare, opera, dance, popular music, and more. Arlington's Signature Theatre stages some of the best musical productions in the area and is only a short trip from downtown Washington, while Synetic Theatre, made nationally famous by its production of Silent Hamlet, is but a Metro stop away in Crystal City. You'll need a car to reach the Birchmere Music Hall, but you'll enjoy an array of country, folk, and popular music nightly.

6

MAJOR VENUES

Center for the Arts. This state-of-the-art performance complex on the suburban Virginia campus of George Mason University satisfies music, ballet, and drama patrons with regular performances in its 1,900-seat concert hall, the 500-seat proscenium Harris Theater, and an intimate 150-seat black-box theater. The 9,500-seat Patriot Center, venue for pop acts and sporting events, is also on campus. ⊠ *Rte. 123 and Braddock Rd., Fairfax* ☎ *703/993–8888, 888/945–2468* ⊕ *cfa.gmu.edu.*

Wolf Trap National Park for the Performing Arts. At the only national park dedicated to the performing arts, the 7,000-seat outdoor Filene Center hosts more than 80 performances from June through September. They range from pop and jazz concerts to dance and musical theater productions. The National Symphony Orchestra is based here in summer, and the Children's Theatre-in-the-Woods delivers 70 free performances. During the colder months the intimate, indoor Barns at Wolf Trap fill with the sounds of musicians playing folk, country, and chamber music, along with many other styles. The park is just off the Dulles Toll Road, about 20 miles from downtown Washington. Wolf Trap provides round-trip bus service from the West Falls Church Metro stop during events. ⊠ *1645 Trap Rd., Vienna* ☎ *703/255–1900, 703/255–1868 Barns at Wolf Trap* ⊕ *www.wolftrap.org* Ⓜ *W. Falls Church.*

MUSIC

PERFORMANCE SERIES

Fodors Choice **The Birchmere Music Hall.** A hidden treasure in Northern Virginia, this
★ legendary music hall is known as one of the venues in the country. You
can eat and drink as you enjoy the likes of Merle Haggard, B.B. King,
Emmylou Harris, and other music legends crooning from the acousti-
cally wonderful stage. You need a car to get here. ⊠ *3701 Mount Vernon Ave., Alexandria* ☎ *703/549–7500* ⊕ *birchmere.com.*

THEATER AND PERFORMANCE ART

Signature Theatre. Led by artistic director Eric Schaeffer, the Tony
Award–winning Signature has earned national acclaim for its presen-
tation of contemporary plays and groundbreaking American musicals,
especially those of Stephen Sondheim. The company performs in a dramatic facility with two performance spaces, the 299-seat MAX and
the 99-seat ARK. ⊠ *4200 Campbell Ave., Arlington* ☎ *703/820–9771*
⊕ *www.sigtheatre.org.*

Synetic Theatre. One of the most distinctive performing arts groups in
the Washington area uses music, dance, high energy, acting, and athleti-
cism to transform the works of Shakespeare, Dante, Edgar Allan Poe,
and Robert Louis Stevenson into visual theatrics that are guaranteed
to leave audiences fascinated. The theater is tucked away in Virginia's
Crystal City, a short Metro ride away from Downtown Washington.
⊠ *1800 S. Bell St., Arlington* ☎ *866/811–4111* ⊕ *synetictheater.org*
Ⓜ *Crystal City.*

SPORTS AND
THE OUTDOORS

Updated by
Doug Rule

Although Washington may be best known for what goes on inside its hallowed corridors, what happens outside is just as entertaining. Washingtonians are an active bunch, and the city provides a fantastic recreational backyard, with dozens of beautiful open spaces in the District and the nearby Maryland and Virginia suburbs. The city's residents take full advantage of these opportunities, biking its many trails, running amid the monuments, and sailing up the Potomac. They are also passionate about their local teams— especially the Redskins, the Capitals, and the Nationals, whose games are sold out year after year.

Visitors to Washington can enjoy a wealth of outdoor attractions. Rock Creek Park is one of the city's treasures, with miles of wooded trails and paths for bikers, runners, and walkers that extend to almost every part of the city. The National Mall connects the Lincoln Memorial and the Capitol and is one of the most scenic green spaces in the world. Around the Tidal Basin you can run, tour the monuments, and rent paddleboats. Theodore Roosevelt Island, a wildlife sanctuary, has several paths for hiking and enjoyable spots for picnics. And these places are just a few among dozens.

PLANNING

WHERE THE PROS PLAY
If you're going to a pro sports event, chances are you'll be headed here.

Nationals Park. D.C.'s baseball team, the Washington Nationals, plays in a spacious, 41,888-seat state-of-the-art park, on the fast-developing Capitol Riverfront in Southeast Washington. Since its opening in 2008, the park has been a catalyst for the renaissance in this area. Inside

FIVE GREAT OUTDOOR EXPERIENCES

Bird-watch on Theodore Roosevelt Island: Take in the spectacular scenery at this tucked-away wildlife sanctuary.

Get a new perspective on the cherry trees: Take a leisurely trip in a paddleboat around the Tidal Basin in spring.

Get moving with picture-postcard motivation: Run or bike on the Mall with Washington's monuments as a unique background.

See the National Zoo's giant pandas: Washington's love affair with the adorable pandas at the National Zoo has gotten a welcome extension; Mei Xiang and Tian Tian are extending their D.C. stay until December 2020.

Walk or ride along the C&O Canal: An excursion along the historic waterway comes with nice views of the Potomac River; you may even see a bald eagle.

the stadium, there are dozens of outstanding food venues and craft beer vendors among other concessions. Tours are available. ✉ *1500 S. Capitol St. SE, Capitol Hill* ☎ *202/675–6287* ⊕ *www.mlb.com/was/ballpark/information* 🎟 *Tours $15* Ⓜ *Navy Yard.*

Robert F. Kennedy Stadium. Soccer is incredibly popular in the nation's capital, finding many of its fans among the international crowds who miss the big matches at home, as well as families whose kids play soccer. Robert F. Kennedy Stadium, the Redskins' and Senators' former residence on Capitol Hill, is currently home to Major League Soccer's D.C. United, though that will soon change when the team moves to its new 20,000-seat stadium near the revitalized Southwest waterfront and just a few blocks from Nationals Park. When Audi Field opens in mid-2018, RFK Stadium will be redeveloped as a 350,000-square-foot recreation and sports complex. ✉ *2400 E. Capitol St. NE at 22nd St., Washington* ☎ *202/587–5000* ⊕ *www.dcunited.com/stadium* Ⓜ *Stadium.*

Verizon Center. One of the country's top-grossing sports and entertainment venues, the 20,000-seat Verizon Center averages more than 200 events each year and has helped to turn the surrounding area into the most vibrant part of Downtown, where you'll find several of the city's best restaurants. But there are also decent food and beverage options inside the Center, going beyond the standard stadium fare of hot dogs, chicken fingers, and light beers, including good local chili from Hard Times Café and Chesapeake Bay crab cakes, paired with craft beers and Angry Orchard Gluten-Free Hard Cider. Sporting events include hockey featuring the Washington Capitals; basketball with the Washington Wizards, Washington Mystics, and Georgetown Hoyas; and figure-skating events. Outside, street musicians of all kinds and styles add to the Center experience. The Metro station is directly below the Center. ✉ *601 F St. NW between 6th and 7th Sts., Chinatown* ☎ *202/628–3200* ⊕ *www.verizoncenter.com* Ⓜ *Gallery Pl./Chinatown.*

7

WASHINGTON FOR EVERY SEASON

With every change of the seasons, D.C. offers new pleasures for sports and outdoors enthusiasts.

In winter you can have an old-fashioned afternoon of ice-skating and hot chocolate in the National Gallery's Sculpture Garden, or go to the Verizon Center to see the Wizards play basketball or the Capitals play hockey.

Come spring, the city emerges from the cold with activities everywhere. Runners throng Rock Creek Park, Frisbee contests and soccer games fill up the Mall, and boats float down the Potomac.

In summer, baseball fans head to Nationals Park for games, and this greenery-laced city seems to become one big outdoor playground.

When fall arrives, the seasonal colors of the trees in Rock Creek Park are a spectacular sight for bikers, hikers, and runners. Tickets to see the Redskins at FedEx Field are among the city's most prized commodities.

PARKS AND NATURE

Washington is more than marble-and-limestone buildings. The city is blessed with numerous parks and outdoor attractions that provide a break from the museums and government facilities. Rock Creek Park extends through much of the city, with entrances to the park near many hotels. Other outdoor spaces, such as the National Mall, Potomac Park, and Constitution Gardens, offer a chance to see nature, combined with the beauty of nearby waterways and the majesty of the city's beloved monuments.

GARDENS

Constitution Gardens. Many ideas were proposed to develop this 50-acre site near the Reflecting Pool and the Vietnam Veterans Memorial. President Nixon is said to have favored something resembling Copenhagen's Tivoli Gardens. The final design was plainer, with paths winding through groves of trees and, on the lake, a tiny island paying tribute to the signers of the Declaration of Independence, their signatures carved into a low stone wall. Naturalization ceremonies for new citizens take place here. ⊠ *Constitution Ave., White House area* ✛ *Between 17th and 23rd Sts. NW* ⊕ *www.nps.gov/coga* Ⓜ *Farragut W/Foggy Bottom.*

| QUICK BITES | At the circular snack bar just west of the lake at Constitution Gardens, you can get hot dogs, potato chips, candy bars, soft drinks, and beer at prices lower than those charged by most street vendors. |

FAMILY

Fodor's Choice

★

Dumbarton Oaks. One of the loveliest places for a stroll in Washington is Dumbarton Oaks, a research institute in residential Georgetown administered by the Trustees for Harvard University. Planned by noted landscape architect Beatrix Farrand, the estate's acres of enchanting gardens incorporate elements of traditional English, Italian, and French styles and include a formal rose garden, an English country garden, and an orangery (circa 1810). A dozen full-time gardeners maintain the

stunning collection of terraces, geometric gardens, tree-shaded brick walks, fountains, arbors, and pools. Plenty of well-positioned benches make this a good place for resting weary feet, too. Public garden tours are at 2:10 pm Tuesday–Thursday and Saturday. In May, the peonies and azaleas in full bloom are spectacular. ■TIP→ **The gardens are closed for extensive renovations from July 2017 to March 2018.** ⊠ *31st and R Sts., Georgetown* ☎ *202/339–6401, 202/339–6400* ⊕ *www.doaks.org* ▧ *$8 mid-Mar.–Oct.; free Nov.–mid-Mar.*

Fodor's Choice
★

Hillwood Estate, Museum and Gardens. Cereal heiress Marjorie Merriweather Post purchased the 25-acre Hillwood Estate in 1955, and devoted as much attention to her gardens as she did to the 40-room Georgian mansion. You can wander through 13 acres of them, including a Japanese rock and waterfall garden, a manicured formal French garden, a rose garden, Mediterranean fountains, and a greenhouse full of orchids. The "Lunar Lawn," where she threw garden parties that were the most coveted invitation in Washington society, is planted with dogwood, magnolia, cherry, and plum trees, as well as azaleas, camellias, lilacs, tulips, and pansies. Tours are offered on a first-come, first-served basis in spring and fall. ⊠ *4155 Linnean Ave. NW, Upper Northwest* ☎ *202/686–5807* ⊕ *www.hillwoodmuseum.org* ▧ *House and grounds $18 (suggested donation)* Ⓜ *Van Ness/UDC.*

Kahlil Gibran Memorial Garden. In a town known for political combat, this tiny urban park is a wonderful place to find some peace. The shady park combines Western and Arab symbols and is perfect for contemplation. From the Massachusetts Avenue entrance, a stone walk bridges a grassy swale. Farther on are limestone benches, engraved with sayings from Gibran that curve around a fountain and a bust of the namesake Lebanese-born poet, who emigrated to the U.S. at the turn of the 20th century and remains one of the best-selling poets of all time. The garden is near the grounds of the United States Naval Observatory and across from the British Embassy. ⊠ *3100 block of Massachusetts Ave. NW, Upper Northwest* ☎ *202/895–6000* ▧ *Free* Ⓜ *Woodley Park or Dupont Circle.*

Kenilworth Park and Aquatic Gardens. Exotic water lilies, lotuses, hyacinths, and other water-loving plants thrive in this 14-acre sanctuary of quiet ponds, protected wetlands, and marshy flats, listed on the National Register of Historic Places. The gardens' wetland animals include turtles, frogs, beavers, spring azure butterflies, and some 40 species of birds. ■TIP→ **In July nearly everything blossoms; early morning is the best time to visit.** There's a tiny child-friendly museum in the visitor center. The nearest Metro stop is a 15-minute walk away, but there is ample free parking. ⚠ **Exit gates are locked promptly at 4.** ⊠ *1550 Anacostia Ave., Anacostia* ✛ *At Douglas St. NE* ☎ *202/692–6080* ⊕ *www. nps.gov/keaq* ▧ *Free* Ⓜ *Deanwood.*

Tudor Place. A little more than a block from Dumbarton Oaks in Georgetown is this neighborhood gem, the former home of Martha Washington's granddaughter, Martha Parke Custis Peter. Preserved as a historic house museum, the property includes 5½ acres of grounds that offer impressive replications of Federal-period gardens with 19th-century specimen trees and boxwoods from Mount Vernon. The self-guiding tour comes with a map and/or an audio tour or there are docent-led tours. ✉ *1644 31st Pl. NW, Georgetown* ☎ *202/965–0400* ⊕ *www. tudorplace.org* ✉ *$10 house and garden; $3 garden only* Ⓜ *Woodley Park or Dupont Circle.*

FAMILY

Fodor'sChoice

★

United States Botanic Garden. Established by Congress in 1820, this is the oldest continually operating botanic garden in North America. The garden conservatory sits at the foot of Capitol Hill, and offers an escape from the stone-and-marble federal office buildings that surround it; inside are exotic rain-forest species, desert flora, and trees from all parts of the world. Walkways suspended 24 feet above the ground provide a fascinating view of the plants. Established in 2006, the National Garden emphasizes educational exhibits and features a Rose Garden, Butterfly Garden, Lawn Terrace, First Ladies' Water Garden, and Regional Garden. ✉ *1st St. at 100 Maryland Ave. SW, Capitol Hill* ☎ *202/225–8333* ⊕ *www.usbg.gov* ✉ *Free* Ⓜ *Federal Center SW.*

Fodor'sChoice

★

United States National Arboretum. During azalea season (mid-April through May) this 446-acre oasis operated by the U.S. Department of Agriculture is a blaze of color. In early summer, clematis, peonies, rhododendrons, and roses bloom. At any time of year the 22 original Corinthian columns from the U.S. Capitol, reerected here in 1990, are striking. All 50 states are represented by a state tree or flower. Since 2014, a pair of American bald eagles have made a home near the azaleas, and the nest can be seen via an unobstructed viewing scope. The arboretum has guided hikes throughout the year, including a Full Moon Hike, and dogs are allowed on the grounds as long as they're on a leash at all times. Check the website for schedules and to register. Visit the Cryptomeria Walk and Japanese Stroll Garden, which are part of the Bonsai and Penjing Museum. On weekends a tram tours the arboretum's curving roadways at 11:30 and on the hour 1–4. ✉ *3501 New York Ave. NE, Northeast* ☎ *202/245–2726* ⊕ *www.usna.usda.gov* ✉ *Free* Ⓜ *Weekends: Union Station, then X6 bus (runs every 40 mins); weekdays: Stadium/Armory, then B2 bus to Bladensburg Rd. and R St.*

7

PARKS

FAMILY

Fodor'sChoice

★

C&O Canal. George Washington was one of the first to advance the idea of a canal linking the Potomac with the Ohio River across the Appalachians. Work started on the Chesapeake & Ohio Canal in 1828, and when it opened in 1850, its 74 locks linked Georgetown with Cumberland, Maryland, 185 miles to the northwest (still short of its intended destination). Lumber, coal, iron, wheat, and flour moved up and down the canal, but it was never as successful as its planners had hoped it would be. Many of the bridges spanning the canal in Georgetown were too low to allow anything other than fully loaded barges to pass underneath, and competition from the Baltimore & Ohio Railroad spelled an end to profitability. Today the canal is part of the National Park System; walkers and cyclists follow the towpath once used by mules, while canoeists paddle the canal's calm waters. You could walk or pedal the length of the canal, but most cyclists stop at Great Falls, Maryland. ⊠ *Georgetown Canal Visitor Center, 1057 Thomas Jefferson St. NW, Georgetown* ☎ *202/653–5190 Georgetown, 301/767–3714 Great Falls* ⊕ *www.nps.gov/choh* ⊠ *3-day pass $5 per person to enter on foot or bicycle, $10 per vehicle; annual pass $30.*

FAMILY **East Potomac Park.** This 328-acre finger of land extends south of the Jefferson Memorial from the Tidal Basin, between the Washington Channel and the new Southwest Waterfront redevelopment neighborhood to the east and the Potomac River to the west. Although in recent years the park has fallen into disrepair with lack of proper upkeep, some locals still consider this a nice retreat, with playgrounds, picnic tables, tennis courts, swimming pools, a driving range, one 18-hole and two 9-hole golf courses, miniature golf, and a pool. There's also a scenic riverfront trail that winds around the park's perimeter. Double-blossoming Japanese cherry trees line Ohio Drive and bloom about two weeks after the single-blossoming variety that attracts throngs to the Tidal Basin each spring. ⊠ *Ohio Dr. SW, Southwest* ☎ *202/426–6841* ⊕ *www.npca.org/parks* Ⓜ *Smithsonian.*

Fort Reno Park. At 429 feet above sea level, this highest point in Washington has been used in different eras as a Civil War fort, the site of telegraph and radio towers, and a reservoir. In 1864 Abraham Lincoln watched nearby as outnumbered Union troops defended the capital from a formidable Confederate advance led by General Early, in the only battle to take place in the capital. Today, the park is enjoyed by soccer players, dog-park regulars, and picnickers. Most of the Civil War–era earthworks are gone, and two curious faux-medieval towers, built in 1929, mark the reservoir site, which is not accessible to the public. Nonetheless, the park has an appealing city view and plenty of room to run around. A popular, free outdoor concert series takes place every summer featuring many of the area's most esteemed indie-rock acts, from Fugazi to Dismemberment Plan to Priests. ⊠ *Chesapeake St. NW at Nebraska Ave. NW, Upper Northwest* ☎ *202/895–6070 visitor information, 202/521–1493 summer concert info only* ⊕ *www.fortreno.com* Ⓜ *Tenleytown/American U.*

Glover-Archbold Park. Groves of beeches, elms, and oaks flourish at this 183-acre park, part of the Rock Creek system, which begins just west of Georgetown and ends, 3½ miles later, near Van Ness Street. Along the way you'll experience a stream valley with ancient trees and possible bird sightings. And chances are you'll have the trail mostly to yourself. ⊠ *Wisconsin Ave. at Van Ness St. NW, Upper Northwest* ⊕ *www.nps.gov/pohe/index.htm* Ⓜ *Tenleytown/American U.*

FAMILY
Fodor's Choice ★
Rock Creek Park. The 1,800 acres surrounding Rock Creek have provided a cool oasis for visitors and D.C. residents ever since Congress set them aside for recreational use in 1890. The bubbling, rocky stream draws nature lovers to the miles of paved walkways. Bicycle routes, jogging and hiking paths, and equestrian trails wind through the groves of dogwoods, beeches, oaks, and cedars, and 30 picnic areas are scattered about. About twice the size of New York City's Central Park, the park bifurcates the length of the city, making entrance and egress easy for short or long exercise excursions.

An asphalt bike path running through the park has a few challenging hills but is mostly flat, and it's possible to bike several miles without having to stop for cars (the roadway is closed entirely to cars on weekends). Bikers can begin a ride at the Lincoln Memorial or Kennedy Center, pass the Washington Zoo, and eventually come to the District line, where the trail separates, with one part continuing to Bethesda and another to Silver Spring. The most popular run in Rock Creek Park is along a trail that follows the creek from Georgetown to the National Zoo, about 4 miles round-trip. In summer there's considerable shade, and there are water fountains and an exercise station along the way. Rangers at the Nature Center and Planetarium introduce visitors to the park and keep track of daily events; guided nature walks leave from the center on weekends at 2. The park is open only during daylight hours. ✉ *5200 Glover Rd. NW, Nature Center and Planetarium, Washington* ☎ *202/895–6070* ⊕ *www.nps.gov/rocr.*

Meridian Hill Park. Landscape architect Horace Peaslee created oft-overlooked Meridian Hill Park, a noncontiguous section of Rock Creek Park, after a 1917 study of the parks of Europe. As a result, the garden contains elements of gardens in France (a long, straight mall bordered with plants), Italy (terraces and wall fountains), and Switzerland (a lower-level reflecting pool based on one in Zurich). John Quincy Adams lived in a mansion here after his presidency in 1829, and the park later served as an encampment for Union soldiers during the Civil War. All 50 states are represented by a state tree or flower. Meridian Hill is also unofficially known as **Malcolm X Park** in honor of the civil rights leader. On weekends you will find a mix of pickup soccer games, joggers running the stairs, and a weekly (weather permitting) drum circle. A statue of **Joan of Arc** poised for battle on horseback stands above the terrace, and a statue of **Dante** is on a pedestal below. A ranger-led tour and cell-phone tours illuminate the history of the landmarks inside the park. Meridian Hill is open year-round during daylight hours. ✉ *16th and Euclid Sts., Adams Morgan* ⊕ *www.nps.gov/mehi* Ⓜ *U St./Cardozo or Columbia Heights.*

Pierce-Klingle Mansion. The renovated 19th-century Pennsylvania Dutch style mansion, also known as Linnaean Hill, was used as the National Park Service's Rock Creek headquarters, but is no longer open to the public. Also in distant areas of the park are Fort Reno, Fort Bayard, Fort Stevens, and Fort DeRussy, remnants of the original ring of forts that guarded Washington during the Civil War, and the Rock Creek Park Golf Course, an 18-hole public course. ✉ *3545 Willliamsburg La. NW, Upper Northwest* Ⓜ *Cleveland Park.*

FAMILY
Fodor'sChoice
★

Tidal Basin. The Tidal Basin is the setting for memorials to Thomas Jefferson, Franklin Delano Roosevelt, Martin Luther King Jr., and George Mason.

Two sculpted heads on the sides of the Inlet Bridge can be seen as you walk along the sidewalk that hugs the basin. The inside walls of the bridge also feature two other sculptures: bronze, human-headed fish that spout water from their mouths. Sculptor Constantine Sephralis played a little joke: these fish heads are actually modeled after the head of Jack Fish, the chief of the park, who was retiring at the time he made the sculptures.

DID YOU KNOW?

The mayor of Tokyo gave Washington, D.C., 3,000 cherry trees in 1912 honoring the friendship between the United States and Japan. The U.S. government reciprocated in 1915 with a gift of dogwood trees.

Once you cross the bridge, continue along the Tidal Basin to the right. This route is especially scenic when the **cherry trees** are in bloom. The first batch of these trees arrived from Japan in 1909. The trees were infected with insects and fungus, however, and the Department of Agriculture ordered them destroyed. A diplomatic crisis was averted when the United States politely asked the Japanese for another batch, and in 1912 First Lady Helen Taft planted the first tree. The second was planted by the wife of the Japanese ambassador, Viscountess Chinda. About 200 of the original trees still grow near the Tidal Basin. (These cherry trees are the single-flowering Akebeno and Yoshino variety.)

The trees are now the centerpiece of Washington's two-week **National Cherry Blossom Festival**, held each spring since 1935. The festivities are kicked off by the lighting of a ceremonial Japanese lantern that rests on the north shore of the Tidal Basin, not far from where the first tree was planted. The celebration has grown over the years to include concerts, a running race, a kite festival, and a parade. The trees are usually in bloom for about 12 days in late March or early April. When winter will not release its grip, parade and festival take place without the presence of blossoms. ⊠ *Bordered by Independence and Maine Aves., The Mall* Ⓜ *Smithsonian.*

FAMILY **West Potomac Park.** Between the Potomac and the Tidal Basin, this park is known for its flowering cherry trees, which bloom for two weeks in late March or early April, and for the World War II Memorial, as well as the memorials for Lincoln, Martin Luther King Jr., Franklin Delano Roosevelt, Jefferson, George Mason, and the Korean and Vietnam War Veterans. It's a nice place to picnic and play ball, where families can relax and admire the views of the water. ⊠ *Bounded by Constitution Ave., 17th St., and Independence Ave., Washington* ⊕ *www.npca.org.*

World War I Memorial. In late 2014 Congress redesignated this quiet, sunken garden, which was formerly named Pershing Park in tribute to General John J. "Black Jack" Pershing, the first—a century ago—to hold the title General of the Armies. An official unit of the National Park System, the World War I Memorial includes engravings on the stone walls recounting pivotal campaigns from World War I, when Pershing commanded the American expeditionary force and conducted other military exploits. Steps and small tables surround a fountain and duck pond, making for a pleasant midday respite. A new design for the memorial was selected in 2016 and groundbreaking was expected in late 2017. This memorial will play a central part in honoring the centennial of the end of World War I in 2018. ⊠ *15th St. and Pennsylvania Ave., White House area* Ⓜ *McPherson Sq.*

SPORTS

Washington is well designed for outdoor sports, with numerous places to play, run, and ride. When the weather is good, it seems all of Washington is out riding a bike, playing softball and volleyball, jogging past monuments, or taking a relaxing stroll. Many of the favorite locations for participation sports are in the shadow of D.C.'s most famous spots, such as Capitol Hill and the White House.

BASEBALL

Washington Nationals. It's been over a decade now since Major League Baseball returned to D.C., where the Washington Nationals of the National League play in the spectacular 41,888-seat, state-of-the-art Nationals Park. The team has enjoyed winning seasons and is hugely popular with the hometown crowd, although seats are usually available at the gate. The Nationals' mascots, "The Racing Presidents," compete during the fourth inning at every game. Tours of the stadium are available when the Nationals are on the road and in the morning when the team has night games. ■ TIP→ **The Metro is a hassle-free and inexpensive way to get to the ballpark. Parking is scarce.** ⊠ *Nationals Park, 1500 S. Capitol St. SE, Southwest* ☎ *202/675–6287* ⊕ *www.mlb. com/nationals* ✉ *$7–$598; tours $15* Ⓜ *Navy Yard.*

BASKETBALL

Georgetown University Hoyas. Former NCAA national champions, the Hoyas are the most prominent Division I men's college basketball team in the area. They became a national basketball powerhouse under coach John Thompson, and remain perennial contenders in the national tourney under their current coach, John Thompson III. The team has produced famous national figures both on and off the court, from Patrick Ewing to Henry Hyde. The Hoyas play home games at the Verizon Center downtown. ⊠ *Verizon Center, 601 F St. NW, Chinatown* ☎ *202/687–4692* ⊕ *guhoyas.com* ✉ *$10–$85* Ⓜ *Gallery Pl./Chinatown.*

Washington Mystics. This WNBA team plays at the Verizon Center in downtown Washington and perennially leads the WNBA in attendance, despite a losing record and having not yet made it even once to the WNBA Finals in two decades of operation. The games are loud, boisterous events. You can buy Mystics tickets at the Verizon Center box office or through Ticketmaster. The women's season runs from late May to August. ⊠ *Verizon Center, 6th and F Sts., Chinatown* ☎ *202/432–7328* ⊕ *www.wnba.com/mystics* ✉ *$19–$300* Ⓜ *Gallery Pl./Chinatown.*

Washington Wizards. From October to April the NBA's Washington Wizards play at the Verizon Center and feature NBA All-Star John Wall. For showtime entertainment look for the G-Wiz, the G-Man, the Wiz Kids, and the Wizard Girls. Buy tickets from the Verizon Center box office, the Wizards' online, or Ticketmaster. ⊠ *Verizon Center, 6th and F Sts. NW, Chinatown* ☎ *202/432–7328* ⊕ *www.nba.com/wizards* ✉ *$18–$2,500* Ⓜ *Gallery Pl./Chinatown.*

7

BICYCLING

The numerous trails in the District and its surrounding areas are well maintained and clearly marked. Washington's large parks are also popular with cyclists. Plus, with new bike lanes on all major roads and the Capital Bikeshare scheme, it's also a great way to get around town. *See also the C&O Canal and Rock Creek Park in Parks, and the National Mall in Running.*

Capital Crescent Trail. Suited for bicyclists, walkers, rollerbladers, and strollers, this paved trail stretches along the old Georgetown Branch, a B&O Railroad line that was completed in 1910 and was in operation until 1985. The 7.5-mile route's first leg runs from Georgetown near Key Bridge to central Bethesda at Bethesda and Woodmont Avenues. At Bethesda and Woodmont the trail heads through a well-lighted tunnel near the heart of Bethesda's lively business area and continues into Silver Spring. The 3.5-mile stretch from Bethesda to Silver Spring is gravel, though the all-volunteer Coalition for the Capital Crescent Trail is spearheading efforts to pave it. The Georgetown Branch Trail, as this section is officially named, connects with the Rock Creek Trail, which goes to Rockville in the north and Memorial Bridge past the Washington Monument in the south. On weekends when the weather's nice, all sections of the trails are crowded ⌧ *Washington* ☎ *202/234–4874 Coalition for the Capital Crescent Trail* ⊕ *www.cctrail.org.*

East Potomac Park. Cyclists might try the 3-mile loop around the golf course in East Potomac Park at Hains Point (entry is near the Jefferson Memorial). This peninsula, though somewhat less scenic than a run around the Mall, is a favorite training course for dedicated local racers and would-be triathletes. Hains Point is a great place to view Fort McNair and the National War College, as well as to watch planes take off and land from Reagan National Airport across the river. ⌧ *14th St. SW, Southwest* ☎ *202/485–9874 National Park Service.*

Mount Vernon Trail. Across the Potomac in Virginia is this multiuse riverside trail, which is split into two sections. The northern part begins near the pedestrian causeway at Theodore Roosevelt Island, across the river from the Kennedy Center. Three and a half miles later it passes Ronald Reagan National Airport and continues on to Mount Vernon, a total distance of 18 miles. This section has slight slopes and almost no interruptions for traffic, making it a delightful biking experience. Even inexperienced bikers enjoy the trail, which provides wonderful views of the Potomac. To access the trail from the District, take the Theodore Roosevelt Bridge or the Rochambeau Memorial Bridge, also known as the 14th Street Bridge. South of the airport, the trail runs down to the Washington Marina. The final mile of the trail's northern section meanders through protected wetlands before ending in the heart of Old Town Alexandria. The trail's 9-mile southern section extends along the Potomac from Alexandria to Mount Vernon, but no bicycles (or motorized vehicles, skateboards, scooters, and Segways) are allowed. ⌧ *Park Headquarters, Turkey Run Park, McLean* ☎ *703/289–2500* ⊕ *www.nps.gov/gwmp* Ⓜ *Arlington Cemetery, Ronald Reagan Washington National Airport, or Rosslyn.*

INFORMATION

Washington Area Bicyclist Association. Members conduct local outreach to encourage biking and do advocacy for a better integrated transportation system linking transit, trails, bicycling, and walking facilities. They also educate the public about bike safety. WABA provides an institutional structure for those looking for organized longer rides, including its fall signature 50 State

BIKING THE MALL

A pleasant loop route begins at the Lincoln Memorial, going north past the Washington Monument, and turning around at the Tidal Basin. Along the way you can take a break at some of the small fountains and parks, and there are places to get a drink of water.

and 13 Colonies event, which offers either a 62-mile ride down all 50 state-named streets in the District, or a 15-mile ride down just the streets in Downtown D.C. named after the original colonies. ✉ *1803 Connecticut Ave. NW, 3rd fl., Dupont Circle* ☎ *202/518–0524* ⊕ *www. waba.org* Ⓜ *Dupont Circle.*

RENTALS AND TOURS

Big Wheel Bikes. This 45-year-old company near the C&O Canal Towpath rents multispeed and other types of bikes hourly or for the day. Rates range $5–$10 per hour and $35–$100 per day. There is a three-hour minimum. Tandem bikes, kids' bikes, and bikes with baby carriers are also available. Other locations are in Bethesda, near the Capital Crescent Trail, and Alexandria, if you want to ride the Mount Vernon Trail. ✉ *1034 33rd St. NW, Georgetown* ☎ *202/337–0254* ⊕ *www. bigwheelbikes.com.*

Bike and Roll. This national multicity company offers several two-hour, 4- to 8-mile guided tours of downtown Washington between early March and Thanksgiving, with bike or Segway rental included in the price. Tours start from Union Station, the Mall, and outside the Museum of American History, as well as from Alexandria for rides to Mount Vernon. Specific tours include Capital Sites or Capital Sites@ Nite and Monuments or Monuments@Nite. Reservations are required. ✉ *50 Massachusetts Ave. NE, Downtown* ☎ *202/842–2453* ⊕ *www. bikeandrolldc.com* ✍ *$16–$85* Ⓜ *Union Station.*

Capital Bikeshare. One of the nation's largest bike-share programs, with more than 2,500 bikes, lets you pick up a bike at one of more than 400 stations around Washington, Arlington, Alexandria and Fairfax County in Virginia, and Montgomery County, Maryland, and then return it to a bike station near your destination. Using a credit card to pay the 24-hour, three-day, one month, or annual membership fee at a bike station kiosk, you receive a code to unlock a bike. The membership entitles you to an unlimited number of rides during the membership period. ✉ *Washington* ☎ *877/430–2453* ⊕ *www.capitalbikeshare.com* ✍ *Membership: $2 for a single trip; $8 for 24 hrs; $17 for 3 days; $28 for a month. Usage fees from $1.50 for 30 mins.*

BOATING AND SAILING

The Chesapeake Bay is one of the great sailing basins of the world. For scenic and historical sightseeing, take a day trip to Annapolis, Maryland, the home of the U.S. Naval Academy. ■TIP➜ The popularity of boating and the many boating businesses in Annapolis make it one of the best civilian sailing centers on the East Coast.

Mather Gorge. Some of the best white-water kayakers and canoeists in the country call Washington home, and on weekends they practice below Great Falls in Mather Gorge, a canyon (named after the first director of the National Park Service, which runs the park) carved by the Potomac River just north of the city, above Chain Bridge. The water is deceptive and dangerous, containing Class I to Class IV rapids. Beginners should watch the experts at play from a post above the gorge. Great Falls Park is now a trash-free zone, so be prepared to carry your trash out when you leave. ⊠ *Great Falls Park, 9200 Old Dominion Dr., McLean* ☎ *703/285–2965 in Virginia, 301/299–3613 in Maryland* ⊕ *www.nps.gov/grfa.*

Potomac River. Canoeing, sailing, and powerboating are popular in the Washington, D.C., area. Several places rent boats along the Potomac River north and south of the city. You can dip your paddle just about anywhere along the "Nation's River"—go canoeing in the C&O Canal, sailing in the widening river south of Alexandria, or kayaking in the raging rapids at Great Falls, a 30-minute drive from the capital. The Potomac Conservancy is a great resource for information about efforts to clean up and improve this great waterway, but more than that it can serve as a starting point for the many activities available, including maps and links to organizations offering paddling, biking, and fishing opportunities. ⊠ *Washington* ☎ *301/608–1188* ⊕ *www.potomac.org.*

RENTALS

Belle Haven Marina. South of Ronald Reagan Washington National Airport and Old Town Alexandria, this quaint marina is owned by the National Park Service, and rents two types of sailboats: Sunfish and Flying Scots. Two-hour rentals are $35 weekdays and $40 on weekends for Sunfish; $50 weekdays and $60 on weekends for Flying Scots. All-day rentals are available. You can also rent canoes, jon boats, and kayaks. Rentals are available from April to October, and the marina takes reservations—useful during peak-season weekends. ⊠ *1201 Belle Haven Rd., Old Town* ✛ *Across from gas station* ☎ *703/768–0018* ⊕ *www.saildc.com.*

The Boathouse at Fletcher's Cove. In business since the 1850s, The Boat House at Fletcher's Cove, on the D.C. side of the Potomac, rents rowboats, canoes, and bicycles and sells tackle, snack foods, and D.C. fishing licenses in season (early March through fall). Here you can catch shad, perch, catfish, striped bass, and other freshwater species. Canoeing is allowed on the canal and on the Potomac, weather permitting. There's a large picnic area along the riverbank. ⊠ *4940 Canal Rd. at Reservoir Rd., Georgetown* ☎ *202/244–0461* ⊕ *www.fletcherscove.com.*

Thompson's Boat Center. The center rents nonmotorized watercraft, including canoes and kayaks (from $16 per hour, $30 per day), all on a first-come, first-served basis. Rowing sculls are also available (from

$17 per hour), but you must demonstrate prior experience and a suitable skill level. Bikes are also available for rent ($11 per hour or $35 per day). The location provides a nice launching point into the Potomac, right in the center of the city, and close to the monuments. In addition to its access to the river, Thompson's is conveniently sited for getting onto the Rock Creek Trail and the C&O towpath. Note: Thompson's closes from Halloween through mid-April, based on the water's temperature. ⊠ *2900 Virginia Ave. NW, Foggy Bottom* ☎ *202/333–9543* ⊕ *www. thompsonboatcenter.com* Ⓜ *Foggy Bottom/GWU.*

Tidal Basin Boathouse. Paddleboat rentals are available from mid-March through mid-October. The entrance is on the east side of the Tidal Basin. You can rent two-passenger boats at $18 per hour and four-passenger boats at $30 per hour. Visit the website for the option of prepaid guaranteed parking nearby. ⊠ *1501 Maine Ave. SW, The Mall* ☎ *202/479–2426* ⊕ *www.boatingindc.com* Ⓜ *Smithsonian.*

Washington Sailing Marina. Sailboats can be rented from this scenic marina from May to October, or until the water gets too cold. Aqua fins are $17 per hour or $68 for the day; 19-foot Flying Scots, holding a maximum of six people, are $25 per hour. All-terrain bikes rent for $11 per hour and $35 per day. The marina is on the Mount Vernon Trail off the George Washington Parkway, south of Ronald Reagan Washington National Airport. ⊠ *1 Marina Dr., Alexandria* ☎ *703/548–9027* ⊕ *www.boatingindc.com/marinas/washington-sailing-marina.*

FOOTBALL

Washington Redskins. The perennially popular Redskins continue to play football in the Maryland suburbs at 82,000-seat FedEx Field. Under ongoing discussion is a name change for the team, since an increasing number of people deem it insensitive to Native Americans. Super Bowl wins in 1983, '88, and '92 have ensured the Redskins a place as one of the top three most valuable franchises in the NFL. Diehard fans snap up season tickets year after year. Individual game-day tickets can be hard to come by when the team is enjoying a strong season. Your best bet is to check out StubHub (*www.stubhub,* the official ticket marketplace of the Redskins).

Several restaurants overlook the field, and the stadium houses the Redskins Hall of Fame. A large installation of solar panels, including one shaped like a giant quarterback and dubbed "Solar Man," powers the lights. Parking is a hassle, so take the Metro or arrive several hours early if you don't want to miss the kickoff.

Game tickets can be difficult to get, but fans can see the players up close and for free at the Bon Secours Training Camp in Richmond, Virginia. Camp begins in July and continues through mid-August. The practices typically last from 90 minutes to two hours. Fans can bring their own chairs, and the players are usually available after practice to sign autographs. Call ahead to make sure the practices are open that day. A practice schedule is on the team's website. ⊠ *FedEx Field, 1600 Fedex Way, Landover* ☎ *301/276–6000 FedEx Field* ⊕ *www.redskins. com* 🎟 *$75–$1,200.*

HIKING

Great hiking is available in and around Washington. Hikes and nature walks are listed in the Friday "Weekend" section of the *Washington Post*. Several area organizations sponsor outings, and many are guided.

Billy Goat Trail. This challenging trail in the Chesapeake and Ohio Canal National Historical Park starts and ends at the C&O Canal Towpath for a total hike of 4.7 miles, providing some outstanding views of the wilder parts of the Potomac, along with some steep downhills, rock hopping, and some climbs. Be prepared—the hike is mostly in the sun, not suitable for small children, and no dogs are allowed. ⊠ *Near Great Falls Tavern Visitor Center, 11710 MacArthur Blvd., Potomac* ☎ *301/413–0720* ⊕ *www.nps.gov/choh.*

Huntley Meadows Park. On this 1,500-acre refuge south of Alexandria in Fairfax County, you can spot more than 200 bird species—from ospreys to owls, egrets to ibis. Much of the park is wetlands, a favorite of aquatic species. A boardwalk circles through a marsh, enabling you to spot beaver lodges, and 4 miles of trails wend through the park, making it likely you'll see deer, muskrats, and river otters as well. The park has an observation tower for good wildlife spotting and a small visitor's center and gift shop. ⊠ *3701 Lockheed Blvd., Alexandria* ☎ *703/768–2525* ⊕ *www.fairfaxcounty.gov/parks/huntley-meadows-park.*

Fodor'sChoice   **Theodore Roosevelt Island.** Designed as a living memorial to the environ-
★   mentally minded 26th U.S. President, this wildlife sanctuary is off the George Washington Parkway near the Virginia side of the Potomac—close to Foggy Bottom, Georgetown, East Potomac Park, and the Kennedy Center. Hikers and bicyclists can reach the island by crossing the Theodore Roosevelt Memorial Bridge or walking for 15 minutes from the Rosslyn Metro, but bikes are not allowed on the island and must be docked instead near the footbridge. Many birds and other animals live in the island's marsh and forests, and rangers are available for an Island Safari, where a statue of Teddy greets you with his arm raised. ⊠ *Washington* ☎ *703/289–2500* ⊕ *www.nps.gov/this* Ⓜ *Rosslyn.*

Woodend Nature Sanctuary. A self-guided nature trail winds through a verdant 40-acre estate featuring a Georgian Revivalist mansion, designed in the 1920s by Jefferson Memorial architect John Russell Pope, that is the suburban Maryland headquarters of the **Audubon Naturalist Society.** So bring those binoculars! You're never far from the trill of birdsong here, as the Audubon Society has turned the place into something of a private nature preserve, forbidding the use of toxic chemicals and leaving some areas in a wild, natural state. Programs include wildlife identification walks, environmental education programs, and Saturday-morning bird walks September through November and March through June. A bookstore stocks titles on conservation, ecology, and birds. The grounds are open daily sunrise to sunset. ⊠ *8940 Jones Mill Rd., Chevy Chase* ☎ *301/652–9188, 301/652–1088 for recent bird sightings* ⊕ *www.audubonnaturalist.org* ⧉ *Free.*

HOCKEY AND ICE-SKATING

FAMILY
Fodor's Choice
★

National Gallery of Art Ice Rink. One of the most popular outdoor winter venues in Washington is surrounded by the museum's Sculpture Garden. The art deco rink is perfect for a romantic date night, a fun daytime kid activity (when it's less crowded), or for just enjoying the wintry views of the National Archives and the sculptures as the sun sets. In spring the rink becomes a fountain. The close proximity of the Gallery's Pavilion Café is a bonus. Open daily mid-November through mid-March, 10–9 (until 11 pm Friday and Saturday, except when it's raining or if the temperature is below 20°F). ⊠ *Constitution Ave. NW, between 7th and 9th Sts., Downtown* ☎ *202/216–9397* ⊕ *www.nga.gov* ⊠ *$8.50; skate rental $3; lockers $0.50, plus a $5 deposit* Ⓜ *Archives/Navy Memorial.*

Washington Capitals. One of pro hockey's top teams, the Washington Capitals play loud and exciting home games October through April at the Verizon Center. The team is led by one of hockey's superstars, Alex Ovechkin, and enjoys a huge, devoted fan base. Tickets are difficult to find but can be purchased at the Verizon Center box office, StubHub, or Ticketmaster. ⊠ *Verizon Center, 601 F St. NW, Chinatown* ☎ *202/266–2222* ⊕ *capitals.nhl.com* ⊠ *$45–$385* Ⓜ *Gallery Pl./Chinatown.*

RUNNING

Running is one of the best ways to see the city, and several uninterrupted scenic trails wend through Downtown Washington and nearby northern Virginia (including the Mount Vernon Trail; *see Bicycling*). The trails of Rock Creek Park close at nightfall and the ones along the C&O Canal (*see Parks for information on both these prime daytime running spots*) and other remote areas—or on the Mall—are not as safe, although the streets are fairly well lit.

Mount Vernon Trail. Across the Potomac in Virginia is the 18-mile paved Mount Vernon Trail. The 3.5-mile northern section begins near the pedestrian causeway leading to Theodore Roosevelt Island and goes past Ronald Reagan Washington National Airport and on to Old Town Alexandria. South of the airport, the trail runs down to the Washington Marina. The 9-mile southern section leads to Mount Vernon. ⊠ *Washington* ⊕ *www.nps.gov/gwmp.*

Fodor's Choice
★

National Mall and Memorial Parks. The most popular running route in Washington is the 4½-mile loop on the Mall. At any time of day hundreds of runners and speed walkers make their way along the gravel pathways. There's relatively little car traffic and, as they travel from the Lincoln Memorial all the way up to the Capitol and back, they can take in some of Washington's finest landmarks, such as the Washington Monument, the Reflecting Pool, and the Smithsonian's many museums. For a longer run, veer south of the Mall on either side of the Tidal Basin and head for the Jefferson Memorial and East Potomac Park, the site of many races. ⊠ *Bounded by Constitution and Independence Aves., The Mall* ⊕ *www.nps.gov/nacc.*

SOCCER

Fodor's Choice ★ **D.C. United.** One of the best Major League Soccer teams has a huge fan base in the nation's capital, finding many of its fans in the international crowds who miss the big matches at home, as well as families whose kids play soccer. International matches, including some World Cup preliminaries, are often played on the grass field of Capitol Hill's RFK Stadium, the Redskins' and Senators' former venue, which is the home to D.C. United until mid-2018 when the new Audi Field in Southwest's Buzzard Point is planned to open. Games are played March through October. You can buy tickets at the RFK Stadium ticket office or through the team's website, which offers special youth pricing. The D.C. Talon, the team mascot, entertains the crowd, along with enthusiastic, horn-blowing fans. ⊠ *Robert F. Kennedy Stadium, 2400 E. Capitol St. SE, Capitol Hill* ☎ *202/587–5000* ⊕ *www.dcunited.com* ✉ *$35–$55* Ⓜ *Stadium.*

SHOPPING

Updated by
Catherine
Sharpe

Despite the fact that going to "the Mall" in D.C. doesn't mean you're going shopping, Washington offers fabulous stores that sell serious or silly souvenirs, designer fashions, recycled and green goods, books about almost everything, and handicrafts. Even if you are headed to the mall, our nation's Mall, that is, you'll discover that plenty of collections housed along the famous greensward, such as the Smithsonian museums and the National Gallery of Art, sell interesting keepsakes in their gift shops.

Beyond the Mall, smaller one-of-a-kind shops, designer boutiques, and interesting specialty collections add to Washington's shopping scene alongside stores that have been part of the landscape for generations. Weekdays, Downtown street vendors add to the mix by offering funky jewelry; brightly patterned ties; buyer-beware watches; sunglasses; and African-inspired clothing, accessories, and art. Discriminating shoppers will find satisfaction at upscale malls on the city's outskirts. Not surprisingly, T-shirts and Capitol City souvenirs are in plentiful supply.

PLANNING

GALLERY HOPPING
Washington has three main gallery districts—Downtown, Dupont Circle, and Georgetown—though small galleries can be found all over in converted houses and storefronts. Whatever their location, many keep unusual hours and close entirely on Sunday and Monday. The *Washington Post* "Weekend" section (⊕ *www.washingtonpost. com*) and *Washington CityPaper* (⊕ *www.washingtoncitypaper.com*), published on Friday, are excellent sources of information on current exhibits and hours.

HISTORIC WALKS

Shopping is the perfect way to acquaint yourself with some of D.C.'s distinguished neighborhoods. A quick diversion down a side street in Georgetown reveals the neighborhood's historic charm and current glamour. Peer around a corner in Dupont or Capitol Hill to see a true D.C. architecture classic—the row house. Wandering Downtown you are sure to bump into one of the nation's great neoclassical structures, whether it is the White House or Ford's Theatre.

HOURS

Store hours vary greatly. In general, Georgetown stores are open late and on Sunday; stores Downtown that cater to office workers close as early as 5 pm and may not open at all on weekends. Some stores extend their hours on Thursday, and in Adams Morgan and along the U Street Corridor some don't open until noon but keep late hours to serve the evening crowds.

HOW TO SAVE MONEY

If you're willing to dig a bit, D.C. can be a savvy shopper's dream. Upscale consignment stores like Secondi in Dupont Circle and discount outlets like Nordstrom Rack in Friendship Heights provide an alternative to the surrounding luxury retail. Secondhand bookstores throughout the city provide hours of browsing and buying at welcoming prices.

WHITE HOUSE AREA

In the area best known for the nation's most famous house, you can also shop for official White House Christmas ornaments and Easter eggs, "red tape" paperweights, and crafts made by living Native American artists and artisans. If you're looking for a tasty treat, grab the fixings for a picnic lunch at the FRESHFARM market held every Thursday, April through October, on the corner of Lafayette Square—the produce that's sold here is said to be as fresh as food grown in the White House garden.

8

CRAFTS AND GIFTS

Fodor's Choice ★ **Indian Craft Shop.** Jewelry, pottery, sand paintings, weavings, and baskets from more than 50 Native American tribes, including Navajo, Pueblo, Zuni, Cherokee, and Lakota, are at your fingertips here—as long as you have a photo ID to enter the federal building. Items range from inexpensive jewelry costing as little as $5 on up to collector-quality art pieces selling for more than $10,000. This shop has been open since 1938. ⊠ *U.S. Department of the Interior, 1849 C St. NW, Room 1023, White House area* ☎ *202/208–4056* ⊕ *www.indiancraftshop.com* ⊙ *Closed weekends and federal holidays, except 3rd Sat. of each month* Ⓜ *Farragut W or Farragut N.*

Fodor's Choice ★ **myArchives Store.** In a town full of museum shops, this store at the National Archives Museum stands out, with exclusive memorabilia, reproductions, apparel, books, gifts, and plenty of Founding Fathers gear that let you own a piece of history. Authentic-looking copies of the Constitution and other historical documents are printed in Pennsylvania.

The popular "red tape" paperweights are crafted in the United States with real red tape that once bound government documents: hence the phrase "cut through the red tape." Other popular products feature Rosie the Riveter and Stars and Stripes bags; Teddy in Hat items for young children; and apparel featuring Franklin, Hamilton, and other founding fathers. Throughout the store, interactive games associated with special exhibits provide entertainment and education into history—of the United States and even you. Enter your last name into the computer and see how many people in the United States share your name and in which states they live. ⊠ *Constitution Ave. between 7th and 9th Sts., The Mall* ☎ *202/357–5271* ⊕ *www.myarchivesstore.org* Ⓜ *Archives/Navy Memorial.*

FAMILY **National Air and Space Museum Store.** One of the most visited museums in the world has a huge gift shop. The lower level of the three-floor, 12,000-square-foot store has tons of toys and games, plenty of souvenirs including T-shirts and totes, and an extensive selection of Star Wars and Star Trek licensed products for sci-fi fans. The upper level showcases a wide assortment of kites and books, but the largest selection of merchandise is on the middle level. Flight suits for both young and young at heart, space pens that work upside down, and freeze-dried "astronaut" ice cream are best sellers. The Einstein Planetarium Store has a fun array of Albert Einstein and space-related puzzles, games, and gadgets that especially appeal to teens and tweens. ⊠ *Independence Ave. and 6th St. SW, The Mall* ☎ *202/633–4510* Ⓜ *L'Enfant Plaza or Smithsonian.*

White House History Shop. The White House Historical Association operates two shops. The flagship store is in the White House Visitor Center, adjacent to the White House between 14th and 15th streets, and this smaller shop is in the historic Decatur House on Lafayette Square just a block from the White House. Both shops sell the Association's official merchandise, which are all well made. You can find everything from top-selling Christmas ornaments to jewelry, ties, T-shirts, books, and accessories. Ten dollars or less will get you cocktail napkins, bookmarks, or a wooden Easter egg. The more expensive items include silk scarves, hand-painted enamel boxes, and jewelry with cameos of the White House. The charming staff offers fun facts about the White House for free. ⊠ *1610 H St. NW, White House area* ☎ *202/218–4337* ⊕ *www.whitehousehistory.org* ⊘ *Closed weekends* Ⓜ *Farragut W.*

White House Visitor Center Flagship Store. Be sure to visit the White House Flagship Store, where you'll discover a trove of wonderful souvenirs and gifts that reflect the beauty, history, and symbolism of the Executive Mansion. For children, there are backpacks, puzzles, games, coloring books, plush presidential pets including Bo, Socks, Fala, Minnie, and Macaroni, and even a LEGO White House building kit. Jewelry selections include American eagle cuff links, tie tacks and money clips for men, and gorgeous Tiffany pearl and American Elm necklaces and earrings for women. You'll also find silk scarves and neckties, great books, journals and stationery, umbrellas, and tote bags that you can use to carry your treasures home. ⊠ *1450 Pennsylvania Ave. NW, Washington* ☎ *202/208–7031* ⊕ *www.whitehousehistory.org* Ⓜ *Federal Triangle.*

FIVE GREAT SHOPPING EXPERIENCES

Eastern Market, Capitol Hill Area: Artists, musicians, farmers, and more make this beautifully restored market a feast for the senses. Most vendors accept only cash.

Kramerbooks & Afterwords, Dupont Circle: Meeting up at Kramerbooks for a lazy Sunday afternoon of brunch and browsing is a quintessential D.C. experience.

Miss Pixie's, U Street Corridor: The color scheme of the store may be bright pink, but everything for sale is "green." Buyers flock to Miss Pixie's for vintage furniture and home goods.

MyArchives Store, The Mall: The hallowed hall where you can see the Declaration of Independence is also home to a store full of all-American gifts, including jewelry made out of real "red tape."

Tiny Jewel Box, Downtown: Since 1930, one family has owned and run this gem of a shop. On the day that her husband was inaugurated, First Lady Michelle Obama presented former First Lady Laura Bush with a custom-made Tiny Jewel Box leather-bound journal and silver pen.

MARKETS

USDA Farmers' Market. Blueberry popcorn anyone? On Fridays from May through October from 9 to 2, you can pick up fresh fruits, vegetables, breads, and other baked goods (and that flavored popcorn) across from the Smithsonian Metro station. During the summer months, the market is also open on Friday evenings from 4 to 7. Appropriately, the market is in the parking lot of the U.S. Department of Agriculture building. ⊠ *12th St and Independence Ave. SW, White House area* ☏ *202/708–0082* ⊕ *www.ams.usda.gov* Ⓜ *Smithsonian.*

FOGGY BOTTOM

Home to George Washington University, the Kennedy Center, the famed Watergate complex, and row houses owned by diplomats and dignitaries, it's a good spot for people-watching and fine dining, but alas there's very little shopping in this area.

MARKETS

FRESHFARM Market. Pick up a crab cake, an empanada, or a Mexican-style ice pop at this farmers market on Wednesday from 3 to 7, in early April through November. Similar fare is available near Lafayette Park (810 Vermont Avenue NW) on Thursday 11–3, April–October. Other FRESHFARM markets are in CityCenterDC (Tuesday 11–2, May–October), Dupont Circle (year-round on Sunday), H Street NE (Saturday morning, April–December), and at Penn Quarter (Thursday afternoon, April–December). All locations sell local fruits and vegetables. ⊠ *I St., between New Hampshire and 24th St. NW, Foggy Bottom* ☏ *202/362–8889* ⊕ *www.freshfarmmarkets.org* Ⓜ *Foggy Bottom.*

CAPITOL HILL

Capitol Hill is surprisingly good territory for shopping. Eastern Market and the unique shops and boutiques clustered around the historic redbrick building are great for browsing. Inside Eastern Market are produce and meat counters, plus places to buy flowers and sweets. ■ TIP→ **The flea market, held on weekends outdoors, presents nostalgia and local crafts by the crateful. There's also a farmers' market on Saturday.** Along 7th Street you can find a number of small shops selling such specialties as art books, handwoven rugs, and antiques. Cross Pennsylvania Avenue and head south on 8th Street for historic Barracks Row, where shops, bars, and restaurants inhabit the charming row houses leading toward the Anacostia River. The other shopping lure on the Hill is Union Station, D.C.'s gorgeous train station, these days actually a shopping mall that happens to also accommodate Amtrak and commuter trains.

Keep in mind that Union Station and Eastern Market are on opposite sides of the Hill. The Eastern Market Metro stop is the midpoint between the Eastern Market strip and Barracks Row; Union Station is several blocks away. You can certainly walk to Union Station from the Eastern Market stop, but it might be taxing after the time already spent on your feet in the shops.

BOOKS

Capitol Hill Books. Pop into this two-story maze of used books to browse through a wonderful collection of out-of-print history titles, political and fiction writings, and mysteries. On the second Saturday of every month, this cozy bookstore hosts a free wine-and-cheese reception from 4 to 7 and all purchases are discounted 10%. ⊠ 657 C St. SE, Capitol Hill ☎ 202/544–1621 ⊕ www.capitolhillbooks-dc.com Ⓜ Eastern Market.

Fodor'sChoice
★
East City Bookshop. A gathering spot for residents and visitors alike, East City stocks a wide selection of books, as well as art supplies, gifts, and toys. Check out the calendar of events, too—there's everything from storytime for children to author-led book discussions to musical performances. ⊠ 645 Pennsylvania Ave. SE, Suite 100, Capitol Hill ☎ 202/290–1636 ⊕ www.eastcitybookshop.com Ⓜ Eastern Market.

FAMILY
Fodor'sChoice
★
Fairy Godmother. This specialty store, in business since 1984, features a delightful selection of books for children, from infants through teens, in English, Spanish, and French, including an extensive nonfiction selection. It also sells puppets, games, dolls, puzzles, and toys. ⊠ 319 7th St. SE, Capitol Hill ☎ 202/547–5474 Ⓜ Eastern Market.

Riverby Books. The Capitol Hill and Eastern Market area loves its books, and Riverby is another great shop that sells everything from bestsellers to out-of-print rarities. ⊠ 417 E. Capitol St. SE, Capitol Hill ☎ 202/543–4342 ⊕ www.riverbybooksdc.com Ⓜ Capitol S.

CHILDREN'S CLOTHING

FAMILY **Dawn Price Baby.** The infant and toddler clothing at this friendly row-house boutique has been carefully selected with an eye for super-comfortable fabrics and distinctive designs. The shop also stocks toys, gifts, strollers, and bibs for baby Democrats and Republicans. There's a second location in Georgetown. ✉ *325 7th St. SE, Capitol Hill* ☎ *202/543–2920* ⊕ *www.dawnpricebaby.com* Ⓜ *Eastern Market.*

CRAFTS AND GIFTS

Woven History/Silk Road. Landmarks in this bohemian neighborhood, these connected stores sell gorgeous, handmade treasures from the mountain communities in India, Nepal, Turkey, Iran, Pakistan, and Tibet. You'll find everything from colorful weavings, pillows, and embroidered quilts to exotic jewelry and bags, as well as antique furniture. Woven History's rugs are made the old-fashioned way, with vegetable dyes and hand-spun wool, and sizes range from 3-by-5 feet to 8-by-10 feet. ✉ *311–315 7th St. SE, Capitol Hill* ☎ *202/543–1705* ⊕ *www.wovenhistory.com* Ⓜ *Eastern Market.*

FOOD

Hill's Kitchen. If you're a cook or looking for a gift for someone who is, pop into this small shop next to the Eastern Market. You'll find cookbooks, baking pans, aprons, towels and pot holders, cookie cutters, barware, grilling tools, specialty foods, and much more. ✉ *713 D St. SE, Eastern Market* ☎ *202/543–1997* ⊕ *www.hillskitchen.com* ⊘ *Closed Mon.* Ⓜ *Eastern Market.*

MARKETS

Fodor's Choice ★ **Eastern Market.** For nearly 145 years, this has been the hub of the Capitol Hill community. Vibrantly colored produce and flowers; freshly caught fish; fragrant cheeses; and tempting sweets are sold at the market by independent vendors. On weekends year-round, local farmers sell fresh fruits and vegetables, and artists and exhibitors sell handmade arts and crafts, jewelry, antiques, collectibles, and furniture from around the world. The city's oldest continuously operating public market continues to be a vibrant and lively gathering place, complete with entertainment, art showings, and a pottery studio for residents and visitors alike. ✉ *7th St. and North Carolina Ave. SE, Capitol Hill* ☎ *202/698–5253* ⊕ *www.easternmarket-dc.com* Ⓜ *Eastern Market.*

Radici. The name means "roots" in Italian, and this little shop has quickly settled its roots into the Capitol Hill neighborhood. The charming owners have created a warm and inviting gathering spot and store with its brick walls, Venetian glass light fixtures, terra-cotta tiles, beautiful food, and handmade Italian gift displays and tables both inside and out. This is a lovely spot for an afternoon pick-me-up of espresso and cannoli or an end-of-day glass of wine and *cicchetti Veneziani* (small bites). You'll also find everything you need for an Italian-themed picnic. Wine tastings are held on Thursday evening. ✉ *303 7th St. SE, Capitol Hill* ☎ *202/758–0086* ⊕ *www.radici-market.com* Ⓜ *Eastern Market.*

Union Station. Resplendent with marble floors and vaulted ceilings, Union Station is a shopping mall as well as a train station. Tenants

8

include such familiar names as Ann Taylor, H&M, Jos. A. Banks Clothiers, MAC Cosmetics, Neuhaus Chocolatier, Swarovski Crystal, and Victoria's Secret, as well as restaurants and a food court with everything from sushi and smoothies to scones. The east hall is filled with vendors of expensive domestic and international wares who sell from open stalls. From April through October an outdoor market is held Monday to Saturday with dozens of vendors selling fresh produce, baked goods and quick snacks, and arts and crafts. The Christmas season brings lights, a train display, and seasonal gift shops. ✉ *50 Massachusetts Ave. NE, Capitol Hill* ☎ *202/289–1908* ⊕ *www.unionstationdc.com* Ⓜ *Union Station.*

WOMEN'S CLOTHING

Forecast. If you like classic, contemporary styles, Forecast should be in your future. It sells silk and wool-blend sweaters in solid, muted tones and bright colors for women seeking elegant but practical clothing from brands like Lafayette 148 and Eileen Fisher. The housewares and gifts selection on the first floor is colorful and of high quality. ✉ *218 7th St. SE, Capitol Hill* ☎ *202/547–7337* ⊕ *www.forecaststore.com* ☻ *Closed Mon.* Ⓜ *Eastern Market.*

TOYS

Labyrinth Games & Puzzles. You won't find any video games in this gem, but instead you'll discover an outstanding selection of handmade wooden puzzles and mazes, collectible card and travel games, board games, and brainteasers. An added bonus to stopping in are the dozens of activities and games for all ages you can play. ✉ *645 Pennsylvania Ave. SE, Eastern Market* ☎ *202/544–1059* ⊕ *www.labyrinthgameshop. com* Ⓜ *Eastern Market.*

DOWNTOWN

Downtown D.C. is spread out and sprinkled with federal buildings and museums. Shopping options run the gamut from the upscale CityCenter complex and Gallery Place shopping center to small art galleries and bookstores. Gallery Place houses familiar chain stores like Urban Outfitters, Bed Bath & Beyond, and Ann Taylor Loft; it also has a movie theater and a bowling alley. Other big names in the Downtown area include Macy's and chain stores like H&M, Target, and Banana Republic. With its many offices, Downtown tends to shut down at 5 pm sharp, with the exception of the department stores and larger chain stores. A jolly happy-hour crowd springs up after work and families and fans fill the streets during weekend sporting events at the Verizon Center. The revitalized Penn Quarter has some of the best restaurants in town peppered among its galleries and specialty stores.

The worthwhile shops are not concentrated in one area, however. The Gallery Place Metro stop provides the most central starting point—you can walk south to the galleries and design shops, or west toward the Metro Center and Farragut North, though this trek is only for the ambitious. Although Gallery Place is a nightlife hot spot, the Metro Center and the Farragut area are largely silent after working hours.

CRAFTS AND GIFTS

Fodor's Choice ★ **Fahrney's Pens.** What began in 1929 as a repair shop and a pen bar—a place to fill your fountain pen before setting out for work—is now a wonderland for anyone who loves a good writing instrument. You'll find pens in silver, gold, and lacquer by the world's leading manufacturers. If you want to improve your handwriting, the store offers classes in calligraphy and cursive. And yes, the store still offers repair services for all writing instruments. ✉ *1317 F St. NW, Downtown* ☎ *202/628–9525* ⊕ *www.fahrneyspens.com* ☽ *Closed Sun.* Ⓜ *Metro Center.*

JEWELRY

Fodor's Choice ★ **Tiny Jewel Box.** Despite its name, this venerable D.C. favorite contains six floors of precious and semiprecious wares, including unique gifts, home accessories, vintage pieces, and works by such well-known designers as David Yurman, Penny Preville, and Alex Sepkus. The Federal Collection on the sixth floor features handmade boxes and paperweights with decoupages of vintage prints of Washington commissioned by the Tiny Jewel Box. *InStore Magazine* has named this family-run store "America's Coolest Jewelry Store." ✉ *1147 Connecticut Ave. NW, Downtown* ☎ *202/393–2747* ⊕ *www.tinyjewelbox.com* ☽ *Closed Sun.* Ⓜ *Farragut N.*

MEN'S CLOTHING

J. Press. Like its flagship store (founded in Connecticut in 1902 as a custom shop for Yale University), this Washington outlet keeps with the Ivy League traditions. Harris tweed and classic navy blazers are the best-sellers. ✉ *1801 L St. NW, Downtown* ☎ *202/857–0120* ⊕ *www. jpressonline.com* ☽ *Closed Sun.* Ⓜ *Farragut N.*

SPAS AND BEAUTY SALONS

Andre Chreky. Housed in an elegantly renovated Victorian town house, this salon offers complete services—hair, nails, facials, waxing, and makeup. Because it's a favorite of the Washington elite, you might just overhear a tidbit or two on who's going to what black-tie function with whom. Adjacent whirlpool pedicure chairs allow two friends to get pampered simultaneously. ✉ *1604 K St. NW, Downtown* ☎ *202/293–9393* ⊕ *www.andrechreky.com* Ⓜ *Farragut N.*

The Grooming Lounge. Most spas are geared to women, but guys are pampered here. You can find old-fashioned hot-lather shaves, haircuts, massages, and business manicures and pedicures—everything a man needs to look terrific. The hair- and skin-care products—from Kiehl's, Billy Jealousy, and Malin+Goetz, to name just a few—are worth a visit even if you don't have time for a service. ✉ *1745 L St. NW, Downtown* ☎ *202/466–8900* ⊕ *www.groominglounge.com* Ⓜ *Farragut N.*

WOMEN'S CLOTHING

Coup de Foudre. The name translates to "love at first sight," and that may be the case when you step into this inviting, elegant boutique. All the upscale lingerie hails from France, England, Belgium, and Italy, and the specialty is friendly, personalized bra fittings. Appointments accepted. ✉ *1001 Pennsylvania Ave. NW, Downtown* ☎ *202/393–0878* ⊕ *www. shopcdf.com* ☽ *Closed Sun.* Ⓜ *Metro Center.*

8

Rizik's. This tony, patrician Washington institution offers women's designer clothing, accessories, outerwear, bridal fashions, and expert advice. The sales staff will help you find just the right style from the store's extensive inventory from worldwide designers. If you're looking for a one-of-kind cocktail or evening dress, this is the place to get it. Take the elevator up from the northwest corner of Connecticut Avenue and L Street. ✉ *1100 Connecticut Ave. NW, Downtown* ☎ *202/223–4050* ⊕ *www.riziks.com* ⊘ *Closed Sun.* Ⓜ *Farragut N.*

SHOPPING MALLS

CityCenterDC. Downtown's newest shopping complex is an upscale gathering of high-end boutiques, restaurants, residential and office buildings, park and open-air plaza, bordered by New York Avenue, 9th, 11th, and H Streets NW. It's all too easy to spend several hundred dollars in just a few minutes here, with leather goods from Longchamp, Louis Vuitton, and Salvatore Ferragamo; designer fashions and accessories from Burberry, Canali, CH Carolina Herrera, Kate Spade, Loro Piana, Paul Stuart, Zadig & Voltaire; outdoor clothing and sporting goods from Arc'teryx; Tumi luggage; and David Yurman jewelry. For a break from shopping or browsing, grab an indulgent treat from Momofuku Milk Bar, Rare Sweets, or a scrumptious gelato from Dolcezza and relax in the plaza with its benches, tables, and fountains. The 10-acre site will also have a luxury hotel, slated for completion in 2018. ✉ *825 10th St. NW, Downtown* ☎ *202/347–6337* ⊕ *www.citycenterdc.com* Ⓜ *Metro Center or Gallery Pl./Chinatown.*

GEORGETOWN

Although Georgetown, the capital's center for famous residents, is not on a Metro line and street parking is tough to find, people still flock here to shop. It's also a hot spot for restaurants, bars, and nightclubs.

National chains and designer shops now stand side by side with the specialty shops that first gave the district its allure, but the historic neighborhood is still charming and its street scene lively. Most stores lie east and west on M Street and to the north on Wisconsin Avenue. The intersection of M and Wisconsin is the nexus for chain stores and big-name designer shops. The farther you venture in any direction from this intersection, the more eclectic and interesting the shops become. Some of the big-name stores are worth a look for their architecture alone; several shops blend traditional Georgetown town-house exteriors with airy modern showroom interiors.

Shopping in Georgetown can be expensive, but you don't have to add expensive parking lot fees. ■TIP➔ **The DC Circulator is your best bet for getting into and out of Georgetown, especially if it's hot or if you are laden down with many purchases. This $1 bus runs along M Street and up Wisconsin Avenue, the major shopping strips.** The nearest Metro station, Foggy Bottom/GWU, is a 10- to 15-minute walk from the shops.

ANTIQUES AND COLLECTIBLES

Cherub Antiques Gallery and Michael Getz Antiques. You might want to keep your sunglasses on as you enter this shop, where the sterling silver is polished to perfection. Two dealers have shared this Victorian row

DID YOU KNOW?

Georgetown, one of D.C.'s oldest and most storied neighborhoods, is a great spot for political celebrity sightings. Heavyweights like former Secretary of State John Kerry, former Secretary of State Madeleine Albright, and journalist Bob Woodward live here.

house since 1983. Michael Getz Antiques carries fireplace equipment and silver. Cherub Antiques Gallery specializes in art nouveau and art deco. A glass case by the door holds a collection of more than 100 cocktail shakers, including Prohibition-era pieces disguised as penguins, roosters, and dumbbells. ⊠ *2918 M St. NW, Georgetown* ☎ *202/337–2224 Cherub Gallery, 202/338–3811 Michael Getz Antiques* ⊕ *www.trocadero.com/cherubgallery* Ⓜ *Foggy Bottom/GWU.*

Marston Luce. House and garden accessories are in the mix here, but the emphasis is on 18th- and 19th-century French and Swedish painted furniture, discovered by the owner on yearly buying trips in Europe. ⊠ *1651 Wisconsin Ave. NW, Georgetown* ☎ *202/333–6800* ⊕ *www.marstonluce.com* Ⓜ *Foggy Bottom/GWU.*

Fodor's Choice
★

Opportunity Shop of the Christ Child Society. This gem of a consignment/thrift store has been a Georgetown landmark since 1954. You'll find gorgeous fine jewelry, antiques, crystal, silver, and porcelain. Prices are moderate, and profits go to a good cause—the Christ Child Society provides for the needs of local children and young mothers. ⊠ *1427 Wisconsin Ave. NW, Georgetown* ☎ *202/333–6635* ⊕ *www.christchilddc.org* ⊘ *Closed Sun.* Ⓜ *Foggy Bottom/GWU.*

ART GALLERIES

Addison Ripley. Stunning, large-scale contemporary work by national and local artists, including painters Manon Cleary and Wolf Kahn and photographer Frank Hallam Day, is exhibited at this well-respected gallery. ⊠ *1670 Wisconsin Ave. NW, Georgetown* ☎ *202/338–5180* ⊕ *www.addisonripleyfineart.com* ⊘ *Closed Sun. and Mon.* Ⓜ *Foggy Bottom/GWU.*

Fodor's Choice
★

Cross MacKenzie Gallery. Vibrant and unusual contemporary ceramic pieces are shown here, plus paintings and photography. There's a new exhibit almost every month, which makes this a stunning showcase of art from D.C.-based and international artists. ⊠ *1675 Wisconsin Ave. NW, Georgetown* ☎ *202/333–7970* ⊕ *www.crossmackenzie.com* ⊘ *Closed Sun.–Tues.* Ⓜ *Foggy Bottom.*

Maurine Littleton Gallery. Even if the prices are as untouchable as the art in this gallery devoted to glass, metal, and ceramics, it's worth a look to see work by some of the world's finest contemporary artists. The intimate, bright space is owned and managed by the daughter of Harvey K. Littleton, founder of the American Studio Glass movement. ⊠ *1667 Wisconsin Ave. NW, Georgetown* ☎ *202/333–9307* ⊕ *www.littletongallery.com* Ⓜ *Foggy Bottom.*

Susan Calloway Fine Arts. Stunning art draws people into this two-floor gallery where a mix of vintage, contemporary, and classical paintings are hung salon-style. You'll find large abstract oils and a lovely selection of landscapes, but don't miss the box full of small original paintings in the back, most priced under $100. ⊠ *1643 Wisconsin Ave., Georgetown* ☎ *202/965–4601* ⊕ *www.callowayart.com* Ⓜ *Foggy Bottom or Dupont Circle.*

BOOKS

Bridge Street Books. This charming independent store focuses on politics, history, philosophy, poetry, literature, music, film, and Judaica. ⊠ *2814 Pennsylvania Ave., NW, Georgetown* ☎ *202/965–5200* ⊕ *www.bridgestreetbooks.com* Ⓜ *Foggy Bottom/GWU.*

CHILDREN'S CLOTHING AND TOYS

Egg by Susan Lazar. Adorable is the world that instantly comes to mind when you step into this boutique from designer Susan Lazar. There are clothes for newborns to size 8 in organic and environmentally friendly material with simple and colorful eye-catching patterns and designs. ⊠ *1661 Wisconsin Ave. NW, Georgetown* ☎ *202/338–9500* ⊕ *www.egg-baby.com* Ⓜ *Foggy Bottom.*

FAMILY **Tugooh Toys.** You might have a difficult time getting your children to leave this fun toy store filled with educational and eco-friendly toys. From puzzles, games, and building toys to dolls, puppets, and dress-up clothes, you are bound to find the perfect gift for youngsters. ⊠ *1355 Wisconsin Ave. NW, Georgetown* ☎ *202/338–9476* ⊕ *www.tugoohtoys.com* Ⓜ *Foggy Bottom.*

CRAFTS

Appalachian Spring. Traditional and contemporary American-made crafts—including art glass, pottery, jewelry, housewares, and toys—fill this lovely shop. The glossy wooden jewelry boxes displayed here are treasures in their own right. There's an outpost in Union Station's East Hall. ⊠ *1415 Wisconsin Ave. NW, Georgetown* ☎ *202/337–5780* ⊕ *www.appalachianspring.com* Ⓜ *Foggy Bottom.*

HOME FURNISHINGS

Fodor's Choice ★ **A Mano.** The name is Italian for "by hand," and it lives up to its name, stocking colorful hand-painted ceramics, hand-dyed tablecloths, blown-glass stemware, hand-embroidered bed linens, and other home and garden accessories by American, English, Italian, and French artisans. Some of the jewelry pieces are simply stunning, and the kids' gifts are adorable. ⊠ *1677 Wisconsin Ave. NW, Georgetown* ☎ *202/298–7200* ⊕ *www.amano.bz.*

Random Harvest. Whether you're looking for something that's decorative or functional (or a combination of both), you'll find it here. Random Harvest sells new and antique treasures for the home, including pillows, mirrors, glassware, barware, and lamps. There's also a nice selection of American and European vintage furniture. ⊠ *1313 Wisconsin Ave. NW, Georgetown* ☎ *202/333–5569* ⊕ *www.randomharvesthome.com* Ⓜ *Foggy Bottom/GWU.*

JEWELRY

Ann Hand. Catering to Washington's powerful and prestigious, this jewelry and gift shop specializing in patriotic pins may seem intimidating, but prices begin at $35. Hand's signature pin, The Liberty Eagle, is $200. Photos on the walls above brightly lit display cases show who's who in Washington wearing you-know-who's designs, making this a worthwhile visit while shopping in Georgetown. ⊠ *3236 Prospect St. NW, Upper Northwest* ☎ *202/333–2979* ⊕ *www.annhand.com* ⊘ *Closed weekends.*

8

MUSIC

Hill & Dale Records. Georgetown's only vinyl record store carries a wonderful collection of new vinyl LPs—yes, it's true, they are new; there's nothing used at this store. Genres include jazz, country, pop, folk, blues, rock, and electronica. From Billie Holiday's "Body and Soul" and Dick Dale & The Del-Tones's "Summer Surf" to Rush's "Clockwork Angels," the selection is bound to delight any music lover. Also on display in this bright and airy spot are photos and posters that celebrate music. ⊠ *1054 31st St. NW, Georgetown* ☎ *202/333–5012* ⊕ *www.hillanddalerecords.com* ⊘ *Closed Mon.*

SHOES

Fodor's Choice
★

Hu's Shoes. This cutting-edge selection would shine in Paris, Tokyo, or New York. Luckily for Washingtonians, it brings ballet flats, heels, and boots from designers like Chloé, Fendi, Manolo Blahnik, Proenza Schouler, and Valentino right to Georgetown. ⊠ *3005 M St. NW, Georgetown* ☎ *202/342–0202* ⊕ *www.husonline.com* Ⓜ *Foggy Bottom/GWU.*

SHOPPING MALLS

Georgetown Park. There's a good mix of retailers at this mall in the center of Georgetown, including Anthropologie, Dean & DeLuca, DSW, Forever 21, H&M, HomeGoods, J. Crew, and T.J. Maxx. Stop at the Georgetown Visitor Center just inside the main entrance to learn about what's happening in the neighborhood. If you need a break from shopping, visit Olivia Macaron's for a coffee and luscious raspberry macaron. You can even try your hand at bocce or bowling at Pinstripes, a bistro and entertainment spot with a wonderful patio. ⊠ *3222 M St. NW, Georgetown* ☎ *202/342–8190* ⊕ *www.georgetownpark.com* Ⓜ *Foggy Bottom/GWU.*

SPAS AND BEAUTY SALONS

Bluemercury. Hard-to-find skin-care lines—Laura Mercier and Trish McEvoy, among others—are what set this homegrown, now national, chain apart. The retail space up front sells soaps, lotions, perfumes, cosmetics, and skin- and hair-care products. Behind the glass door is the "skin gym," where you can treat yourself to facials, waxing, and oxygen treatments. You'll also find branches in Dupont Circle and Downtown. ⊠ *3059 M St. NW, Georgetown* ☎ *202/965–1300* ⊕ *www.bluemercury.com* Ⓜ *Foggy Bottom/GWU.*

WOMEN'S CLOTHING

Fodor's Choice
★

Ella-Rue. Although it's a small shop, you'll find a wonderful selection of high-end consignment clothing, shoes, and handbags here. On any given day, you might discover pieces by designers like Bulgari, Carolina Herrera, Stella McCartney, or Zac Posen. The staff is especially helpful and works hard to help you find the perfect ensemble for your next special event or important meeting. ⊠ *3231 P St. NW, Georgetown* ☎ *202/333–1598* ⊕ *www.ella-rue.com.*

Hu's Wear. Ladies looking for just-off-the-runway looks to go with their Hu's Shoes just need to cross the street to find designs by The Row, Isabel Marant, and Stella McCartney. ⊠ *2906 M St. NW, Georgetown* ☎ *202/342–2020* ⊕ *www.husonline.com* Ⓜ *Foggy Bottom.*

Fodor'sChoice **The Phoenix.** All under one roof (with 30 solar panels) in a delightful
★ shop owned and operated by the Hays family since 1955, you can find
contemporary clothing in natural fibers by designers such as Eileen
Fisher, OSKA, White+Warren, Michael Stars, and Lilla P. There's also
a stunning selection of jewelry from Germany, Turkey, Israel, and Italy;
gorgeous leather handbags by Annabel Ingall; whimsical pewter kitchen
accessories from South African designer Carrol Boyes; and fine- and
folk-art pieces from Mexico. ⊠ *1514 Wisconsin Ave. NW, Georgetown*
☎ *202/338–4404* ⊕ *www.thephoenixdc.com* Ⓜ *Foggy Bottom.*

Reddz Trading. You can't miss the bright red storefront of this consignment shop which sells clothing, accessories, jewelry, and shoes. Unlike
traditional consignment stores, Reddz buys its merchandise for cash
or trade so inventory is added regularly. It's not uncommon to find
pieces with the price tags still attached. ⊠ *1413 Wisconsin Ave. NW,
Georgetown* ☎ *202/506–2789* ⊕ *www.reddztrading.com.*

relish. In fashionable Cady's Alley, this dramatic space holds a women's
collection handpicked seasonally by the owner. Modern, elegant, and
practical selections include European classics and well-tailored modern designers, such as Marc Jacobs, Sacai, Thom Browne, Veronique
Branquinho, and Dries Van Noten. ⊠ *3312 Cady's Alley NW, Georgetown* ☎ *202/333–5343* ⊕ *www.relishdc.com* ☉ *Closed Sun.* Ⓜ *Foggy
Bottom/GWU.*

Fodor'sChoice **Violet Boutique.** Women looking for fashion-forward styles at decent
★ prices will find plenty to love here—everything is under $200. Alluring
dresses, silk wraps and jackets, chic clutches, and gorgeous accessories from Los Angeles–based jeweler Lilli Klein are sure to turn heads.
⊠ *3289 M St. NW, Georgetown* ☎ *202/621–9225* ⊕ *www.violetdc.com.*

8

DUPONT CIRCLE AND LOGAN CIRCLE

You might call Dupont Circle a younger, less staid version of Georgetown—almost as pricey, but with more apartment buildings than
houses. Its many restaurants, offbeat shops, and specialty stores give it
a cosmopolitan air. The street scene here is more urban than Georgetown's, with bike messengers and chess aficionados filling up the park.
The Sunday farmers' market attracts shoppers with organic food, artisanal cheeses, homemade soap, and hand-spun wool. To the south of
Dupont Circle proper are several boutiques and familiar retail stores
close to the Farragut and Farragut North Metro stops. Burberry and
Thomas Pink both have stores in this area of Dupont.

ART GALLERIES

Fodor'sChoice **Hemphill Fine Arts.** This spacious showcase for contemporary art shows
★ mid-career and established artists such as William Christenberry, John
Dreyfuss, Linling Lu, and Julie Wolfe, with works in all media. ⊠ *1515
14th St. NW, 3rd fl., Logan Circle* ☎ *202/234–5601* ⊕ *www.hemphill-
finearts.com* ☉ *Closed Sun. and Mon.* Ⓜ *Dupont Circle.*

Hillyer Art Space. Featuring art from local, regional, and international contemporary artists, this gallery also offers life drawing classes on Monday
nights and artists' presentations. Exhibits change frequently and highlight

works in all mediums. It also attracts a big crowd during Dupont Circle's gallery crawl every first Friday of the month from 6 to 9 pm. ✉ *9 Hillyer Ct. NW, Dupont Circle* ☎ *202/338–0325* Ⓜ *Dupont Circle.*

Marsha Mateyka Gallery. Just around the corner from the Phillips Collection sits this gallery that showcases the work of nearly 20 contemporary artists. You'll find paintings, sculptures, photography, and works on paper by international artists including Athena Tacha, Jae Ko, and William Wiley, among others. ✉ *2012 R St. NW, Dupont Circle* ☎ *202/328–0088* ⊕ *www.marshamateykagallery.com* Ⓜ *Dupont Circle.*

Fodor's Choice
★
Studio Gallery. Founded in 1956 by Jennie Lea Knight (whose work is in the collections of many D.C. museums), Studio exhibits contemporary work by internationally acclaimed artists, as well as emerging local artists. The spacious gallery encompasses two floors in an elegant town house and exhibitions change frequently. Don't miss the sculpture garden in the back of the house. ✉ *2108 R St. NW, Dupont Circle* ☎ *202/232–8734* ⊕ *www.studiogallerydc.com* ☉ *Closed Sun.* Ⓜ *Dupont Circle.*

BOOKS

Fodor's Choice
★
Kramerbooks & Afterwords Café. One of Washington's best-loved independent bookstores has a choice selection of fiction and nonfiction. Open all night on Friday and Saturday, it's a convenient meeting place. Kramerbooks shares space with Afterwords Café, which has all-day dining and coffee. ✉ *1517 Connecticut Ave. NW, Dupont Circle* ☎ *202/387–1400* ⊕ *www.kramers.com* Ⓜ *Dupont Circle.*

Second Story Books. One of the largest used and rare book stores in the country, Second Story Books sells not only books, but also maps, posters, manuscripts, CDs, prints, and DVDs. A knowledgeable staff is always on hand to help you shop. ✉ *2000 P St. NW, Dupont Circle* ☎ *202/659–8884* ⊕ *www.secondstorybooks.com* Ⓜ *Dupont Circle.*

CLOTHING

Fodor's Choice
★
Betsy Fisher. Catering to women of all ages and sizes in search of contemporary and trendy styles, the selection here includes one-of-a-kind accessories, clothes, shoes, and jewelry by American, Canadian, and European designers. ✉ *1224 Connecticut Ave. NW, Dupont Circle* ☎ *202/785–1975* ⊕ *www.betsyfisher.com* Ⓜ *Dupont Circle.*

Marine Layer. This San Francisco–based retailer is known for its soft, eco-friendly, and durable T-shirts. The company's signature fabric, Micro-Modal, is made from beech-wood pulp and woven into the product line for men and women. In addition to T-shirts, you'll find equally comfortable dresses, pants, outerwear, loungewear, sweaters, and hats. ✉ *1627 14th St. NW, Logan Circle* ☎ *202/864–6686* ⊕ *www.marinelayer.com* Ⓜ *U St./African American Civil War Memorial/Cardozo.*

Fodor's Choice
★
Proper Topper. As its name suggests, this gem of a boutique carries a delightful collection of hats for women, men, and children for any occasion or season. But upon entering, you'll find so much more: unusual gifts for the home, delightful clothes and shoes for the young ones in your life, funky jewelry, clothing from designers like Tracy Reese and Yoana Baraschi, and a wonderfully varied assortment of accessories

for men and women. ⊠ *1350 Connecticut Ave. NW, Dupont Circle* ☏ *202/842–3055* ⊕ *propertopper.com.*

Fodor'sChoice ★ **Secondi.** One of the city's finest consignment stores carries a well-chosen selection of women's designer and casual clothing, accessories, and shoes. The brands carried include Isabel Marant, Louis Vuitton, Donna Karan, Prada, and Chanel. ⊠ *1702 Connecticut Ave. NW, 2nd fl., Dupont Circle* ☏ *202/667–1122* ⊕ *www.secondi.com* Ⓜ *Dupont Circle.*

CRAFTS AND GIFTS

Beadazzled. A rainbow of ready-to-string beads fills the cases, and the stock also includes jewelry as well as books on crafts history and techniques. Check the website for a class schedule. ⊠ *1507 Connecticut Ave. NW, Dupont Circle* ☏ *202/265–2323* ⊕ *www.beadazzled.com* Ⓜ *Dupont Circle.*

The Chocolate Moose. This store is simple, sheer fun for adults and kids alike. Looking for clacking, windup teeth? You can find them here, along with unusual greeting cards, whimsical and colorful socks, and unique housewares and handicrafts. If playing with all those fun toys makes you hungry, you can pick up a select line of premium European chocolates. ⊠ *1743 L St., NW, Dupont Circle* ☏ *202/463–0992* ⊕ *www. chocolatemoosedc.com* ☾ *Closed Sun.* Ⓜ *Farragut N.*

HOME FURNISHINGS

Fodor'sChoice ★ **Salt & Sundry.** Bohemian-chic is the best way to describe the knickknacks, tableware, gifts, and other household items you'll find in the delightful Salt & Sundry. Frames, pillows, and small-batch food products like tonics and maple syrup are just a handful of the items stocked by owner Amanda McClements. She also hosts special events, tastings, and presentations with local bartenders, chefs, and food purveyors. There's a second outpost in Union Market. ⊠ *1625 14th St. NW, Logan Circle* ☏ *202/556–1866* ⊕ *www.shopsaltandsundry.com* Ⓜ *U St./African American Civil War Memorial/Cardozo.*

Tabletop. Evoking a museum gift shop, this is a delightful place to find tiles by Canadian designer Xenia Taler; colorful Joseph Joseph kitchen gadgets; charming, eco-friendly trays, games, and bookends from Wolfum; Anorak tote and toiletry bags with kissing stags, hedgehogs, or robins; and Daphne Olive jewelry. For the younger set, there are charming Cate & Levy animal pillows, hand puppets made from upcycled sweaters, and Food Face dinner plates that will make even the pickiest eater clean their plate. ⊠ *1608 20th St. NW, Dupont Circle* ☏ *202/387–7117* ⊕ *www.tabletopdc.com* Ⓜ *Dupont Circle.*

JEWELRY

Fodor'sChoice ★ **Bloom.** As its name suggests, this shop has a wonderful selection of jewelry that is as dazzling as a garden in full bloom. Whether you're looking for a simple pair of earrings for a job interview or a stunning statement piece for a New Year's Eve party, you'll find it here. Rings, pendants, necklaces, and bracelets are beautifully displayed and prices are affordable. The sterling silver jewelry with precious and semiprecious stones from Turkey are gorgeous. There's also a small collection of handmade makeup pouches, wall hangings, linens, and

8

purses. ✉ *1710 Connecticut Ave. NW, Washington* ☎ *202/621–9049* Ⓜ *Dupont Circle.*

lou lou. A "blingful" boutique, jam-packed with costume jewelry and bags at price points that please the purse, draws lots of ladies looking for the latest trendy item. Lou Lou Clothing, a few doors down at 1623 Connecticut, sells boho-contemporary apparel, arranged by color and style. You'll also find lou lou boutiques in Georgetown, the U Street Corridor, and two Downtown locations. ✉ *1601 Connecticut Ave. NW, Dupont Circle* ☎ *202/588–0027* ⊕ *www.loulouboutiques. com* Ⓜ *Dupont Circle.*

ADAMS MORGAN

Scattered among the dozens of Latin, Ethiopian, and international restaurants in this most bohemian of Washington neighborhoods is a score of eccentric shops. If quality is what you seek, Adams Morgan and nearby Woodley Park can be a minefield; tread cautiously. Still, this is good turf for the bargain hunter. ■TIP→ **If bound for a specific shop, you may wish to call ahead to verify hours.** The evening hours bring scores of revelers to the row, so plan to go before dark unless you want to couple your shopping with a party pit stop.

How to get there is another question. Though the Woodley Park/Zoo/ Adams Morgan Metro stop is relatively close to the 18th Street strip (where the interesting shops are), getting off here means that you will have to walk over the bridge on Calvert Street. Five minutes longer, the walk from the Dupont Circle Metro stop is more scenic; you cruise north on 18th Street through tree-lined streets of row houses and embassies. You can also easily catch Metrobus No. 42 or a cab from Dupont to Adams Morgan.

BOOKS

Idle Time Books. Since 1981, this multilevel used-book store has been selling "rare to medium rare" books with plenty of meaty titles in all genres, especially out-of-print literature. ✉ *2467 18th St. NW, Adams Morgan* ☎ *202/232–4774* ⊕ *www.idletimebooks.com* Ⓜ *Woodley Park/Zoo.*

CHOCOLATE

The Chocolate House. For chocoholics with a gourmet palate, this is one-stop shopping. Offerings are both foreign (Michel Cluizel from France and Amedei from Italy) and domestic (Askinosie from Missouri and Amano from Utah). Selections from D.C.-area chocolatiers make for tasty souvenirs. ✉ *1904 18th St. NW, Adams Morgan* ☎ *202/903–0346* ⊕ *www.thechocolatehousedc.com* Ⓜ *Dupont Circle.*

CLOTHING

Meeps & Treasury. Catering to fans of retro glamour and low prices, this shop near the bottom of the Adams Morgan strip stocks vintage clothes and costumes for women and men from the '60s through the '90s. ✉ *2104 18th St. NW, Adams Morgan* ☎ *202/265–6546* ⊕ *www. meepsdc.com* Ⓜ *Dupont Circle.*

Mercedes Bien Vintage. Carefully selected vintage clothing and shoes include everything from cocktail dresses to cowboy boots. You will also find jewelry and belts, all handpicked by the owner, Mercedes. This small shop offers exceptional, personal service. ✉ *2423 18th St. NW, Adams Morgan* ☎ *202/360–8481* ✆ *Closed weekdays* Ⓜ *Woodley Park/Zoo.*

SHOES

Fleet Feet Sports Shop. The expert staff at this friendly shop will assess your feet and your training schedule before recommending the perfect pair of new running shoes. Shoes, along with apparel and accessories for running, swimming, soccer, and cycling, crowd the small space. ✉ *1841 Columbia Rd. NW, Adams Morgan* ☎ *202/387–3888* ⊕ *www. fleetfeetdc.com* Ⓜ *Woodley Park/Zoo.*

U STREET CORRIDOR

In the 1930s and 1940s U Street was known for its classy theaters and jazz clubs. After decades of decline following the 1968 riots, the neighborhood has been revitalized. The area has gentrified at lightning speed, but has retained a diverse mix of multiethnic young professionals and older, working-class African Americans. U Street resident and Associate Justice of the Supreme Court Sonia Sotomayor says, "U Street is the East Village." At night the neighborhood's club, bar, and restaurant scene comes alive. During the day the street scene is more laid-back, with more locals than tourists occupying the distinctive shops.

ANTIQUES AND COLLECTIBLES

Fodor's Choice
★
GoodWood. It's described by its owners as an American mercantile and dry goods store, but when you open the door, you'll feel as if you've been invited into a friend's warm and inviting loft. Displays throughout the store beautifully showcase 19th-century American furniture. You'll also discover leather goods; vintage mirrors and other decorative home items; men's and women's grooming products and perfumes from around the world; Peruvian alpaca and wool scarves; Swedish clogs; and comfortable dresses, sweaters, and tops from American and international designers. ✉ *1428 U St. NW, U Street* ☎ *202/986–3640* ⊕ *www.goodwooddc.com* Ⓜ *U St./Cardozo.*

HOME FURNISHINGS

Home Rule. Here you can find some of the latest design elements for the bathroom, kitchen, and dining room. There are also playful tissue holders and other fun and affordable household items in cheerful colors. ✉ *1807 14th St. NW, U Street* ☎ *202/797–5544* ⊕ *www.homerule.com* Ⓜ *U St./Cardozo.*

Fodor's Choice
★
Miss Pixie's. The well-chosen collectibles—handpicked by Miss Pixie herself—include gorgeous textiles, antique home furnishings, lamps, mirrors, glass- and silverware, and artwork. The reasonable prices will grab your attention, as will the location, in an old car-dealer showroom. ✉ *1626 14th St. NW, U Street* ☎ *202/232–8171* ⊕ *www.misspixies.com* Ⓜ *U St./Cardozo or Dupont Circle.*

Zawadi. The name means "gift" in Swahili, but you may want to buy the beautiful African art, textiles, home accessories, and jewelry for

8

yourself. ⊠ *1524 U St. NW, U Street* ☎ *202/232–2214* ⊕ *www.zawa-diarts.com* ☾ *Closed Sun., Tues., and Wed.* Ⓜ *U St./Cardozo.*

CLOTHING

Current Boutique. Don't be fooled by the new dresses in the front—this shop is a consignment shopper's dream. "Current" styles from brands such as Tory Burch, BCBG, Marc Jacobs, and Diane Von Furstenberg just might fit better when you buy them at a third of their original price. ⊠ *1809 14th St. NW, U Street* ☎ *202/588–7311* ⊕ *www.currentbou-tique.com* Ⓜ *U St./Cardozo.*

Kit & Ace. This Vancouver-based retailer sells sportswear for men and women made from the company's proprietary fabric family, Qemir, in cashmere, silk, and ponte knit. Pieces are not only comfortable, but washable and long-wearing. And be sure to check out the wall highlighting local artists. ⊠ *1921 8th St. NW, Suite 115, Shaw* ☎ *844/548–6223* ⊕ *www.kitandace.com* Ⓜ *Shaw/Howard U.*

Fodor'sChoice ★ **Lettie Gooch Boutique.** Named after the owner's grandmother, this hip boutique attracts many of D.C.'s fashionistas with its wonderful collection of cutting-edge designers, including Prairie Underground, Collective Concepts, The Odells, Curator, Bridge and Burn, and Acoté, among others. Many of the lines are created with environmentally sustainable materials. After you've selected that perfect party dress, check out the bold and colorful jewelry, shoes, and purses for an outfit that is uniquely yours. And if you need a souvenir for friends back home, the shop carries a selection of handmade soaps and candles from emerging artisans. ⊠ *1921 8th St. NW, Suite 110, U Street* ☎ *202/332–4242* ⊕ *www.lettiegooch.com.*

Read Wall. Well-tailored, American-made men's sportswear is the speciality at Read Wall. You'll find sport coats, chinos, dress pants, cashmere sweaters, bright wax jackets, shorts, and lambswool scarves. The company also offers custom tailoring. ⊠ *1921 8th St. NW, Suite 105, Shaw* ☎ *202/733–1913* ⊕ *www.readwall.com* Ⓜ *Shaw/Howard U.*

Redeem. With street-smart clothes and accessories from all over the globe, women and men who are stuck in a fashion rut can find redemption here with brands like Bad Form, Oak, and Won Hundred. There's also a nice selection of chic jewelry, candles, and perfumes. ⊠ *1810 14th St. NW, U Street* ☎ *202/332–7447* ⊕ *www.redeemus.com* Ⓜ *U St./Cardozo.*

SPECIALTY STORES

Shinola. Once a Studebaker showroom in the 1920s, this gorgeous shop is now one of Michigan-based Shinola's nationwide flagship stores. With its floor-to-ceiling windows and quarterly art exhibits by local artists, it's easy to spend some time here. You'll find leather-band watches; supple leather bags, coats, and journals; elegant and classic silver, gold, and rose gold jewelry designed by Pamela Love; home accessories; and yes, even bicycles. ⊠ *1631 14th St. NW, U Street* ☎ *202/470–0200* ⊕ *www.shinola.com* Ⓜ *U St./African American Civil War Memorial/Cardozo.*

UPPER NORTHWEST

The major thoroughfare, Wisconsin Avenue, runs northwest through the city from Georgetown toward Maryland. It crosses the border in the midst of the Friendship Heights shopping district, which is also near Chevy Chase. It's at this border where you'll find the Chevy Chase Pavilion with retailers including H&M, J.Crew, Marshalls, Nordstrom Rack, Old Navy, and World Market, among others. Other chains like Anthropologie, Saks Fifth Avenue, and Bloomingdale's can be found at The Shops at Wisconsin Avenue and at Mazza Gallerie. This neighborhood also boasts stand-alone designer stores like Christian Dior, Jimmy Choo, Ralph Lauren, and Tiffany and Co. There are a few local gems in the surrounding area. Other neighborhoods in the District yield more interesting finds and offer more enjoyable shopping and sightseeing, but it's hard to beat Friendship Heights/Upper Northwest for sheer convenience and selection.

BOOKS

Fodor's Choice ★ **Politics and Prose.** After being bought by two former *Washington Post* reporters in 2011, this legendary independent continues the tradition of jam-packed author events and signings. In the coffee shop and wine bar downstairs, The Den, you can debate the issues of the day or read a book while enjoying a casual meal or snack. ⊠ *5015 Connecticut Ave. NW, Upper Northwest* ☎ *202/364–1919* ⊕ *www.politics-prose.com* Ⓜ *Van Ness.*

CLOTHING

Fodor's Choice ★ **Catch Can.** Bright and breezy clothes made of mostly natural fibers, plus comfortable but playful shoes and funky rain boots, make casual wear as fun as it is practical. The owners' love of color continues with a sizeable collection of jewelry, greeting cards, housewares, and soaps. ⊠ *5516 Connecticut Ave. NW, Upper Northwest* ☎ *202/686–5316* ⊕ *www.catchcan.com* ☉ *Closed Tues.* Ⓜ *Friendship Heights.*

Everett Hall. D.C.'s own Everett Hall designs men's suits that are richly classic in their material and cutting-edge in their design, color, and sensibility. At $1,495 and up, the suits appeal to professionals who want something unique. ⊠ *Chevy Chase Pavillion, 5301 Wisconsin Ave. NW, Friendship Heights* ☎ *202/362–0191* ⊕ *www.everetthallboutique.com* Ⓜ *Friendship Heights.*

Julia Farr. Women who lobby on Capitol Hill and lunch at the country club look to Julia for a professional and polished look. Decorated in soothing sea shades, her boutique carries classic styles from emerging and established designers. Farr also has her own fashion line of classic and elegant wardrobe staples including skirts, blouses, jackets, and dresses inspired by D.C.'s historical and cultural landmarks. And, since they're named after these landmarks, any item would make a beautifully practical souvenir. Appointments are welcomed. ⊠ *5232 44th St. NW, Upper Northwest* ☎ *202/364–3277* ⊕ *www.juliafarrdc.com* ☉ *Closed Sun. and Mon.* Ⓜ *Friendship Heights.*

8

Tabandeh. Located in the Mazza Gallerie, this avant-garde women's collection includes an expertly selected cache of Rick Owens tops and Ann Demeulemeester clothing, along with accessories including stunning leather belts and handbags. The jewelry pieces in the store are dazzling—rings, necklaces, earrings, and pendants made with precious and semiprecious stones from designers like Samiar 13 and Erickson Beamon—and are sure to add panache to your wardrobe. ☒ *5300 Wisconsin Ave. NW, Upper Northwest* ☎ *202/966–5080* ⊕ *www.tabandehjewelry.com* Ⓜ *Friendship Heights.*

FOOD AND WINE

Calvert Woodley Fine Wines and Spirits. In addition to the excellent selection of wine and hard liquor, 200 kinds of cheese and other picnic and cocktail-party fare is on hand. The international offerings have made this a favorite pantry for embassy parties. ☒ *4339 Connecticut Ave. NW, Upper Northwest* ☎ *202/966–4400* ⊕ *www.calvertwoodley.com* Ⓜ *Van Ness/UDC.*

Rodman's Discount Foods and Drugstore. The rare store that carries wine, cheese, and space heaters, Rodman's is a fascinating hybrid of Target and Dean & DeLuca. The appliances are downstairs, the imported peppers and chocolates upstairs. ☒ *5100 Wisconsin Ave. NW, Upper Northwest* ☎ *202/363–3466* ⊕ *www.rodmans.com* Ⓜ *Friendship Heights.*

GIFTS

Periwinkle Gifts. A panoply of gift options are available in these warm and welcoming surroundings: boutique chocolates, cases of nutty and gummy treats, handmade jewelry, Stonewall Kitchen snacks, hand-designed wrapping paper, scented bath products, and printed note cards. ☒ *3815 Livingston St. NW, Upper Northwest* ☎ *202/364–3076* ⊕ *www.periwinklegiftsdc.com* Ⓜ *Friendship Heights.*

SIDE TRIPS FROM
WASHINGTON, D.C.

WELCOME TO SIDE TRIPS FROM WASHINGTON, D.C.

TOP REASONS TO GO

★ **Walk in Washington's shadow:** The minute you step onto the grounds of Mount Vernon, you'll be transported back in time to colonial America.

★ **Travel back in time:** Delve into colonial history in Old Town Alexandria, then fast-forward to the 21st century with funky shops, artists' galleries, hot restaurants, boutiques, and bars. Don't miss Alexandria's farmers' market, held every Saturday year-round from 7 am to noon. Believe it or not, it has been around since George Washington's produce was sold here.

★ **Feast on some crabs:** Head east to Annapolis on the Chesapeake Bay and enjoy a Maryland specialty: blue crabs by the bushel (the bib is optional).

1 **Alexandria.** Alexandria is across the Potomac and 7 miles downstream from Washington. As a commercial port, it competed with Georgetown in the days before Washington was a city. It's now a big small town loaded with historic homes, shops, and restaurants.

2 Mount Vernon, Woodlawn, and Gunston Hall. Three splendid examples of plantation architecture remain on the Virginia side of the Potomac. Sixteen miles south of D.C. is George Washington's beautifully preserved Mount Vernon, the most visited historic house in America; Woodlawn was the estate of Martha Washington's granddaughter; and Gunston Hall was the residence of George Mason, a patriot and author of the document on which the Bill of Rights was based.

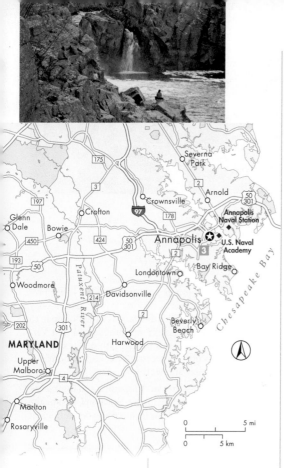

GETTING ORIENTED

There's no question that Washington, D.C., has enough sights, sounds, and experiences to keep you busy for a week or more without seeing everything on your itinerary. The three destinations highlighted here help enrich your experience whether you're a history buff, foodie, outdoors enthusiast, or boater. With just a bit of planning, any one of these trips can be done in a day or even an afternoon. Follow the locals' example and escape the heat of the capital with a trip to the countryside—or the banks of the Potomac or shores of Chesapeake Bay.

9

3 **Annapolis, Maryland.** Maryland's capital is a popular destination for seafood lovers and boating fans. Warm, sunny days bring many boats to the City Dock, where they're moored against a background of waterfront shops and restaurants. The city's nautical reputation is enhanced by the presence of the U.S. Naval Academy. It also has one of the country's largest assemblages of 18th-century architecture.

Updated by Catherine Sharpe

Within an hour of D.C. are getaway destinations connected to the nation's first president, naval history, and colonial events.

Alexandria was once a bustling colonial port, and its Old Town preserves this flavor with cobblestone streets, historic taverns, and a busy waterfront. Cycle 7 miles downriver along the banks of the Potomac to get here, or hop on the Metro for a quick 30-minute ride. Mount Vernon, George Washington's plantation, is 8 miles south of Alexandria. Make a day of it, and visit two other interesting plantation homes—Woodlawn and Gunston Hall—that are nearby.

Another option is to get out on the water in Annapolis, a major center for boating and home to the U.S. Naval Academy. Feast on Chesapeake Bay's famous crabs, then watch the midshipmen parade on campus at the academy.

PLANNING

TRAVELING WITH KIDS

No matter the ages of your children or the weather, Mount Vernon can keep everyone amused with activities that delight the senses. See where George and Martha Washington and their slaves lived, hear the Revolutionary rifles fired in animated movies, taste hoecakes, and smell the herbs in the garden. A dress-up room in the education center gives children the chance to look like colonial kids.

In Annapolis, find out what it takes to become a midshipman at the **U.S. Naval Academy** 's exhibit in the visitor center.

■ TIP→ Even kids who don't "dig" history might like sifting through dirt for artifacts in Alexandria during Family Dig Days at the archaeology museum in the Torpedo Factory.

TO GET TO ...	BY CAR:	BY METRO OR BUS:
Alexandria	George Washington Memorial Pkwy. or Jefferson Davis Hwy. (Rte. 1) south from Arlington (10 mins)	The Blue or Yellow Line to the King St. Metro stop (25 mins from Metro Center)
Mount Vernon	Exit 1 off the Beltway; follow signs to George Washington Memorial Pkwy. southbound (30 mins)	The Yellow Line to the Huntington Metro stop. From there, take Fairfax County Connector Bus No. 101, 151, or 159 (45–50 mins)
Woodlawn	Rte. 1 southwest to the second Rte. 235 intersection; entrance is on the right at the traffic light (40 mins)	Bus No. 101, 151, or 159 from Huntington Metro station (45–50 mins)
Gunston Hall	Rte. 1 south to Rte. 242; turn left and go 3½ miles to entrance (30 mins)	No Metro or bus
Annapolis	U.S. 50 east to the Rowe Blvd. Exit (35–45 mins, except during weekday rush hour when it may take twice as long)	Amtrak from Union Station to BWI; MTA Light Rail from BWI to Patapsco Light Rail Station; transfer to Bus No. 14 (2 hrs)

ALEXANDRIA, VIRGINIA

A short drive (or bike ride) from Washington, Alexandria provides a welcome break from the monuments and hustle and bustle of the District. Here you encounter America's colonial heritage. Founded in 1749 by Scottish merchants eager to capitalize on the booming tobacco trade, Alexandria became one of the most important colonial ports and has been associated with the most significant personages of the colonial, Revolutionary, and Civil War periods. In Old Town this colorful past is revived through restored 18th- and 19th-century homes, churches, and taverns; on the cobblestone streets; and on the revitalized waterfront, where clipper ships docked and artisans displayed their wares. Alexandria also has a wide variety of small- to medium-size restaurants and pubs, plus a wealth of boutiques and antiques dealers vying for your time and money.

GETTING HERE AND AROUND

Take either the George Washington Memorial Parkway or Jefferson Davis Highway (Route 1) south from Arlington to reach Alexandria. ■TIP➔ **Stop at the Alexandria Visitors Center at Ramsay House (221 King Street) to get oriented.**

The King Street/Old Town Metro stop (about 25 minutes from Metro Center) is right next to the Masonic Memorial and a 10-block walk on King Street from the center of Old Town. ■TIP➔ **A free King Street Trolley runs daily between the King Street Metrorail station and the Potomac River Waterfront. Hours are 10 am to 10:15 pm Sunday–Wednesday and 10 am to midnight Thursday–Saturday.**

TOURS

A great way to learn more about Alexandria's fascinating history is on a walking tour with Alexandria Colonial Tours, Footsteps to the Past, or Old Town Experience. All tours depart from the Alexandria Visitors Center at Ramsay House.

FAMILY   **Alexandria Colonial Tours.** On the Ghost & Graveyard Tour, 18th-century costumed guides carrying traditional lanterns take visitors through the streets of Alexandria and share spine-tingling tales of some of Alexandria's most famous and notorious ghosts. ⊠ *Old Town* ☎ *703/519–1749* ⊕ *www.alexcolonialtours.com* ✉ *$13.*

FAMILY   **Footsteps to the Past.** Want to see where George Washington trained his troops, influenced politics, and dined and danced? Join costumed guides for an hour-long walking History Tour. Or you can learn about life in the city during the Civil War, while it was under military occupation and thousands of wounded soldiers were treated here. If you'd rather hunt for Alexandria's resident ghosts using actual paranormal investigation equipment, sign up for a Historical Haunt Tour. ⊠ *Old Town* ☎ *703/683–3451* ⊕ *www.footstepstothepast.com* ✉ *From $10.*

FAMILY   **Old Town Experience.** Explore the history, legends, and folklore of Alexandria on a 90-minute walking tour. You'll visit the Carlyle House, Gadsby's Tavern, Christ Church, Captain's Row, and Old Presbyterian Meeting House, among others. ⊠ *Old Town* ☎ *703/836–0694* ⊕ *www. oldtowntour-alexandriava.com* ✉ *$15.*

ESSENTIALS

Visitor Information Alexandria Visitors Center. ⊠ *Ramsay House, 221 King St.* ☎ *703/746–3301, 800/388–9119* ⊕ *www.visitalexandriava.com.*

EXPLORING

TOP ATTRACTIONS

Appomattox Confederate Statue. In 1861, when Alexandria was occupied by Union forces, the 800 soldiers of the city's garrison marched out of town to join the Confederate Army. In the middle of Washington and Prince Streets stands a statue marking the point where they assembled. In 1885 Confederate veterans proposed a memorial to honor their fallen comrades. This statue, based on John A. Elder's painting *Appomattox*, is of a lone soldier glumly surveying the battlefields after General Robert E. Lee's surrender. The names of 100 Alexandria Confederate dead are carved on the base. ⊠ *Washington and Prince Sts., Old Town* Ⓜ *King St.*

Boyhood Home of Robert E. Lee. This childhood home of the commander of the Confederate forces of Virginia is a fine example of a 19th-century Federal town house. The house is privately owned and not open to visitors. ⊠ *607 Oronoco St., Old Town* Ⓜ *King St.*

Carlyle House. Alexandria forefather and Scottish merchant John Carlyle built this grand house, which was completed in 1753 and modeled on a country manor in the old country. Students of the French and Indian War will want to know that the dwelling served as General Braddock's headquarters. The house retains its original 18th-century woodwork and contains Chippendale furniture and Chinese porcelain. An architectural exhibit

Alexandria Black History Museum **10**

Appomattox Confederate Statue **15**

Athenaeum **4**

Boyhood Home of Robert E. Lee **9**

Captain's Row ... **5**

Carlyle House ... **7**

Christ Church .. **12**

Friendship Fire House Museum **14**

Gadsby's Tavern Museum **1**

George Washington Masonic National Memorial **13**

Lee-Fendall House Museum and Garden **8**

Lloyd House ... **11**

Lyceum **16**

Old Presbyterian Meeting House **3**

Stabler-Leadbeater Apothecary Museum **2**

Torpedo Factory Art Center **6**

on the second floor explains how the house was built; outside there's an attractive garden of colonial-era plants. ⊠ *121 N. Fairfax St., Old Town* ☎ *703/549–2997* ⊕ *www.carlylehouse.org* ⊠ *$5* ⊙ *Closed Mon.* Ⓜ *King St.*

Christ Church. George Washington and Robert E. Lee were pewholders in this Episcopal church, which remains in nearly original condition. (Washington paid quite a lot of money for pews 59 and 60.) Built in 1773, it's a fine example of an English Georgian country-style church with its Palladian window, interior balcony, and English wrought-brass-and-crystal chandelier. Docents give tours during visiting hours. ⊠ *118 N. Washington St., Old Town* ☎ *703/549–1450* ⊕ *www.historicchrist-church.org* ⊠ *$5 donation suggested* Ⓜ *King St.*

FAMILY **Gadsby's Tavern Museum.** George Washington celebrated his birthdays in the ballroom here, and Thomas Jefferson and John Adams were other notable patrons of the two buildings—a circa-1785 tavern and the 1792 City Hotel—that were centers of political and social life. They now form a museum, in which the taproom, dining room, assembly room, ballroom, and communal bedrooms have been restored to their original appearances. Special events include costumed reenactments, balls, afternoon teas, and free tours on President's Day, Mother's Day, and Father's Day. ⊠ *134 N. Royal St., Old Town* ☎ *703/746–4242* ⊕ *www.gadsbystavern.org* ⊠ *$5* Ⓜ *King St.*

George Washington Masonic National Memorial. Because Alexandria, like Washington, D.C., has no really tall buildings, the spire of this memorial dominates the surroundings and is visible for miles. The building overlooks King and Duke Streets, Alexandria's major east–west arteries. Reaching the memorial requires a respectable uphill climb from the King Street Metrorail and bus stations. From the ninth-floor observation deck (reached by elevator) you get a spectacular view of Alexandria and Washington, but access above the first two floors is by guided tour only. The building contains furnishings from the first Masonic lodge in Alexandria. George Washington became a Mason in 1752 in Fredericksburg, and became Charter Master of the Alexandria lodge when it was chartered in 1788, remaining active in Masonic affairs during his tenure as president, from 1789 to 1797. Daily guided tours are included with admission. ⊠ *101 Callahan Dr., Old Town* ☎ *703/683–2007* ⊕ *www.gwmemorial.org* ⊴ *$15* Ⓜ *King St.*

Lee-Fendall House Museum and Garden. Built in 1785 at historic Lee Corner, the Lee-Fendall House was, over the course of the next 118 years, home to 37 members of the Lee family and also served as a Union hospital. The house and its furnishings, of the 1850–70 period, present an intimate study of 19th-century family life. Highlights include a splendid collection of Lee heirlooms, period pieces produced by Alexandria manufacturers, and the beautifully restored, award-winning garden, which can be visited without buying a ticket for the museum. ⊠ *614 Oronoco St., Old Town* ☎ *703/548–1789* ⊕ *www.leefendallhouse.org* ⊴ *$5* ⊙ *Closed Mon. and Tues.* Ⓜ *King St.*

Lyceum. Built in 1839 and one of Alexandria's best examples of Greek Revival design, the Lyceum is also a local history museum. Restored in the 1970s for the Bicentennial, it has an impressive collection, including examples of 18th- and 19th-century silver, tools, stoneware, and Civil War photographs taken by Mathew Brady. Over the years the building has served as the Alexandria Library, a Civil War hospital, a residence, and offices. ⊠ *201 S. Washington St., Old Town* ☎ *703/838–4994* ⊕ *www.alexandriava.gov/Lyceum* ⊴ *$2* Ⓜ *King St.*

FAMILY **Torpedo Factory Art Center.** Torpedoes were manufactured here by the U.S. Navy during World War II, but now the building houses six galleries, as well as the studios and workshops of about 160 artists and artisans. You can observe printmakers, jewelers, sculptors, painters, potters, textile artists, and glass makers as they create original work in their studios. The Torpedo Factory also houses the Alexandria Archaeology Museum, which displays artifacts such as plates, cups, pipes, and coins from an early tavern, and Civil War soldiers' equipment. If archaeological activities interest you, call to sign up for the well-attended public digs (offered once a month from June through September and twice in October). If you need a quick bite, stop in at EatsPlace on the ground level of the Torpedo Factory for a "bronut" (a combination brownie and doughnut), as well as other sweet and savory delights including cold and hot sandwiches, soups, salads, and cheese plates. ⊠ *105 N. Union St., Old Town* ☎ *703/838–4565, 703/746–4399 Archaeology Museum* ⊕ *www.torpedofactory.org* ⊴ *Free* Ⓜ *King St.*

WORTH NOTING

Alexandria Black History Museum. This collection, devoted to the history of African Americans in Alexandria and Virginia, is housed in part in the Robert H. Robinson Library, a building constructed in the wake of a landmark 1939 sit-in protesting the segregation of Alexandria libraries. The Watson Reading Room, next to the Museum, holds a vast collection of books, periodicals, videos, and historical documents detailing the social, economic, and cultural contributions of African Americans who helped shape the city's growth since its establishment in 1749. The federal census of 1790 recorded 52 free African Americans living in the city, but the port town was one of the largest slave exporting points in the South, with at least two highly active slave markets. ⊠ *902 Wythe St., Old Town* ☎ *703/746–4356* ⊕ *www.alexblackhistory.org* ⊠ *$2* ☉ *Closed Sun. and Mon.* Ⓜ *King St.*

> ## ALEXANDRIA'S FARMERS' MARKET
>
> If it's Saturday and you're up early, join the locals at Alexandria's Farmers' Market, one of the oldest continually operating farmers' markets in the country—open for business since the 1700s. The market is held from 7 am to noon year-round at Market Square (*301 King St.*). In addition to incredible produce, you'll find artisans selling handmade jewelry, dolls, quilts, purses, sweaters, and more. You'll also find ham biscuits, baked treats, and other snack items for a quick meal on the go or a picnic later in the day.

Athenaeum. One of the most noteworthy structures in Alexandria, this striking Greek Revival edifice at the corner of Prince and Lee Streets stands out from its many redbrick Federal neighbors. Built in 1852 as a bank (Robert E. Lee had an account here) and later used as a Union commissary headquarters, then as a talcum powder factory for the Stabler-Leadbeater Apothecary, the Athenaeum now houses the gallery of the Northern Virginia Fine Arts Association, which hosts free rotating art exhibitions and receptions throughout the year. This block of Prince Street between Fairfax and Lee Streets is known as **Gentry Row,** after the 18th- and 19th-century inhabitants of its imposing three-story houses. ⊠ *201 Prince St., Old Town* ☎ *703/548–0035* ⊕ *www.nvfaa. org* ⊠ *Free* ☉ *Closed Mon.–Wed.* Ⓜ *King St.*

Captain's Row. Many of Alexandria's sea captains once lived on this block, which gives visitors the truest sense of what the city looked like in the 1800s. The stone pavement is not original, but nicely replicates the stones laid down during the Revolution, which were taken from sailing ships that used them to balance the vessels during the passage. ⊠ *Prince St., between Lee and Union Sts., Old Town* Ⓜ *King St.*

FAMILY **Friendship Firehouse Museum.** Alexandria's showcase firehouse dates from 1855 and is filled with typical 19th-century implements, but the resident Friendship Fire Company was established in 1774 and bought its first engine in 1775. Among early fire engines on display is a hand pumper built in Philadelphia in 1851. Most everything can be seen through the windows even when the firehouse is closed. ⊠ *107 S. Alfred St., Old Town* ☎ *703/746–3891* ⊠ *$2* ☉ *Closed weekdays* Ⓜ *King St.*

9

Lloyd House. This fine example of Georgian architecture was built in 1797 and is owned by the City of Alexandria and used for offices for the Office of Historic Alexandria. The interior has nothing on display, so the house is best admired from outside. ✉ *220 N. Washington St., Old Town* [M] *King St.*

Old Presbyterian Meeting House. Except from 1899 through 1949, the Old Presbyterian Meeting House has been the site of an active Presbyterian congregation since 1772. Scottish pioneers founded the church, and Scottish patriots used it as a gathering place during the Revolution. Four memorial services were held for George Washington here. The tomb of an unknown soldier of the American Revolution lies in a corner of the small churchyard, where many prominent Alexandrians—including Dr. James Craik, physician and best friend to Washington, and merchant John Carlyle—are interred. The original sanctuary was rebuilt after a lightning strike and fire in 1835. The interior is appropriately plain; if you'd like to visit the sanctuary you can borrow a key in the church office at 323 South Fairfax Street, or just peek through the many wide windows along both sides. ✉ *321 S. Fairfax St., Old Town* ☎ *703/549–6670* 🌐 *www.opmh.org* 🎟 *Free* [M] *King St.*

Stabler-Leadbeater Apothecary Museum. Once patronized by Martha Washington and the Lee family, the Stabler-Leadbeater Apothecary is among the oldest apothecaries in the country (the reputed oldest is in Bethlehem, Pennsylvania). The shop now houses a museum of apothecary memorabilia, including one of the finest collections of apothecary bottles in the country. In fact, they have so many of these original bottles that it took six years to process them all. Tours include discussions of Alexandria life and medicine, as well as the history of the family that owned and ran the shop for 141 years. ✉ *105–107 S. Fairfax St., Old Town* ☎ *703/746–3852* 🌐 *www.apothecarymuseum.org* 🎟 *$5* 🕒 *Closed Mon. and Tues. Nov.–Mar.* [M] *King St.*

WHERE TO EAT

$ MEXICAN FUSION

🍴 **Don Taco.** As its name suggests, tacos are the specialty at this lively spot in the heart of Alexandria's busy King Street. With choices like sweet and spicy mahimahi, smoked short rib, chipotle quinoa sweet potato, pomegranate-glazed skirt steak, and roasted chicken Sriracha, you might be tempted to order one of everything. **Known for:** eclectic selection of tacos; late night happy hour (until 2 am) during the week; Nutella banana split dessert tacos. [$] *Average main: $12* ✉ *808 King St., Old Town* ☎ *703/343–9456* 🌐 *www.dontacova.com.*

$ IRISH FAMILY

🍴 **Eamonn's A Dublin Chipper.** A nod to his native Ireland, this fish-and-chips joint is chef Cathal Armstrong's most casual outpost in his growing Old Town Alexandria empire he also runs such other acclaimed spots as Restaurant Eve and Society Fair. This 20-seat, counter-service, chipper-with-attitude serves up crispy cod and fries with your choice of seven different sauces from classic tartar to curry. **Known for:** fish-and-chips from a real Irishman; fried Mars bars for dessert; 21st-century speakeasy upstairs. [$] *Average main: $10* ✉ *728 King St.* ☎ *703/299–8384* 🌐 *www.eamonnsdublinchipper.com* [M] *King St.*

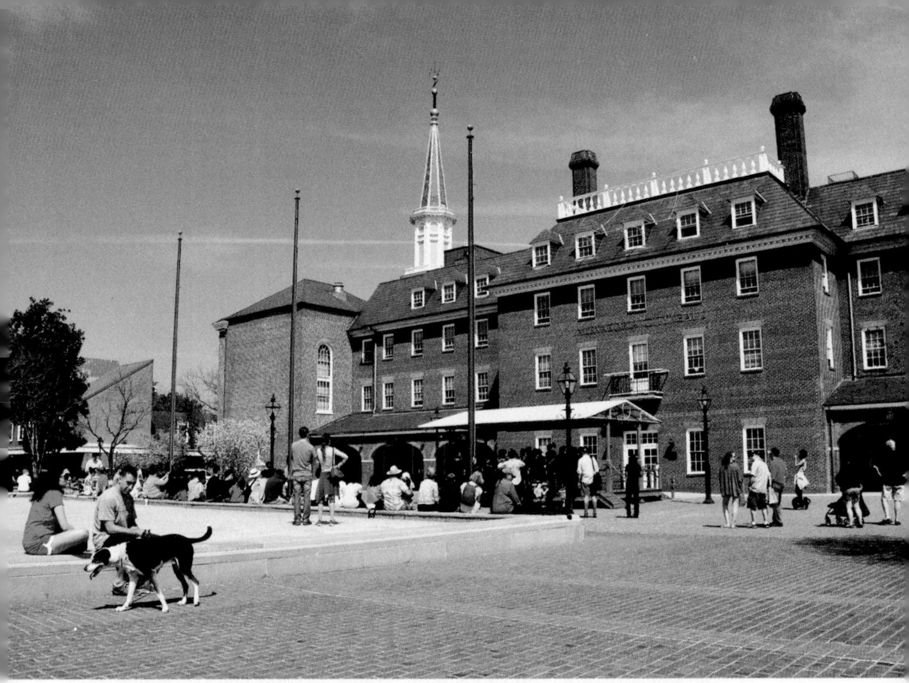

King Street is the heart of historic Old Town Alexandria, Virginia, with lively restaurants and shops.

$$ AMERICAN Fodor's Choice ★ 🍴 **Hank's Oyster Bar.** This classic raw bar is consistently busy thanks to a nice mix of locals and visitors. No doubt it's because the oysters, clams, and lobster rolls are incredibly fresh and the service is outstanding. **Known for:** amazing oysters, duh; non-seafood dinner specials; daily raw bar deals. [$] *Average main: $25* ✉ *1026 King St., Old Town* ☎ *703/739–4265* 🌐 *www.hanksoysterbar.com.*

$$$ FRENCH 🍴 **Le Refuge.** At this local favorite, run by Jean François Chaufour and his wife, Françoise, for more than 30 years, lovingly prepared French country fare is served with beaucoup flavor. Popular selections include trout, bouillabaisse, garlicky rack of lamb, frogs' legs, and beef Wellington. **Known for:** authentic French cuisine with no pretension; three-course prix-fixe lunch and dinner options; tasty profiteroles for dessert. [$] *Average main: $30* ✉ *127 N. Washington St.* ☎ *703/548–4661* 🌐 *www.lerefugealexandria.com* 🕒 *Closed Sun.* [M] *King St.*

$$ CONTEMPORARY Fodor's Choice ★ 🍴 **Mason Social.** The depth of Mason Social's menu made it a hit right from the get-go. Adventurous eaters will relish apps like the pork belly with polenta in a sriracha glaze while those happier with more traditional staples will be delighted with the fried green tomatoes, fried chicken, or swordfish kabobs. **Known for:** adventurous comfort food; long list of craft cocktails; bone marrow burger. [$] *Average main: $24* ✉ *728 N. Henry St.* ☎ *703/548–8800* 🌐 *www.mason-social.com* [M] *Braddock Rd.*

$$$$ JAPANESE FUSION 🍴 **Nasime.** A tiny gem in the area, Nasime serves an exquisite five-course tasting menu of both traditional and contemporary Japanese flavors. The selections change frequently based on the season and availability of products, but always include a wonderful blend of raw, grilled, fried, and baked dishes, plus dessert. **Known for:** stunning, artlike dishes; revolving menu of fresh sushi; intimate seating. [$] *Average main: $48*

✉ *1209 King St., Old Town* ☎ *703/757–0146* ⊕ *www.nasimerestaurant.com* ⊘ *Closed Mon.*

$$
MODERN GREEK

✕**Taverna Cretekou.** Whitewashed stucco walls and colorful macramé tapestries bring a bit of the Mediterranean to the center of Old Town. The menu takes diners on a trip around Greece—each dish identifies its region of origin. **Known for:** Greek favorites spanning the whole country; extensive Greek-only wine list; live music on Thursdays; romantic canopied garden. 💲 *Average main: $22* ✉ *818 King St.* ☎ *703/548–8688* ⊕ *www.tavernacretekou.com* ⊘ *Closed Mon.* Ⓜ *King St.*

$$$
MODERN
AMERICAN
Fodor's Choice
★

✕**Vermilion.** Be sure to make reservations because foodies flock here for a taste of chef William Morris's award-winning modern American menu. Morris favors locally sourced, sustainable ingredients, though quality trumps local here, so you may find a Scottish salmon alongside a Shenandoah beef fillet on this mid-Atlantic menu. **Known for:** casual, hip interior with exposed brick and gas lamps; popular weekend brunch; live music on Tuesdays and Wednesdays. 💲 *Average main: $32* ✉ *1120 King St.* ☎ *703/684–9669* ⊕ *www.vermilionrestaurant.com* ⊘ *No lunch Tues.* Ⓜ *King St.*

$$
AMERICAN

✕**Virtue Feed & Grain.** Housed in what was once a feed house in the 1800s, this American tavern serves an all-day menu and weekend brunch. Now beautifully restored with reclaimed wood, antique bricks, and glass panes, you can sample grilled teriyaki chicken wings, pork barbacoa tacos, and Chesapeake Benedict, among many other options. **Known for:** unique rustic space; classic farm-to-table cuisine with some spice; fried chicken and waffles for brunch. 💲 *Average main: $20* ✉ *106 S. Union St., Old Town* ☎ *571/970–3669* ⊕ *www.virtuefeedgrain.com.*

WHERE TO STAY

$$
HOTEL
FAMILY

🏨 **Embassy Suites Alexandria – Old Town.** A location across from the Metro station makes this all-suites hotel a convenient base for city exploration. **Pros:** large rooms; good breakfast; complimentary fitness center. **Cons:** small indoor pool is often crowded; parking costs $32 per day; popular with school groups. 💲 *Rooms from: $270* ✉ *1900 Diagonal Rd., Old Town* ☎ *703/684–5900, 800/362–2779* ⊕ *embassysuites3.hilton.com* ⇗ *288 rooms* ⦿❘ *Breakfast.*

$$$
HOTEL

🏨 **Kimpton Lorien Hotel & Spa.** Service is top-notch at this casually elegant boutique hotel in the heart of Old Town Alexandria. **Pros:** central to Old Town sights; full-service spa (only one in town); free use of bikes; well-appointed fitness center. **Cons:** no pool; daily fee for valet-only parking; some rooms are small. 💲 *Rooms from: $339* ✉ *1600 King St.* ☎ *877/956–7436, 703/894–3434* ⊕ *www.lorienhotelandspa.com* ⇗ *107 rooms* ⦿❘ *No meals* Ⓜ *King St.*

$$$
HOTEL

🏨 **Morrison House, Autograph Collection.** Housed in a charming brick manor-style home a half block off bustling King Street, this hotel is a quiet escape for couples and business travelers. **Pros:** in the heart of Old Town; delightful literary theme, including on-site library; modern building with historic charm. **Cons:** about a 15-minute walk from Metro and train stations; daily fee for valet-only parking; fee for in-room Wi-Fi. 💲 *Rooms from: $329* ✉ *116 S. Alfred St.* ☎ *703/838–8000, 888/236–2427* ⊕ *www.marriott.com* ⇗ *45 rooms* ⦿❘ *No meals* Ⓜ *King St.*

$$ **The Westin Alexandria.** The staff seems genuinely happy to see you
HOTEL come through the door at this hotel just 1½ miles from the cobbled
streets of Old Town Alexandria, and if you don't need or want to be in
D.C.—only 20–25 minutes away by Metro—you'll get more for your
travel dollar here. **Pros:** rooms have pretty views; indoor heated pool
and 24-hour gym are complimentary; free shuttle service to waterfront
and Old Town Alexandria; close to airport and Metro. **Cons:** outside
the city; half-hour walk to waterfront; fee for in-room Wi-Fi. **$** *Rooms
from: $283* ✉ *400 Courthouse Sq., Old Town* ☎ *703/253–8600* ⊕ *www.
westin.com/alexandria* ⤴ *319 rooms* �’❍❘ *No meals.*

MOUNT VERNON, WOODLAWN, AND GUNSTON HALL

Long before Washington, D.C., was planned, wealthy traders and
gentlemen farmers had parceled the shores of the Potomac into planta-
tions. Most traces of the colonial era were obliterated as the capital
grew in the 19th century, but several splendid examples of plantation
architecture remain on the Virginia side of the Potomac, 15 miles or
so south of D.C. In one day you can easily visit three such mansions:
Mount Vernon, the home of George Washington and one of the most
popular sites in the area; Woodlawn, the estate of Martha Washington's
granddaughter; and Gunston Hall, the home of George Mason, author
of the document on which the Bill of Rights was based. Set on hillsides
overlooking the river, these estates offer magnificent vistas and bring
back to vivid life the more palatable aspects of the 18th century.

MOUNT VERNON, VIRGINIA

16 miles southeast of Washington, D.C., 8 miles south of Alexandria.

Once a vibrant plantation in the 18th century, Mount Vernon is an
enduring reminder of the life and legacy of George Washington. This
historic site features an authentically interpreted 18th-centry home,
lush gardens and grounds, captivating museum galleries, and immersive
educational programs.

GETTING HERE AND AROUND

To reach Mount Vernon by car from the Capital Beltway (Route 495),
take Exit 1 and follow the signs to George Washington Memorial Parkway
southbound. Mount Vernon is about 8½ miles south. From downtown
Washington, cross into Arlington on Key Bridge, Memorial Bridge, or
the 14th Street Bridge and drive south on the George Washington Memo-
rial Parkway past Ronald Reagan National Airport through Alexandria
straight to Mount Vernon. The trip from D.C. takes about a half hour.

Getting to Mount Vernon by public transportation requires that you
take both the Metro and a bus. Begin by taking the Yellow Line train
to the Huntington Metro station. From here, take Fairfax County Con-
nector Bus No. 101 ($1.75 cash or $1.25 with SmarTrip card). Buses on
each route leave about once an hour—more often during rush hour—
and operate weekdays from about 5 am to 9:15 pm, weekends from
about 6:30 am to 7 pm.

TOURS

BOAT TOURS The *Spirit of Mount Vernon* makes a pleasant day trip from Washington down the Potomac to Mount Vernon mid-March through mid-October. Boarding begins at 8 am for the narrated cruise down the Potomac River. Once you arrive at Mount Vernon, you'll have three hours to tour the estate before reboarding at 1:15. Tickets cost about $50 and include admission to the estate.

BUS TOURS Gray Line runs a nine-hour Mount Vernon and Arlington National Cemetery tour, Friday through Sunday in January through mid-March and daily mid-March through December. Priced at $90, which includes admission to the mansion and grounds, the tour departs at 8 am from Union Station.

ESSENTIALS

Boat Information Spirit of Mount Vernon. ⊠ *Pier 4, 6th and Water Sts. SW, Southwest* ☎ *866/302–2469 boat reservations* ⊕ *www.spiritcruises.com.*

Bus Information Fairfax County Connector. ☎ *703/339–7200* ⊕ *www.fairfaxconnector.com.*

Bus Tour Information Gray Line. ☎ *800/862–1400* ⊕ *www.graylinedc.com.*

Metro Information Washington Metro Area Transit Authority. ☎ *202/637–7000* ⊕ *www.wmata.com.*

EXPLORING

FAMILY   **Mount Vernon.** This plantation and the surrounding lands had been
Fodor'sChoice   in the Washington family for nearly 70 years by the time the future
★   president inherited it all in 1743. Before taking over command of the Continental Army, Washington was an accomplished farmer, managing the 8,000-acre plantation and operating five farms on the land. He oversaw the transformation of the main house from an ordinary farm dwelling into what was, for the time, a grand mansion. The inheritance of his widowed bride, Martha, is partly what made that transformation possible.

The red-roof main house is elegant though understated, with a yellow pine exterior that's been painted and coated with layers of sand to resemble white-stone blocks. The first-floor rooms are quite ornate, especially the formal large dining room, with a molded ceiling decorated with agricultural motifs. As you tour the mansion, guides are stationed throughout the house to describe the furnishings and answer questions.

You can stroll around the estate's 500 acres and three gardens, visiting workshops, kitchen, carriage house, greenhouse, slave quarters, and—down the hill toward the boat landing—the tomb of George and Martha Washington. There's also a pioneer farmer site: a 4-acre hands-on exhibit with a reconstruction of George Washington's 16-side treading barn as its centerpiece.

But some of the most memorable experiences at Mount Vernon, particularly for kids, are in the Museum and Education Center. Interactive displays, movies with special effects straight out of Hollywood, life-size models, and Revolutionary artifacts illustrate Washington's life and contributions.

U.S. Navy and Coast Guard ships salute ("render honors") when passing Mount Vernon during daylight hours.

Actors in period dress who portray General Washington and his wife welcome visitors at special occasions throughout the year, including President's Day, Mother's and Father's Day, and July 4. Evening candlelight tours are offered weekend evenings in late November and early December.

George Washington's **Gristmill and Distillery**—both reproductions—operate on their original sites. In 1799, the distillery was the largest American whiskey producer. Today, using the same recipe and processes thanks to the excellent records kept by Washington, small batches of his whiskey are made and sold here. During guided tours, led by costumed interpreters, you'll meet an 18th-century miller and watch the water-powered wheel grind grain into cornmeal and watch the grains being distilled. The mill and distillery, open from April through October, are 3 miles from Mount Vernon on Route 235 toward U.S. 1, almost to Woodlawn. General-admission tickets to Mount Vernon include the gristmill and distillery. ⊠ *Southern end of George Washington Pkwy.* ☎ *703/780–2000* ⊕ *www.mountvernon. org* ⊠ *$20 ($18 if booked online), includes admission to distillery and gristmill.*

SPORTS AND THE OUTDOORS
An asphalt bicycle path leads from the Virginia side of Key Bridge (across from Georgetown), past Ronald Reagan National Airport, and through Alexandria all the way to Mount Vernon. Bikers in moderately good condition can make the 16-mile trip in less than two hours. You can rent bicycles at several locations in Washington.

A great place to rent a bike is the **Washington Sailing Marina** (☎ 703/548–9027 ⊕ *www.washingtonsailingmarina.com*), which is beside the Mount Vernon Bike Trail just past the airport. A 12-mile ride south will take you right up to the front doors of Mount Vernon. Cruiser bikes rent for $8.50 per hour or $30 per day. The marina is open 9–5 daily.

WOODLAWN, VIRGINIA

3 miles west of Mount Vernon, 15 miles south of Washington, D.C.

Woodlawn was once part of the Mount Vernon estate, and from here you can still see the trees of the bowling green that fronted Washington's home. The mansion was built for Martha Washington's granddaughter, Nelly Custis, who married George Washington's nephew, Lawrence Lewis. Also on the grounds of Woodlawn is one of Frank Lloyd Wright's "Usonian" homes, the **Pope-Leighey House.** The structure, which belongs to the National Trust for Historic Preservation, was completed in 1941 at a cost of $7,000 and is one of only three homes in Virginia designed by Wright.

GETTING HERE AND AROUND

To drive to Woodlawn, travel southwest on Route 1 to the second Route 235 intersection (the first leads to Mount Vernon). The entrance to Woodlawn is on the right at the traffic light. From Mount Vernon, travel northwest on Route 235 to the Route 1 intersection; Woodlawn is straight ahead through the intersection.

To use public transportation, take Bus No. 101, 151, or 159 ($1.75 cash or $1.25 with SmarTrip card) from Huntington Metro station. Buses returning to the station have the same numbers but are marked Huntington.

EXPLORING

FAMILY **Woodlawn & Pope-Leighey House.** Completed in 1805, Woodlawn was designed by William Thornton, a physician and amateur architect who drew up the original plans for the U.S. Capitol and designed Tudor Place and the Octagon House in Washington, D.C. Built on a site selected by George Washington, the mansion has commanding views of the surrounding countryside and the Potomac River beyond. In the tradition of mansions from this period, Woodlawn has a central passage that provides a cool refuge in summer. Woodlawn was once an estate where more than 100 people, most of them slaves, lived and worked. Guides explain how the family entertained and architectural details of the house.

The modest and sparsely furnished Pope-Leighey House, designed by Frank Lloyd Wright, provides a stark contrast to Woodlawn. It was moved here from Falls Church, Virginia, in 1964, to save it from destruction during the building of Route 66. Built to bring nature inside, the 1,200-square-foot, two-bedroom, one-bath home features Tidewater red cypress, brick, a flat roof, and tall glass windows and doors. Even the furniture was designed by Wright. The home was commissioned by journalist Lauren Pope and his wife, Charlotte—one lender declined to

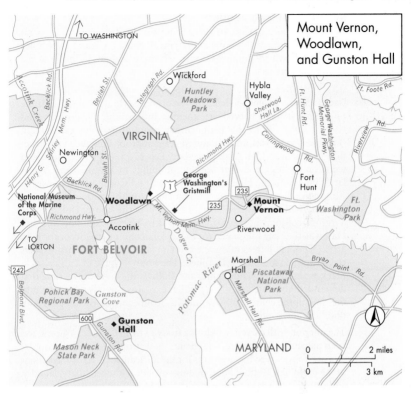

Mount Vernon,
Woodlawn,
and Gunston Hall

give the Popes a loan, calling it a "white elephant." The Popes lived here for six years and in 1946 sold it to Robert and Marjorie Leighey. ✉ *9000 Richmond Hwy., Alexandria* ☎ *703/780–4000* ⊕ *www.wood-lawnpopeleighey.org* 💲 *$10 for Woodlawn, $15 for Pope-Leighey, $20 for both* ⊙ *Closed Tues.–Thurs.*

GUNSTON HALL, VIRGINIA

12 miles south of Woodlawn, 25 miles south of Washington, D.C.

Down the Potomac from Mount Vernon is the home of another important George. Gentleman-farmer George Mason was a colonel of the Virginia militia and author of the Virginia Declaration of Rights, the model for the U.S. Bill of Rights, which called for freedom of the press, tolerance of religion, and other fundamental democratic principles. Mason was a framer of the Constitution but refused to sign the final document because it didn't stop the importation of slaves, adequately restrain the powers of the federal government, or include a bill of rights. Mason's objections spurred the movement for the inclusion of the Bill of Rights into the Constitution. This 18th-century Georgian mansion was located at the center of a 5,500 acre plantation. You can tour the home and grounds of Gunston Hall, a National Historic Landmark.

GETTING HERE AND AROUND

You'll have to use a car to get to Gunston Hall because there is no bus stop within walking distance. Travel south on Route 1, 9 miles past Woodlawn to Route 242; turn left there and go 3½ miles to the plantation entrance.

EXPLORING

FAMILY
Fodor'sChoice
★

George Mason's Gunston Hall. The Georgian-style mansion has some of the finest hand-carved ornamented interiors in the country and is the handiwork of the 18th-century's foremost architect, William Buckland, who was an indentured servant from England. Construction of Gunston Hall took place between 1755 and 1759. Buckland went on to design several notable buildings in Virginia and Maryland, including the Hammond-Harwood and Chase-Lloyd houses in Annapolis. It is believed he worked closely with another indentured servant, William Bernard Sears, to complete the house. Unlike other Virginia colonial homes which tended to be very simple, Gunston Hall was the only house known to have had chinoiserie decoration. In 1792, Thomas Jefferson traveled to Gunston Hall to pay his respects to George Mason on his deathbed. The house is built of native brick, black walnut, and yellow pine, and follows the style of the time that demanded absolute symmetry, which explains the false door set into one side of the center hallway and the "robber" window on a second-floor storage room.

The interior, with carved woodwork in styles from Chinese to Greek, has been meticulously restored, with paints made from the original formulas and carefully carved replacements for the intricate mahogany medallions in the moldings. Restored outbuildings include a kitchen, dairy, laundry, and smokehouse, and a schoolhouse has also been reconstructed.

The formal gardens, recently excavated by a team of archaeologists, are famous for their boxwoods—some were planted during George Mason's time, making them among the oldest in the country. The Potomac is visible past the expansive deer park, and Mason's landing road to the river was recently found. Special programs, such as archaeology tutelage and a plantation Christmas celebration, are available. Guided tours are offered daily every half hour between 9:30 am and 4:30 pm. On Mondays at 10:15 am and Thursdays at 1:15 pm, longer, more detailed tours are offered. Plan on spending about an hour at Gunston Hall. ✉ 10709 Gunston Rd., Mason Neck ☎ 703/550–9220 ⊕ www.gunstonhall.org ✍ $10.

OFF THE
BEATEN
PATH

National Museum of the Marine Corps. The glassy atrium of this 118,000-square-foot homage to the military's finest soars into the sky next to the Marine Corps Base Quantico. The design was inspired by the iconic photograph of Marines lifting the American flag on Iwo Jima. Inside the museum, visitors are able to see the flag itself, as well as experience the life of a Marine. The museum is completely interactive, from the entrance where drill instructors yell at new "recruits" in surround-sound, to the Korean War exhibit, where visitors walk through a snowy mountain pass and shiver from the cold while listening to the 2nd Platoon fight on the other side of the mountain. The museum also has a staggering collection of tanks, aircraft, rocket launchers, and other weapons. There is even a rifle range simulator, where guests of all ages can learn how to hold a laser rifle and practice hitting targets. Family Day at the Museum is held the second Saturday of the month with activities and crafts. There also are gallery hunts for children ages 4–10 that encourage exploration of the museum. ✉ *18900 Jefferson Davis Hwy., Triangle* ☎ *877/635–1775* ⊕ *www. usmcmuseum.org* ✉ *Free.*

ANNAPOLIS, MARYLAND

32 miles east of Washington, D.C.

This beautiful city, the capital of Maryland, offers something for everyone. Whether you spend one or several days here, you'll discover fascinating history; exciting sporting, visual, and performing arts events; great dining, shopping, and nightlife; and dozens of recreation activities. There are more 18th-century brick homes in Annapolis than in any other city in the nation, and, because the city is so walkable, it is truly a walk down memory lane. It's also a popular boating destination and on warm sunny days, the waters off City Dock become center stage for boats of all sizes. If you love the water, the Chesapeake Bay and the area's winding inlets, creeks, and rivers provide wonderful opportunities for paddleboarding, kayaking, sailing, or fishing. One of Annapolis's longest-standing institutions is the U.S. Naval Academy, which has been training officers for the U.S. Navy and Marine Corps since 1845. As you stroll through downtown, you'll often see uniformed midshipmen in their crisp white uniforms in summer and navy blue in winter. A visit to the Naval Academy campus, to learn about its lengthy and proud history and get a close-up look at what life as a midshipman is like, is a must.

GETTING HERE AND AROUND

The drive (east on U.S. 50 to the Rowe Boulevard exit) normally takes 35–45 minutes from Washington. During rush hour (weekdays 3:30–6:30 pm), however, it takes about twice as long. Also, beware of Navy football Saturdays.

Parking spots on the historic downtown streets of Annapolis are scarce, but there are some parking meters for $2 an hour (maximum two hours). You can park on some residential streets for free for two hours. The public parking garage adjacent to the Annapolis Visitors Center charges $2 per hour with a daily maximum of $15. The Annapolis Circulator offers free trolley transportation within the Historic Area. On Sunday morning from 6 am to 1 pm, most parking is free.

TOURS

Walking tours are a great way to see the historic district, and Discover Annapolis Tours and Watermark run historical and ghost tours. Watermark and Schooner *Woodwind* Cruises offer boat trips.

Discover Annapolis Tours. Narrated trolley tours, departing from the visitor center, introduce you to the history and architecture of Annapolis. ✉ *26 West St.* ☎ *410/626–6000* ⊕ *www.townetransport.com/tours* ✉ *From $15.*

9

Schooner Woodwind Cruises. Two 74-foot sailboats, *Woodwind* and *Woodwind II*, make daily trips and overnight excursions. ⊠ *Annapolis Marriott Hotel dock, 80 Compromise St.* ☎ *410/263–7837, 410/263–7837* ⊕ *www.schoonerwoodwind.com* ⌕ *From $43.*

Fodor'sChoice ★ **Watermark.** Tour guides wearing colonial-style dress take you to the State House, St. John's College, and the Naval Academy on their very popular twice-daily, 2¼-hour "Four Centuries Walking Tour." There's also a "Historic Ghost Walk" on weekends. Watermark also runs boat tours, lasting from 40 minutes to 7½ hours, going as far as St. Michael's on the Eastern Shore where there's a maritime museum as well as dining and boutiques. ⊠ *1 Dock St.* ☎ *410/268–7601* ⊕ *www.watermarkjourney.com* ⌕ *From $16.*

ESSENTIALS

Visitor Information Annapolis & Anne Arundel County Conference and Visitors Bureau. ⊠ *26 West St.* ☎ *410/280–0445, 888/302–2852* ⊕ *www.visitannapolis.org.* **Information Booth.** ⊠ *Ego Alley, Dock St.* ☎ *410/280–0445.*

EXPLORING

TOP ATTRACTIONS

FAMILY **Banneker-Douglass Museum.** Maryland's official museum of African American heritage is named for abolitionist Frederick Douglass and scientist Benjamin Banneker. This former church and its next-door neighbor make up a museum that tells the stories of African Americans in Maryland through performances, lectures, educational programs, and both permanent and changing exhibits. Audio and visual presentations and hands-on exhibits make the museum especially engaging for kids. ⊠ *84 Franklin St.* ☎ *410/216–6180* ⊕ *www.bdmuseum.maryland.gov* ⌕ *Free* ☉ *Closed Sun. and Mon.*

▌NEED A BREAK **Old Fox Books and Coffeehouse.** This is more than just a bookstore. Relax in the café with a hot or cold beverage, freshly baked pastry, soup or sandwich, and then head to the back to see the charming Fairy Garden and book house, which is literally made of books. With a carefully selected collection of new, used, and rare books, the store is an oasis from the ubiquitous chains. As befits its Annapolis location, the shop specializes in maritime books, as well as classics, poetry, and children's books. ⊠ *35 Maryland Ave.* ☎ *410/626–2020* ⊕ *www.oldfoxbooks.com.*

Hammond-Harwood House. Based on the Villa Pisani in Stra, Italy, by Andrea Palladio, this 1774 home was designed by premier colonial architect William Buckland and is considered America's greatest colonial high-style residence. Called the architectural "Jewel of Annapolis," the residence was greatly admired by Thomas Jefferson when he sketched the house in 1783. The wood carvings surrounding the front door and enriching the dining room are some of the best surviving of their kind in America. The site today exhibits famous colonial art by Charles Willson Peale, Rembrandt Peale, James Peale, John Trumbull, John Hesselius, Jeremiah Theus, and John Beale Bordley, as well as

Banneker-
Douglass
Museum **2**

Hammond-
Harwood
House **7**

Historic
Annapolis
Museum **9**

Historic London
Town and
Gardens **1**

Kunta
Kinte–Alex Haley
Memorial **10**

Maryland State
House **4**

St. Anne's
Church **3**

St. John's
College **5**

U.S. Naval
Academy **11**

U.S. Naval
Academy
Museum **8**

William Paca
House and
Garden **6**

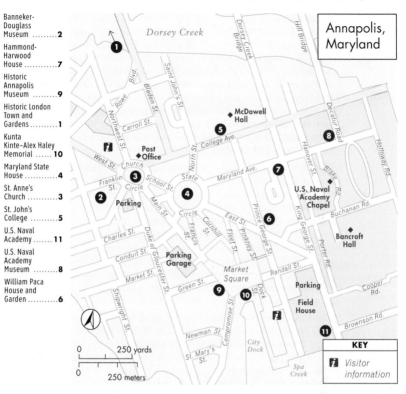

an extensive decorative arts collection covering everything from Chinese-export porcelain to Georgian-period silver. Also on display is the world's largest collection of colonial cabinetwork by Annapolis native John Shaw. The property's Colonial Revival garden is lovely. ⊠ *19 Maryland Ave.* ☎ *410/263–4683* ⊕ *www.hammondharwoodhouse. org* ⊴ *$10* ⊙ *Closed Mon. and Jan.–Mar.*

Historic London Town and Gardens. The 17th-century tobacco port of London, on the South River a short car ride from Annapolis, was made up of 40 dwellings, shops, and taverns. London all but disappeared in the 18th century, its buildings abandoned and left to decay, but the excavation of the town is underway, and buildings are continually being restored. One of the few original colonial structures is a three-story waterfront brick house, built by William Brown between 1758 and 1764, with dramatic river views. Walk around on your own or take a 30-minute docent-led tour; allow more time to wander the house grounds, woodland gardens, and a visitor center with an interactive exhibit on the archaeology and history of London Town and Anne Arundel County. ⊠ *839 Londontown Rd., Edgewater* ☎ *410/222–1919* ⊕ *www.historiclondontown.org* ⊴ *$12 mid-Mar.–Nov.; $5 mid-Jan.– mid-Mar.* ⊙ *Closed Dec.–mid-Jan., weekends in mid-Jan.–mid-Mar., and Mon. and Tues. in mid-Mar.–Nov.*

Fodor'sChoice ★ **Maryland State House.** Originally constructed between 1772 and 1780, the State House is the oldest state capitol in continuous legislative use; it's also the only one in which the U.S. Congress has sat (1783–84). General George Washington resigned as commander in chief of the Continental Army here in 1783 and the Treaty of Paris was ratified in 1784, ending the Revolutionary War. Both events took place in the Old Senate Chamber. The Maryland Senate and House hold their sessions in two other chambers in the building. Also on the grounds is the oldest public building in Maryland, the tiny redbrick treasury, built in 1735. Visit the Office of Interpretation on the first floor to pick up self-guided tour information. You must have a photo ID to enter the State House.

In the State House Square is the **Thurgood Marshall Memorial,** an 8-foot statue of Thurgood Marshall as a young lawyer, benches with images of students for whom he fought for integration, and plaques commemorating his achievements. Born in Baltimore, Marshall (1908–93) was the first African American Supreme Court Justice and one of the 20th century's foremost leaders in the struggle for equal rights under the law. He won the decision in 1954's *Brown v. Board of Education,* in which the Court overturned the doctrine of "separate but equal." Marshall was appointed as U.S. Solicitor General in 1965 and to the Supreme Court in 1967 by President Lyndon B. Johnson. ✉ *100 State Circle* ⊕ *msa.maryland.gov/ msa/mdstatehouse/html/visitor.html* 🎟 *Free.*

St. John's College. The Annapolis campus of St. John's, the third-oldest college in the country (after Harvard and William and Mary), once held the last Liberty Tree, under which the Sons of Liberty convened to hear patriots plan the Revolution. Damaged in a 1999 hurricane, the 400-year-old tree was removed; its progeny stands to the left of McDowell Hall. St. John's adheres to a Great Books program, and all students follow the same four-year, liberal-arts curriculum, which includes philosophy, mathematics, music, science, Greek, and French. Students are immersed in the classics through small classes conducted as discussions rather than lectures. Start a visit here by climbing the slope of the long, brick-paved path to the cupola of McDowell Hall.

Down King George Street toward the water is the **Carroll-Barrister House,** now the college admissions office. Once home to Charles Carroll (not the signer of the Declaration but his cousin), the house was built in 1722 at Main and Conduit Streets and moved onto campus in 1955. The **Elizabeth Myers Mitchell Art Gallery,** on the east side of Mellon Hall, presents world-class exhibits and special programs that relate to the fine arts. ✉ *60 College Ave., at St. John's St.* ☎ *410/263–2371* ⊕ *www.sjc.edu* 🎟 *Mitchell Gallery free* ☉ *Mitchell Gallery closed Mon.*

Fodor'sChoice ★ **United States Naval Academy.** Probably the most interesting and important site in Annapolis, the Naval Academy occupies 328 waterfront acres along the Severn River and abuts downtown. Men and women enter the USNA, established in 1845 on the site of a U.S. Army fort, from every part of the United States and foreign countries to undergo rigorous study in subjects that include literature, navigation, and nuclear engineering. Midshipmen (the term used for both women and men) go to classes, conduct military drills, and practice or compete in intercollegiate and intramural sports.

Your visit to "The Yard" (as the USNA grounds are nicknamed) will start at the **Armel-Leftwich Visitor Center.** Note that all visitors 18 years and older must have a government-issued photo ID to be admitted through the academy's gates. Park on the street or in Annapolis public parking and walk through the Visitor Access Center at Gate 1—only cars on official Department of Defense business are allowed on campus. The visitor center features an exhibit, *The Quarter Deck,* which introduces visitors to the Academy's mission, including a 13-minute film, "The Call to Serve," and a well-stocked gift shop. From here you can join one of the hour-long guided walking tours of the Academy.

The centerpiece of the campus is the bright copper-clad dome of the interdenominational **U.S. Naval Academy Chapel.** Beneath it lies the crypt of the Revolutionary War naval hero John Paul Jones, who, in a historic naval battle with a British ship, uttered the inspirational words, "I have not yet begun to fight!" Bancroft Hall is one of the largest dormitories in the world—it houses the entire 4,000-member Brigade of Midshipmen. You can't see how shipshape the middies' quarters are, but you can go inside Bancroft and see a sample room and the glorious Memorial Hall, a tribute to Academy grads who died in military operations. In front of Bancroft is the Statue of Tecumseh, a bronze replica of the USS *Delaware*'s wooden figurehead, "Tamanend," which midshipman decorate for athletics events. ■ TIP➔ If you're here at noon on weekdays in fair weather, watch the midshipmen form up outside Bancroft Hall and parade to lunch accompanied by the Drum and Bugle Corps. You also can have lunch on campus either at Drydock in Dahlgren Hall or the Naval Academy Club. ⊠ *Off Prince George St. or Randall St.* ☎ *410/293–8687* ⊕ *www.usna. edu/visit/index.php* ⊠ *Guided tour $11.*

FAMILY **U.S. Naval Academy Museum.** Displays of model ships and memorabilia from naval heroes and fighting vessels tell the story of the U.S. Navy. The Rogers Ship Model Collection has nearly 80 models of sailing ships built for the British Admiralty, the largest display of 17th- and 18th-century ship models in North America. Kids of all ages will enjoy watching the restoration and building of model ships on the ground level and might even learn a few tricks of the trade should they wish to purchase a model ship kit to build when they get home. ⊠ *118 Maryland Ave.* ☎ *410/293–2108* ⊕ *www.usna.edu/ Museum/* ⊠ *Free.*

William Paca House and Garden. A signer of the Declaration of Independence, Paca (pronounced "PAY-cuh") was a Maryland governor from 1782 to 1785. His house was built from 1763 through 1765, and its original garden was finished by 1772. The main floor (furnished with 18th-century antiques) retains its original Prussian blue and soft gray color scheme and the second floor houses more 18th-century pieces. The adjacent 2-acre garden provides a longer perspective on the back of the house, plus worthwhile sights of its own: upper terraces, a Chinese Chippendale bridge, a pond, a wilderness area, and formal arrangements. An inn, Carvel Hall, once stood in the gardens, now planted with 18th-century perennials. You can take a self-guided tour of the garden, but to see the house you must go on the docent-led tour, which leaves every hour at half past the hour. The last tour leaves 1½ hours before closing. ✉ *186 Prince George St.* ☎ *410/990–4543* ⊕ *www.annapolis. org* 🖃 *$10 house and garden, $8 1st floor of house and garden, $5 garden only* ⊘ *Closed Jan.–mid-Mar.*

WORTH NOTING

Historic Annapolis Museum. Light-filled and modern, this little museum occupies a historic building that once held supplies for the Continental Army during the Revolutionary War. The current exhibit, *Freedom Bound: Runaways of the Chesapeake,* which continues at least through 2015, tells the stories of individuals who resisted servitude during the 1760s–1860s, through artifacts and displays, video, and hands-on activities. The Museum Store sells a wonderful array of history books, beautiful ceramic pieces, crafts made by local artisans, and nautical gifts. Nearby, the Historic Annapolis Waterfront Warehouse at 4 Pinkney Street, which was used in the early 19th century to store tobacco before it was shipped to England, serves as a great orientation site for historic Annapolis properties with its detailed diorama of Annapolis during the 1790s. ✉ *99 Main St.* ☎ *410/267–6656* ⊕ *www. annapolis.org* 🖃 *Free.*

Kunta Kinte–Alex Haley Memorial. *The Story Wall,* comprising 10 plaques along the waterfront, recounts the story of African Americans in Maryland. These granite-framed markers lead to a sculpture group depicting Alex Haley, famed author of *Roots,* reading to a group of children. Here you'll also see a plaque that commemorates the 1767 arrival of the African slave Kunta Kinte, who was immortalized in Haley's novel. Across the street is "The Compass Rose," a 14-foot-diameter inlaid bronze map of the world oriented to true north with Annapolis in the center. This is a lovely place that may inspire you to reflect on African American history and the importance of family, reading, and passing oral history from one generation to another. ✉ *Market Sq.* ⊕ *www.kintehaley.org.*

St. Anne's Church. Residing in the center of one of the historic area's busy circles, this brick building is one of the city's most prominent places of worship. King William III donated the communion silver when the parish was founded in 1692, but the first St. Anne's Church wasn't completed until 1704. The second church burned in 1858, but parts of its walls survived and were incorporated into the present structure, which was built the following year. Free guided tours are offered the first and third Monday of every month at 10 and every Wednesday at 12:30.

The churchyard contains the grave of the last colonial governor, Sir Robert Eden. ✉ *Church Circle* ☎ *410/267–9333* ⊕ *www.stannes-annapolis.org* 🖃 *Free.*

WHERE TO EAT

In the beginning, there was crab: crab cakes, crab soup, whole crabs to crack. This Chesapeake Bay specialty is still found in abundance, but Annapolis has broadened its horizons to include eateries—many in the Historic District—that offer many sorts of cuisines. Ask for a restaurant guide at the visitor center.

$$ SEAFOOD FAMILY 🍴 **Buddy's Crabs & Ribs.** Family owned and operated since 1988, with a central location overlooking Main Street and City Dock, the biggest restaurant in Annapolis is fun and informal and features all kinds of seafood and shellfish. There are also pastas, chicken, and steak selections, and specialty sandwiches and salads. **Known for:** "Big Buddy" crab cakes and all-you-can-eat buffets; great deals for kids; casual, family atmosphere. [$] *Average main: $25* ✉ *100 Main St.* ☎ *410/626–1100* 🌐 *www.buddysonline.com.*

$$$ FRENCH 🍴 **Café Normandie.** Wood beams, skylights, and a four-sided fireplace provide a cozy ambience, and out of the open kitchen comes an astonishingly good French onion soup. Bouillabaisse, puffy omelets, crepes, and seafood dishes are other specialties. **Known for:** sustainable and local ingredients; French onion soup made entirely from scratch; delightful weekend breakfast. [$] *Average main: $28* ✉ *185 Main St.* ☎ *410/263–3382* 🌐 *www.cafenormandie.com.*

$$ SEAFOOD Fodor's Choice ★ 🍴 **Cantler's Riverside Inn.** Jimmy Cantler, a native Marylander who worked as a waterman on Chesapeake Bay, founded this local institution 40 years ago. The no-nonsense interior has nautical items laminated beneath tabletops, and steamed mussels, clams, and shrimp as well as Maryland vegetable crab soup, seafood sandwiches, crab cakes, and much more. **Known for:** seasonal outdoor dining right next to the water; steamed crabs served on a "tablecloth" of brown paper; a classic casual Maryland seafood experience; long waits during the summer. [$] *Average main: $26* ✉ *458 Forest Beach Rd.* ☎ *410/757–1311* 🌐 *www.cantlers.com.*

9

$$$ AMERICAN 🍴 **Carrol's Creek.** You can walk, catch a water taxi from City Dock, or drive over the Spa Creek drawbridge to this local favorite in Eastport. Whether you dine indoors or out, the view of historic Annapolis and its harbor is spectacular. **Known for:** à la carte Sunday brunch; upscale (but not too pricey) seafood specialties; amazing city and harbor views. [$] *Average main: $29* ✉ *410 Severn Ave., Eastport* ☎ *410/263–8102* 🌐 *www.carrolscreek.com.*

$ AMERICAN 🍴 **Chick and Ruth's Delly.** Deli sandwiches, burgers, subs, crab cakes, and milk shakes are the fare at this very busy counter-and-booth institution. Built in 1899, the edifice was just a sandwich shop when Baltimoreans Ruth and Chick Levitt purchased it in 1965. **Known for:** legendary sandwiches named after local politicians; giant milk shakes (including a six-pounder); patriotic decor (and a daily reciting of the Pledge of Allegiance); homemade pies and breads. [$] *Average main: $11* ✉ *165 Main St.* ☎ *410/269–6737* 🌐 *www.chickandruths.com.*

$ ECLECTIC 🍴 **49 West Coffeehouse, Winebar and Gallery.** In what was once a hardware store, this casual eatery has one interior wall of exposed brick and another of exposed plaster; both are used to hang art for sale by local artists. Daily specials are chalked on a blackboard. **Known for:**

DID YOU KNOW?

The Navy's Blue Angels fly over each graduating class at the U.S. Naval Academy in Annapolis to celebrate their accomplishments.

live music every night; eclectic coffeehouse vibe; flatbread pizzas, deli sandwiches, and coffee galore. $ *Average main: $15* ✉ *49 West St.* ☎ *410/626–9796* ⊕ *49westcoffeehouse.com.*

$$ ✕**Galway Bay.** Step inside this Irish pub and you'll be welcomed like a member of the family. As you would expect, the corned beef and cabbage and other traditional Irish menu items (along with classic Annapolis bar food like crab and oysters) are fantastic. **Known for:** traditional Irish grub and hospitality; authentic house-made corned-beef hash; Sunday brunch with live music. $ *Average main: $21* ✉ *63 Maryland Ave.* ☎ *301/263–8333* ⊕ *www.galwaybaymd.com.*

IRISH

Fodor'sChoice ★

$$$ ✕**Harry Browne's.** In the shadow of the State House, this understated establishment has long held a reputation for quality food and attentive service that ensures bustle year-round, especially during the busy days of the legislative session (early January into early April) and special weekend events at the Naval Academy. The menu clearly reflects the city's maritime culture, but also has seasonal specialties. **Known for:** political clientele; green approach to sourcing and recycling; champagne brunch on Sunday. $ *Average main: $30* ✉ *66 State Circle* ☎ *410/263–4332* ⊕ *www.harrybrownes.com.*

AMERICAN

Fodor'sChoice ★

$$ ✕**Iron Rooster.** There's often a line of hungry diners waiting for a table at this comfort-food haven located on the city dock where the portions are generous and service first-rate. You can enjoy breakfast all day— Benedicts and omelets are top sellers, as are the chicken and waffles and the shrimp and grits. **Known for:** daily homemade pop-tart specials; Southern-inspired all-day breakfast (including amazingly light and fluffy biscuits); long lines. $ *Average main: $18* ✉ *12 Market Space* ☎ *410/990–1600* ⊕ *www.ironroosterallday.com.*

AMERICAN

Fodor'sChoice ★

$$$ ✕**Osteria 177.** This might be the only local Italian restaurant that doesn't offer pizza or spaghetti. Instead, Osteria serves seafood from all over the world, meat, and pasta made on the premises. **Known for:** politicians and lobbyists at lunchtime; authentic coastal Italian cuisine; unique seafood and asparagus linguine pasta. $ *Average main: $33* ✉ *177 Main St.* ☎ *410/267–7700* ⊕ *www.osteria177.com.*

MODERN ITALIAN

$$$ ✕**Preserve.** Jars of pickled chard stems and radishes, preserved lemons, and pepper jelly line the shelves at this lively spot on Main Street run by a husband-and-wife team who both have impressive culinary resumes and a shared passion for pickling, fermenting, and preserving. That edible art peeks through the lunch, dinner, and brunch menus and makes the very seasonal dishes come alive. **Known for:** varied dishes that highlight unique preservation methods; kimchi and sauerkraut galore; lots of seasonal veggies. $ *Average main: $27* ✉ *164 Main St.* ☎ *443/598–6920* ⊕ *www.preserve-eats.com* ☾ *Closed Mon.*

AMERICAN

$ ✕**Vin 909.** If it wasn't for the sign out front, you might think you're at someone's Eastport home given the charming front porch and well-tended gardens. But walk through the doors and you'll discover a casually hip and always crowded restaurant serving organic, sustainable, and seasonally focused food that's simply fantastic. **Known for:** crispy pizza with farm-to-table toppings; huge wine menu by the glass and bottle; diverse selection of beers. $ *Average main: $16* ✉ *909 Bay Ridge Ave.* ☎ *410/990–1846* ⊕ *www.vin909.com* ☾ *Closed Mon.*

AMERICAN

Fodor'sChoice ★

9

WHERE TO STAY

$$$ **Annapolis Waterfront Hotel.** You can practically fish from your room at
HOTEL   the city's only waterfront hotel, where rooms have either balconies over
FAMILY   the water or large windows with views of the harbor or the historic district. **Pros:** a "pure room" is available for the allergy sensitive; accessible
for travelers with disabilities; on-site restaurant and bar; complimentary
Wi-Fi throughout. **Cons:** some rooms have no waterfront view, some
have only partial views; chain hotel lacks charm; parking is pricey.
$ *Rooms from: $395* ⊠ *80 Compromise St.* ☎ *410/268–7555* ⊕ *www.
annapolismarriott.com* ⌐ *150 rooms* ¶⊙¶ *No meals.*

$ **Country Inn & Suites.** Although this hotel is 5 miles from the historic
HOTEL   Annapolis waterfront, there's a free shuttle, and the two-room suites
with pullout sofas are perfect for families. **Pros:** reliable and inexpensive option; free shuttle services; complimentary Wi-Fi. **Cons:** distance
from the dock; tiny gym; small indoor heated pool can be crowded at
times. $ *Rooms from: $119* ⊠ *2600 Housely Rd.* ☎ *410/571–6700,
800/456–4000* ⊕ *www.countryinns.com* ⌐ *100 rooms* ¶⊙¶ *Breakfast.*

$$ **Gibson's Lodgings.** Just half a block from the water, the three detached
HOTEL   houses that form this hotel come from three centuries—1780, 1890, and
1980—and all the guest rooms are furnished with pre-1900 antiques.
Pros: conveniently located between the Naval Academy and downtown;
free parking in the courtyards; free continental breakfast. **Cons:** cannot
accommodate children under the age of eight; two of the rooms share a
bathroom; no elevator, although three rooms are on the ground floor.
$ *Rooms from: $229* ⊠ *110–114 Prince George St.* ☎ *410/268–5555,
877/330–0057* ⊕ *www.gibsonslodgings.com* ⌐ *20 rooms* ¶⊙¶ *Breakfast.*

$$ **Historic Inns of Annapolis.** Three 18th-century properties in the his-
B&B/INN   toric district—the Governor Calvert House, Robert Johnson House, and
Maryland Inn—are grouped as one inn, all offering guest rooms individually decorated with antiques and reproductions. **Pros:** historic properties;
within walking distance of activities; lemonade or spiced cider served daily
in the Calvert House. **Cons:** prices vary greatly; some rooms are small.
$ *Rooms from: $249* ⊠ *58 State Circle* ☎ *410/263–2641, 800/847–8882*
⊕ *www.historicinnsofannapolis.com* ⌐ *138 rooms* ¶⊙¶ *No meals.*

$ **Scotlaur Inn.** On the two floors above Chick and Ruth's Delly in the
B&B/INN   heart of the historic district, this family-owned B&B is cozy and characterful. **Pros:** a chance to stay above one of Annapolis's landmarks
right in the center of town; half off in nearby parking garage. **Cons:**
not for those who prefer modern style and don't like chintz; rooms are
on the small side; no elevator. $ *Rooms from: $149* ⊠ *165 Main St.*
☎ *410/268–5665* ⊕ *www.scotlaurinn.com* ⌐ *10 rooms* ¶⊙¶ *Breakfast.*

$$$ **The Westin Annapolis Hotel.** About a mile from City Dock, in a rapidly
HOTEL   gentrifying neighborhood, this hotel is the centerpiece of a European-
themed planned community, complete with restaurants, shops, and
condominiums. **Pros:** the complete Starwood hotel experience; modern hotel with many amenities. **Cons:** distance from the City Dock;
Wi-Fi only free in public areas. $ *Rooms from: $398* ⊠ *100 Westgate
Circle* ☎ *410/972–4300* ⊕ *www.westin.com/annapolis* ⌐ *225 rooms*
¶⊙¶ *No meals.*

TRAVEL SMART
WASHINGTON, D.C.

GETTING HERE AND AROUND

Although it may not appear so at first glance, there's a system to addresses in D.C., albeit one that's a bit confusing for newcomers. The city is divided into the four quadrants of a compass (NW, NE, SE, SW), with the U.S. Capitol at the center. Because the Capitol doesn't sit in the exact center of the city, Northwest is the largest quadrant. Northwest also has most of the important landmarks, although Northeast and Southwest have their fair share. The boundaries are North Capitol Street, East Capitol Street, South Capitol Street, and the National Mall.

If someone tells you to meet them at 6th and G, ask them to specify the quadrant, because there are actually four different 6th and G intersections (one per quadrant). Within each quadrant, numbered streets run north to south, and lettered streets run east to west (the letter *J* was omitted to avoid confusion with the letter *I*). The streets form a fairly simple grid—for instance, 900 G Street NW is the intersection of 9th and G Streets in the NW quadrant of the city. Likewise, if you count the letters of the alphabet, skipping *J*, you can get a good approximation of an address for a numbered street. For instance, 1600 16th Street NW is close to Q Street, Q being the 16th letter of the alphabet if you skip *J*.

As if all this weren't confusing enough, Major Pierre L'Enfant, the Frenchman who originally designed the city, threw in diagonal avenues recalling those of Paris. Most of D.C.'s avenues are named after U.S. states. You can find addresses on avenues the same way you find those on numbered streets, so 1200 Connecticut Avenue NW is close to M Street, because M is the 12th letter of the alphabet when you skip *J*.

▮ AIR TRAVEL

A flight to D.C. from New York takes a little less than an hour. It's about 1½ hours from Chicago, 3 hours from Denver or Dallas, and 5 hours from San Francisco. Passengers flying from London should expect a trip of about 6 hours. From Sydney it's an 18-hour flight.

Airline Contacts American Airlines/American Eagle. ☎ *800/433–7300* ⊕ *www.aa.com.* **Delta Airlines.** ☎ *800/221–1212* ⊕ *www. delta.com.* **JetBlue.** ☎ *800/538–2583* ⊕ *www. jetblue.com.* **Southwest Airlines.** ☎ *800/435–9792* ⊕ *www.southwest.com.* **United Airlines.** ☎ *800/864–8331* ⊕ *www.united.com.*

Airline Security Issues Transportation Security Administration. ☎ *866/289–9673* ⊕ *www.tsa.gov.*

Air Travel Resources in Washington, D.C. U.S. Department of Transportation Aviation Consumer Protection Division. ☎ *202/366–2220* ⊕ *www.transportation.gov/airconsumer.*

AIRPORTS

The major gateways to D.C. are **Ronald Reagan Washington National Airport (DCA)** in Virginia, 4 miles south of Downtown Washington; **Dulles International Airport (IAD)**, 26 miles west of Washington, D.C.; and **Baltimore/Washington International–Thurgood Marshall Airport (BWI)** in Maryland, about 30 miles to the northeast.

Reagan National Airport is closest to Downtown D.C. and has a Metro stop in the terminal. East Coast shuttles and shorter flights tend to fly in and out of this airport. Dulles is configured primarily for long-haul flights, although as a United hub, it's also well-connected regionally. BWI offers blended service, with its many gates for Southwest Air, as well as international flights. Although Metro trains don't serve Dulles or BWI, there is affordable and convenient public transportation to and from each airport. Be aware that the

Mid-Atlantic region is prone to quirky weather that can snarl air traffic, especially on stormy summer afternoons.

Airport Information Baltimore/Washington International–Thurgood Marshall Airport (*BWI*). ☎ *800/435-9294* ⊕ *www. bwiairport.com*. **Dulles International Airport** (*IAD*). ☎ *703/572-2700* ⊕ *www.flydulles. com*. **Ronald Reagan Washington National Airport** (*DCA*). ☎ *703/417-8000* ⊕ *www. flyreagan.com*.

GROUND TRANSPORTATION: REAGAN NATIONAL (DCA)

By Car: Take the George Washington Memorial Parkway north for approximately 1 mile. Exit on I–395 North; bear left onto U.S. 1 North toward Downtown. For the city center, turn left on Madison Drive NW and turn right on 15th Street NW. The drive takes 20–30 minutes, depending on traffic and your destination.

By Metro: The Metro station is within easy walking distance of Terminals B and C, and a free airport bus shuttles between the station and Terminal A. The Metro ride to Downtown takes about 20 minutes and costs between $2 and $4, depending on the time of day and your final destination.

By Shuttle: SuperShuttle, a fleet of bright blue vans, will take you to any hotel or residence in the city. The length of the ride varies, depending on traffic and the number of stops. The approximately 20-minute ride from Reagan National to Downtown averages $16.

By Taxi: Expect to pay $20–$25 to get from National to Downtown. Note that a $3 surcharge is added to the metered fare from this airport. Taxi rip-offs have decreased since the District introduced meters, but if the fare seems astronomical, get the driver's name and cab number and contact the D.C. Taxi Commission.

Contacts SuperShuttle. ☎ *800/258-3826, 703/416-7873* ⊕ *www.supershuttle.com*. **Taxicab Commission.** ☎ *311, 202/645-6018* ⊕ *www.dfhv.dc.gov*. **Washington Metropolitan Area Transit Authority.** ☎ *202/637-7000, 202/638-3780 TTY* ⊕ *www.wmata.com*.

GROUND TRANSPORTATION: BALTIMORE/WASHINGTON INTERNATIONAL (BWI)

By Car: Exit BWI and follow I–95 West. Take Exit 2B to MD–295 South for 24 miles; exit on U.S. 50 West toward Washington. Continue on New York Avenue for about 3 miles; continue on Mount Vernon Place NW for 2 miles. Continue on Massachusetts Avenue NW; turn left on Vermont Avenue NW at Thomas Circle. Turn right on K Street NW; take a left on 17th Street NW and you're now basically in the city center. The distance is about 34 miles and should take 50–60 minutes.

By Public Transit: Amtrak and Maryland Rail Commuter Service (MARC) trains run between BWI and Washington, D.C.'s, Union Station from around 6 am to 10 pm. The cost of the 30-minute ride averages between $16 and $32 on Amtrak; MARC's Penn Line, which runs seven days a week, is a much more affordable $7. A free shuttle bus transports passengers between airline terminals and the train station (which is in a distant parking lot).

Washington Metropolitan Area Transit Authority (WMATA) operates express bus service (Bus No. B30) between BWI and the Greenbelt Metro station. Buses run between 6 am and 10 pm, with more limited hours on weekends. The fare is $7.

By Shuttle: SuperShuttle will take you to any hotel or residence in the city. The ride from BWI, which takes approximately 60 minutes, averages $37.

By Taxi: The fare from BWI is about $90.

Contacts Amtrak. ☎ *800/872-7245* ⊕ *www. amtrak.com*. **Maryland Rail Commuter Service.** ☎ *410/539-5000, 410/539-3497 TTY, 866/743-3682* ⊕ *www.mta.maryland.gov*. **SuperShuttle.** ☎ *800/258-3826, 410/859-3427* ⊕ *www.supershuttle.com*. **Washington Metropolitan Area Transit Authority.** ☎ *202/637-7000, 202/638-3780 TTY* ⊕ *www. wmata.com*.

GROUND TRANSPORTATION: DULLES (IAD)

By Car: From Dulles Airport, exit onto Dulles Airport Access Road and follow this for 14 miles; merge onto VA–267 East. Merge onto I–66 East; follow this for approximately 6 miles and exit to the left on E Street Expressway. Take the ramp to E Street NW. Total distance from the airport to Downtown is about 27 miles and should take about 45 minutes.

By Public Transit: Silver Line Express links Dulles International Airport and the Wiehle Avenue station. The 30-minute bus ride is $5 each way for adults, free for children under six. Buses run every 15–20 minutes from 6 am to 10:40 pm. All coaches are accessible to those in wheelchairs. Fares may be paid with cash or credit card at the ticket counter near Door 4 at the Arrivals/Baggage Claim Level. Board the bus just outside the door.

The Washington Metropolitan Area Transit Authority (WMATA) operates express bus service between Dulles and several stops in Downtown D.C., including the L'Enfant Plaza Metro station and Rosslyn Metro station in Arlington, Virginia, just across the river from Georgetown. Bus No. 5A, which costs $7, runs every hour between 5:50 am and 11:35 pm from curb location 2E in the second lane on the (lower) arrivals level in front of the terminal. Make sure to have the exact fare or a rechargeable SmarTrip card, as drivers cannot make change.

By Shuttle: The roughly 45-minute ride from Dulles on the SuperShuttle runs $30 for one person, $10 for each additional person. Sign in with the attendants at the lower-level doors, down the ramp when you exit the terminal.

By Taxi: The fare to Washington D.C. from Dulles is about $60–$70.

Contacts SuperShuttle. ☎ 800/258–3826, 703/416–7873 ⊕ www.supershuttle.com. **Washington Flyer.** ☎ 888/927–4359 ⊕ www.flydulles.com/iad/washington-flyer. **Washington Metropolitan Area Transit Authority.** ☎ 202/637–7000, 202/638–3780 TTY ⊕ www.wmata.com.

▌ BUS TRAVEL

CITY BUSES

Most of the sightseeing neighborhoods (the Mall, Capitol Hill, Downtown, Dupont Circle) are near Metro rail stations, but a few (Georgetown, Adams Morgan) are more easily reached via Metrobus, blue-and-white buses operated by the Washington Metropolitan Area Transit Authority. Bus No. 42 travels from the Dupont Circle Metro stop to, and through, Adams Morgan. Georgetown is a hike from the closest Metro rail station, but you can take a Georgetown Metro Connection shuttle to any Metrobus stop from the Foggy Bottom or Dupont Circle Metro stations in D.C. or the Rosslyn Metro station in Arlington, Virginia.

The D.C. Circulator is another option for getting around the city; it has five routes and charges $1. The Potomac Avenue–Skyland via Barracks Row, Union Station–Navy Yard via Capitol Hill, and Woodley Park–Adams Morgan–McPherson Square Metro routes cut a path from north to south; the Georgetown–Union Station and Rosslyn–Georgetown–Dupont routes go east to west.

Complete bus and Metro maps for the metropolitan D.C. area, which note museums, monuments, theaters, and parks, can be picked up free of charge at the Metro Center sales office.

FARES AND TRANSFERS

All regular buses within the District are $1.75; express buses, which make fewer stops, are $4. For every adult ticket purchased, two children under the age of four travel free. Children ages five and older pay the regular fare. Bus fares are payable with cash (exact change only) or a SmarTrip card, a rechargeable pass you can use on buses and is required for Metro trains. Just touch the card to the SmarTrip logo on the fare box. Bus-to-bus transfers are free within a two-hour window. You'll also get a $0.50 discount by using a SmarTrip card on bus-to-rail and rail-to-bus transfers.

D.C. Circulator passengers can pay cash when boarding (exact change only) or use Metro SmarTrip cards, and one-day, three-day, or weekly Circulator passes. Passes can be purchased online at ⊕ *www. commuterdirect.com*. You only have to wait about 5–10 minutes at any of the stops for the next bus.

PAYMENT AND PASSES

Buses require exact change in bills, coins, or both. You can eliminate the exact-change hassle by purchasing a seven-day Metrobus pass for $17.50, or the $2 rechargeable SmarTrip card online before your trip or at any Metrorail station. The SmarTrip card is required on the Metrorail system.

Information D.C. Circulator. ☏ *202/962–1423* ⊕ *www.dccirculator.com.* **Washington Metropolitan Area Transit Authority.** ☏ *202/637–7000, 202/638–3780 TTY* ⊕ *www. wmata.com.*

REGIONAL BUSES

Several bus lines run between New York City and the Washington, D.C., area, including BoltBus, BestBus, Megabus, Peter Pan Bus Lines, Tripper Bus, Vamoose, and Washington Deluxe. Tripper and Vamoose routes run between NYC and Metro stations in Bethesda, Maryland, and Arlington, Virginia. All the buses are clean, the service satisfactory, and the price can't be beat. Believe it or not, with advance planning, you might be able to get a round-trip ticket for just $2. Megabus also has bus service from Toronto, Canada, and a handful of other U.S. cities. Several of the bus lines offer power outlets, Wi-Fi, and a frequent-rider loyalty program.

Information BestBus. ☏ *202/332–2691* ⊕ *www.bestbus.com.* **BoltBus.** ☏ *877/265–8287* ⊕ *www.boltbus.com.* **Megabus.** ☏ *877/462–6342* ⊕ *us.megabus.com.* **Peter Pan Bus Lines.** ☏ *800/343–9999* ⊕ *www. peterpanbus.com.* **Tripper Bus.** ☏ *877/826–3874* ⊕ *www.tripperbus.com.* **Vamoose.** ☏ *877/393–2828* ⊕ *www.vamoosebus.com.* **Washington Deluxe.** ☏ *866/287–6932* ⊕ *www.washny.com.*

▌ CAR TRAVEL

A car is often a drawback in Washington, D.C. Traffic is awful, especially at rush hour, and driving is often confusing, with many lanes and some entire streets changing direction suddenly during rush hour. Most traffic lights stand at the side of intersections (instead of hanging suspended over them), and the streets are dotted with giant potholes. The city's most popular sights are all within a short walk of a Metro station, so do yourself a favor and leave your car at the hotel. If you're visiting sights in Maryland or Virginia or need a car because of reduced mobility, time your trips to avoid D.C. rush hours, 7–10 am and 3–7 pm.

With Zipcar, an urban car-rental membership service, you can rent a car for a couple of hours or a couple of days from convenient Downtown parking lots. A onetime application fee of $25, an annual membership fee of $70, plus hourly rates starting at $7.75, or $66 per day, buys you gas, insurance, parking, and satellite radio. Reserve online or by phone.

Like the comfort of a car but don't want to drive? Uber is your answer. You can request a ride through the mobile app or the Uber website. Drivers are available seven days a week, 24 hours a day. Once you request your ride, you'll be able to see exactly where the driver is and how long you'll have to wait. The fare for a Black (sedan) is $7 base charge, plus $3.40/mile (traveling more than 11 mph) and $0.40/minute (traveling less than 11 mph); the SUV fare is $14 base charge, plus $3.65/mile and $0.45/minute; the economy option, uberX, charges a $1.15 base rate plus $1.02 per mile and $0.17 per minute. After registering, your credit card information is kept on file and your card is charged upon completion of your ride. When demand is high due to weather, holidays or special events, rates can be considerably higher. Other ride-sharing apps like Lyft offer similar options.

Information **Lyft.** ⊕ *www.lyft.com.* **Uber.** ⊕ *www.uber.com.* **Zipcar.** ☎ *866/494-7227* ⊕ *www.zipcar.com.*

GASOLINE

Gas is more expensive in the District than it is in Maryland or Virginia, and gas stations can be hard to find, especially around Pennsylvania Avenue and the National Mall. Your best bets are the BP station at the corner of 18th and S Streets NW, the Mobil station at the corner of 15th and U Streets NW, the Exxon station at 2150 M Street NW, and the Mobil station at the corner of 22nd and P Streets NW. The no-name station at Wisconsin and Q in Georgetown has the cheapest gas in Northwest D.C.—cash only.

LAY OF THE LAND

Interstate 95 skirts D.C. as part of the Beltway, the six- to eight-lane highway that encircles the city. The eastern half of the Beltway is labeled both I–95 and I–495; the western half is just I–495. If you're coming from the south, take I–95 to I–395 and cross the 14th Street Bridge to 14th Street in the District. From the north, stay on I–95 South. Take the exit to Washington, which will place you on the Baltimore–Washington (B–W) Parkway heading south. The B–W Parkway will turn into New York Avenue, taking you into Downtown Washington, D.C.

Interstate 66 approaches the city from the southwest. You can get Downtown by taking I–66 across the Theodore Roosevelt Bridge to Constitution Avenue.

Interstate 270 approaches Washington, D.C., from the northwest before hitting I–495. To reach Downtown, take I–495 East to Connecticut Avenue South, toward Chevy Chase.

PARKING

Parking in D.C. is a question of supply and demand—little of the former, too much of the latter. The police are quick to ticket, tow away, or boot any vehicle parked illegally, so check complicated parking signs and feed the meter before you go. If you find you've been towed

from a city street, call *311* or *202/737–4404*. Be sure you know the license-plate number, make, model, and color of the car before you call.

Most of the outlying, suburban Metro stations have parking lots, though these fill quickly with city-bound commuters. If you plan to park in one of these lots, arrive early.

Downtown private parking lots often charge around $5–$10 an hour and $25–$40 a day. Most of the streets along the Mall have metered parking and, although there are some free, three-hour parking spots on Constitution, Jefferson, and Madison Avenues, these spots are almost always filled. There is no parking near the Lincoln or Roosevelt memorials. The closest free parking is in three lots in East Potomac Park, south of the 14th Street Bridge.

RENTAL CARS

If you're staying in D.C., skip it. Public transportation in the city is convenient and affordable, and driving here is no fun.

However, if you're staying in Virginia or Maryland and your hotel doesn't have a shuttle into D.C. and isn't within walking distance of the Metro, then a car may be your best transportation option.

Daily rental rates in Washington, D.C., begin at about $40 during the week and about $22 on weekends for an economy car with air-conditioning, automatic transmission, and unlimited mileage. This does not include airport facility fees or the tax on car rentals.

In Washington, D.C., many agencies require you to be at least 25 to rent a car. However, younger employees of major corporations and military or government personnel on official business should check with rental companies and their employers for exceptions.

Major Rental Agencies Alamo. ☎ *844/357-5138, 844/354-6962 reservations* ⊕ *www.alamo.com.* **Avis.** ☎ *800/633-3469* ⊕ *www.avis.com.* **Budget.** ☎ *800/218-7992* ⊕ *www.budget.com.* **Hertz.** ☎ *800/654-3131* ⊕ *www.hertz.com.* **National Car Rental.** ☎ *877/222-9058* ⊕ *www.nationalcar.com.*

ROADSIDE EMERGENCIES

Dial *911* to report accidents on the road and to reach police, the highway patrol, or the fire department. For police non-emergencies, dial *311*.

Emergency Services U.S. Park Police.
☎ 202/610–7500 ⊕ www.nps.gov.

RULES OF THE ROAD

In D.C. you may turn right at a red light after stopping if there's no oncoming traffic and no signs indicate otherwise. When in doubt, wait for the green. Be alert for one-way streets, "no left turn" intersections, and blocks closed to car traffic. The use of handheld mobile phones while operating a vehicle is illegal in Washington, D.C. Drivers can also be cited for "failure to pay full time and attention while operating a motor vehicle." The speed limit in D.C. is 25 mph except on the Whitehurst Freeway.

Radar detectors are illegal in Washington, D.C., and Virginia.

During the hours of 6–9 am (inbound) and 3:30–6 pm (outbound), HOV (high-occupancy vehicle) lanes on I–395 and I–95 are reserved for cars with three or more people. From 6:30 to 9 am (inbound) and 4 to 6:30 pm (outbound), all the lanes of I–66 inside the Beltway are reserved for cars carrying two or more, as are some of the lanes on the Dulles Toll Road and on I–270.

Always strap children under a year old or under 20 pounds into approved rear-facing child-safety seats in the back seat. In Washington, D.C., children weighing 20–40 pounds must also ride in a car seat in the back, although it may face forward. Children cannot sit in the front seat of a car until they are at least four years old and weigh more than 80 pounds.

▌ METRO TRAVEL

The Metro, which opened in 1976, is clean and safe and provides a convenient way to get around the city—if you're staying near a Metro stop. Visit Metro's website and click on Metrorail maps to locate the station nearest your hotel. The Metro operates from 5 am weekdays and from 7 am weekends; it shuts down at midnight seven days a week, although there are proposals to extend those hours on weekends. Check for updates before ruling out a later ride home. Don't get to the station at the last minute, as trains from the ends of the lines depart before the official closing time. During the weekday peak periods (5–9:30 am and 3–7 pm), trains come along every three to six minutes. At other times and on weekends and holidays, trains run about every 12–15 minutes. Lighted displays at the platforms show estimated arrival times of trains, as well as the number of cars available. Eating, drinking, smoking, and littering in stations and on the trains are strictly prohibited.

FARES

The Metro's base fare is $1.75; the actual price you pay depends on the time of day and the distance traveled, which means you might end up paying close to $6 if you're traveling to a distant station at rush hour. All rides now require a SmarTrip card, a rechargeable fare card that can be used throughout the Metro, bus, and parking system. Up to two children under age four ride free when accompanied by a paying passenger.

PAYMENT AND PASSES

Buy your SmarTrip card at a vending machine in any station; they accept cash, credit cards, and debit cards. You can buy one-day passes for $14.50 and seven-day passes for $59.25. To enter the Metro platform, just touch your card to the SmarTrip logo on the turnstile. Passes and SmarTrip cards can also be purchased online.

Metro Information Washington Metropolitan Area Transit Authority (WMATA).
✉ Downtown ☎ 202/637–7000, 202/638–3780 TTY, 202/962–1195 lost and found
⊕ www.wmata.com.

▮ TAXI TRAVEL

Taxis are easy to hail in commercial districts, less so in residential ones. If you don't see one after a few minutes, walk to a busier street. If you call, make sure to have an address—not just an intersection—and be prepared to wait, especially at night. D.C. cabs are independent operators and the various companies' cars all have a different look. If you're traveling to or from Maryland or Virginia, your best bet is to call a Maryland or Virginia cab, which generally are more reliable. But they're not allowed to take you from point to point in the District or pick you up there if you hail them, so don't be offended if one passes you by.

FARES

The base rate for the first one-eighth mile is $3.25. Each additional one-eighth mile is $0.27, and each minute stopped or traveling at less than 10 mph is $0.58. A charge of $1 is tacked on for additional passengers, regardless how many. The telephone dispatch fee is $2. During D.C.-declared snow emergencies, there is an additional $15 fee. Cab rates in Virginia differ by county, but immediately surrounding D.C., riders should expect to pay $3–$6 for the first quarter mile and between $0.50 and $0.65 for each additional quarter mile. Extra passengers usually face a $1 surcharge.

Taxi Companies Barwood. ☎ 301/984–1900 ⊕ www.barwoodtaxi.com. **Diamond.** ☎ 202/387–6200. **Red Top.** ☎ 703/522–3333 ⊕ www.redtopcab.com. **Taxi Transportation.** ☎ 202/398–0500 ⊕ www.dctaxionline.com. **Yellow.** ☎ 202/544–1212 ⊕ www.dcyellow-cab.com.

▮ TRAIN TRAVEL

More than 80 trains a day arrive at Washington, D.C.'s, Union Station. Amtrak's regular service runs from D.C. to New York in 3¼–3¾ hours and from D.C. to Boston in 7¾–8 hours. Acela, Amtrak's high-speed service, travels from D.C. to New York in 2¾–3 hours and from D.C. to Boston in 6½ hours.

Two commuter lines—Maryland Rail Commuter Service (MARC) and Virginia Railway Express (VRE)—run to the nearby suburbs. They're cheaper than Amtrak, but the VRE doesn't run on weekends, and only one MARC line (the Penn Line) does.

Amtrak tickets and reservations are available at Amtrak stations, by telephone, or online. Amtrak schedule and fare information can be found at Union Station as well as online.

Amtrak has both reserved and unreserved trains available. If you plan to travel during peak times, such as a Friday night or near a holiday, you'll need to get a reservation and a ticket in advance. Some trains at off-peak times are unreserved, with seats assigned on a first-come, first-served basis.

Information Amtrak. ☎ 800/872–7245 ⊕ www.amtrak.com. **Maryland Rail Commuter Service (MARC).** ☎ 866/743–3682 ⊕ www.mta.maryland.gov. **Union Station.** ✉ 50 Massachusetts Ave. NE, Washington ☎ 202/289–1908 ⊕ www.unionstationdc.com. **Virginia Railway Express (VRE).** ☎ 703/684–1001 ⊕ www.vre.org.

ESSENTIALS

▌ BUSINESS SERVICES AND FACILITIES

Imagine two Washington monuments laid end to end, and you will have an idea about the size of the Washington Convention Center, the District's largest building. Recognized nationally for its architectural design, the center also has a $4 million art collection featuring 120 sculptures, oil paintings, and photographs from artists around the world.

FedEx Office, across the street from the Convention Center and at many other locations citywide, provides everything from photocopying and digital printing to shipping and receiving packages. In addition, several companies provide translation and interpretation services, including Capital Communications Group, which also offers multilingual city tours, and Comprehensive Language Center.

Business Services FedEx Office Print & Ship Center. ✉ *901 Massachusetts Ave. NW, Downtown* ☎ *202/783-8412,* ⊕ *www.fedex. com* Ⓜ *Mt. Vernon Sq./7th St. Convention Center.*

Convention Center Walter E. Washington Convention Center. ✉ *801 Mt. Vernon Pl. NW, Downtown* ☎ *202/249-3000* ⊕ *www. dcconvention.com* Ⓜ *Mt. Vernon Sq/7th St. Convention Center.*

▌ COMMUNICATIONS

INTERNET

Every major hotel offers high-speed access in rooms and/or lobbies and business centers. In addition, dozens of D.C.-area restaurants and coffee shops provide free wireless broadband Internet service, including branches of Starbucks and Così all over town. The Martin Luther King Jr. Memorial Public Library and 25 other branches of the D.C. Library System offer Wi-Fi access free of charge to all library visitors, and most have computers available to use,

also at no cost. At Busboys and Poets, a popular restaurant, bar, and bookstore, you can also pick up free Wi-Fi while taking in near-nightly literary events.

Contacts Busboys and Poets. ✉ *2021 14th St. NW, Washington* ☎ *202/387-7638* ⊕ *www. busboysandpoets.com* Ⓜ *U St./Cardozo.* **Così.** ⊕ *www.getcosi.com.* **Martin Luther King Jr. Memorial Library.** ✉ *901 G St. NW, China- town* ☎ *202/727-0321* ⊕ *www.dclibrary.org/ mlk* Ⓜ *Metro Center or Gallery Pl. Chinatown.*

▌ HOURS OF OPERATION

If you're getting around on the Metro, remember that it closes at midnight—an inconvenience to anyone barhopping on weekends, when bars close at 3 am. Give yourself enough time to get to the station, because at many stations the last trains leave earlier than the closing times. If it's a holiday, be sure to check the schedule before you leave the station, as trains may be running on a different timetable. Bars and nightclubs close at 2 am on weekdays and 3 am on weekends.

▌ MONEY

Washington is an expensive city, comparable to New York. On the other hand, many attractions, including most of the museums, are free.

ITEM	AVERAGE COST
Cup of Coffee	$1–$4
Glass of Wine	$7–$10 and up
Pint of Beer	$5–$7
Sandwich	$5–$7
One-Mile Taxi Ride	$5–$10
Museum Admission	Usually free

Prices in this guide are given for adults. Substantially reduced fees are almost always available for children, students, and senior citizens.

▌PACKING

A pair of comfortable shoes is your must-pack item. This is a walking town, and if you fail to pack for it, your feet will pay. D.C. isn't the most fashionable city in the country but people do look neat and presentable; business attire tends to be fairly conservative, and around college campuses and in hip neighborhoods like U Street Corridor or Adams Morgan, styles are more eclectic.

The most important element to consider, however, is the weather: D.C.'s temperatures can be extreme, and the right clothes are your best defense.

Winters are cold but sunny, with nighttime temperatures in the 20s and daytime highs in the 40s and 50s. Although the city doesn't normally get much snow, when it does, many streets won't be plowed for days, so if you're planning a visit for winter, bring a warm coat and hat and shoes that won't be ruined by snow and salt. Summers are muggy and very hot, with temperatures in the 80s and 90s and high humidity. Plan on cool, breathable fabrics, a hat for the sun, a sweater for overzealous air-conditioning, and an umbrella for daily thunderstorms. Fall and spring are less challenging, with temperatures in the 60s and occasional showers. Pants, lightweight sweaters, and light coats are appropriate.

▌RESTROOMS

Restrooms are found in all of the city's museums and galleries. Most are accessible to people in wheelchairs, and many are equipped with changing tables for babies. Locating a restroom is often difficult when you're strolling along the Mall. There are facilities at the Washington Monument, the Lincoln Memorial, the Jefferson Memorial, and Constitution Gardens, near the Vietnam Veterans Memorial, but these are not always as clean as they should be. The White House Visitors Center at 1450 Pennsylvania Avenue NW has a very nice public restroom.

Restrooms are also available in restaurants, hotels, and department stores. Unlike in many other cities, these businesses are usually happy to help out those in need. There's one state-of-the-art public restroom in the Huntington Station on the Metro. All other stations have restrooms available in cases of emergency; ask one of the uniformed attendants in the kiosks.

▌SAFETY

Washington, D.C., is a fairly safe city, but as with any major metropolitan area it's best to stay alert. Keep an eye on purses and backpacks, and be aware of your surroundings before you use an ATM, especially one that is outdoors. Assaults are rare but they do happen, especially late at night in Adams Morgan, Capitol Hill, Northeast D.C., and U Street Corridor. Public transportation is quite safe, but late at night, choose bus stops on busy streets over those on quiet ones. If someone threatens you with violence, it's best to hand over your money and seek help from police later. Also be careful with smartphones and other electronics, as it's not uncommon for thieves to snatch those devices straight from the hands of unsuspecting pedestrians and Metro riders.

▌TAXES

Washington's hotel tax is a whopping 14.5%. Maryland and Virginia charge hotel taxes of 5%–10%. The effective sales tax is 5.75% in D.C., 6% in Maryland, and 6% in Northern Virginia.

▌TIME

Washington, D.C., is in the Eastern time zone. It's 3 hours ahead of Los Angeles, 1 hour ahead of Chicago, 5 hours behind London, and 15 hours behind Sydney.

▍ TIPPING

Bartender	$1–$5 per round of drinks, depending on the number of drinks
Bellhop	$1–$5 per bag, depending on the level of the hotel
Coat Check	$1–$2 per coat
Hotel Concierge	$5 or more, depending on the service
Hotel Doorman	$1–$5 for help with bags or hailing a cab
Hotel Maid	$2–$5 a day (either daily or at the end of your stay, in cash)
Hotel Room Service Waiter	$1–$2 per delivery, even if a service charge has been added
Porter at Airport or Train Station	$1 per bag
Restroom Attendants	$1 or small change
Skycap at Airport	$1–$3 per bag checked
Spa Personnel	15%–20% of the cost of your service
Taxi Driver	15%, but round up the fare to the next dollar amount
Tour Guide	10% of the cost of the tour
Valet Parking Attendant	$2–$5, each time your car is brought to you
Waiter	15%–20%, with 20% being the norm at high-end restaurants; nothing additional if a service charge is added to the bill

▍ TOURS

For more tours, please see "The Best Tours in D.C." section in the Experience chapter.

GUIDED TOURS

Several tour companies provide multi-day tours that either focus on or include Washington, D.C., in their itineraries.

Recommended Companies Mayflower Tours. ☎ 800/323–7604 ⊕ www.mayflowertours.com. **Smithsonian Journeys.** ☎ 855/330–1542 ⊕ www.smithsonianjourneys.org. **Tauck.** ☎ 800/788–7885 ⊕ www.tauck.com.

SPECIAL-INTEREST TOURS

Road Scholar. Presented in conjunction with the Close Up Foundation, the nation's largest nonprofit citizenship education organization, Road Scholar offers a series of distinct tours through Washington. "Monumental D.C." is a four-night program that includes seminars on many of the figures memorialized on and near the National Mall. "A Capital Intergenerational Adventure" caters to kids accompanied by their grandparents. It features a wide array of visits through Mount Vernon, the monuments, Smithsonian museums, and the Spy Museum. "Discover Washington, D.C.: The Best of the Capital" is a five-night stay targeting all of the city's most prominent historical and cultural wonders, guided by scholars and local experts throughout. There's even a four-night genealogy tour that lets visitors dig deep into their ancestry at the National Archives and the Library of Congress. ☎ 800/454–5768 ⊕ www.roadscholar.org ➳ From $999.

DAY TOURS AND GUIDES

There are various excellent tour options for discovering the nation's capital, many of them led by highly qualified experts, some with a touch of theater, and all worth an hour, a day, or more of your time. You are sure to learn something you wouldn't have found out on your own.

For families we recommend the bike tours (or Segway tours if all kids are over 16), the DC Ducks tour (younger kids will get a kick out of the quackers that are given to all riders), a mule-drawn barge ride on the C&O Canal, and any of Natalie Zanin's historic strolls, especially the Ghost Story Tour of Washington.

BICYCLE TOURS

Adventure Cycling Association. ☎ 800/755–2453 ⊕ www.adventurecycling.org. **Capital Bikeshare.** ☎ 877/430–2453 ⊕ www.capital-bikeshare.com.

BOAT TOURS

Washington tour operators make the most of the city's waterways, which offer a unique perspective on the sights and a relaxing experience. Some cruises include meals on board, some have a historical focus, and DC Ducks and the Potomac Riverboat Company's pirate cruises appeal particularly to children.

Contacts C&O Canal Barges. ⊠ Great Falls Tavern Visitor Center, 11710 MacArthur Blvd., Potomac ☎ 301/739–4200 ⊕ www.nps.gov/choh. **Capitol River Cruises.** ⊠ Washington Harbor, 31st and K Sts. NW, Georgetown ☎ 301/460–7447, 800/405–5511 ⊕ www.capitolrivercruises.com. **DC Sail.** ⊠ 600 Water St., SW, D.C. Waterfront ☎ 202/547–1250 ⊕ www.dcsail.org. **Odyssey III and Spirit of Washington.** ⊠ 600 Water St. SW, D.C. Waterfront ☎ 202/488–6010, 866/306–2469 ⊕ www.odysseycruises.com. **Potomac Riverboat Company.** ⊠ 205 The Strand, Alexandria ☎ 877/511–2628, 703/684–0580 ⊕ www.potomacriverboatco.com.

BUS AND TROLLEY TOURS

A number of companies run hop-on, hop-off services that give you the freedom to see all the major sights and disembark to explore the ones that hold the most interest for you. The two-day tickets are good value, particularly as it's unlikely you'll see everything you want to in just one day.

Contacts Arlington National Cemetery Tours. ☎ 866/754–9014 ⊕ www.arlington-tours.com. **Big Bus Tours.** ☎ 877/332–8689 ⊕ www.bigbustours.com. **Gray Line.** ☎ 202/779–9894, 800/862–1400 ⊕ www.graylinedc.com. **On Board D.C. Tours.** ☎ 301/839–5261 ⊕ www.washingtondctours.onboardtours.com.

GOVERNMENT BUILDING TOURS

Special tours of government buildings with heavy security, including the White House and the Capitol, can be arranged through your U.S. representative or senator's office. Limited numbers of these so-called VIP tickets are available, so plan up to six months in advance of your trip. Foreign visitors should contact their embassy in Washington, D.C., as far in advance as possible. Governmental buildings close to visitors when the Department of Homeland Security issues a high alert, so call ahead.

MEDIA TOURS

Contacts National Public Radio. ⊠ 1111 N. Capitol St. NE, Northeast ☎ 202/513–2000 ⊕ www.npr.org Ⓜ New York Ave./Gallaudet University - Red Line. **Voice of America.** ⊠ 330 Independence Ave. SW, Capitol Hill ☎ 202/203–4990 ⊕ www.voatour.com.

PHOTO TOURS

Contacts City Photo Walking Tours. ☎ 202/246–5683 ⊕ www.cpwtours.com. **Washington Photo Safari.** ☎ 202/537–0937 ⊕ www.washingtonphotosafari.com.

PRIVATE GUIDES

There's no better way to get the best out of your visit to Washington, D.C., than to hire someone to take you exactly where you want to go and dedicate their expertise to you and your party alone.

Contacts A Tour de Force. ☎ 703/525–2948 ⊕ www.atourdeforce.com. **D.C. Sightseeing.** ☎ 301/437–2345 ⊕ www.dcsightseeing.com.

SEGWAY AND SCOOTER TOURS

Rest your feet and glide by the monuments, museums, and major attractions aboard a Segway. Guided tours usually last between two and three hours. D.C. city ordinance requires that riders be at least 16 years old; some tour companies have weight restrictions of 250 pounds. Tours, limited to 6 to 10 people, begin with an instruction session.

Contacts Capital Segway. ☎ 202/682–1980 ⊕ www.capitalsegway.com Ⓜ McPherson Sq. **City Segway Tours.** ☎ 877/734–8687 ⊕ www.citysegwaytours.com. **Scootaround Inc.** ☎ 888/441–7575 ⊕ www.scootaround.com. **Segs in the City.** ☎ 800/734–7393 ⊕ www.segsinthecity.com.

WALKING TOURS

Variety is the spice of the many walking tours that explore the city, ranging from standard sightseeing to themed tours with a focus on anything from historical events to hauntings to neighborhood culinary heritage.

Contacts Capitol Historical Society. ☎ 202/543–8919 ⊕ www.uschs.org. **DC Metro Food Tours.** ☎ 202/683–8847, 800/979–3370 ⊕ www.dcmetrofoodtours.com. **DC Walkabout.** ☎ 202/421–4053 ⊕ www.dcwalkabout.com. **History on Foot.** ☎ 202/347–4833 ⊕ www.fords.org. **Natalie Zanin's Historic Strolls.** ☎ 301/346–5303 ⊕ www.historicstrolls.com. **The Smithsonian Associates.** ☎ 202/633–3030 ⊕ www.smithsonianassociates.org. **Spies of Washington Tour.** ☎ 703/569–1875 ⊕ www.spiesofwashingtontour.com. **U.S. National Arboretum.** ☎ 202/245–2726 ⊕ www.usna.usda.gov.

▌ VISITOR INFORMATION

Destination D.C.'s free, 85-page publication, the *Official Visitors' Guide,* is full of sightseeing tips, maps, and contacts. You can order a copy online or by phone, or pick one up in their office (enter on I Street).

Most of the popular sights in D.C. are run by either the National Park Service (NPS) or the Smithsonian, both of which have recorded information about locations and hours of operation.

Events and Attractions National Park Service. ☎ 202/619–7275 "Dial-a-Park" ⊕ www.nps.gov. **Smithsonian.** ☎ 202/633–1000, 202/633–5285 TTY ⊕ www.si.edu. **White House Visitor Center.** ✉ 1450 Pennsylvania Ave. NW, White House area ☎ 202/208–1631 ⊕ www.nps.gov/whho.

State Information State of Maryland. ☎ 866/639–3526 ⊕ www.visitmaryland.org. **Virginia Tourism Corporation.** ☎ 800/847–4882 ⊕ www.virginia.org.

Tourist Information Destination DC. ✉ 901 7th St. NW, 4th fl., Downtown ☎ 202/789–7000, 800/422–8644 ⊕ www.washington.org.

FODORS.COM CONNECTION

Before your trip, be sure to check out what other travelers are saying in the Forums on ⊕ www.fodors.com.

ALL ABOUT WASHINGTON, D.C.

Cultural Tourism D.C. (⊕ *www.culturaltourismdc.org*) is a nonprofit coalition whose mission is to highlight the city's arts and heritage. Their website is loaded with great information about sights, special events, and neighborhoods, including self-guided walking tours.

DowntownDC Business Improvement District (⊕ *www.downtowndc.org*) is a nonprofit that oversees the 140-block area from the White House to the U.S. Capitol. The website has special events, shopping, and dining listings and information about the wonderful red-, white-, and blue-uniformed D.C. SAMs, roving hospitality specialists linked to a central dispatcher by radio. In spring and summer, SAMs (which stands for Safety, Administration, and Maintenance) are available to help visitors with directions, information, and emergencies. You'll spot their hospitality kiosks near Metro stops and major attractions.

The **Smithsonian website** (⊕ *www.si.edu*) is a good place to start planning a trip to the Mall and its museums. The **National Gallery** has its own website, too (⊕ *www.nga.gov*). You can check out the exhibitions and events that will be held during your visit.

GAY AND LESBIAN

Washington, D.C., is a very inclusive town, with an active gay community and plenty of gay-friendly hotels, nightlife, and events. In addition to news and features, both *Washington Blade* (⊕ *www.washingtonblade.com*) and *Metro Weekly* (⊕ *www.metroweekly.com*) have guides to gay bars and clubs, including calendars of events.

KIDS AND FAMILIES

Washingtonfamily.com (⊕ *www.washingtonfamily.com*) compiles a "Best for Families" feature, as voted on by area families. Families may also want to check out **washingtonparent.com** (⊕ *www.washingtonparent.com*) and **kidfriendlydc.com** (⊕ *www.kidfriendlydc.com*), a blog with loads of kid-friendly events, deals, and activities.

NEWS AND HAPPENINGS

The website of the *Washington Post* (⊕ *www.washingtonpost.com*) has a fairly comprehensive listing of what's going on around town. Also check out the site of *Washington CityPaper* (⊕ *www.washingtoncitypaper.com*), a free weekly newspaper. The *Washingtonian* (⊕ *www.washingtonian.com*) is a monthly magazine.

CultureCapital (⊕ *www.culturecapital. org*), a nonprofit group promoting the city's culture and arts, has an online link (⊕ *www.ticketplace.org*) with dozens of theater, dance, music, and opera performances offering half-price tickets.

For personalized emails of things to do, member reviews, and listings of half-price show and event tickets in D.C. and other major cities nationwide, register for free at ⊕ *www.goldstar.com*, an online entertainment company.

INDEX

A

A Mano (shop), *245*
Adam's Inn ⊞, *173*
Adams Morgan area, 14,
  100–102
  dining, 103, 143–144
  exploring, 100, 103
  lodging, 173–174
  nightlife, 188–189
  performing arts, 209
  shopping, 250–251
  transportation, 103
Addresses, *13*
African-American Civil War
  Memorial, *22, 107*
Air travel, *12–13, 284–285*
Akwaaba D.C. ⊞, *171*
Alexandria, Virginia, *256,
  259–267*
Alexandria Black History
  Museum, *263*
Alexandria's Farmers' Market,
  263
American Red Cross, *58*
American Revolution Institute of
  the Society of the Cincinnati,
  95, 98
American Veterans Disabled for
  Life Memorial, *87*
Amsterdam Falafel ✕, *103*
Anacostia Riverwalk, *78*
Annapolis (Maryland), *257,
  273–282*
Annapolis Waterfront Hotel
  ⊞, *282*
Appomattox Confederate
  Statue, *260*
Arena Stage, *204*
Arlington and Northern Vir-
  ginia, 14, 113–124
  dining, 115, 149–150
  exploring, 113, 116–124
  lodging, 175–176
  nightlife, 195–196
  performing arts, 211–212
  transportation, 114, 120
Arlington House, *122*
Arlington National Cemetery,
  17, 113, 114, 117–123
Arsenal at Bluejacket, The ✕,
  132
Art and Soul ✕, *129*
Art galleries ⇨ *See* Museums
  and galleries
Art Museum of the Americas,
  58

Arts, *197–212*
Ashby Inn ✕, *149*
Athenaeum, *263*
Avenue Suites Georgetown
  ⊞, *162*

B

Banneker-Douglass Museum,
  274
Barracks Row, *65*
Bars and lounges
  Adams Morgan, 188–189
  *Arlington and Northern Vir-
    ginia, 195–196*
  *Capitol Hill and Northeast
    D.C., 180, 181*
  Downtown, 182–183
  *Dupont Circle and Logan
    Circle, 185–186, 187*
  Georgetown, 184
  U Street Corridor, 190–193
  *White House area and Foggy
    Bottom, 179–180*
Barmini, *182–183*
Baseball, *225*
Basketball, *225*
Bayou ✕, *139*
Beau Thai ✕, *132–133*
Belga Café ✕, *129*
Belmont-Paul Women's Equality
  National Monument, *66*
Ben's Chili Bowl ✕, *22, 107,
  145*
Betsy Fisher (shop), *248*
Bibiana Osteria and Enoteca
  ✕, *133*
Bicycling, *20, 219–220,
  226–227, 269–270, 294*
Biergartenhaus (bar), *181*
Birchmere, The (club), *181, 196*
Birchmere Music Hall, The, *212*
Bishop's Garden, *109*
Bistro Bis ✕, *129–130*
Bistrot du Coin ✕, *141*
Bistrot Lepic ✕, *148*
"Black Broadway," *22.* ⇨ *See
  also* U Street Corridor
Black Cat (club), *194*
Black Salt ✕, *148*
Bloom (shop), *249–250*
Blue Duck Tavern ✕, *128–129*
Blues Alley (club), *181,
  184–185*
Boat tours, *20–21, 294*
  Annapolis, 274
  C&O Canal, 219–220
  Mount Vernon, 268

Boating and sailing, *228–229*
  *White House area and Foggy
    Bottom, 57*
Bombay Club ✕, *133*
Bourbon Steak ✕, *139*
Boyhood home of Robert E.
  Lee, *260*
Brasserie Beck ✕, *133*
Buddy's Crabs & Ribs ✕, *279*
Bureau of Engraving and Print-
  ing, *25, 52*
Bus tours, *20, 268, 294*
Bus travel, *12, 286–287*
Busboys and Poets ✕, *107*
Business hours, *291*
  nightlife, 179
  restaurants, 127
  shops, 235
Business services, *291*

C

C&O Canal, *91, 219–220*
Café Normandie ✕, *279*
Cantler's Riverside Inn ✕, *279*
Capital Pride Festival, *26*
Capitol Building, *62*
Capitol Hill and Northeast D.C.,
  14, 16, 62–78
  dining, 129–132
  exploring, 62–66, 70–78
  lodging, 164–165
  nightlife, 180–181
  performing arts, 203–205
  shopping, 238–240
  transportation, 80
Capitol Hill Hotel ⊞, *164*
Capitol Hilton ⊞, *165*
Capitol Steps (comedy club),
  183
Capitol Visitor Center, *65,
  70, 77*
Captain's Row (Alexandria),
  263
Car rental, *288*
Car travel, *12, 287–289*
Carlyle Hotel Dupont Circle
  ⊞, *171*
Carlyle House, *260–261*
Carrol's Creek ✕, *279*
Catch Can (shop), *253*
Cava Mezze ✕, *130*
Cemeteries
  *Arlington National Cemetery,
    17, 113, 114, 117–123*
  Congressional Cemetery, 75
Chamber music, *207, 208*

Cherry Blossom Festival, 26, 224

Chez Billy Sud ✕, 91

Chick and Ruth's Delly ✕, 279

Children, attractions for, 25, 296

Banneker-Douglass Museum, 274

Bureau of Engraving and Printing, 25, 52

C&O Canal, 91, 219–220

Capitol Visitor Center, 65, 70, 77

D.C. Ducks, 25

Daughters of the American Revolution Museum (DAR), 59

Discovery Theater, 25

Dumbarton Oaks, 17, 89, 91, 93, 216, 218

Eastern Market, 65, 237, 239

Friendship Fire House, 263

Gadsby's Tavern Museum, 261

Georgetown, 89

Gunston Hall, 256, 267, 271–273

International Spy Museum, 25, 80, 81

lodging, 159, 162, 163, 164–165, 167, 169, 171–172, 173, 174, 176

Mount Vernon, 25, 268–270

National Air and Space Museum, 25, 37, 39–43

National Archives, 80, 81, 82–83

National Building Museum, 81, 84

National Geographic Society, 94–95, 96

National Museum of American History, 25, 46–47

National Museum of Natural History, 25, 47–48

National Museum of the American Indian, 47

National Museum of the Marine Corps, 273–273

National Museum of the US Navy, 78

National Portrait Gallery, 80, 81, 84

National Postal Museum, 75–76

National Zoo, 17, 25, 109, 111

Newseum, 80, 81, 85–86

President Lincoln's Cottage, 112

restaurants, 128, 130, 131, 132, 133, 135, 136, 137, 138, 142, 145, 147, 148, 149, 150

shopping, 236, 238, 239, 245

Smithsonian American Art Museum, 81, 86

Smithsonian National Museum of African Art, 48

Smithsonian National Postal Museum, 75–76

Stabler-Leadbeater Apothecary Museum, 264

Thompson's Boat Center, 57

Torpedo Factory Art Center, 262

Tudor Place, 91, 93, 218–219

U.S. Naval Academy Museum, 277

United States Botanic Garden, 65

United States National Arboretum, 219

Washington Monument, 16, 51

Washington National Cathedral, 17, 77, 109, 111, 112

Washington Navy Yard, 78

White House, 55

Woodlawn, 270–271

zoos, 17, 25, 47, 109, 111

China Chilcano ✕, 136

Chinatown, 136–139, 168, 168

Ching Ching Cha ✕, 91

Choral music, 202, 204, 210–211

Christ Church, 261

Christian Heurich House Museum, 99

Churches, mosques, and synagogues

Christ Church, 261

Old Presbyterian Meetinghouse, 264

St. Anne's Church, 278

United States Naval Academy Chapel, 277

Washington National Cathedral, 17, 77, 109, 111, 112

Churchill Hotel Near Embassy Row 🏨, 173

Climate, 12

Columbia Room (bar), 191

Comedy clubs, 183

Comfort Inn Downtown D.C/ Convention Center 🏨, 165–166

Comic Ping Pong ✕, 148

Communications, 291

Congress, 60

Congressional Cemetery, 75

Convivial ✕, 143

Cork ✕, 145

Cork Wine Bar, 191

Courtyard Washington Capitol Hill/Navy Yard 🏨, 164

Courtyard Washington/Dupont Circle 🏨, 173–174

Credit cards, 7

D

D.C. Ducks, 25

Dabney, The ✕, 143

Daikaya ✕, 136

Dance, 201, 203

Dance clubs

Adams Morgan, 189

Downtown, 183

Dupont Circle and Logan Circle, 187

U Street Corridor, 193–194

White House area and Foggy Bottom, 180

Das ✕, 139

Daughters of the American Revolution Museum (DAR), 59

DC Improv, 183

Department of State, 54

Department of State's Diplomatic Reception Room, 57

Department of the Interior, 59, 61

Department of the Interior Museum, 59, 61

DBGB Kitchen and Bar ✕, 133

DGS Delicatessen ✕, 96, 141

Dining. ⇨See Restaurants

Dirty Habit ✕, 136

Discovery Theater, 25

District of Columbia War Memorial, 52

District Taco ✕, 133

Doi Moi ✕, 145

Don Taco ✕, 264

Donovan House 🏨, 166

Douglass, Frederick, 76

Downtown Washington, 14, 79–88

dining, 81, 132–136

exploring, 79, 82–88

lodging, 165–168

nightlife, 182–183

performing arts, 205–207

safety, 81

shopping, 240–242

transportation, 80

Dubliner (bar), 180

Dumbarton Oaks, 17, 89, 91, 93

Dupont Circle, 14, 94–99

dining, 96, 141–143

exploring, 94–95, 98–99

lodging, 171–173

nightlife, 185–187

performing arts, 207–209

shopping, 247–250
transportation, 97
Dupont Circle Hotel, The ⌧,
171

E

Eamonn's A Dublin Chipper
×, 264
East City Bookshop, 238
East Potomac Park, 220, 226
Eastern Market, 65, 237, 239
EatBar ×, 130
Echostage (club), 182
Eighteenth Street Lounge, 185
El Camino ×, 145
Ella-Rue (shop), 246
Embassy Circle Guest House
⌧, 171
Embassy Row Hotel, The ⌧,
171
Embassy Suites Alexandria-Old
Town ⌧, 266
Embassy Suites Washington
D.C. ⌧, 162
Emergencies, 289
Eno ×, 139
Epic Smokehouse ×, 115
Estadio ×, 143
Ethiopic ×, 130
Exploring, 28–124
Extreme Pizza ×, 115

F

Fahrney's Pens (shop), 241
Fairfax at Embassy Row, The
⌧, 171
Fairfield Inn & Suites Washing-
ton DC/Downtown ⌧, 168
Fairmont, Washington, D.C.
Georgetown, The ⌧, 162
Fairy Godmother (shop), 238
Farmers' market, 263
Federal Reserve Building, 61
Festivals and seasonal events
Capital Fringe Festival, 204
Capital Pride Festival, 26
Cherry Blossom Festival, 26,
224
Flower Mart, 26
free events, 24
Georgetown French Market, 26
Independence Day, 26
National Book Festival, 26
National Cathedral Flower
Mart, 26
National Cherry Blossom
Festival, 26
National Christmas Tree Light-
ing/Pageant of Peace, 26

National Symphony Orchestra
Labor Day Concert, 26
Restaurant Week, 26
Smithsonian Folklife Festival, 26
Smithsonian Institution, 200
Veterans Day, 26
Washington Auto Show, 26
Washington International Horse
Show, 26
Washington Shakespeare The-
atre Free for All, 26
Film
Downtown, 205
Dupont Circle, 208
festivals, 208
White House area, 200
Fiola ×, 134
Flash (dance club), 193
Fodor's choice, 7
Foggy Bottom, 54–61
dining, 57, 128–129
lodging, 162–164
nightlife, 180
performing arts, 201–203
shopping, 237
transportation, 57
Fojol Brothers (food truck), 135
Folger Shakespeare Library,
66, 204
Folger Theater, 205
Food trucks, 135
Football, 229
Ford's Theatre, 79
Fort Reno Park, 220
49 West Coffeehouse, Winebar
and Gallery ×, 279, 281
Founding Farmers ×, 57
Four Seasons Hotel, Washing-
ton, D.C. ⌧, 169
Franklin Delano Roosevelt
Memorial, 16, 30–31
Frederick Douglass National
Historic Site, 76
Free attractions and events, 24
Freer Gallery of Art, 31
Fresh Farm Market, 237
Friendship Firehouse Museum,
263
Friendship Heights, 111
Full Kee ×, 136–137

G

Gadsby's Tavern Museum, 261
Galleries. ⇨ See Museums and
galleries
Galway Bay ×, 281
Gardens, 216, 218–219
Bishop's Garden, 109

Dumbarton Oaks, 17, 89, 91,
93, 216, 218
Hillwood Estate, Museum and
Gardens, 108, 218
Hirshhorn Museum and Sculp-
ture Garden, 31, 34
Historic London Town and
Gardens, 275
Kenilworth Park & Aquatic
Gardens, 218
Kahlil Gibran Memorial Gar-
den, 218
Lee Fendall House Museum &
Garden, 362
Tudor Place, 91, 93, 218–219
United States Botanic Garden,
65, 219
United States National Arbore-
tum, 219
William Paca House and Gar-
den, 277–278
Gay and lesbian, 186, 295
George Washington Masonic
National Memorial, 262
George Washington University
Museum, 98
Georgetown, 14, 89–93
dining, 91, 139–140
exploring, 89, 93
history, 92
lodging, 169–170
nightlife, 184–185
performing arts, 207
shopping, 242–247
transportation, 91
Georgetown French Market, 26
Georgetown Suites ⌧, 169
Glover Park Hotel ⌧, 174
Good Stuff Eatery ×, 130
GoodWood (shop), 251
Government building tours,
72, 294
Graffiato ×, 137
Graham Georgetown, The ⌧,
169
Grand Hyatt Washington ⌧,
166
Granville Moore's Brickyard ×,
130–131, 181
Guided tours, 72, 293
Gunston Hall, 256, 267,
271–272

H

H Street Country Club, 181
Hamilton, The ×, 134, 179
Hamilton Crowne Plaza ⌧, 166
Hammond-Harwood House,
274–275

Hank's Oyster Bar ✕, 141, 185
Harry Browne's ✕, 281
Hay-Adams Hotel 🔲, 160
Hazel ✕, 145
Hemphill Fine Arts (shop), 247
Henley Park Hotel 🔲, 166
Heurich House Museum, 99
Hiking, 230
Hill Country ✕, 137
Hillwood Estate, Museum and Gardens, 108, 218
Hilton Garden Inn/U.S. Capitol 🔲, 164
Hirshhorn Museum and Sculpture Garden, 31, 34
Historic Annapolis Museum, 278
Historic Inns of Annapolis 🔲, 282
Historic London Town and Gardens, 275
Hockey, 231
Holiday Inn Capitol 🔲, 164–165
Homewood Suites by Hilton, Washington 🔲, 171–172
Hotel George, The 🔲, 165
Hotel Hive 🔲, 162–163
Hotel Lombardy 🔲, 163
Hotel Madera 🔲, 172
Hotel Monaco 🔲, 166
Hotel Rouge 🔲, 172–173
Hotels. ➯See Lodging
Howard Theatre, 22, 209
Hula Girl (food truck), 135
Hu's Shoes (shop), 246
Hyatt Centric Arlington 🔲, 175
Hyatt Place Washington DC/Georgetown/West End 🔲, 163

I

Ice skating, 231
Independence Day, 26
Indian Craft Shop, 61, 235
Inn at Little Washington ✕, 149
International Spy Museum, 25, 80, 81
Internet, 291
Iron Gate ✕, 141
Iron Rooster ✕, 281
Itineraries, 18–19
Izakaya Seki ✕, 145–146

J

Jack Rose Dining Saloon ✕, 146
Jaleo ✕, 137
Jazz and blues clubs

Capitol Hill and Northeast D.C., 181
Georgetown, 184–185
northeast D.C., 182
suburban Virginia, 196
U Street Corridor, 194–195
Jefferson, The 🔲, 166–167
Jimmy T's Place ✕, 131
John F. Kennedy Center for the Performing Arts, 57, 201, 202
Julia's Empanadas ✕, 103
JW Marriott 🔲, 167

K

Kabob Palace ✕, 150
Kafe Leopold ✕, 140
Kapnos ✕, 146
Kaz Sushi Bistro ✕, 134
Kenilworth Park & Aquatic Gardens, 218
Kennedy Center, 57, 201, 202
Kennedy Graves, 122
Key Bridge Marriott 🔲, 175
Kimpton Lorien Hotel & Spa 🔲, 266
Kinship ✕, 137
Komi ✕, 141–142
Korean War Veterans Memorial, 17, 34
Kramerbooks & Afterwords ✕, 96, 142, 237, 248
Kreeger Museum, 112
Kunta Kinte–Alex Haley Memorial, 278

L

La Chaumière ✕, 140
Landmark's E Street Cinema, 205
Lapis ✕, 143–144
Le Diplomate ✕, 146
Le Méridien Arlington 🔲, 175
Le Refuge ✕, 265
Lectures, 206
Lee, Robert E., boyhood home of, 260
Lee-Fendall House Museum & Garden, 262
Lettie Gooch Boutique, 252
Liaison Capitol Hill, The 🔲, 165
Libraries
Folger Shakespeare Library, 66, 204
Library of Congress, 62–63, 65, 77
Library of Congress, 62–63, 65, 77

Lincoln Memorial, 16, 34–36
Lincoln Theater, 210
Little Serow ✕, 142
Lloyd House, 264
Lodging, 7, 157–176
atlas, 151–156
children, 159, 162, 163, 164–165, 167, 169, 171–172, 173, 174, 176
facilities, 159
hotel bars, 170
neighborhoods, 161
parking, 159
prices, 159–160
reservations, 159
side trips, 266–267
Loews Madison Hotel 🔲, 167
Logan Circle, 14, 94–99, 143, 170–173, 187–188
Lyceum, 262

M

M Street, 91
Madame Tussauds, 87
Madison Building Cafeteria ✕, 65
Makoto ✕, 148–149
Malcolm X Park, 221
Mall, The, 14, 32–53, 231
Mansion on O Street 🔲, 172
Marcel's ✕, 129
Marian Koshland Science Museum, 81, 87
Marijuana, 11
Marine Corps Barracks and Commandant's House, 76
Market Lunch, The ✕, 131
Markets, 237, 239–240
Marriott Marquis Washington D.C. 🔲, 167
Martin Luther King Jr. National Memorial, 17, 36–37
Maryland
Annapolis, 257, 273–282
dining, 274, 279, 281
lodging, 282
Maryland State House, 276
Mason & Rook 🔲, 172
Mason Social ✕, 265
Mayflower Hotel, Autograph Collection, The 🔲, 167
Media tours, 294
Melrose Georgetown Hotel 🔲, 169
Memorial Parks, 231
Meridian Hill Park, 221
Metro (subway), 12, 289
minibar by José Andrés ✕, 137
Mintwood Place ✕, 144

Miss Pixie's (shop), 237, 251
Momofuku CCDC ✕, 134
Money matters, 291
Monuments and memorials
African-American Civil War
 Memorial, 22
American Veterans Disabled for
 Life Memorial, 87
Appomattox Confederate
 Statue, 260
Arlington National Cemetery,
 17, 113, 114, 117–123
Belmont-Paul Women's Equality
 National Monument, 66
District of Columbia War
 Memorial, 52
Franklin Delano Roosevelt
 Memorial, 16, 30–31
George Washington Masonic
 National Memorial, 262
Jefferson Memorial, 16
Korean War Veterans Memorial,
 17, 34
Kunta Kinte–Alex Haley Memo-
 rial, 278
Lincoln Memorial, 16, 34–36
Martin Luther King Jr. National
 Memorial, 17, 36–37
National Law Enforcement
 Officers Memorial, 87–88
National World War II Memo-
 rial, 17, 48
Park Rangers, 52
Pentagon Memorial, 116
Statue of Tecumseh, 277
Thomas Jefferson, 49
Thurgood Marshall, 276
Tidal Basin, 25, 221, 224, 229
Tomb of the Unknowns, 123
United States Air Force Memo-
 rial, 114, 124
United States Marine Corps War
 Memorial, 114
United States Navy Memorial,
 88
Vietnam Veterans Memorial,
 17, 50–51
Washington Monument, 16, 51
Morrison-Clark Historic Inn
 ☴, 167
Morrison House ☴, 266
Motorcades, 13
Mount Vernon (Virginia), 25,
 256, 267–270
Mr. Henry's (club), 181
Museums and galleries, 234
Alexandria Black History
 Museum, 263

American Revolution Institute
 of the Society of the Cincin-
 nati, 95, 98
Art Museum of the Americas, 58
Athenaeum, 263
Banneker-Douglass Museum,
 274
Carlyle House, 260–261
Christian Heurich House
 Museum, 99
Cross MacKenzie Gallery, 244
Daughters of the American Rev-
 olution Museum (DAR), 59
Department of the Interior
 Museum, 59–61
Dumbarton Oaks, 17, 89, 91,
 93
Folger Shakespeare Library,
 66, 204
Frederick Douglass National
 Historic Site, 76
Freer Gallery of Art, 31
Gadsby's Tavern Museum, 261
George Washington University
 Museum, 98
Hammond-Harwood House,
 274–275
Hemphill Fine Arts, 247
Heurich House Museum, 99
Hillwood Estate, Museum and
 Gardens, 108, 218
Hirshhorn Museum and Sculp-
 ture Garden, 31, 34
Historic Annapolis Museum,
 278
International Spy Museum, 25,
 80, 81
Kreeger Museum, 112
Lee-Fendall House, 362
Lyceum, 262
Madame Tussauds, 87
Marian Koshland Science
 Museum, 81, 87
National Air and Space
 Museum, 25, 37, 39–43
National Air and Space Museum
 Steven F. Udvar-Hazy Center,
 39, 114, 116
National Archives, 80, 81,
 82–83
National Book Festival, 26
National Building Museum,
 81, 84
National Gallery of Art, East
 Building, 37, 44
National Gallery of Art, West
 Building, 44
National Gallery of Art Ice
 Rink, 231

National Geographic Society,
 94–95, 96
National Law Enforcement
 Officers Memorial, 87–88
National Museum of African
 American History and Cul-
 ture, 10–11, 44, 46
National Museum of American
 History, 25, 46–47
National Museum of Natural
 History, 25, 47–48
National Museum of the Ameri-
 can Indian, 47
National Museum of the Marine
 Corps, 272–273
National Museum of the US
 Navy, 76–77
National Museum of Women in
 the Arts, 88
National Portrait Gallery, 80,
 81, 84
National Postal Museum, 75–76
Newseum, 80, 81, 85–86
Old Stone House, 93
Phillips Collection, 95, 96
President Lincoln's Cottage, 112
Renwick Gallery, 55
Smithsonian American Art
 Museum, 81, 86
Smithsonian National Museum
 of African Art, 48
Smithsonian National Postal
 Museum, 75–76
Stabler-Leadbeater Apothecary
 Museum, 264
Textile Museum, 98
Thurgood Marshall Memorial,
 276
Torpedo Factory Art Center,
 262
Tudor Place, 91, 93
U.S. Naval Academy Museum,
 277
United States Holocaust Memo-
 rial Museum, 49–50
Washington Navy Yard, 78
Woodrow Wilson House, 96, 99
Music
Capitol Hill and Northeast
 D.C., 204
Dupont Circle, 188, 208
Foggy Bottom, 202–203
Georgetown, 184–185, 207
U Street Corridor, 107,
 194–195, 210
Upper Northwest, 210–211
White House area and Foggy
 Bottom, 200

Music clubs
Adams Morgan, *189*
Arlington and Northern Virginia, *195*
Capitol Hill, *181*
Northeast D.C., *182*
U Street Corridor, *107, 194–195*
Music performance series, *200, 203, 211, 212*
myArchives Store, *235–236, 237*

N

Nasime ✕, *265–266*
National Air and Space Museum, *25, 37, 39–43*
National Air and Space Museum Steven F. Udvar-Hazy Center, *39, 114, 116*
National Air and Space Museum Store, *236*
National Archives, *80, 81, 82–83*
National Book Festival, *26*
National Building Museum, *81, 84*
National Cathedral Flower Mart, *26*
National Cherry Blossom Festival, *26*
National Christmas Tree Lighting/Pageant of Peace, *26*
National Gallery of Art, East Building, *37, 44*
National Gallery of Art, West Building, *44*
National Geographic Society, *94–95, 96*
National Law Enforcement Officers Memorial, *87–88*
National Mall, *14, 32–53, 231*
National Museum of African American History and Culture, *10–11, 44, 46*
National Museum of American History, *25, 46–47*
National Museum of Natural History, *25, 47–48*
National Museum of the American Indian, *47*
National Museum of the Marine Corps, *272–273*
National Museum of the US Navy, *76–77*
National Museum of Women in the Arts, *88*
National Portrait Gallery, *80, 81, 84*
National Postal Museum, *75–76*

National Symphony Orchestra Labor Day Concert, *26*
National Theater, *206*
National World War II Memorial, *17, 48*
National Zoo, *17, 25, 109, 111*
Nationals Park, *214–215*
Newseum, *80, 81, 85–86*
Nightlife, *177–196*
9:30 Club, *194*
Nora ✕, *142*
Normandy Hotel, The 🏨, *174*
Northeast DC, *14, 76–78*
exploring, 76–78
nightlife, 181–182
performing arts, 203–205

O

Obelisk ✕, *142*
Old Ebbitt Grill ✕, *134*
Old Presbyterian Meeting-house, *264*
Old Stone House, *93*
Omni Shoreham Hotel 🏨, *174*
On Rye ✕, *81*
Oohhs & Aahhs ✕, *146*
Opera, *202*
Opportunity Shop of the Christ Child Society, *244*
Orchestras, *202*
Osteria Morini ✕, *134*
Osteria 177 ✕, *281*
Oval Room, The ✕, *135*
Oyamel ✕, *138*

P

P.O.V. (club), *179–180, 181*
Packing for the trip, *292*
Paddleboating, *25*
Palomar, Washington D.C. 🏨, *172*
Park Hyatt, Washington 🏨, *163*
Parks, *219–221, 224*
Partisan, The ✕, *138*
Paul ✕, *135*
Pearl Dive Oyster Palace ✕, *146*
Pentagon, *113, 116*
Pentagon Memorial, *116*
Performance series (music), *200, 201*
Performance venues
Adams Morgan, 209
Arlington and Northern Virginia, 211–212
Capitol Hill and Northeast D.C., 203
Downtown, 205

Dupont Circle and Logan Circle, 207–209
Foggy Bottom, 201
Georgetown, 207
U Street Corridor, 209–210
Upper Northwest, 210–211
White House area, 199–200
Performing arts, *197–212*
Petersen House, *79*
Phillips Collection, *95, 96*
Phoenix, The (shop), *247*
Phoenix Park Hotel 🏨, *165*
Photo tours, *294*
Pineapple and Pearls ✕, *131*
POD Hotel DC 🏨, *168*
Politics & Prose (shop), *253*
Preserve ✕, *281*
President Lincoln's Cottage, *112*
Prices, *7, 127–128, 160, 291*
Private guides, *293, 294*
Proof ✕, *138*
Proper Topper (shop), *248–249*

R

Range ✕, *149*
Rasika ✕, *138*
Readings and lectures, *206*
Red Apron Butcher ✕, *81*
Red Hen ✕, *147*
Red Hook Lobster Pound (food truck), *135*
Renaissance Arlington Capitol View Hotel 🏨, *176*
Renaissance Washington, D.C. Downtown Hotel 🏨, *168*
Renwick Gallery, *55*
Residence Inn Arlington Pentagon City 🏨, *176*
Residence Inn Washington, D.C./Dupont Circle 🏨, *172*
Restaurant Week, *26*
Restaurants, *7, 11, 125–156*
Afghan, 143–144
American, 130, 131, 134, 138, 140, 142, 143, 145, 146, 147, 149
Asian, 134, 136
Asian fusion, 136
atlas, 151–156
Austrian, 140
barbecue, 137
Belgian, 129, 130–131, 133, 140
brasserie, 146
cafés, 142, 147
cafeteria, 65
Cajun, 139
children, 128, 130, 131, 132, 133, 135, 136, 137, 138, 142, 145, 147, 148, 149, 150

Chinese, 136–137
Chiu Chow, 145
contemporary, 130, 131, 132, 135, 137, 138, 144, 149
deli, 81, 141
diner, 132
dress, 127
eclectic, 134, 142
Ethiopian, 107, 130, 139
food trucks, 135
French, 129–130, 133, 135, 140, 141, 143, 144, 148, 149
Fusion, 136
Greek, 130, 146
hours, 127
Indian, 133, 138
Italian, 133, 134, 142
Japanese, 134, 140, 145–146, 148–149
Lao, 147
Latin American, 147
Mediterranean, 141–142
Mexican, 133, 138, 145
Middle Eastern, 138–139
modern American, 128–129, 131, 137, 138, 150
modern Asian, 145
modern Italian, 134, 137
Pakistani, 150
Peruvian, 136
pizza, 131–132, 148, 149
prices, 127–128
Ramen, 136, 144
reservations, 127
seafood, 141, 146, 148
side trips, 264–266, 274, 279, 281
smoking, 128
southern, 129, 146
Spanish, 137, 143
steak, 139
takeout, 57
taxes, 128
Thai, 132–133, 142
tipping, 128
wine bar, 132, 139, 145, 147–148
Restrooms, *292*
RFK Stadium, *215*
Ripple ✕, *149*
Ritz-Carlton Georgetown ☐, *169–170*
Ritz-Carlton Pentagon City ☐, *176*
Ritz-Carlton Washington, D.C. ☐, *163*
Robert F. Kennedy Stadium, *215*
Rock Creek Park, *220–221*

Ronald Reagan Building and International Trade Center, *88*
Roofers Union ✕, *144*
Room 11 ✕, *147*
Roosevelt Memorial, *16, 30–31*
Rose's Luxury ✕, *131*
Rosewood Washington D.C. ☐, *170*
Rouge Hotel ☐, *172–173*
Running, *231*

S

Safety concerns, *13, 292*
downtown, 81
U Street Corridor, 107
St. Anne's Church, *278*
St. Gregory Hotel & Suites ☐, *163*
St. John's College, *276*
St. Regis Washington, D.C. ☐, *168*
Sakuramen ✕, *144*
Salt & Sundry (shop), *249*
Scooter tours, *294*
Scotlaur Inn ☐, *282*
Sculpture Garden (Hirshhorn Museum), *31, 34*
Secondi (shop), *249*
Segway tours, *294*
1789 Restaurant ✕, *140*
Seventh Hill ✕, *131–132*
Shake Shack ✕, *115, 138*
Shakespeare Theatre Company, *206*
Shopping, *107, 233–254*
Side trips, *255–282*
Sightseeing tours, *20–21, 57,72*
Smithsonian American Art Museum, *81, 86*
Smithsonian Castle Information Center, *52–53*
Smithsonian Institution, *200*
Smithsonian National Museum of African Art, *48*
Smithsonian National Postal Museum, *75–76*
Smithsonian National Zoological Park, *17, 25, 109*
Smoking, *128*
Soccer, *232*
Sofitel Washington D.C. Lafayette Square ☐, *160*
Sonoma ✕, *132*
Sovereign, The ✕, *140*
Special-interest tours, *293*
Sports and outdoor activities, *213–232*
Stabler-Leadbeater Apothecary Museum, *264*

Streetcars, *10, 12*
Studio Gallery, *248*
Studio Theater, *208*
Subways, *12, 289*
Supreme Court Building, *63, 65, 66*
Sushiko ✕, *140*
Swann House ☐, *173*
Sweetgreen ✕, *142*
Symbols, *7*

T

Tabard Inn ✕, *143*
Tail Up Goat ✕, *144*
Taverna Cretekou ✕, *266*
Taxes, *128, 292*
Taxi travel, *12–13, 290*
Taylor Gourmet ✕, *147*
Teaism ✕, *136*
Tecumseh statue, *277*
Ted's Bulletin ✕, *132*
Textile Museum, *98*
Theater, *204–205, 208–209, 211, 212*
Theater District, *80*
Theodore Roosevelt Island, *63, 230*
Thip Khao ✕, *147*
Thomas Jefferson Memorial, *49*
Thompson's Boat Center, *57*
Thurgood Marshall Memorial, *276*
Tico ✕, *147*
Tidal Basin, *25, 221, 224, 229*
Time zone, *292*
Tiny Jewel Box (shop), *237, 241*
Tipping, *128, 293*
Tomb of the Unknowns, *123*
Torpedo Factory Art Center, *262*
Tours and packages, *20–21, 57, 72, 227, 260, 268, 273–274, 293–295*
Train travel, *290*
Transportation, *80, 259, 267, 268, 270, 273, 284–290*
Treasury Building, *61*
Trolley tours, *20, 294*
Tryst ✕, *103, 189*
Tudor Place, *91, 93, 218–219*
2941 Restaurant ✕, *150*
2 Amys ✕, *149*
2 Birds, 1 Stone (bar), *193*

U

U Street Corridor, *14, 104–107*
dining, 107, 144–148
exploring, 104–107
nightlife, 189–195

performing arts, 209–210
safety, 107
shopping, 251–252
transportation, 107
U.S. Naval Academy Museum,
277
U.S. Naval Observatory, *111*
Union Station, 239–240
United States Air Force Memo-
rial, *114, 124*
United States Botanic Garden,
65, 219
United States Holocaust Memo-
rial Museum, 49–50
United States Marine Corps
War Memorial, *114*
United States National Arbore-
tum, *219*
United States Naval Academy,
276–277
United States Naval Academy
Chapel, 277
United States Navy Memorial,
88
Upper Northwest, *14,* 108–112
dining, 111, 148–149
exploring, 108–112
lodging, 174–175
performing arts, 210–211
shopping, 111, 253–254
transportation, 111

V

Verizon Center, 215
Vermilion ✕, 266
Veterans Day, 26
Vietnam Veterans Memorial,
17, 50–51
Vin *909* ✕, 281
Vinoteca ✕, *147–148*
Violet Boutique (shop), 247
Virginia
Alexandria, 256, 259–267

Arlington, 113–116
Arlington National Cemetery,
17, 113, 114, 117–123
dining and lodging, 149–150,
175–176
Gunston Hall, 256, 267,
271–272
Mount Vernon, 25, 256,
267–271
Woodlawn, 256, 267, 270–271
Virtue Feed & Grain ✕, 266
Visitor information, *13,* 295
Alexandria, 260
Annapolis, 274
Bicycling, 227
gay and lesbian, 295
Mount Vernon, 268
nightlife, 179
performing arts, 199

W

Walking tours, *21,* 295
Alexandria, 260
Annapolis, 273, 274
Arlington, 121
shopping, 235–254
Washington, 21
Washington Auto Show, 26
Washington Harbour and
Waterfront Park, *91*
Washington Hilton 🛏, *174*
Washington International Horse
Show, 26
Washington Marriott at Metro
Center 🛏, 168
Washington Marriott Wardman
Park 🛏, *174–175*
Washington Monument, *16, 51*
Washington National Cathe-
dral, *17,* 77, 109, 111, 112
Washington Navy Yard, 78
Washington Shakespeare The-
atre Free for All, 26

Watergate Hotel, The 🛏,
163–164
Watermark (tour guides), 274
We, the Pizza ✕, 65
Weather, 12
West Potomac Park, 224
Westin Alexandria 🛏, 267
Westin Annapolis Hotel 🛏, 282
Westin Georgetown, Washing-
ton D.C. 🛏, 164
Wharf, The, *11*
White House, *16, 55*
White House area, *14, 54–61*
dining, 57, 128–129
lodging, 160, 162
nightlife, 179–180
performing arts, 199–200
transportation, 57
Willard Inter-Continental 🛏,
162
William Paca House and Gar-
den, 277–278
Wolfgang Puck's The Source
✕, 136
Woodlawn (Virginia), 256, 267,
270–271
Woodlawn & Pope-Leighey
House, 270–271
Woodley Park Guest House
🛏, 175
Woodrow Wilson House, 96, 99
Woolly Mammoth Theater
Company, 207
World War I Memorial, 224
WTF (Woodward Takeout Food)
✕, 57

Z

Zaytinya ✕, 138–139
Zoos, *17, 25, 47, 109, 111*

PHOTO CREDITS

Front cover: David Sucsy/iStockphoto [Description: Tidal Basin lake, Washington D.C.]. 1, Smithsonian Institution and the National Museum of African American History and Culture. 2-3, Spencer Grant/age fotostock. 5, Smithsonian Institution. **Chapter 1: Experience Washington:** 8-9, Lunamarina | Dreamstime.com. 16 (left), graham s. klotz/Shutterstock. 16 (top center), S.Borisov/Shutterstock. 16 (top right), Kevin D. Oliver/Shutterstock. 16 (bottom right), Wadester16/wikipedia.org. 17 (left), alykat/ wikipedia.org. 17 (top center), taylorandayumi/Flickr. 17 (top right), Jeremy R. Smith Sr./Shutterstock. 17 (bottom right), Kropotov Andrey/Shutterstock. **Chapter 2: Exploring:** 27, jemaerca/iStockphoto.28, F11photo | Dreamstime.com. 30, Revoc9 | Dreamstime.com. 33, Appalachianviews | Dreamstime.com, 36, tomwachs/iStockphoto. 38 and 39, Eric Long/NASM, National Air and Space Museum, Smithsonian Institution. 40 (top left), NASA/wikipedia.org. 40 (top right), Son of Groucho/Flickr. 40 (bottom), Henristosch/ wikipedia.org. 41 (top left), cliff1066/Flickr. 41 (top left center), dbking/Flickr. 41 (top right center), Eric Long/NASM, National Air and Space Museum, Smithsonian Institution. 41 (top right and bottom), Mr. T in DC/Flickr. 42-43, Smithsonian Institution. 45, Smithsonian Institution and the National Museum of African American History and Culture. 50, Crimestudio | Dreamstime.com. 53, Kcphotos | Dreamstime.com. 54, Ron Blunt, courtesy Smithsonian American Art Museum. 57, Orhan Çam | Dreamstime.com. 59, Sepavo | Dreamstime.com. 62, Hartemink | Dreamstime.com. 65, Etstock | Dreamstime.com. 67 (left), Bartomeu Amengual/age fotostock. 67 (top right), kimberlyfaye/Flickr. 67 (bottom right), SuperStock. 68 (top left and bottom left), Library of Congress Prints & Photographs Division. 68, (top right), Classic Vision/age fotostock. 68 (bottom right), Prints and Photographs Division Library of Congress. 69 (left), Architect of the Capitol. 69 (top right), José Fuste Raga/age fotostock. 69 (bottom), Architect of the Capitol/wikipedia.org. 70, U.S. Capitol Visitor Center. 71 (left), Wadester/wikipedia.org. 71 (right), wikipedia.org. 72 (left), MShades/Flickr. 72 (right), Architect of the Capitol/wikipedia.org. 74 (left), U.S. Senate, 110th Congress, Senate Photo Studio/wikipedia.org. 74 (top right), DCstockphoto.com/Alamy. 74 (center right), SCPhotos/Alamy. 74 (bottom right), United States Congress/wikipedia.org. 75, Gary Blakeley / Shutterstock. 79, Appalachianviews | Dreamstime.com. 81, EdStock / iStockphoto. 83, International Spy Museum. 85, Groovysoup | Dreamstime.com. 89, Kruck87 | Dreamstime.com. 91, Dumbarton Oaks/DC Gardens/Flickr, [CC BY 2.0]. 94, Art Kowalsky/Alamy. 97, Avmedved | Dreamstime.com. 98, Sarah Sampsel/Flickr, [CC BY-ND 2.0]. 100 and 101, Philip Scalia / Alamy. 103, Shootalot | Dreamstime.com. 104, NCinDC/Flickr. 105, Destination DC. 107, G. Byron Peck/City Arts Inc. 108, Condor 36 / Shutterstock. 111, Rokusfocuspix | Dreamstime.com. 113, Vacclav | Dreamstime.com. 115, Americanspirit | Dreamstime.com. 117, Condor 36/Shutterstock. 118, SuperStock/age fotostock. 119 (top left), Scott S. Warren/Aurora Photos. 119 (bottom left), Dennis Brack/Aurora Photos. 119 (right), vario images GmbH & Co.KG/Alamy. 120, Jeremy R. Smith Sr/Shutterstock. 122 (top left), Ken Hackett/Alamy. 122 (top right), Rough Guides/Alamy. 122 (bottom), National Archives and Records Administration. 123 (top left), William S. Kuta/Alamy. 123 (top right), Chris A Crumley/Alamy. 123 (bottom), Jeremy R. Smith/Shutterstock. **Chapter 3: Where to Eat:** 125, Greg Powers/Inn at Little Washington. 126, Andrew Cebulka/The Dabney. **Chapter 4: Where to Stay:** 157, Ron Blunt/Hotel Monaco.158, Ron Blunt/The Watergate Hotel. **Chapter 5: Nightlife:** 177, Elan Fleisher/age fotostock. 178, dk/Alamy. **Chapter 6: Performing Arts:** 197, Travelwide / Alamy. 198, Karin Cooper. **Chapter 7: Sports and the Outdoors:** 213, Avmedved | Dreamstime.com. 214, Davidpark | Dreamstime.com. 217, Anosmia/Flickr. 222-223, Debratos | Dreamstime.com. **Chapter 8: Shopping:** 233, Lucas Bojarowski. 234, Courtesy of The Phoenix. 243, Alex Segre/Alamy. **Chapter 9: Side Trips:** 255, Appalachianviews | Dreamstime.com. 256, 2265524729/Shutterstock. 257, rpongsaj/Flickr 258, Jnevitt | Dreamstime.com. 265, Lee Snider Photo Images/Shutterstock. 269, Jeff Greenberg/age Fotostock. 280, Vittorio sciosia/ age fotostock. **Back cover, from left to right:** Orhancam | Dreamstime.com; graham s. klotz/Shutterstock; SurangaWeeratunga/Shutterstock. **Spine:** Tim Mainiero/Shutterstock. **About Our Writers:** All photos are courtesy of the writers except for the following: Mike Lillis, courtesy of Greg Nash; Robert Michael Oliver, courtesy of Franc Rosario; Cathy Sharp, courtesy of Gary Sharp; Will O'Bryan, courtesy of Carmen Gilotte.

NOTES

NOTES

NOTES

NOTES

NOTES

NOTES

NOTES

NOTES

NOTES

NOTES

NOTES

NOTES

NOTES

NOTES

ABOUT OUR WRITERS

A native of the Boston area, highlights of then-14-year-old Zach Everson's first trip to Washington, D.C., included having a Roy Rogers in his hotel's basement, eating at a family seafood restaurant that let kids pick plastic toys out of a treasure chest, and being introduced to deep-dish pizza. Now a freelance journalist living just across the D.C. border in Bethesda, Maryland, Zach updated the Where to Eat chapter this edition—and, no, Roy Rogers didn't make the cut.

Born and raised in Virginia, Mike Lillis now lives in Washington, D.C., where he covers politics for *The Hill* newspaper. Many weekends find him in a canoe, paddling the rocky streams of the region. He updated the Experience Washington, D.C. and Travel Smart chapters.

Co-founder of the Sanctuary Theatre and its Performing Knowledge Project, Robert Michael Oliver works as a director, an actor, and a playwright. He is currently the D.C. metro editor at *Maryland Theatre Guide*. He updated the Performing Arts chapter.

D.C. Nightlife and Sports and the Outdoors updater Doug Rule has immersed himself in the life and culture of the nation's capital since moving there in 1996. A freelance writer and editor, he has written for D.C.-based nonprofits and foundations as well as covered the arts and nightlife for publications including the *Washington City Paper* and *Metro Weekly*, where he serves as contributing editor. He's lived in various Mid-City neighborhoods since 2000; he currently lives in Shaw.

Cathy Sharpe, a freelance writer with more than 20 years of experience in travel, has lived in the Maryland suburbs of Washington since 1998. She loves seeing the metro area's wonders through the eyes of her four children. She updated the Exploring, Where to Stay, Shopping, and Side Trips chapters.